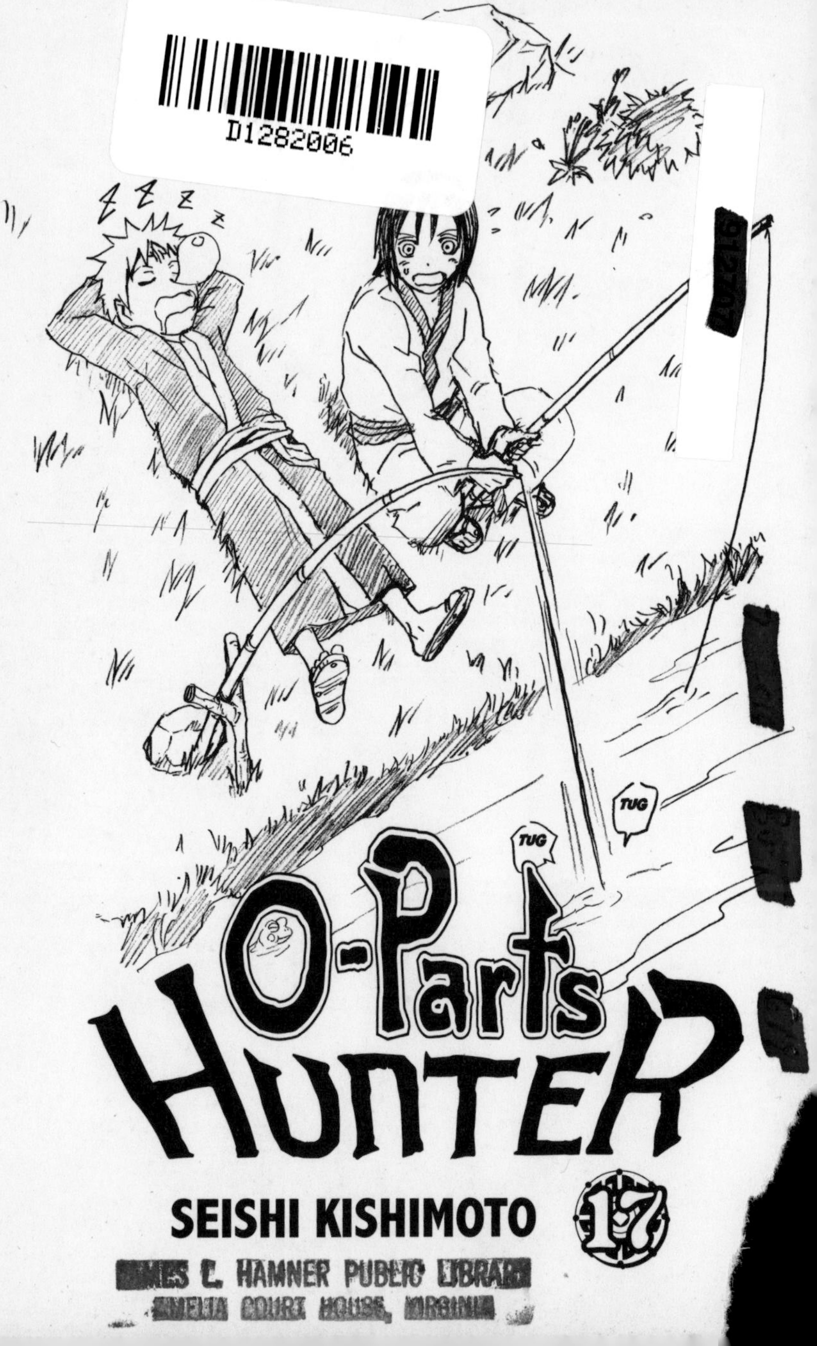
TUG
TUG

O-Parts HUNTER

SEISHI KISHIMOTO

17

CHARACTERS of O-Parts HUNTER

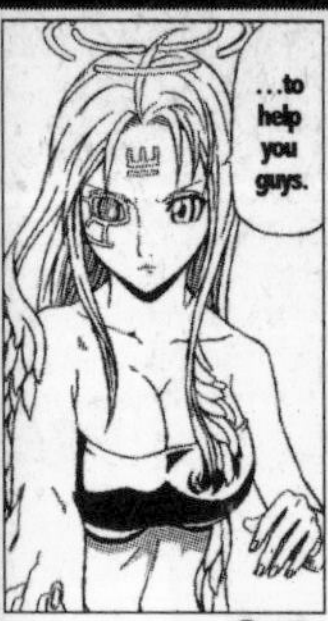

…to help you guys.

Having gotten close to her true Angel form, she is now able to wield Sandalphon's powers, but her true powers are yet to be seen…

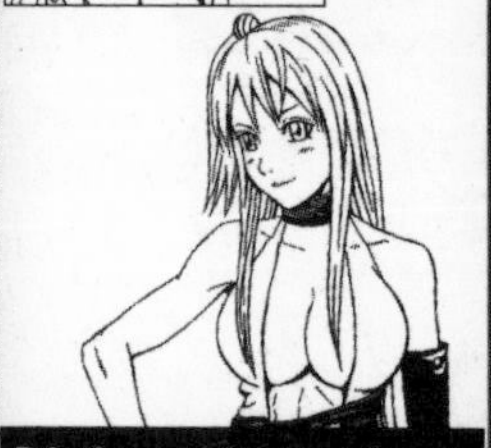

Ruby Crescent: A treasure hunter in search of the Legendary O-Part and her missing father. Rescued from Stea HQ, she turns out to be a Recipe for the Kabbalah. Jio brings her back into this world.

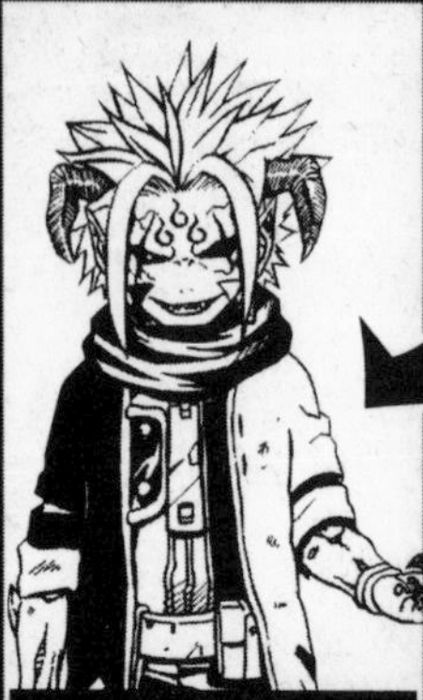

Satan: An alternate personality that exists inside Jio's body. The ultimate weapon of the Kabbalah who holds earth-shattering powers.

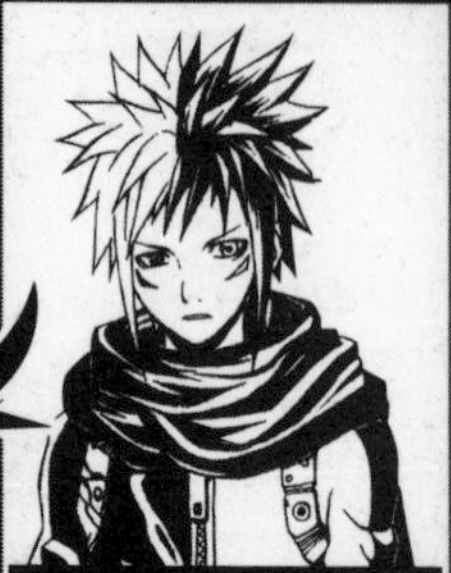

Jio Freed: A wild O.P.T. boy whose dream is world domination. He has been emotionally hurt from his experiences in the past but has become strong after meeting Ruby. Ever since the Rock Bird incident, he has had Ruby's soul inside him.

Jio's Friends

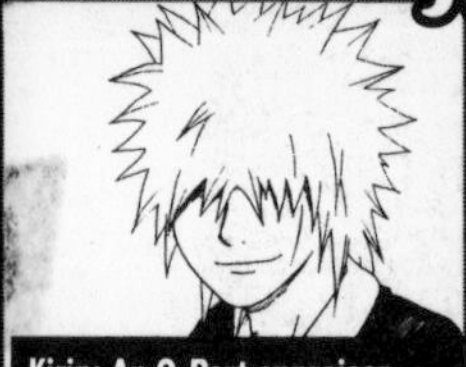

Kirin: An O-Part appraiser and a master of dodging attacks. He trained Jio and Ball into strong O.P.T.s.

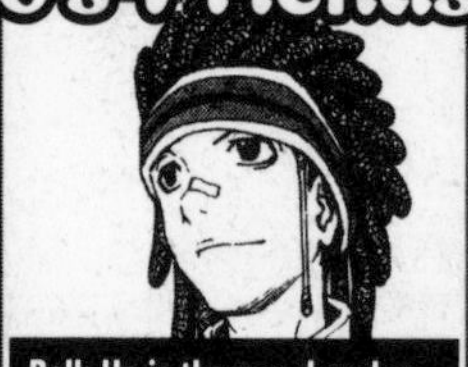

Ball: He is the mood-maker of the group and the kind of person who cares about his friends.

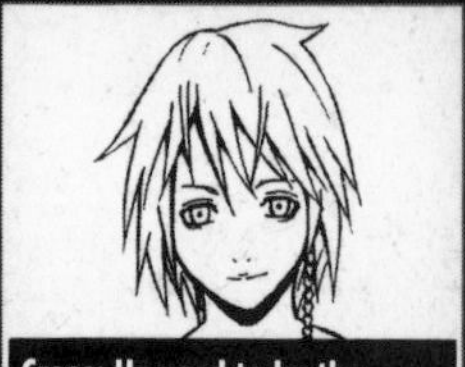

Cross: He used to be the Commander in Chief of the Stea Government's battleship. His sister was killed by Satan.

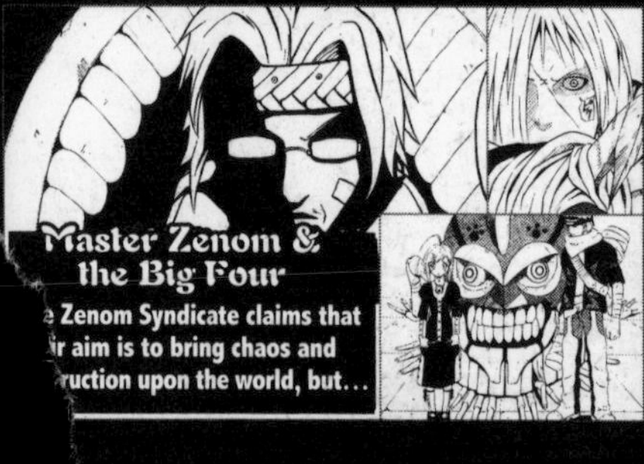

Master Zenom & the Big Four

e Zenom Syndicate claims that ir aim is to bring chaos and ruction upon the world, but…

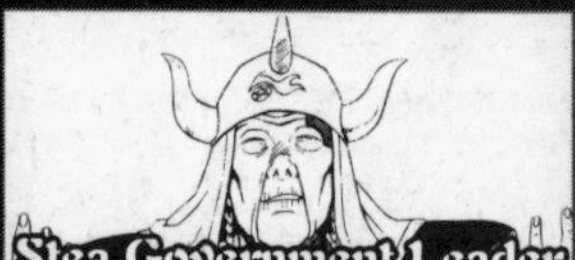

Stea Government Leader Amaterasu Miko

The very person who turned the Stea Government into a huge military state. Rumor has it that she has been alive for at least a century…

KABBALAH

the keyword of 666

A legacy left by the Ancient Race who are said to have con from the Blue Planet. The Kabbalah is the Ultima Memorization Weapon, which absorbs every kind "information" that makes up this world, and evolves alo with the passing of time! It consists of two counterpar the Formal Kabbalah and the Reverse Kabbalah.

10i
Nahema
(Materialism)
9i
Lilith
(Instability)
7i
Baal
(Lust)
8i
Adramelech
(Avarice)
6i
Belphegor
(Odiousness)
4i
Astaroth
(Apathy)
5i
Asmodeus
(Cruelty)
2i
Beelzebub
(Stupidity)
3i
Lucifuge
(Rejection)
1i
Satan
(Atheism)

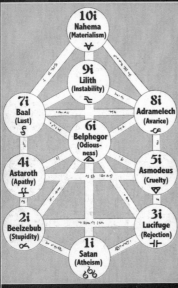

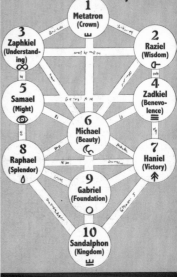

Reverse Kabbalah

The symbol of destruction with the names of the powerful archdemons listed on the sephirot from one to ten.

1
Metatron
(Crown)
3
Zaphkiel
(Understanding)
2
Raziel
(Wisdom)
5
Samael
(Might)
4
Zadkiel
(Benevolence)
6
Michael
(Beauty)
8
Raphael
(Splendor)
7
Haniel
(Victory)
9
Gabriel
(Foundation)
10
Sandalphon
(Kingdom)

Formal Kabbalah

The symbol of creation with the names of the great archangels listed on the sephirot from one to ten.

STORY

Ascald: a world where people fight amongst themselves to get their hands on mystical objects left behind by an ancient civilization…the O-Parts.

In that world, a monster that strikes fear into the hearts of the strongest of men is rumored to exist. Those who have seen the monster all tell of the same thing–that the number of the beast, 666, is engraved on its forehead.

***

Jio and his friends enter Stea Government HQ in order to free Ruby. Amaterasu Miko, Stea's leader, sends her chief of staff Longinus, the true Angel Michael and May's long-missing brother Tsubame to stop them. These are all overcome, but this leads to the discovery that Miko has replaced her human body with a robot one. Jio destroys the robot body, but the question is… where is Miko now?

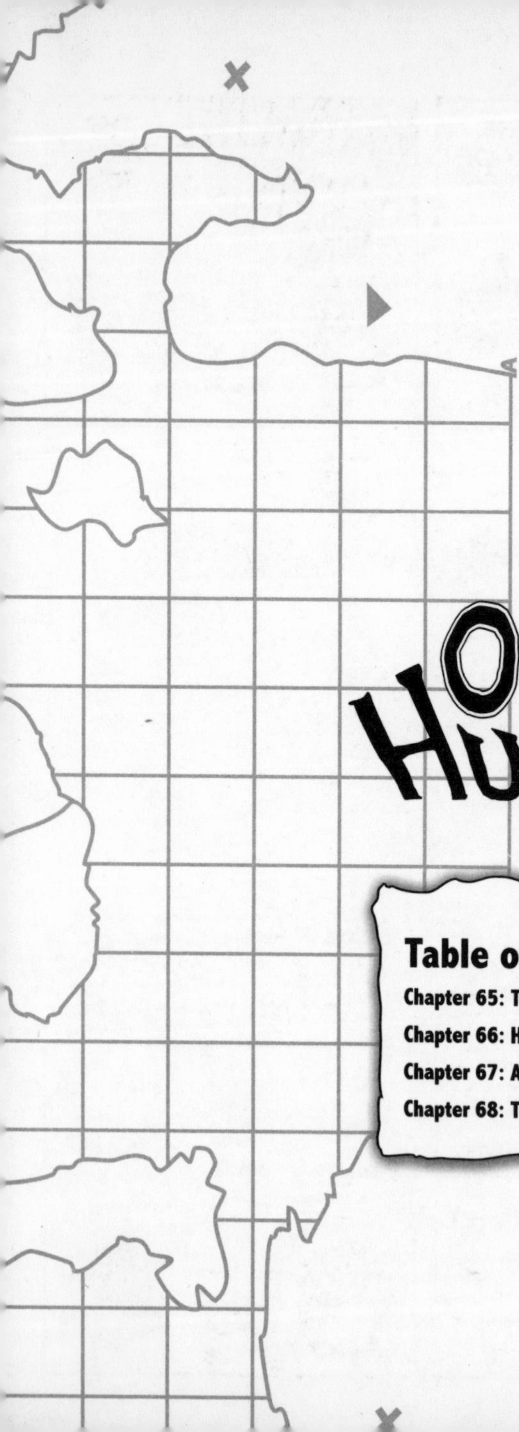

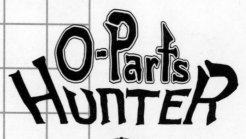

O-Parts Hunter

17

Table of Contents

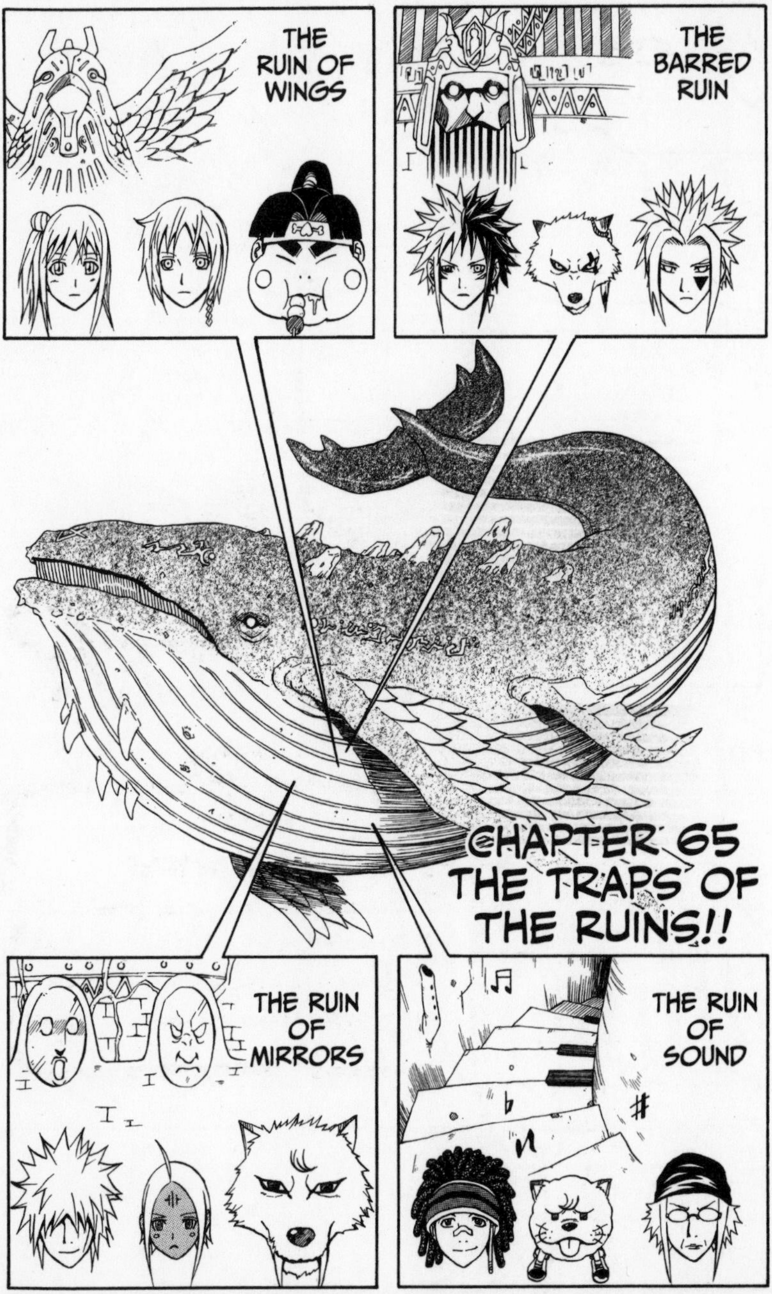
THE BARRED RUIN
THE RUIN OF WINGS
CHAPTER 65 THE TRAPS OF THE RUINS!!
THE RUIN OF SOUND
THE RUIN OF MIRRORS

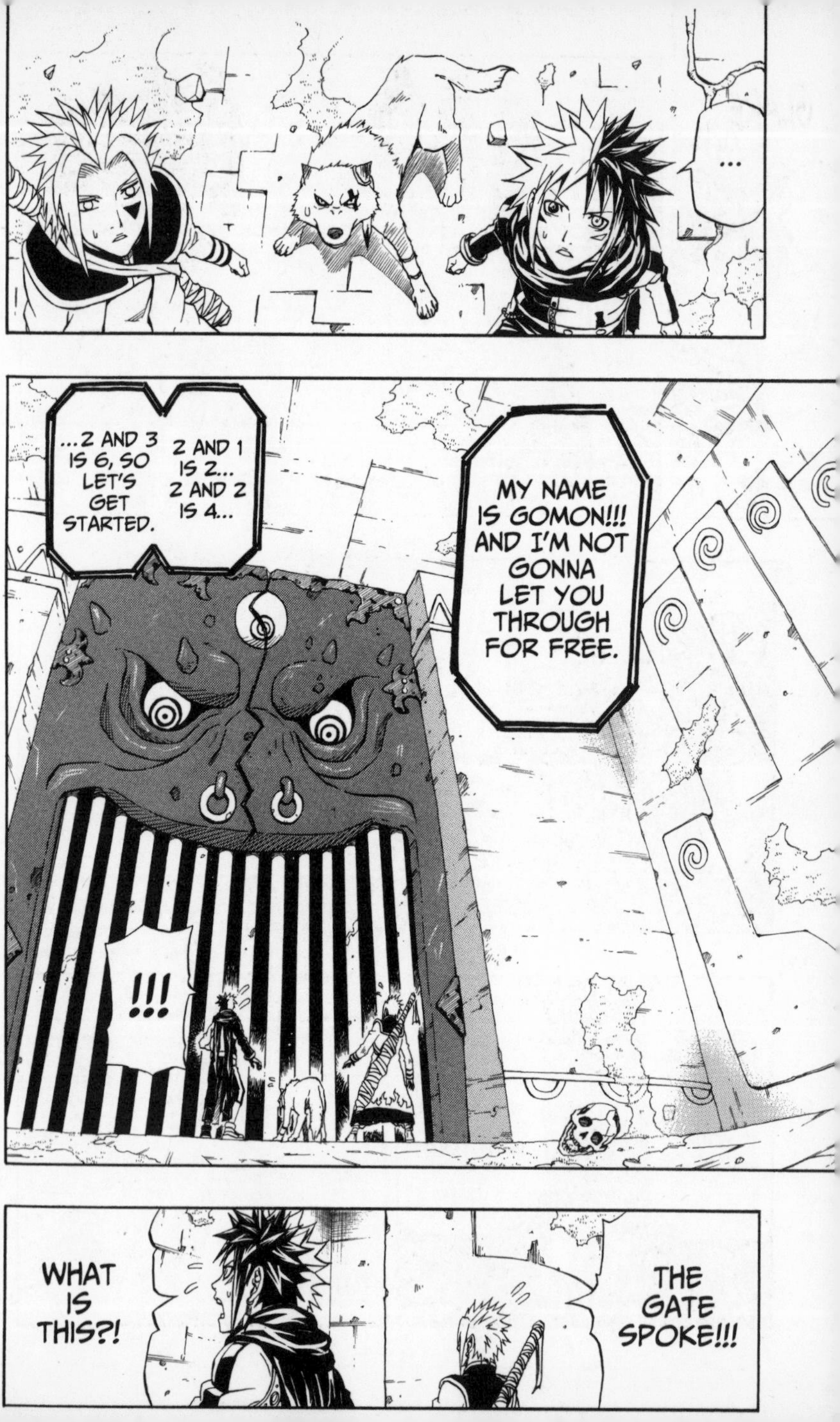
...
MY NAME IS GOMON!!! AND I'M NOT GONNA LET YOU THROUGH FOR FREE.
2 AND 1 IS 2... 2 AND 2 IS 4...
...2 AND 3 IS 6, SO LET'S GET STARTED.
!!!
THE GATE SPOKE!!!
WHAT IS THIS?!

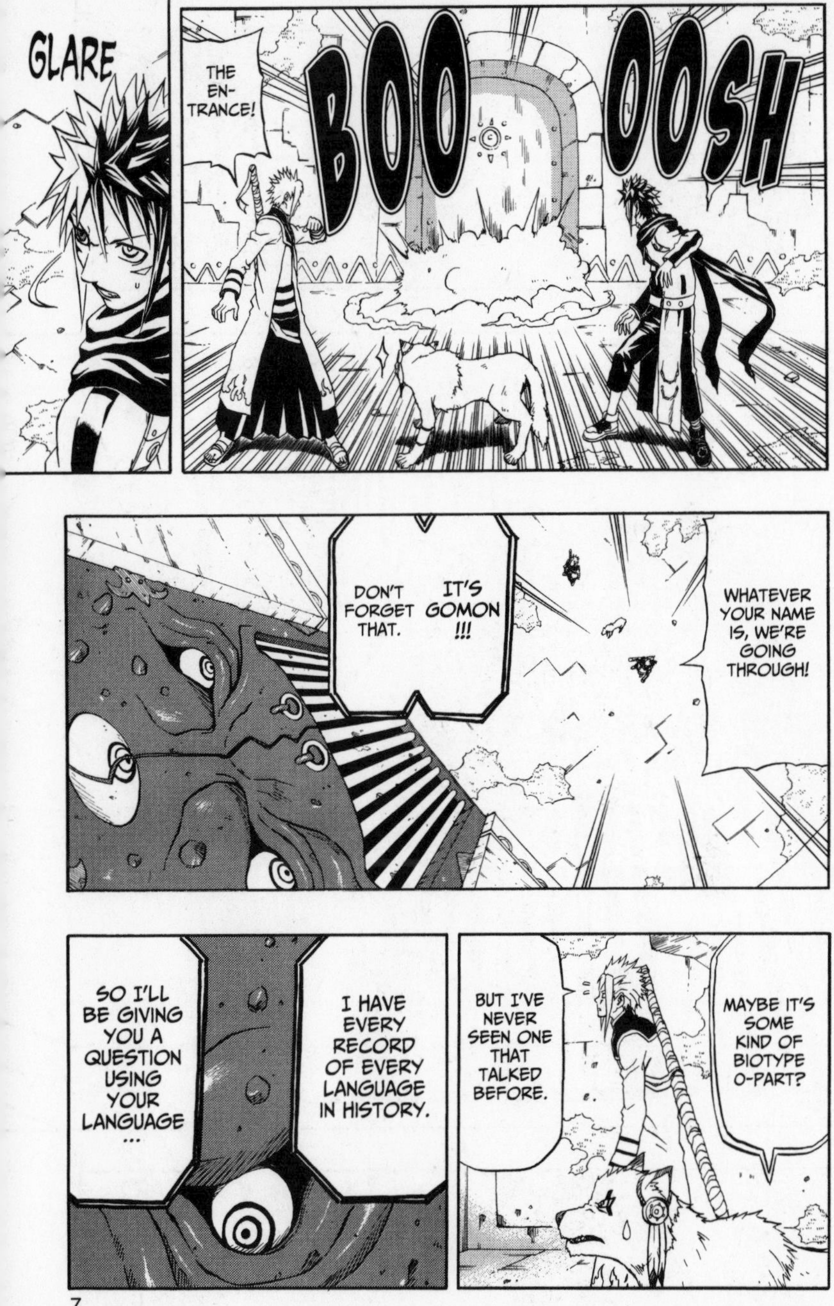
BOOOOSH
THE EN-TRANCE!
GLARE
WHATEVER YOUR NAME IS, WE'RE GOING THROUGH!
IT'S GOMON!!!
DON'T FORGET THAT.
MAYBE IT'S SOME KIND OF BIOTYPE O-PART?
BUT I'VE NEVER SEEN ONE THAT TALKED BEFORE.
I HAVE EVERY RECORD OF EVERY LANGUAGE IN HISTORY.
SO I'LL BE GIVING YOU A QUESTION USING YOUR LANGUAGE...

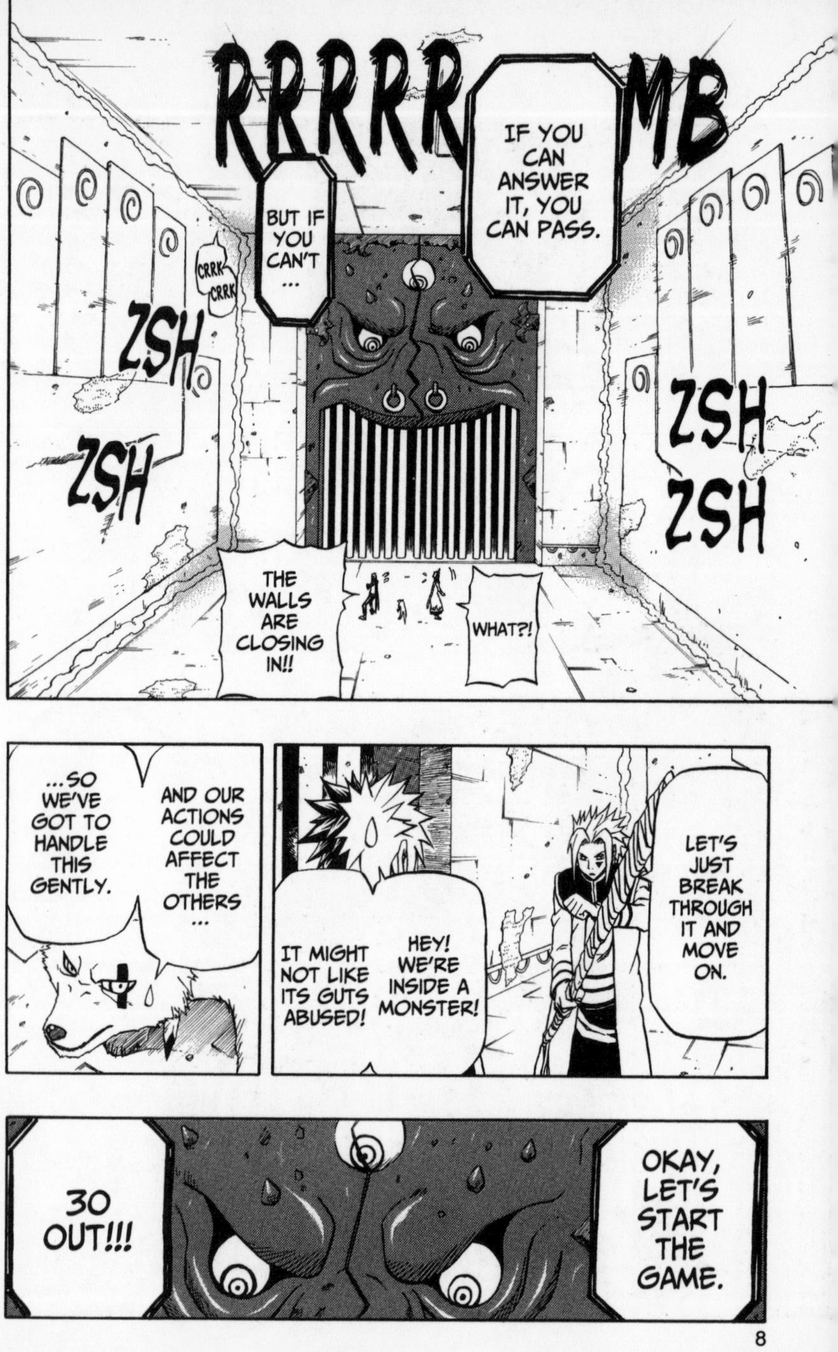
RRRRR
MB
IF YOU CAN ANSWER IT, YOU CAN PASS.
BUT IF YOU CAN'T ...
ZSH
ZSH
CRRK
CRRK
ZSH
ZSH
WHAT?!
THE WALLS ARE CLOSING IN!!
LET'S JUST BREAK THROUGH IT AND MOVE ON.
HEY! WE'RE INSIDE A MONSTER!
IT MIGHT NOT LIKE ITS GUTS ABUSED!
AND OUR ACTIONS COULD AFFECT THE OTHERS ...
...SO WE'VE GOT TO HANDLE THIS GENTLY.
OKAY, LET'S START THE GAME.
30 OUT!!!

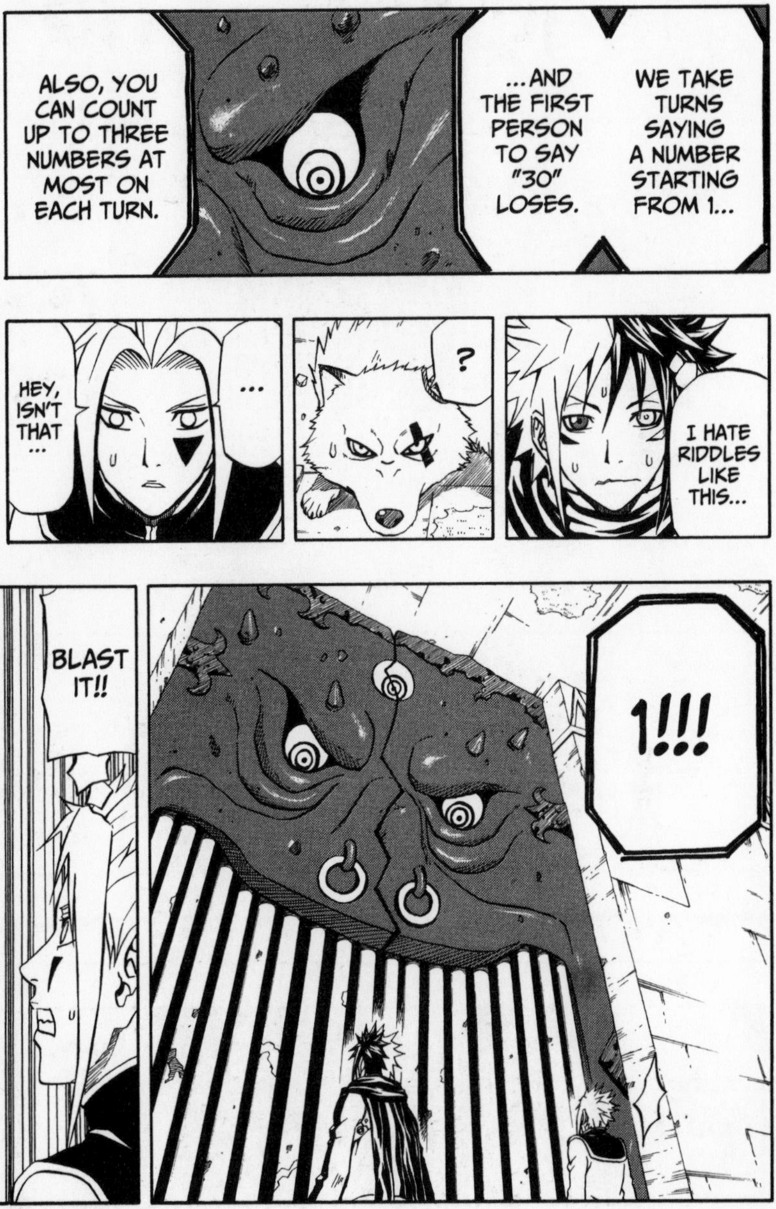
WE TAKE TURNS SAYING A NUMBER STARTING FROM 1...
...AND THE FIRST PERSON TO SAY "30" LOSES.
ALSO, YOU CAN COUNT UP TO THREE NUMBERS AT MOST ON EACH TURN.
I HATE RIDDLES LIKE THIS...
?
...
HEY, ISN'T THAT ...
1!!!
BLAST IT!!

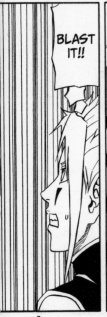

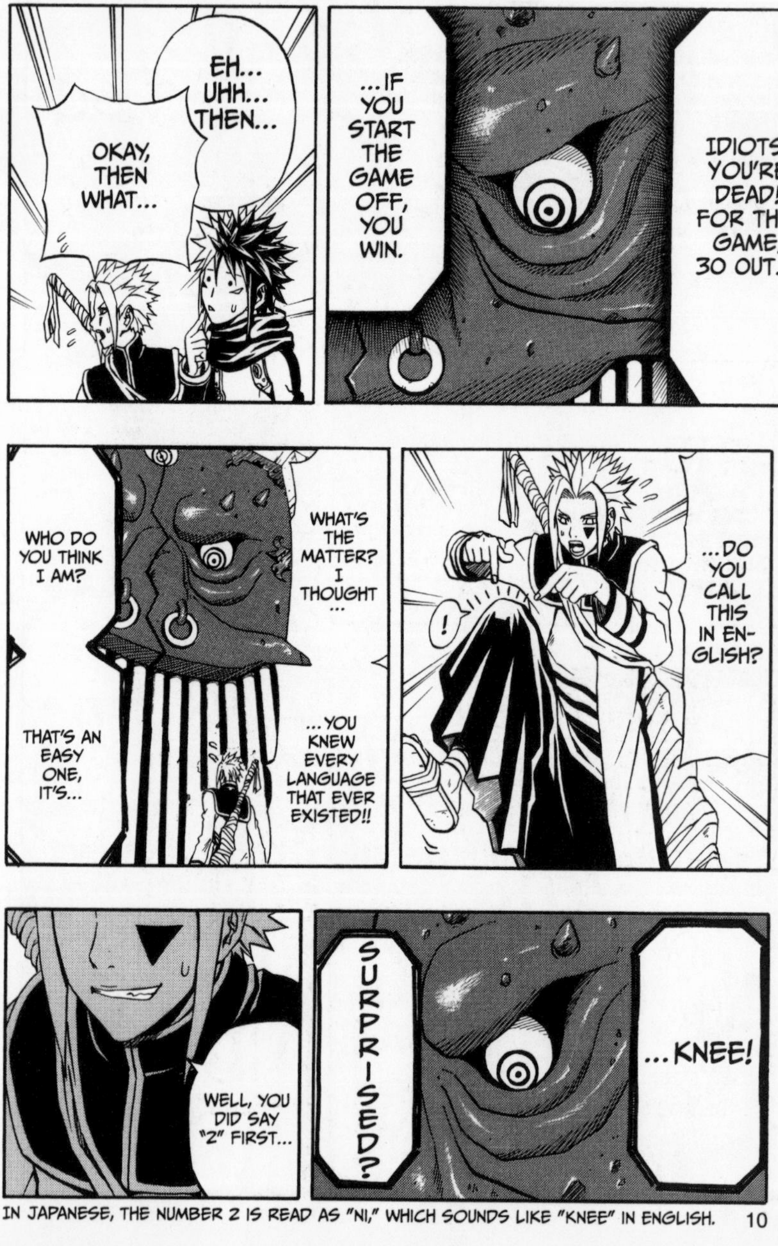
IDIOTS! YOU'RE DEAD! FOR THIS GAME, 30 OUT...
...IF YOU START THE GAME OFF, YOU WIN.
EH... UHH... THEN...
OKAY, THEN WHAT...
...DO YOU CALL THIS IN ENGLISH?
!
WHAT'S THE MATTER? I THOUGHT ...
...YOU KNEW EVERY LANGUAGE THAT EVER EXISTED!!
WHO DO YOU THINK I AM?
THAT'S AN EASY ONE, IT'S...
...KNEE!
SURPRISED?
WELL, YOU DID SAY "2" FIRST...

IN JAPANESE, THE NUMBER 2 IS READ AS "NI," WHICH SOUNDS LIKE "KNEE" IN ENGLISH.

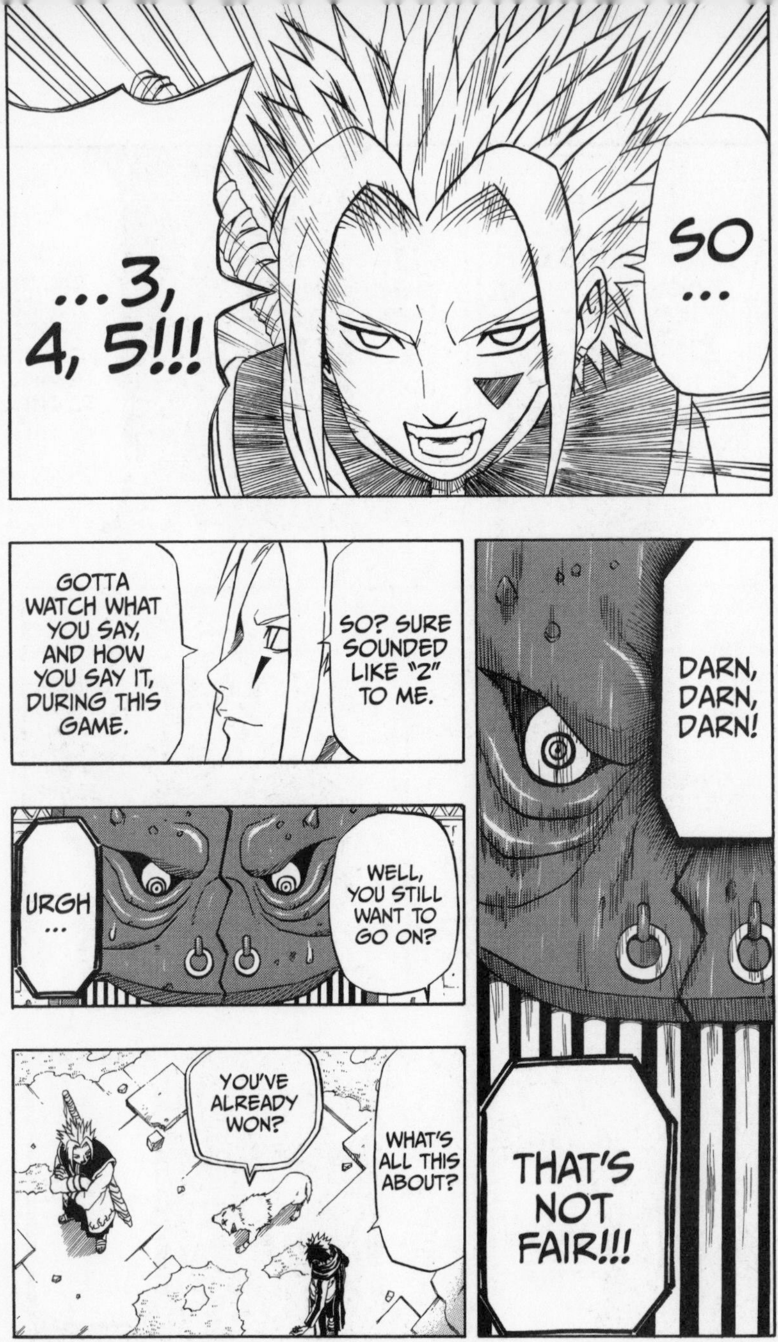

SO ...
...3, 4, 5!!!
DARN, DARN, DARN!
THAT'S NOT FAIR!!!
SO? SURE SOUNDED LIKE "2" TO ME.
GOTTA WATCH WHAT YOU SAY, AND HOW YOU SAY IT, DURING THIS GAME.
WELL, YOU STILL WANT TO GO ON?
URGH ...
WHAT'S ALL THIS ABOUT?
YOU'VE ALREADY WON?

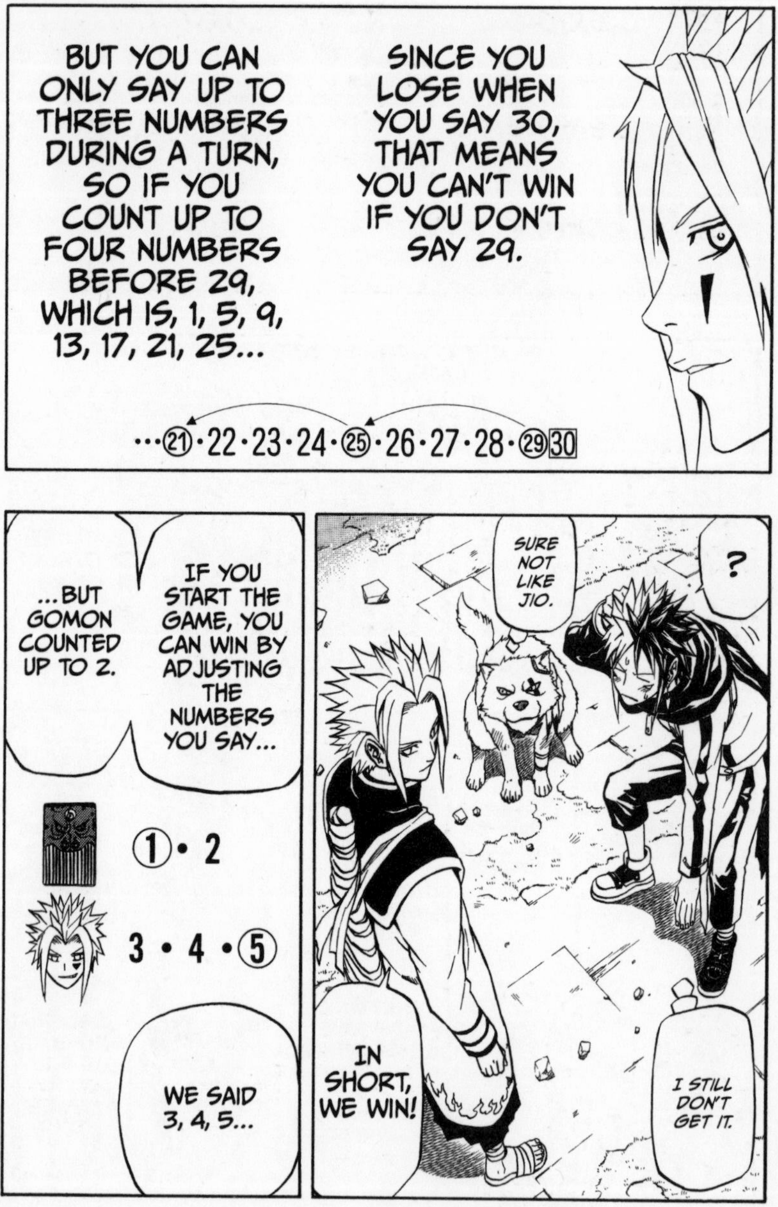
SINCE YOU LOSE WHEN YOU SAY 30, THAT MEANS YOU CAN'T WIN IF YOU DON'T SAY 29.
BUT YOU CAN ONLY SAY UP TO THREE NUMBERS DURING A TURN, SO IF YOU COUNT UP TO FOUR NUMBERS BEFORE 29, WHICH IS, 1, 5, 9, 13, 17, 21, 25...
...㉑・22・23・24・㉕・26・27・28・㉙30
?
SURE NOT LIKE JIO.
I STILL DON'T GET IT.
IN SHORT, WE WIN!
IF YOU START THE GAME, YOU CAN WIN BY ADJUSTING THE NUMBERS YOU SAY...
...BUT GOMON COUNTED UP TO 2.
①• 2
3 • 4 •⑤
WE SAID 3, 4, 5...

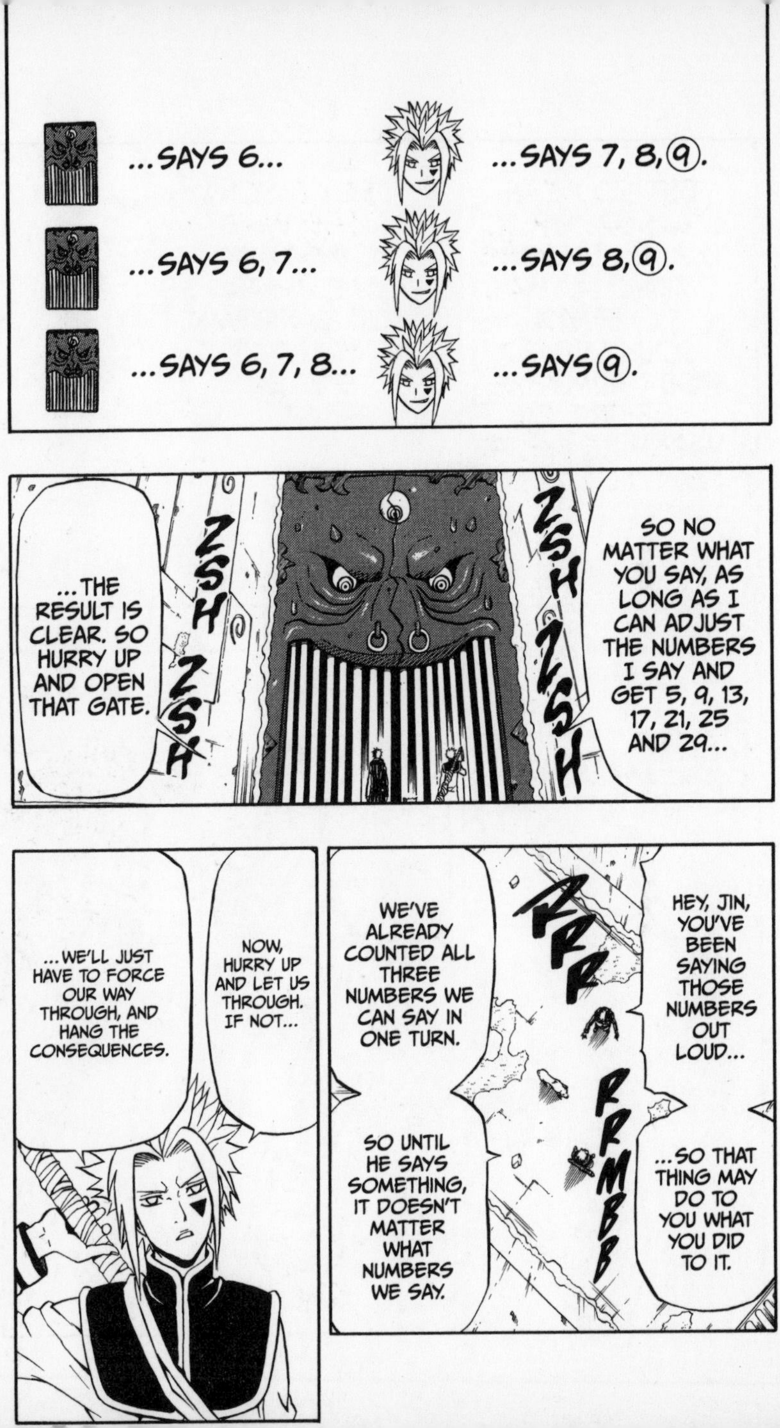
...SAYS 6...
...SAYS 7, 8, ⑨.
...SAYS 6, 7...
...SAYS 8, ⑨.
...SAYS 6, 7, 8...
...SAYS ⑨.
SO NO MATTER WHAT YOU SAY, AS LONG AS I CAN ADJUST THE NUMBERS I SAY AND GET 5, 9, 13, 17, 21, 25 AND 29...
ZSH ZSH
ZSH ZSH
...THE RESULT IS CLEAR. SO HURRY UP AND OPEN THAT GATE.
HEY, JIN, YOU'VE BEEN SAYING THOSE NUMBERS OUT LOUD...
...SO THAT THING MAY DO TO YOU WHAT YOU DID TO IT.
RRR RRMBB
WE'VE ALREADY COUNTED ALL THREE NUMBERS WE CAN SAY IN ONE TURN.
SO UNTIL HE SAYS SOMETHING, IT DOESN'T MATTER WHAT NUMBERS WE SAY.
NOW, HURRY UP AND LET US THROUGH. IF NOT...
...WE'LL JUST HAVE TO FORCE OUR WAY THROUGH, AND HANG THE CONSEQUENCES.

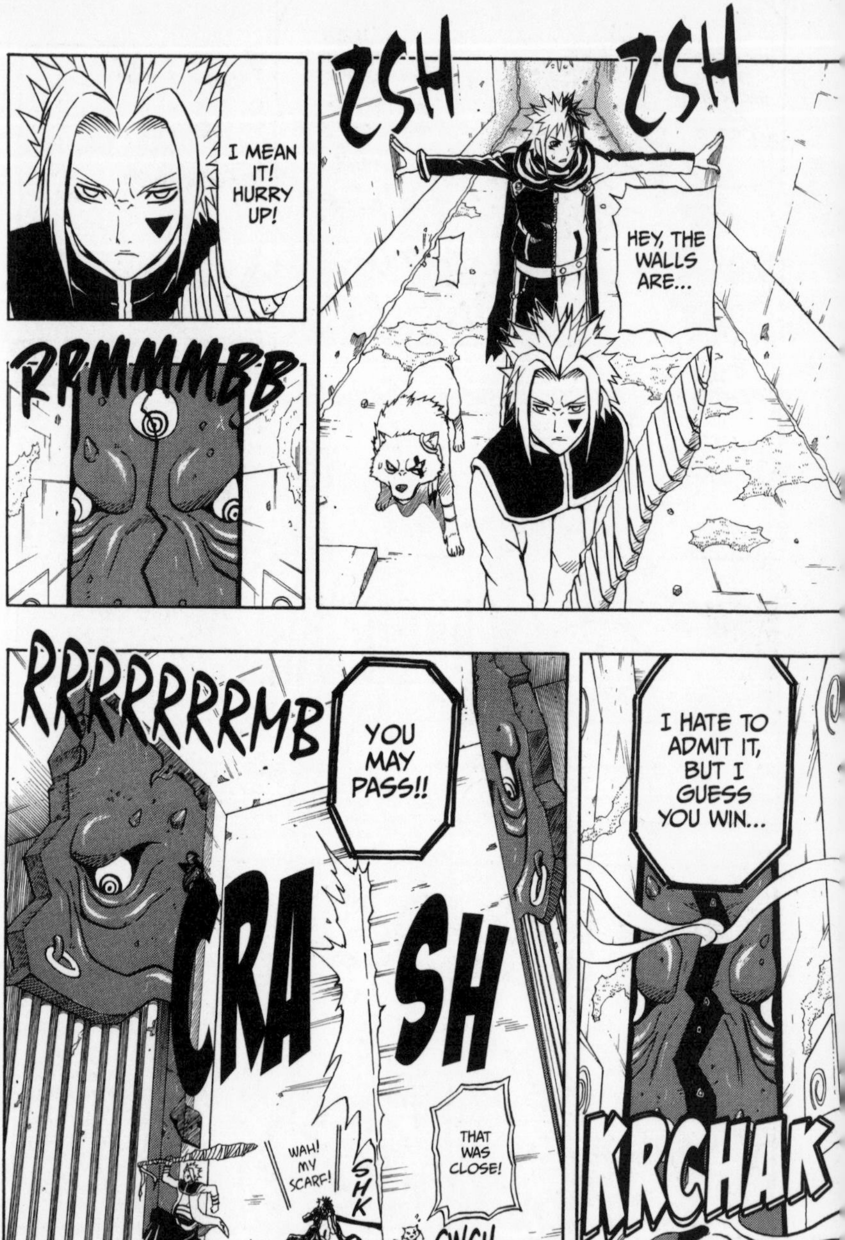
ZSH
ZSH
HEY, THE WALLS ARE...
I MEAN IT! HURRY UP!
RRMMMBB
I HATE TO ADMIT IT, BUT I GUESS YOU WIN...
KRCHAK
RRRRRRRRMB
YOU MAY PASS!!
CRASH
THAT WAS CLOSE!
SHK
SWSH
WAH! MY SCARF!

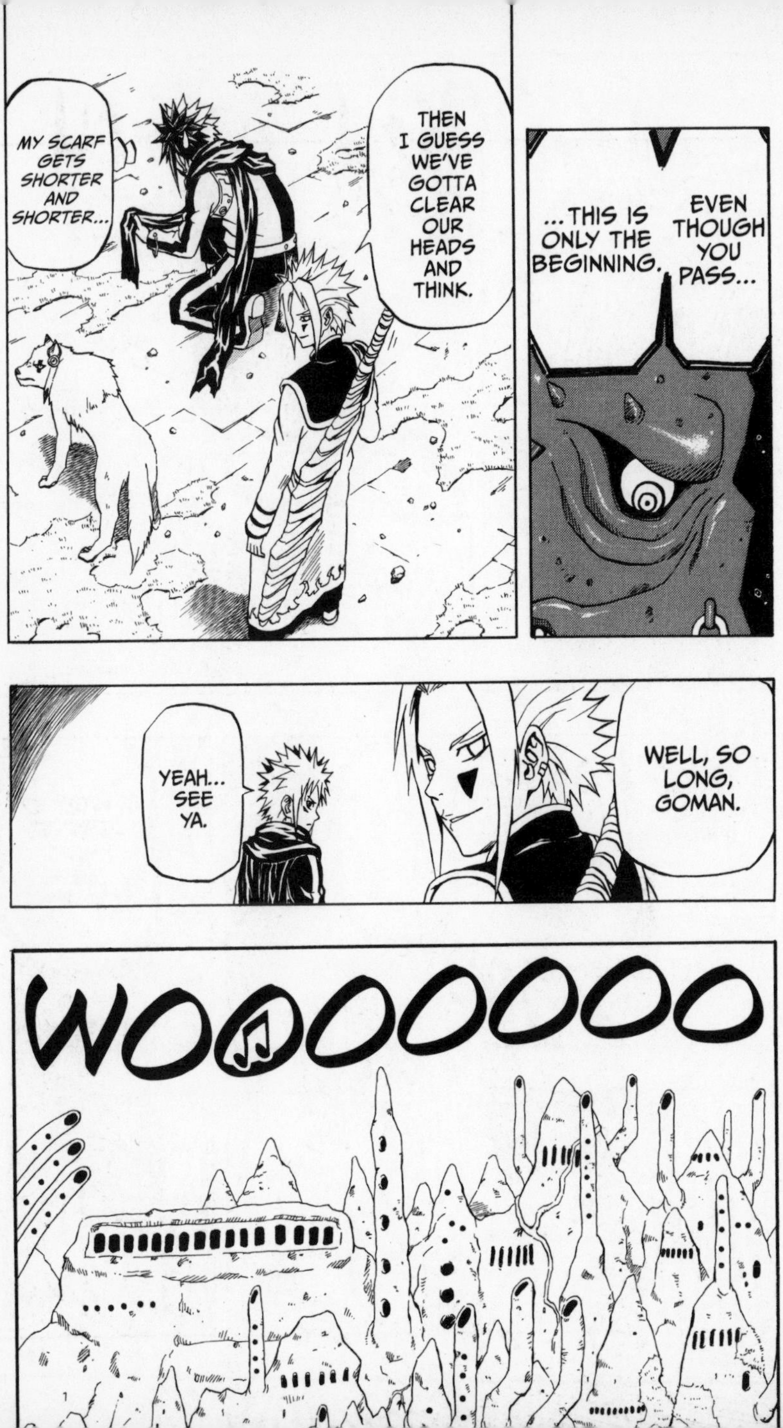
EVEN THOUGH YOU PASS...
...THIS IS ONLY THE BEGINNING.
THEN I GUESS WE'VE GOTTA CLEAR OUR HEADS AND THINK.
MY SCARF GETS SHORTER AND SHORTER...
WELL, SO LONG, GOMAN.
YEAH... SEE YA.
WOOOOOOO

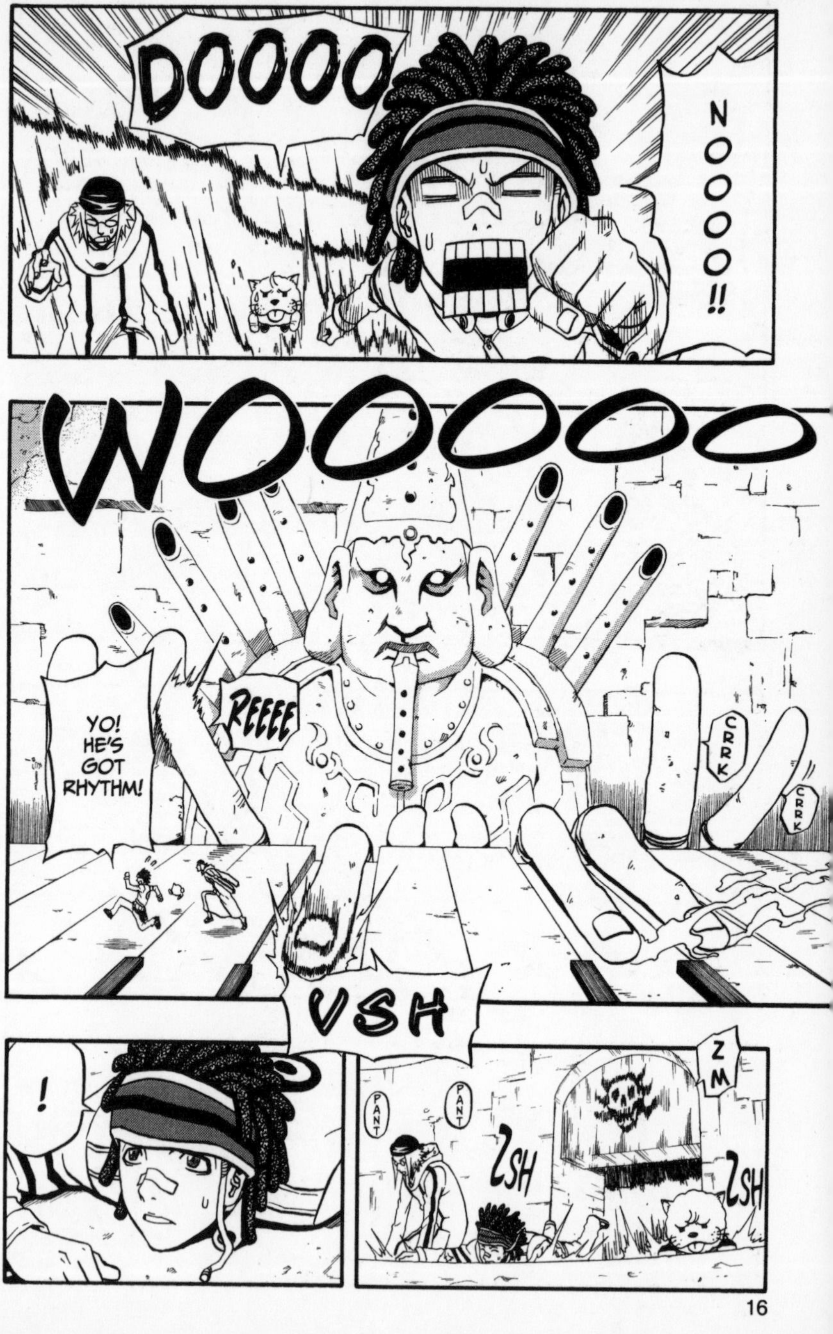
DOOOO
NOOOOO!!
WOOOOO
REEEE
CRRK
CRRK
YO! HE'S GOT RHYTHM!
VSH
ZM
PANT
PANT
ZSH
ZSH
!

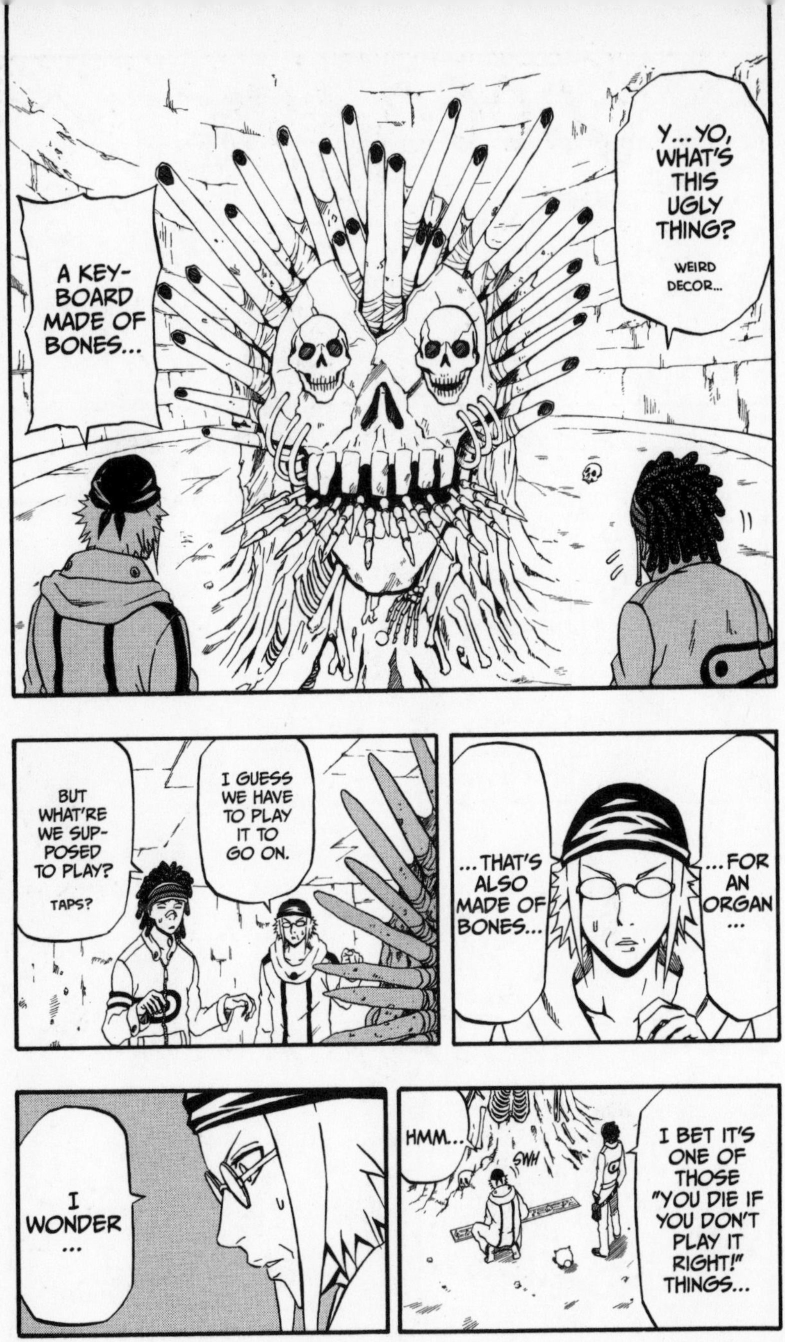
Y...YO, WHAT'S THIS UGLY THING?
WEIRD DECOR...
A KEY-BOARD MADE OF BONES...
...FOR AN ORGAN...
...THAT'S ALSO MADE OF BONES...
I GUESS WE HAVE TO PLAY IT TO GO ON.
BUT WHAT'RE WE SUP-POSED TO PLAY?
TAPS?
I BET IT'S ONE OF THOSE "YOU DIE IF YOU DON'T PLAY IT RIGHT!" THINGS...
SWH
HMM...
I WONDER...

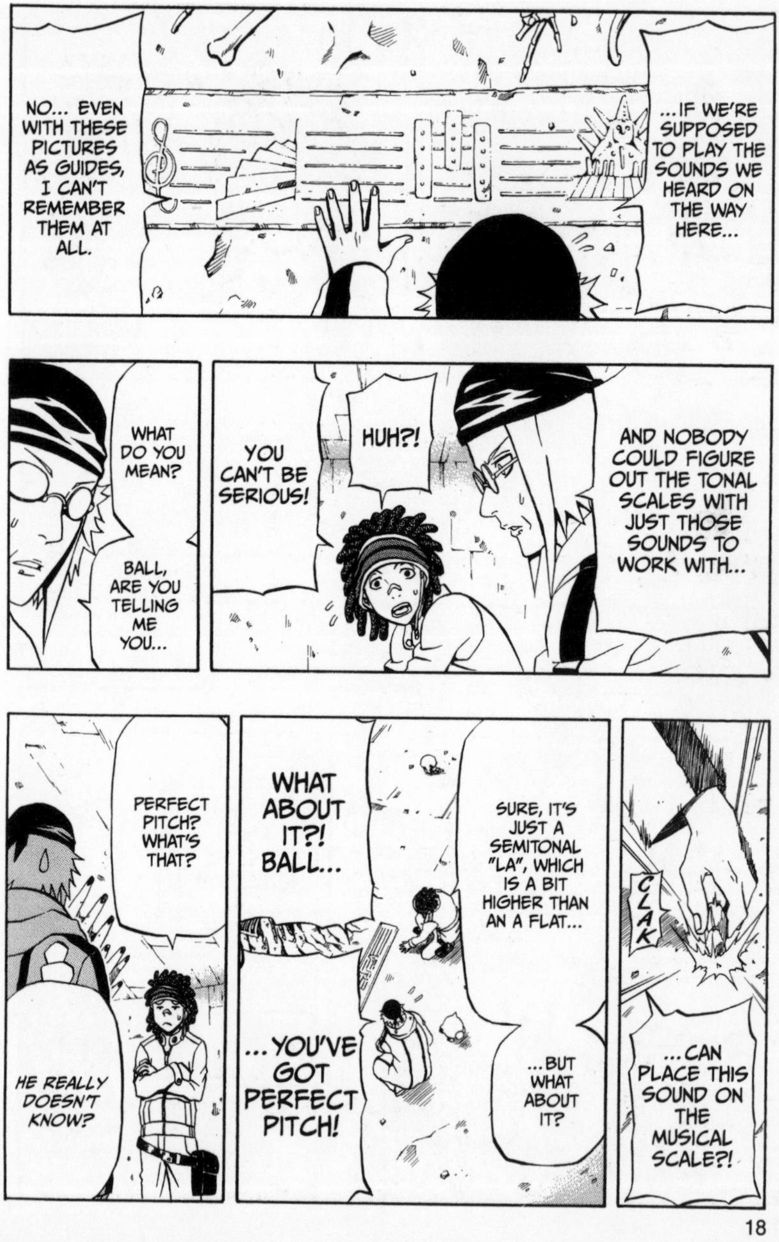
...IF WE'RE SUPPOSED TO PLAY THE SOUNDS WE HEARD ON THE WAY HERE...
NO... EVEN WITH THESE PICTURES AS GUIDES, I CAN'T REMEMBER THEM AT ALL.
AND NOBODY COULD FIGURE OUT THE TONAL SCALES WITH JUST THOSE SOUNDS TO WORK WITH...
HUH?!
YOU CAN'T BE SERIOUS!
WHAT DO YOU MEAN?
BALL, ARE YOU TELLING ME YOU...
CLAK
...CAN PLACE THIS SOUND ON THE MUSICAL SCALE?!
SURE, IT'S JUST A SEMITONAL "LA", WHICH IS A BIT HIGHER THAN AN A FLAT...
...BUT WHAT ABOUT IT?
WHAT ABOUT IT?! BALL...
...YOU'VE GOT PERFECT PITCH!
PERFECT PITCH? WHAT'S THAT?
HE REALLY DOESN'T KNOW?

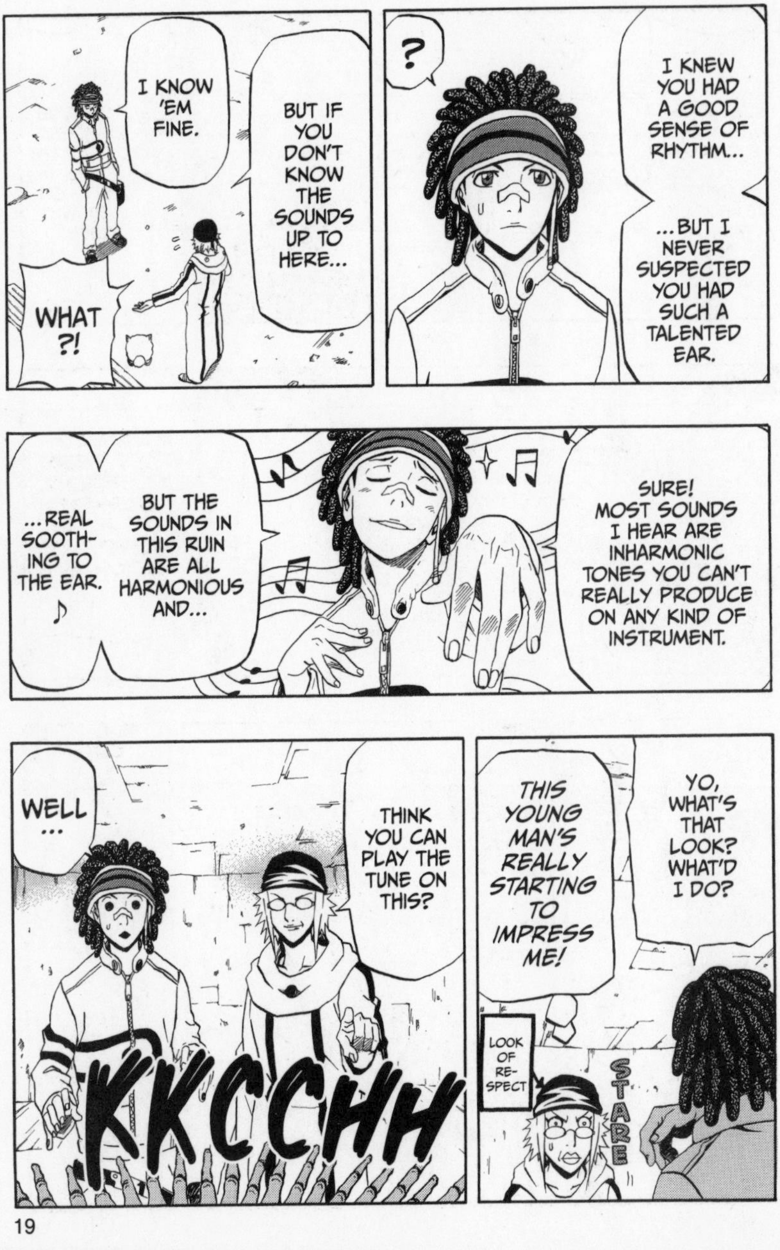
I KNEW YOU HAD A GOOD SENSE OF RHYTHM...
...BUT I NEVER SUSPECTED YOU HAD SUCH A TALENTED EAR.
?
BUT IF YOU DON'T KNOW THE SOUNDS UP TO HERE...
I KNOW 'EM FINE.
WHAT?!
SURE! MOST SOUNDS I HEAR ARE INHARMONIC TONES YOU CAN'T REALLY PRODUCE ON ANY KIND OF INSTRUMENT.
BUT THE SOUNDS IN THIS RUIN ARE ALL HARMONIOUS AND...
...REAL SOOTHING TO THE EAR. ♪
YO, WHAT'S THAT LOOK? WHAT'D I DO?
THIS YOUNG MAN'S REALLY STARTING TO IMPRESS ME!
LOOK OF RE-SPECT
STARE
THINK YOU CAN PLAY THE TUNE ON THIS?
WELL ...
KKCCHH

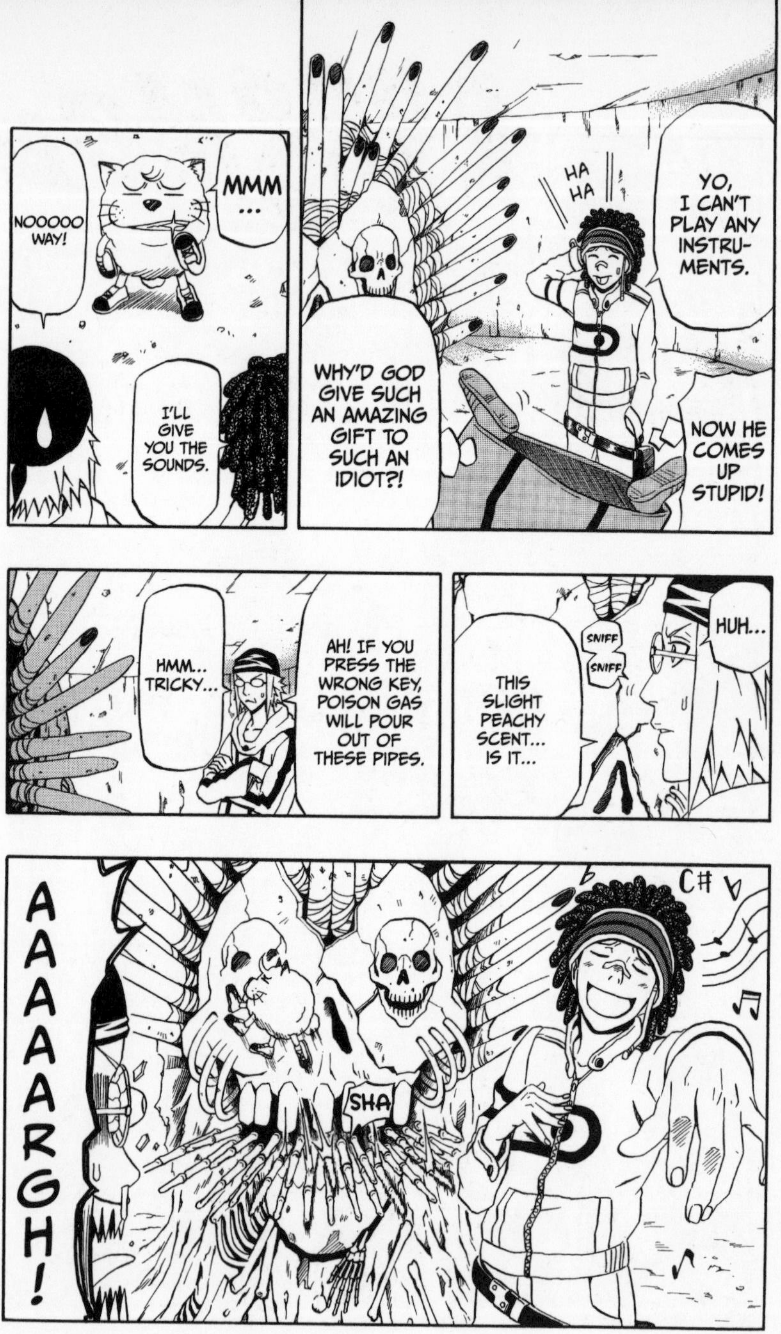
HA HA
YO, I CAN'T PLAY ANY INSTRUMENTS.
NOW HE COMES UP STUPID!
WHY'D GOD GIVE SUCH AN AMAZING GIFT TO SUCH AN IDIOT?!
MMM ...
NOOOOO WAY!
I'LL GIVE YOU THE SOUNDS.
HUH...
SNIFF
SNIFF
THIS SLIGHT PEACHY SCENT... IS IT...
AH! IF YOU PRESS THE WRONG KEY, POISON GAS WILL POUR OUT OF THESE PIPES.
HMM... TRICKY...
C#
SHA
AAAAARGH!

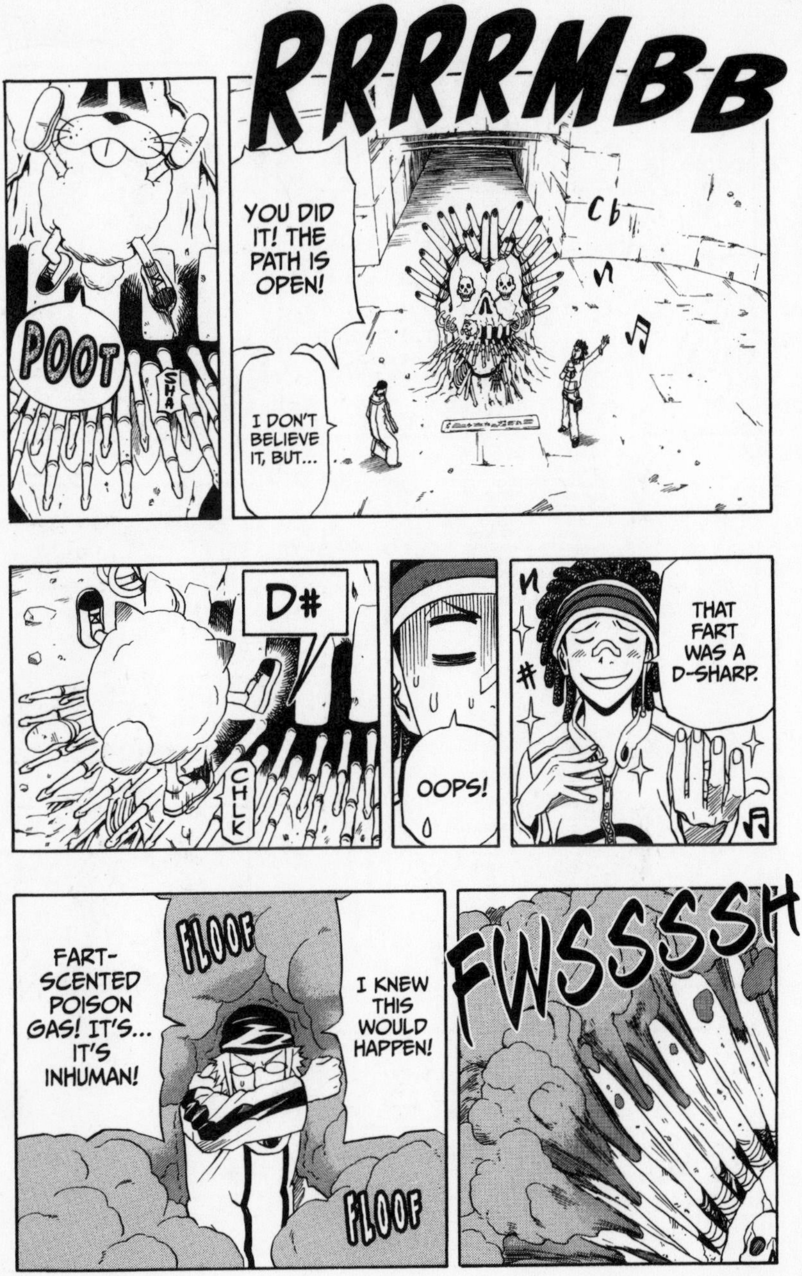
RRRRMBB
YOU DID IT! THE PATH IS OPEN!
I DON'T BELIEVE IT, BUT...
Cb
POOT
SHA
THAT FART WAS A D-SHARP.
OOPS!
D#
CHLK
FWSSSSH
FLOOF
I KNEW THIS WOULD HAPPEN!
FART-SCENTED POISON GAS! IT'S... IT'S INHUMAN!
FLOOF

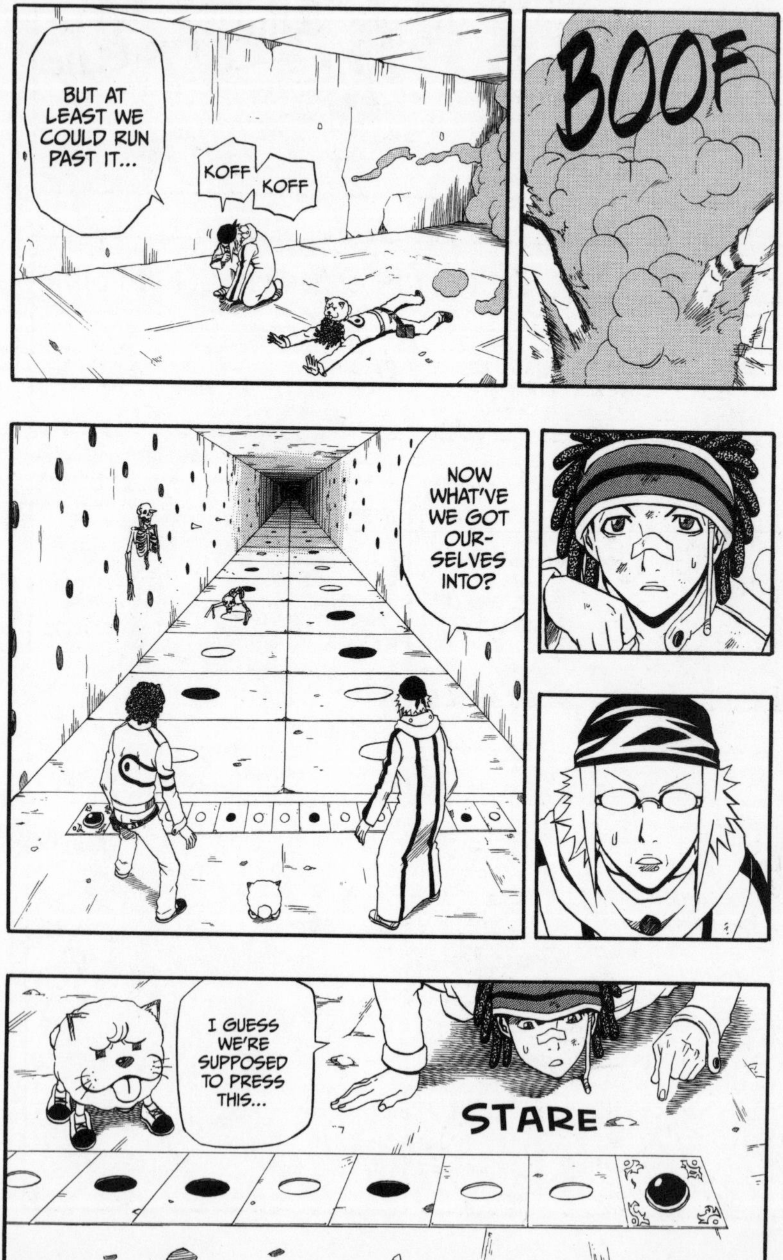
BOOF
BUT AT LEAST WE COULD RUN PAST IT...
KOFF
KOFF
NOW WHAT'VE WE GOT OUR-SELVES INTO?
I GUESS WE'RE SUPPOSED TO PRESS THIS...
STARE

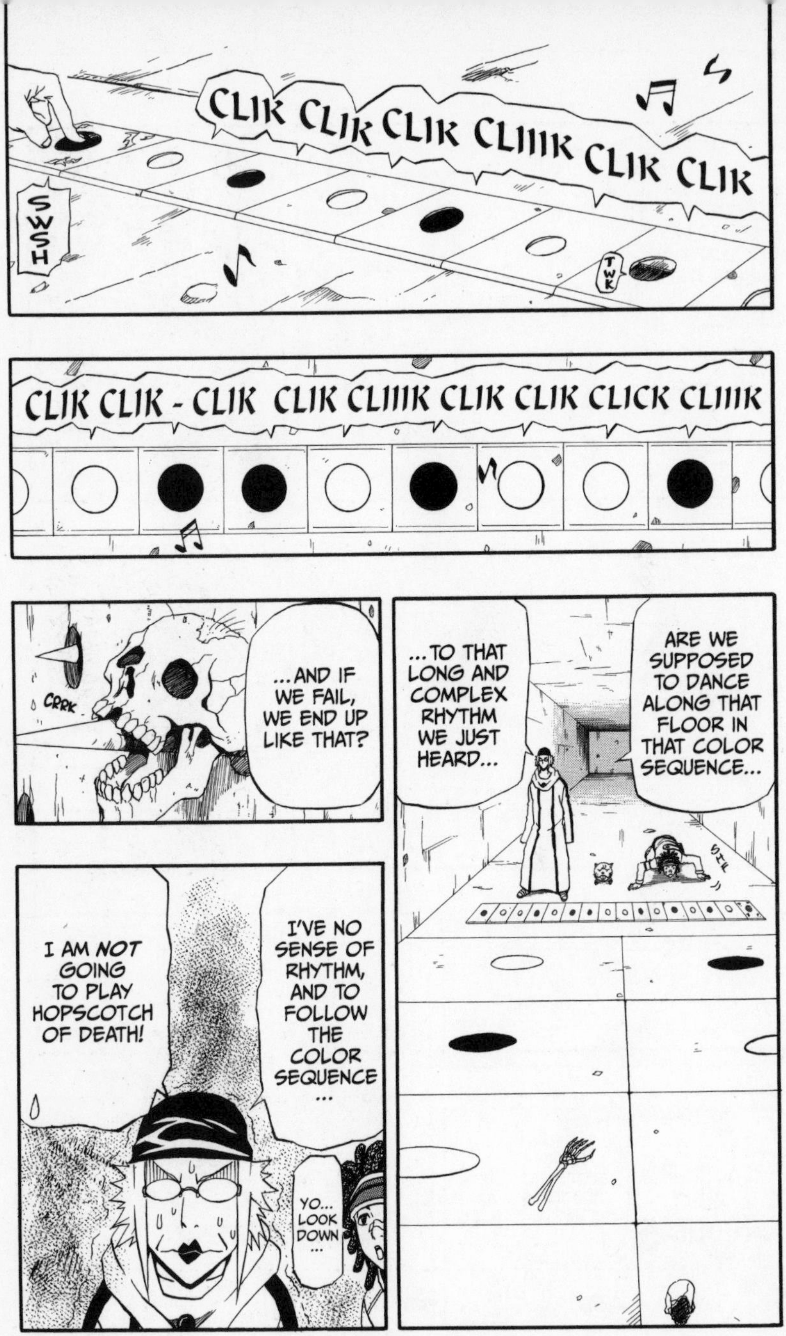
CLIK CLIK CLIK CLIIIK CLIK CLIK
SWSH
TWK
CLIK CLIK - CLIK CLIK CLIIIK CLIK CLIK CLICK CLIIIK
ARE WE SUPPOSED TO DANCE ALONG THAT FLOOR IN THAT COLOR SEQUENCE...
...TO THAT LONG AND COMPLEX RHYTHM WE JUST HEARD...
SIL
...AND IF WE FAIL, WE END UP LIKE THAT?
CRRK
I'VE NO SENSE OF RHYTHM, AND TO FOLLOW THE COLOR SEQUENCE ...
I AM *NOT* GOING TO PLAY HOPSCOTCH OF DEATH!
YO... LOOK DOWN ...

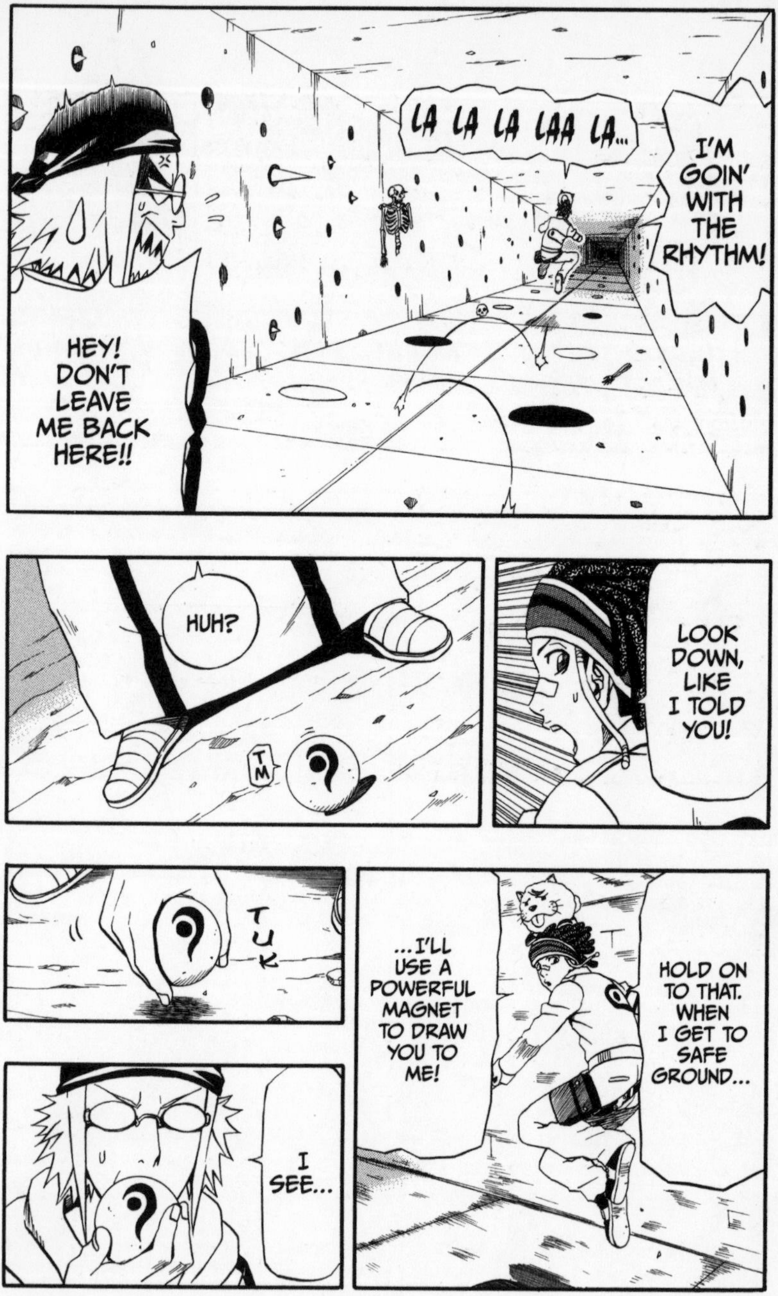
I'M GOIN' WITH THE RHYTHM!
LA LA LA LAA LA...
HEY! DON'T LEAVE ME BACK HERE!!
LOOK DOWN, LIKE I TOLD YOU!
HUH?
TM
HOLD ON TO THAT. WHEN I GET TO SAFE GROUND...
...I'LL USE A POWERFUL MAGNET TO DRAW YOU TO ME!
TUK
I SEE...

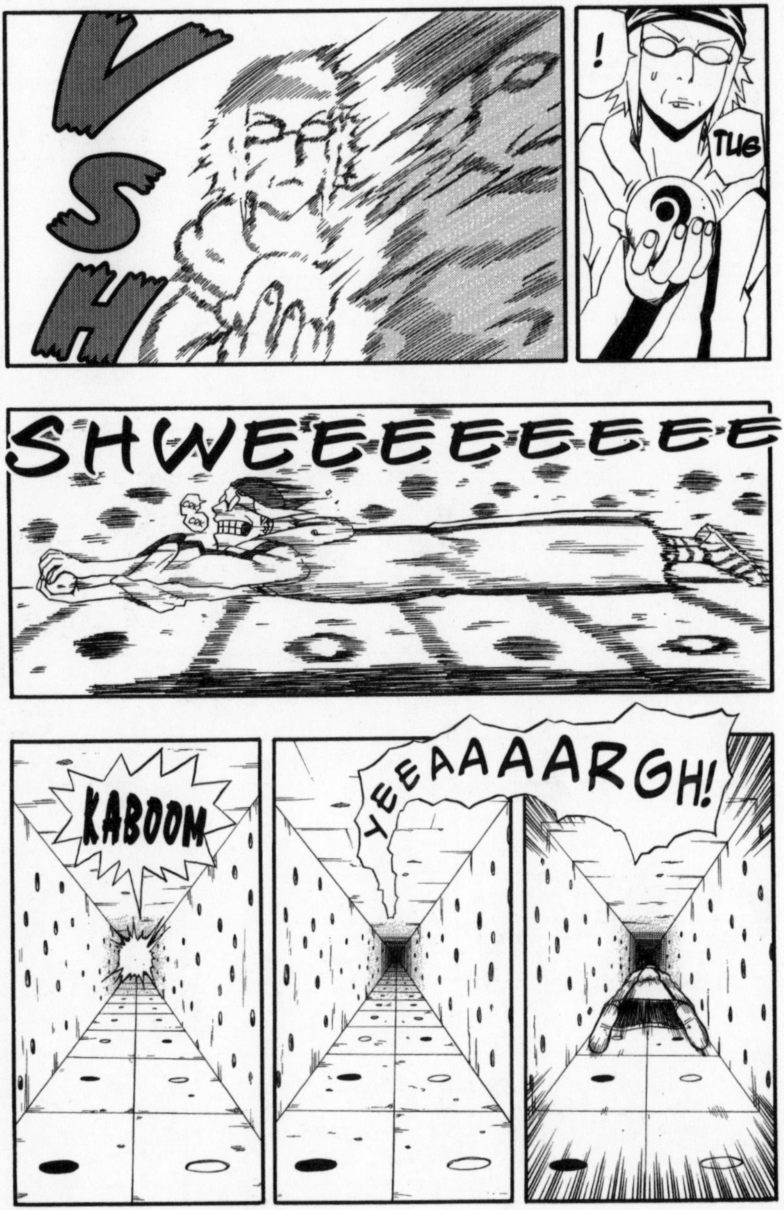
!
TUG
VSH
SHWEEEEEEEEE
CRK
CRK
YEEAAAARGH!
KABOOM

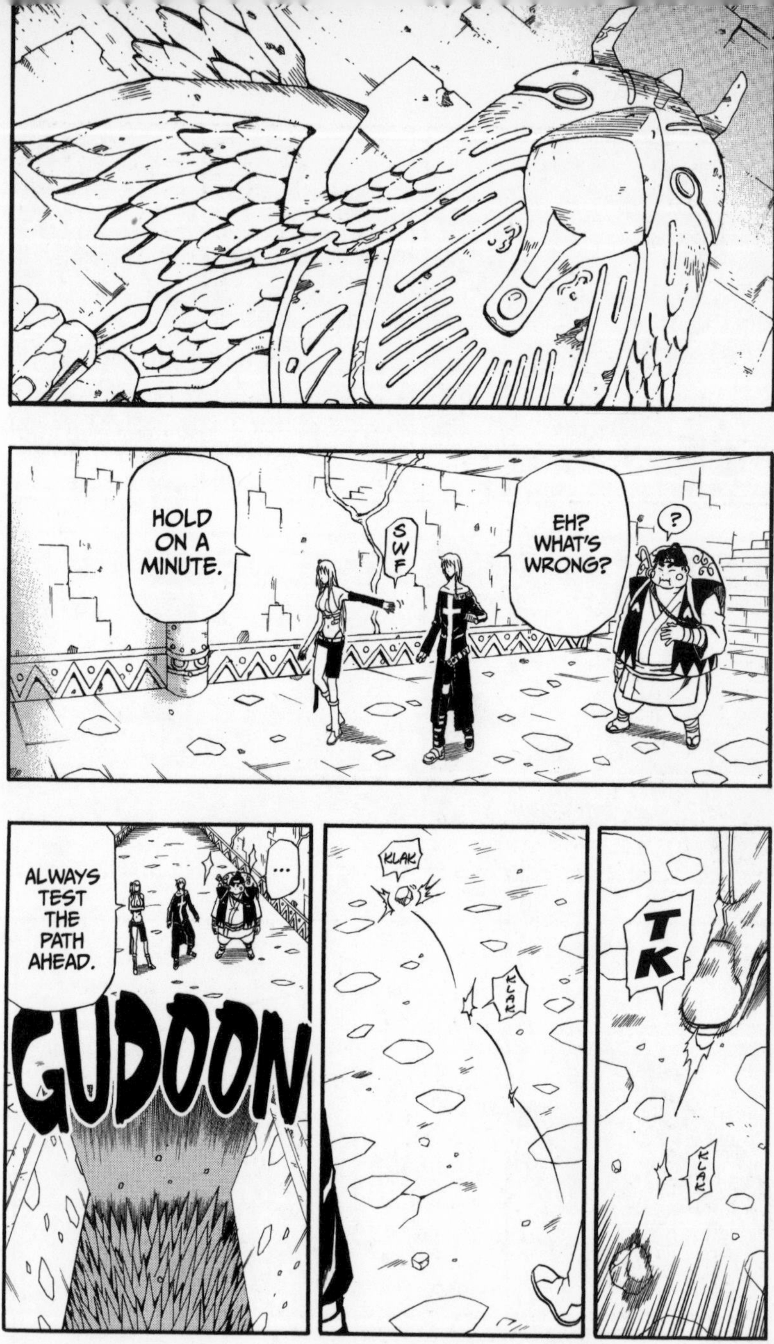
?
EH? WHAT'S WRONG?
SWF
HOLD ON A MINUTE.
TK
KLAK
KLAK
KLAK
...
ALWAYS TEST THE PATH AHEAD.
GUDOON

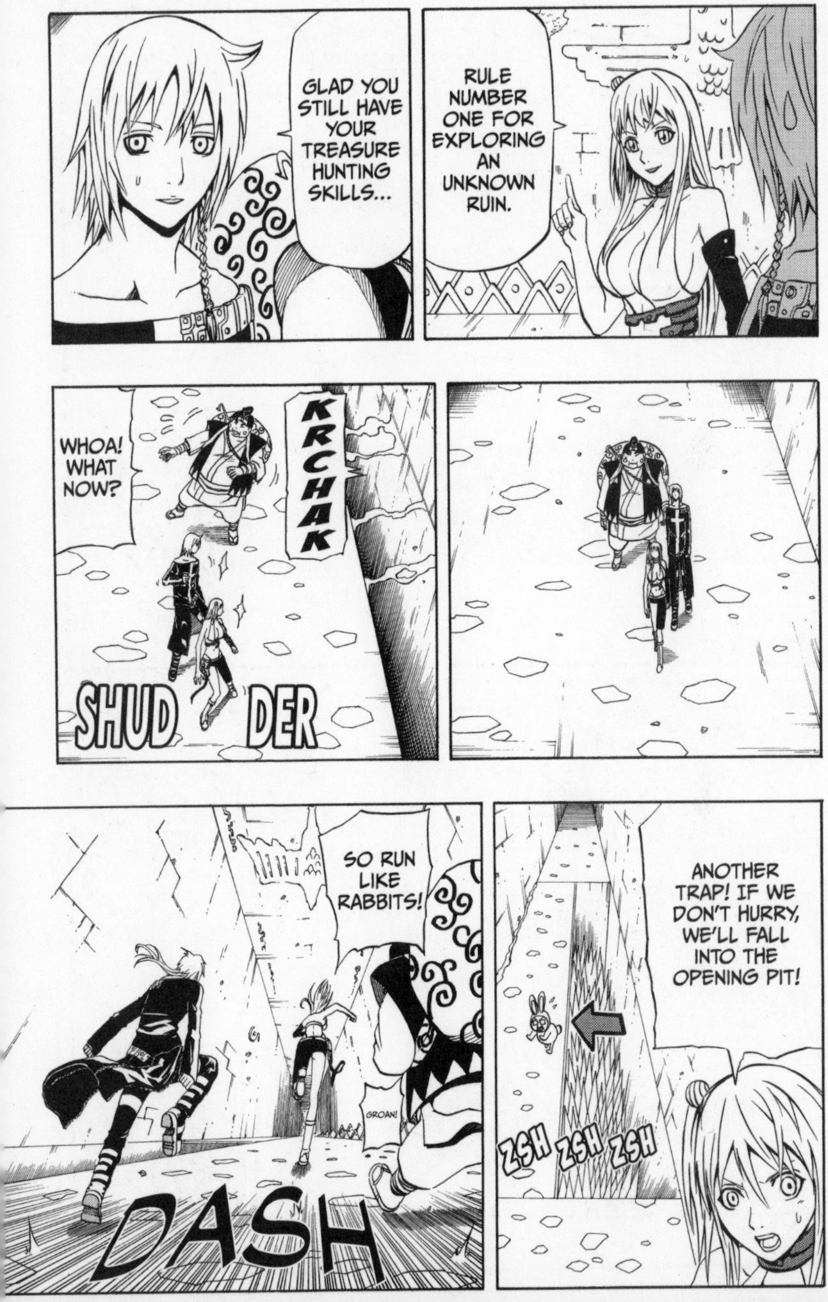
RULE NUMBER ONE FOR EXPLORING AN UNKNOWN RUIN.
GLAD YOU STILL HAVE YOUR TREASURE HUNTING SKILLS...
KRCHAK
WHOA! WHAT NOW?
SHUD DER
ANOTHER TRAP! IF WE DON'T HURRY, WE'LL FALL INTO THE OPENING PIT!
ZSH ZSH ZSH
SO RUN LIKE RABBITS!
GROAN!
DASH

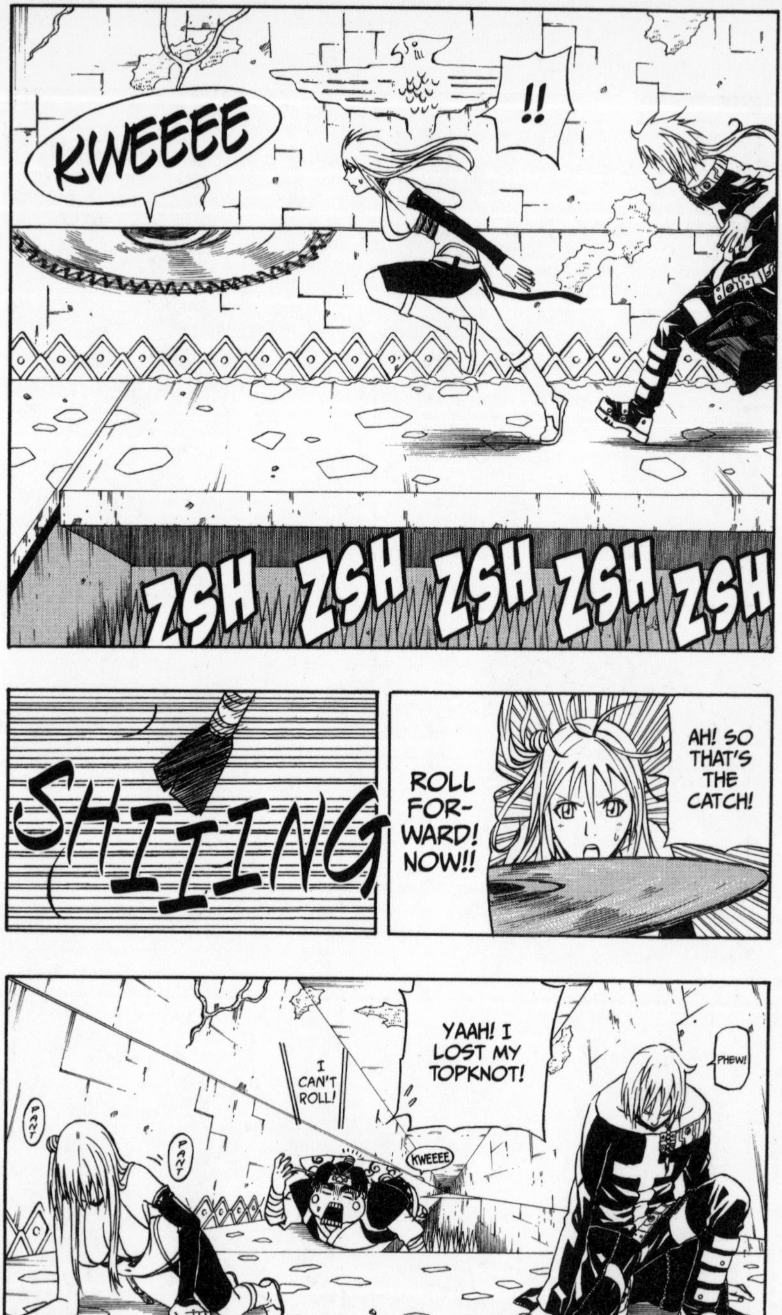
!!
KWEEEE
ZSH ZSH ZSH ZSH ZSH
AH! SO THAT'S THE CATCH!
ROLL FOR-WARD! NOW!!
SHIIING
PHEW!
YAAH! I LOST MY TOPKNOT!
I CAN'T ROLL!
KWEEEE
PANT
PANT

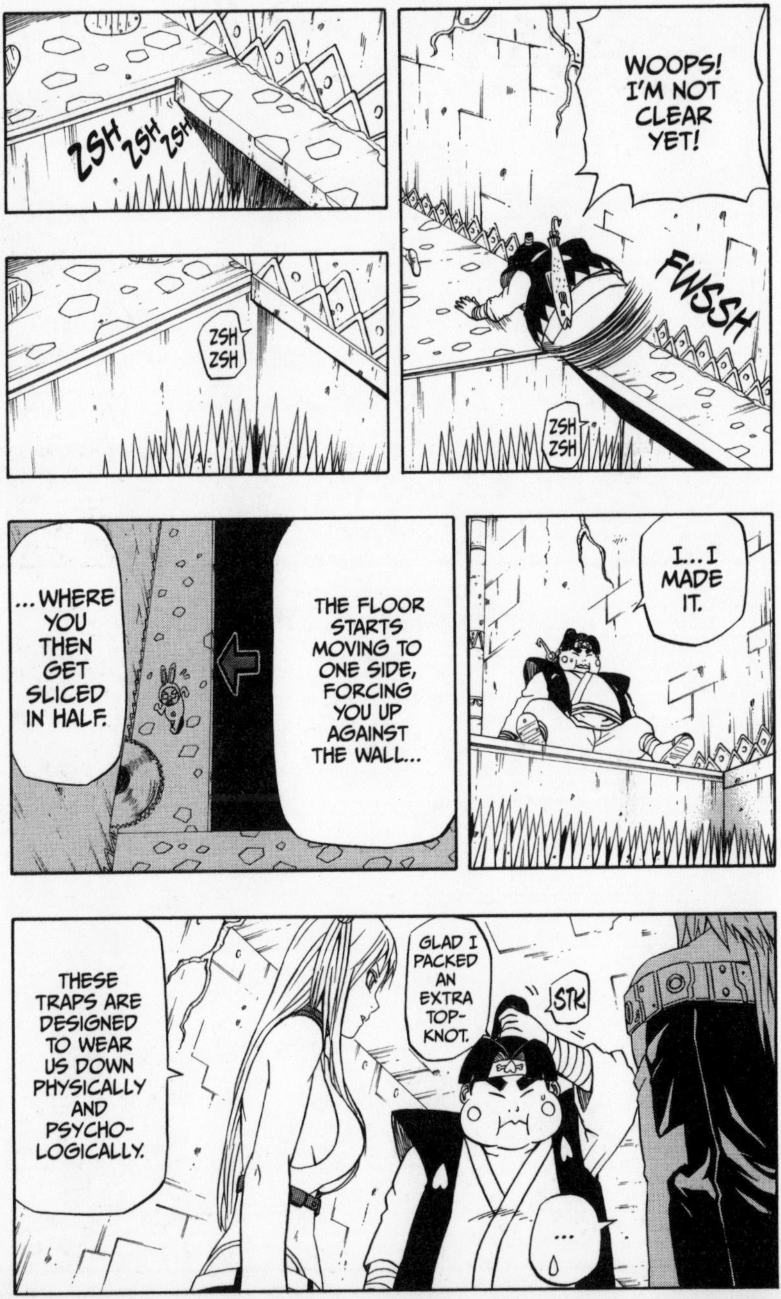
WOOPS! I'M NOT CLEAR YET!
FWSSH
ZSH ZSH
ZSH ZSH ZSH
ZSH ZSH
I... I MADE IT.
THE FLOOR STARTS MOVING TO ONE SIDE, FORCING YOU UP AGAINST THE WALL...
...WHERE YOU THEN GET SLICED IN HALF.
STK
GLAD I PACKED AN EXTRA TOP-KNOT.
THESE TRAPS ARE DESIGNED TO WEAR US DOWN PHYSICALLY AND PSYCHO-LOGICALLY.
...

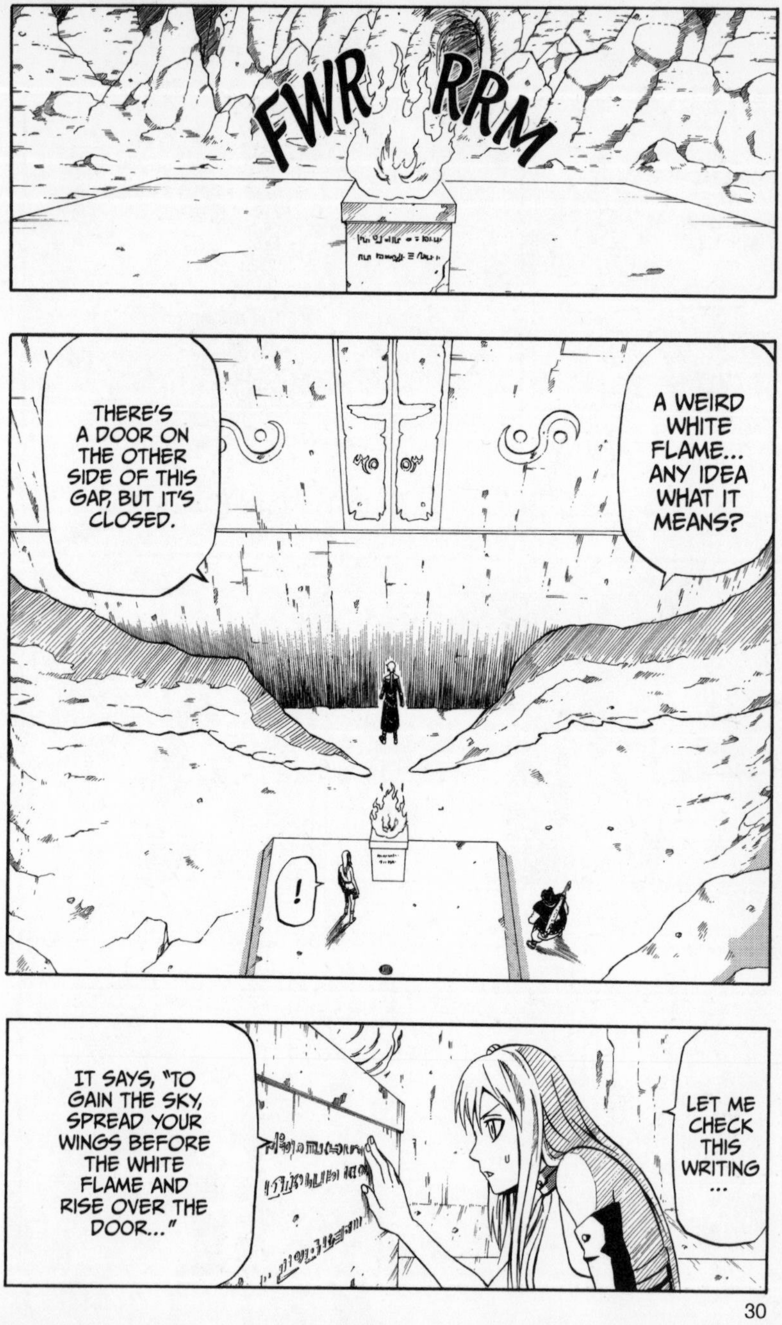
FWR RRM
A WEIRD WHITE FLAME... ANY IDEA WHAT IT MEANS?
THERE'S A DOOR ON THE OTHER SIDE OF THIS GAP, BUT IT'S CLOSED.
!
LET ME CHECK THIS WRITING ...
IT SAYS, "TO GAIN THE SKY, SPREAD YOUR WINGS BEFORE THE WHITE FLAME AND RISE OVER THE DOOR..."

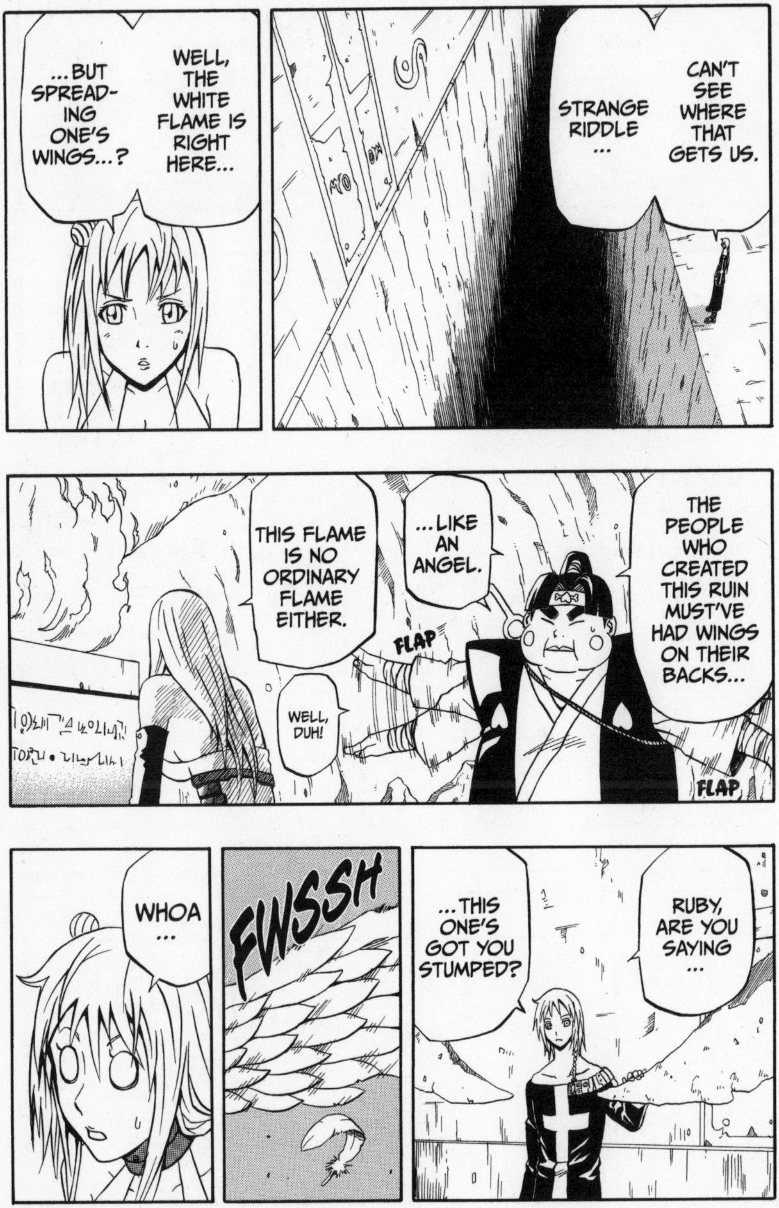
CAN'T SEE WHERE THAT GETS US.
STRANGE RIDDLE ...
WELL, THE WHITE FLAME IS RIGHT HERE...
...BUT SPREADING ONE'S WINGS...?
THE PEOPLE WHO CREATED THIS RUIN MUST'VE HAD WINGS ON THEIR BACKS...
FLAP
...LIKE AN ANGEL.
FLAP
THIS FLAME IS NO ORDINARY FLAME EITHER.
WELL, DUH!
RUBY, ARE YOU SAYING ...
...THIS ONE'S GOT YOU STUMPED?
FWSSH
WHOA ...

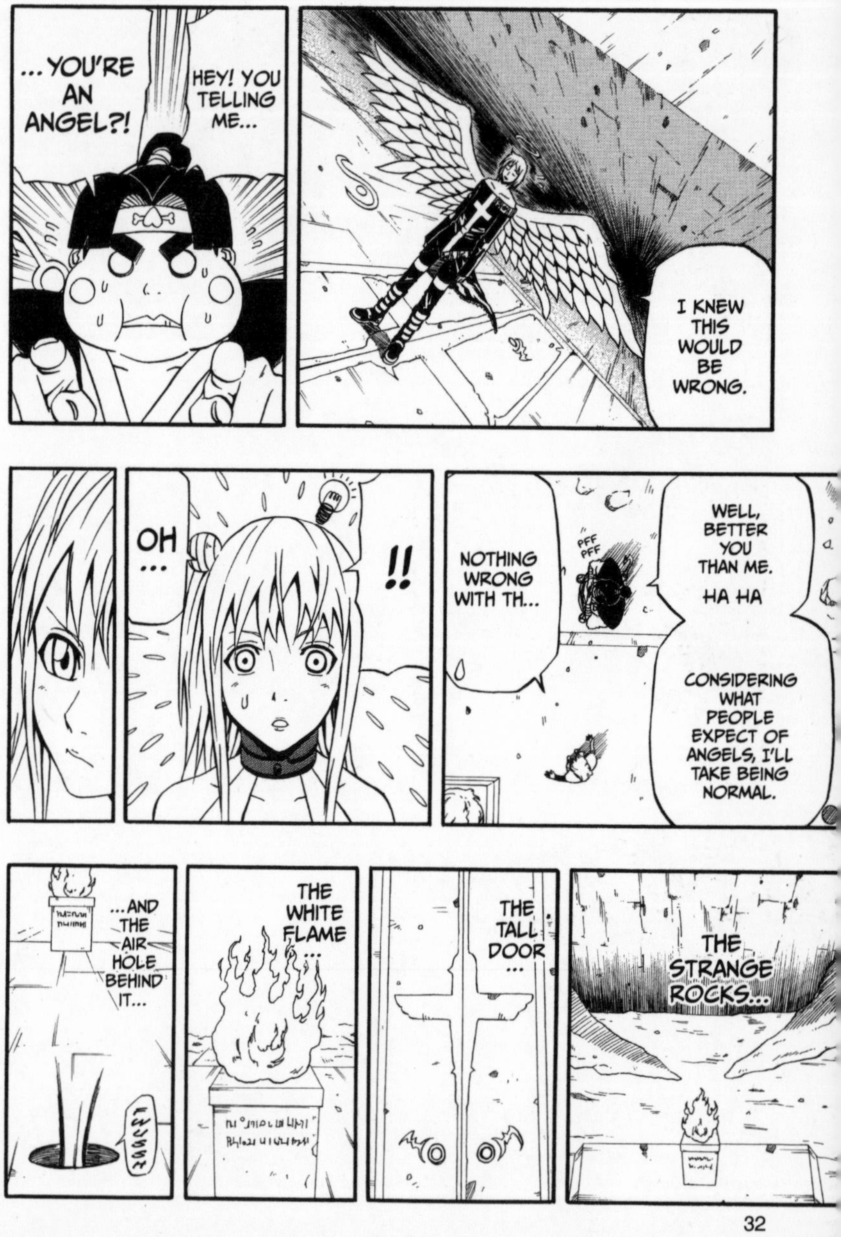
I KNEW THIS WOULD BE WRONG.
HEY! YOU TELLING ME...
...YOU'RE AN ANGEL?!
WELL, BETTER YOU THAN ME.
HA HA
CONSIDERING WHAT PEOPLE EXPECT OF ANGELS, I'LL TAKE BEING NORMAL.
PFF PFF
NOTHING WRONG WITH TH...
!!
OH ...
THE STRANGE ROCKS...
THE TALL DOOR ...
THE WHITE FLAME ...
...AND THE AIR HOLE BEHIND IT...
FWUSSH

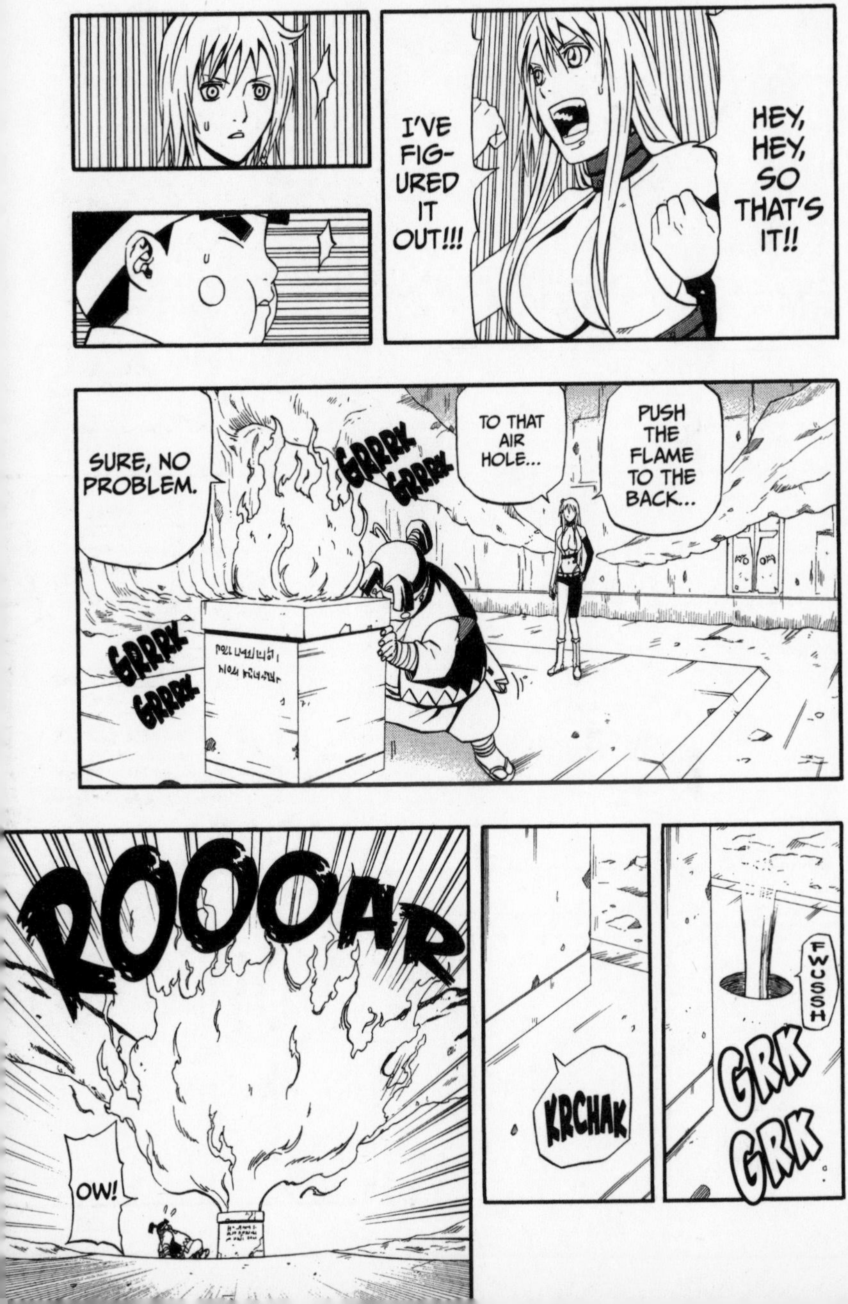
HEY, HEY, SO THAT'S IT!!
I'VE FIG-URED IT OUT!!!
PUSH THE FLAME TO THE BACK...
TO THAT AIR HOLE...
GRRRK GRRRK
SURE, NO PROBLEM.
GRRRK GRRRK
FWUSSH
GRK GRK
KRCHAK
ROOOAR
OW!

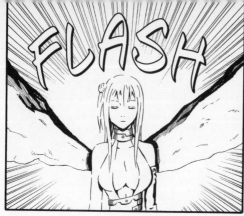

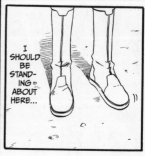

I SHOULD BE STAND-ING ABOUT HERE...
FLASH
SHWOOO
ROOOAR
RISE OVER THE DOOR BEFORE THE WHITE FLAME...
...WITH YOUR WINGS SPREAD OUT...
THAT'S THE FORMULA!
ZSH ZSH ZSH

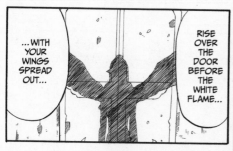

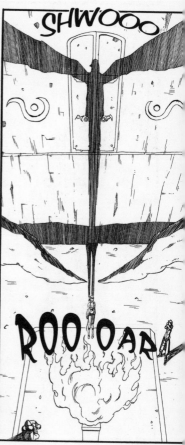

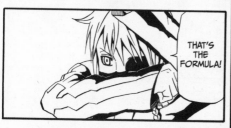

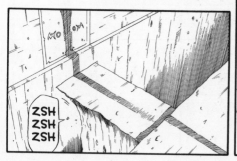

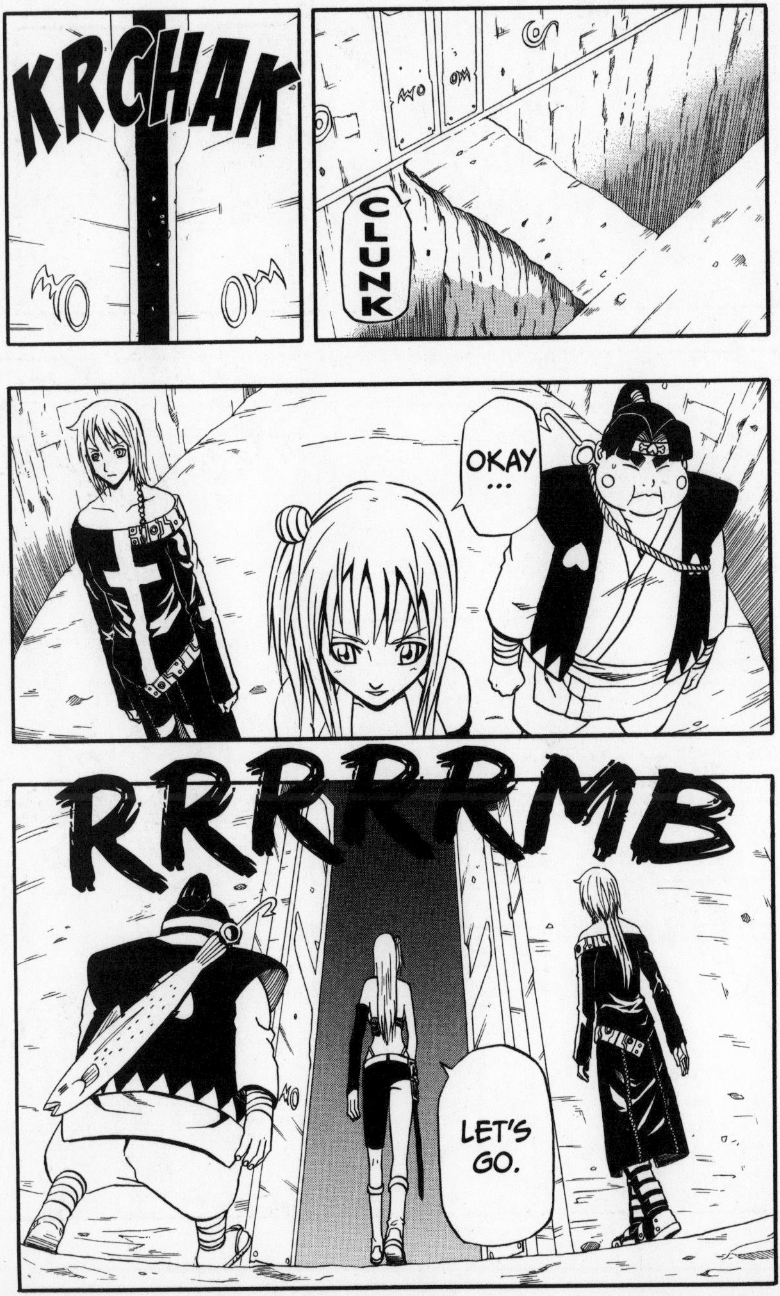
CLUNK
KRCHAK
OKAY...
RRRRRMB
LET'S GO.

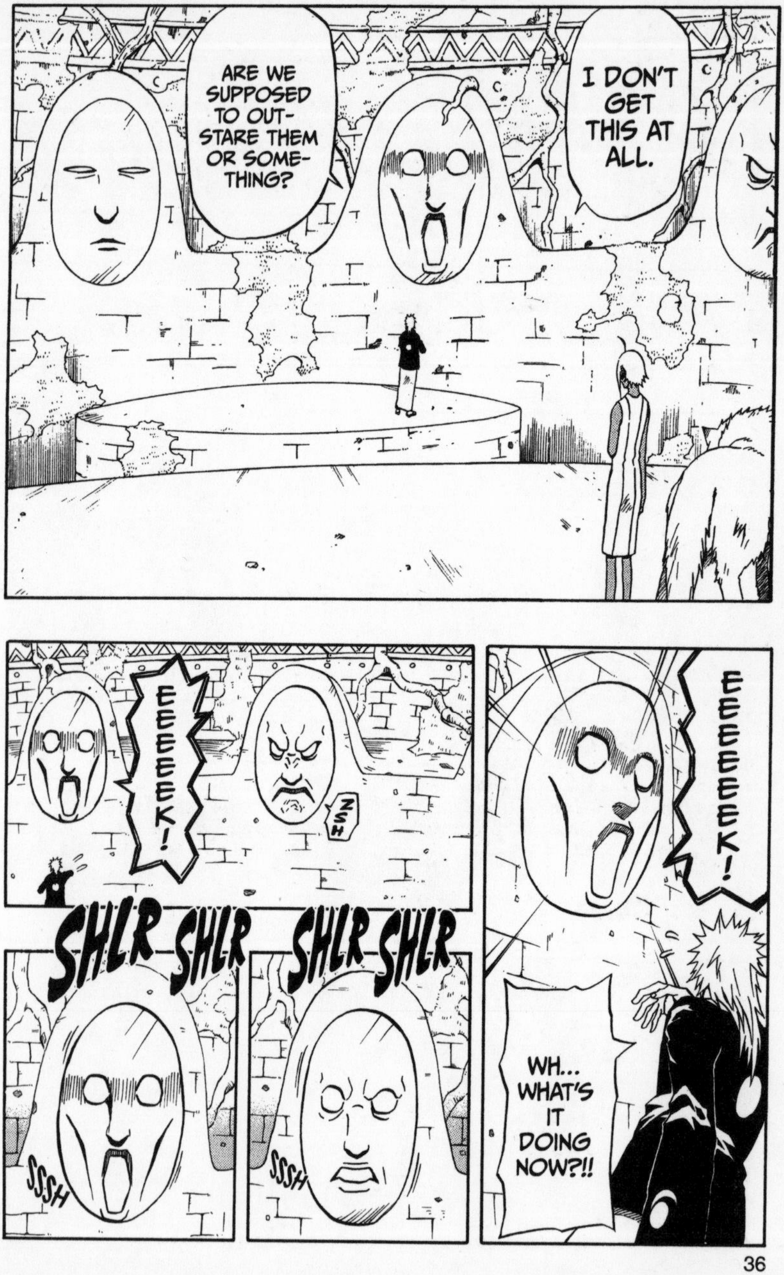
I DON'T GET THIS AT ALL.
ARE WE SUPPOSED TO OUT-STARE THEM OR SOME-THING?
EEEEEEEK!
WH... WHAT'S IT DOING NOW?!!
EEEEEEK!
ZSH
SHLR SHLR
SSSH
SHLR SHLR
SSSH

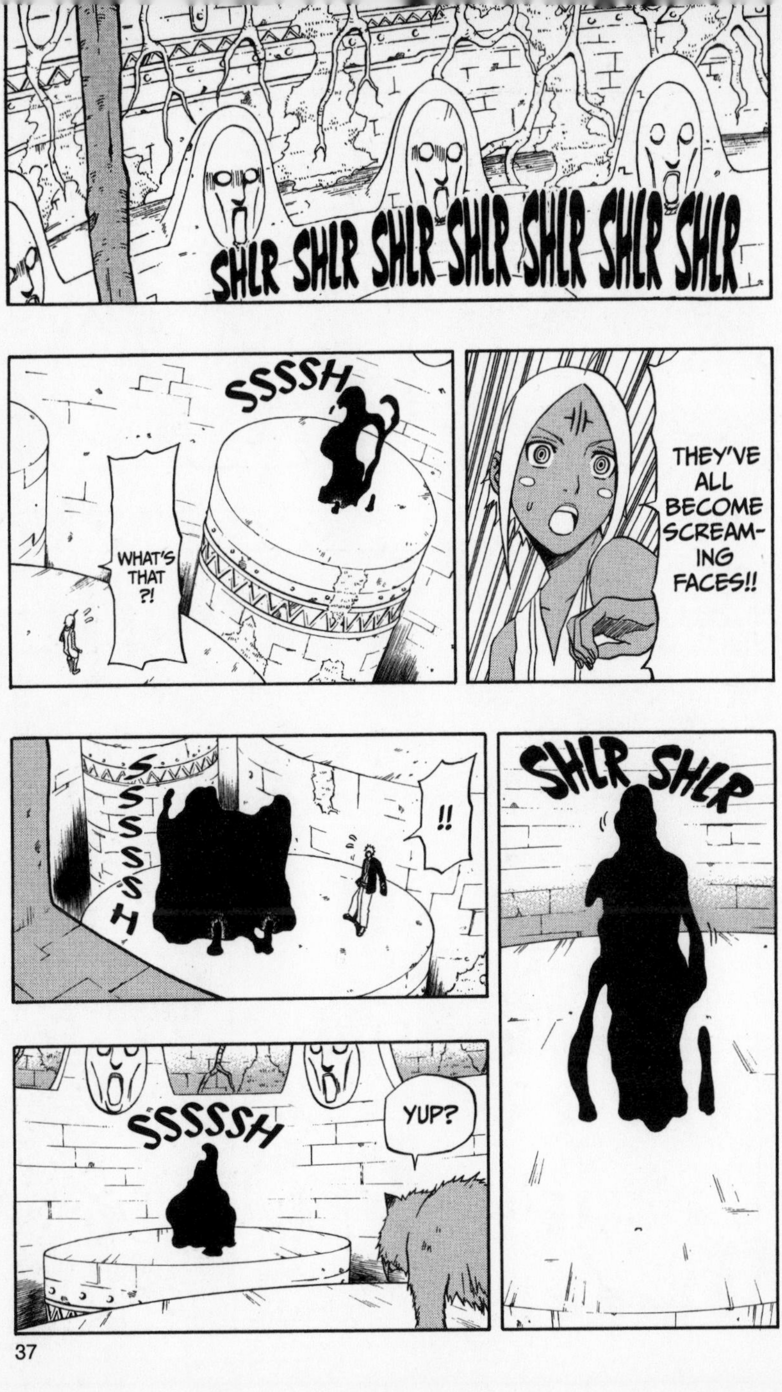
SHLR SHLR SHLR SHLR SHLR SHLR SHLR
THEY'VE ALL BECOME SCREAM-ING FACES!!
SSSSH
WHAT'S THAT ?!
SHLR SHLR
SSSSSH
!!
SSSSSH
YUP?

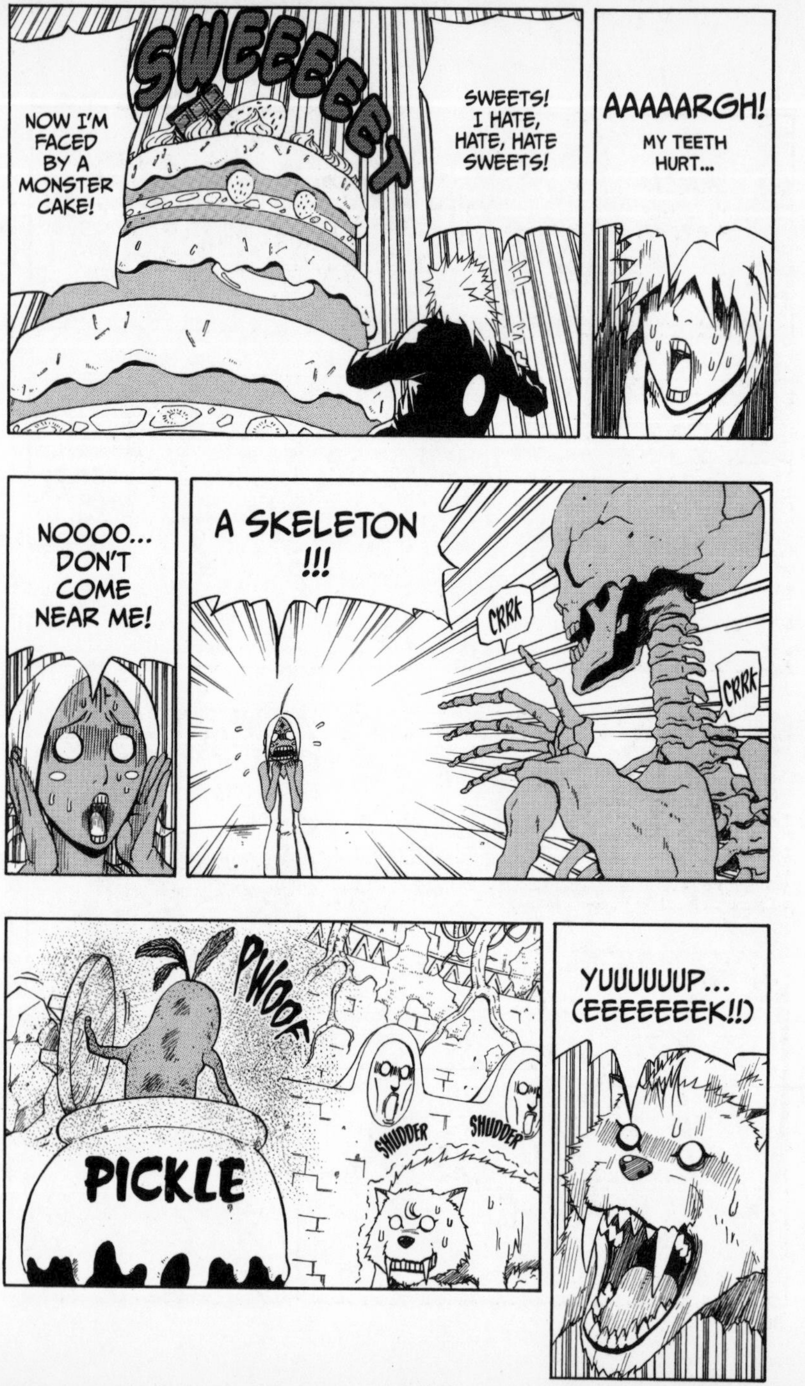
AAAAARGH!
MY TEETH HURT...
SWEETS! I HATE, HATE, HATE SWEETS!
SWEEEEEET
NOW I'M FACED BY A MONSTER CAKE!
A SKELETON !!!
CRRK
CRRK
NOOOO... DON'T COME NEAR ME!
YUUUUUUP... (EEEEEEEK!!)
PWOOF
SHUDDER
SHUDDER
PICKLE

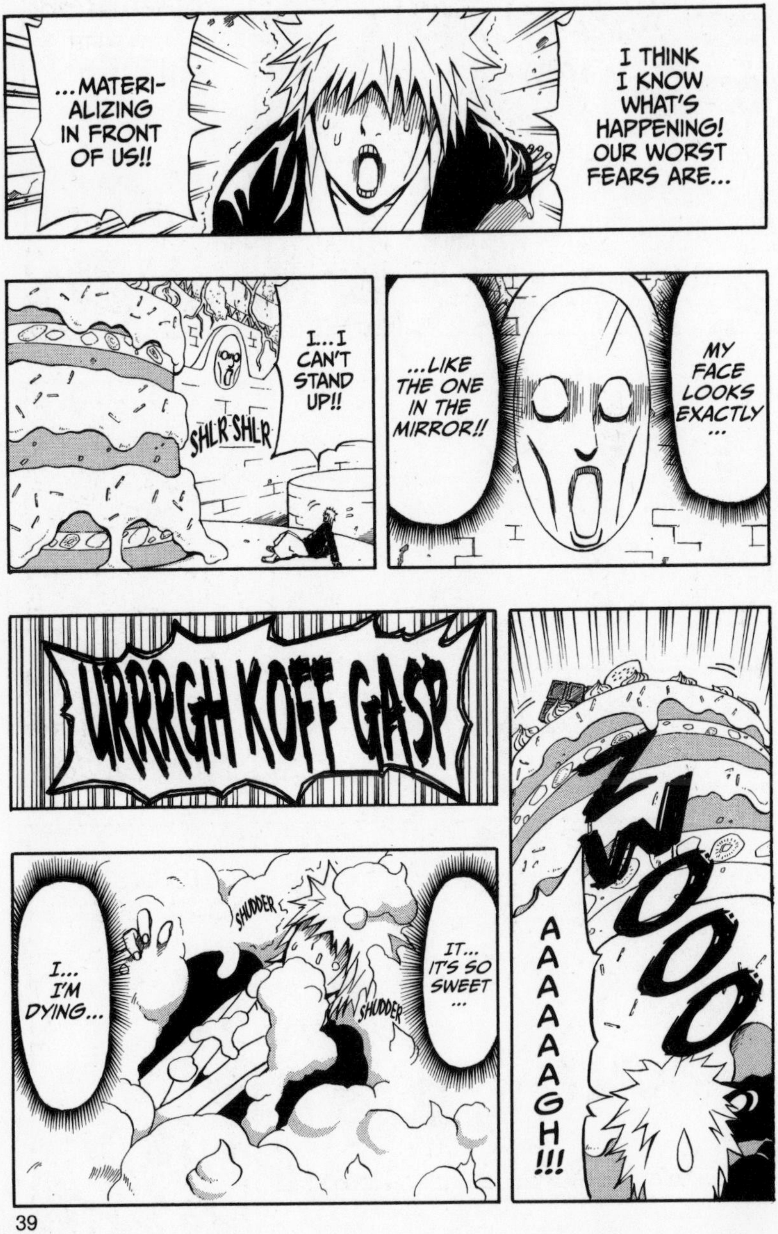

I THINK I KNOW WHAT'S HAPPENING! OUR WORST FEARS ARE...
...MATERI-ALIZING IN FRONT OF US!!
MY FACE LOOKS EXACTLY...
...LIKE THE ONE IN THE MIRROR!!
I...I CAN'T STAND UP!!
SHLR SHLR
NOOOO
AAAAAAAGH!!!
URRRGH KOFF GASP
IT... IT'S SO SWEET...
SHUDDER
SHUDDER
I... I'M DYING...

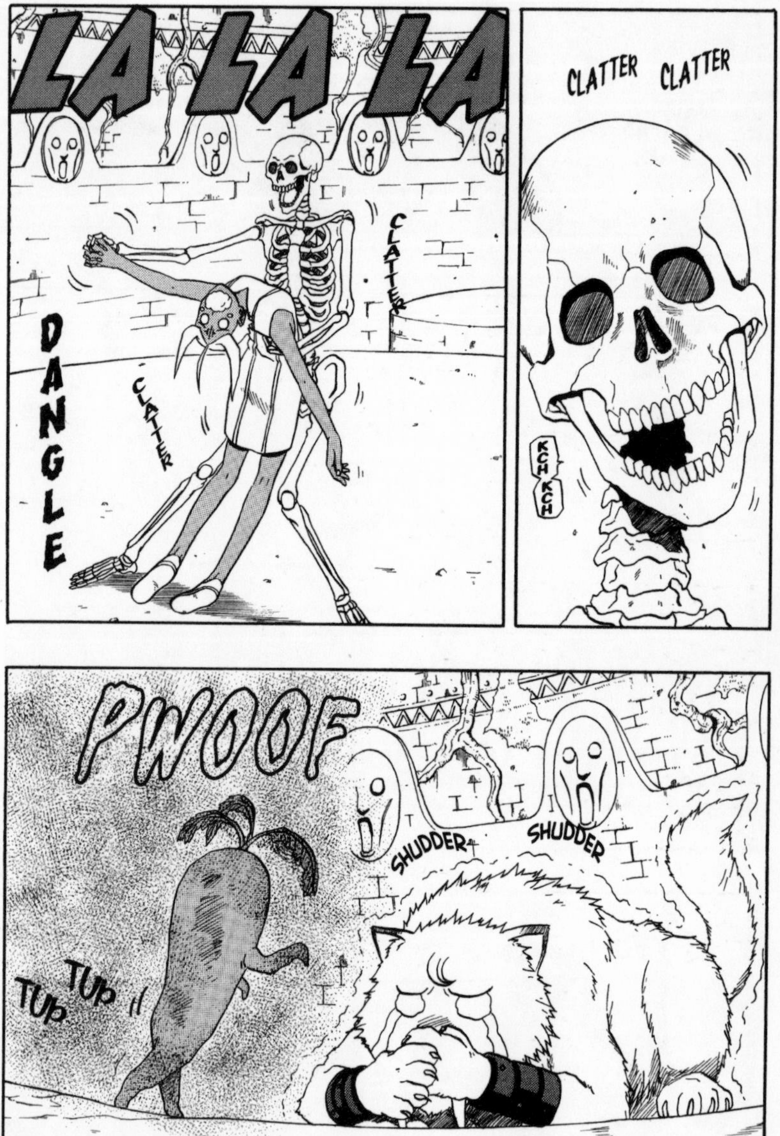
CLATTER CLATTER
KCH KCH
LA LA LA
CLATTER
DANGLE
CLATTER
PWOOF
SHUDDER SHUDDER
TUP TUP

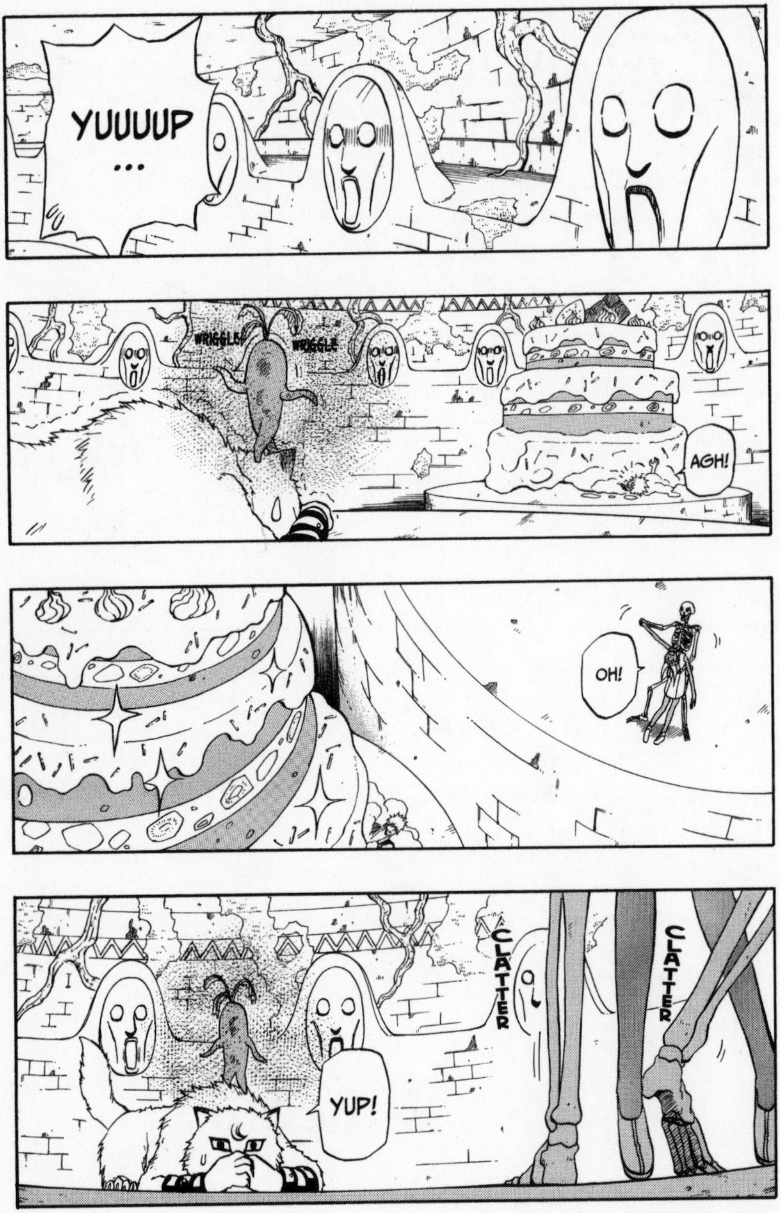
YUUUUP ...
AGH!
WRIGGLE
WRIGGLE
OH!
CLATTER
CLATTER
YUP!

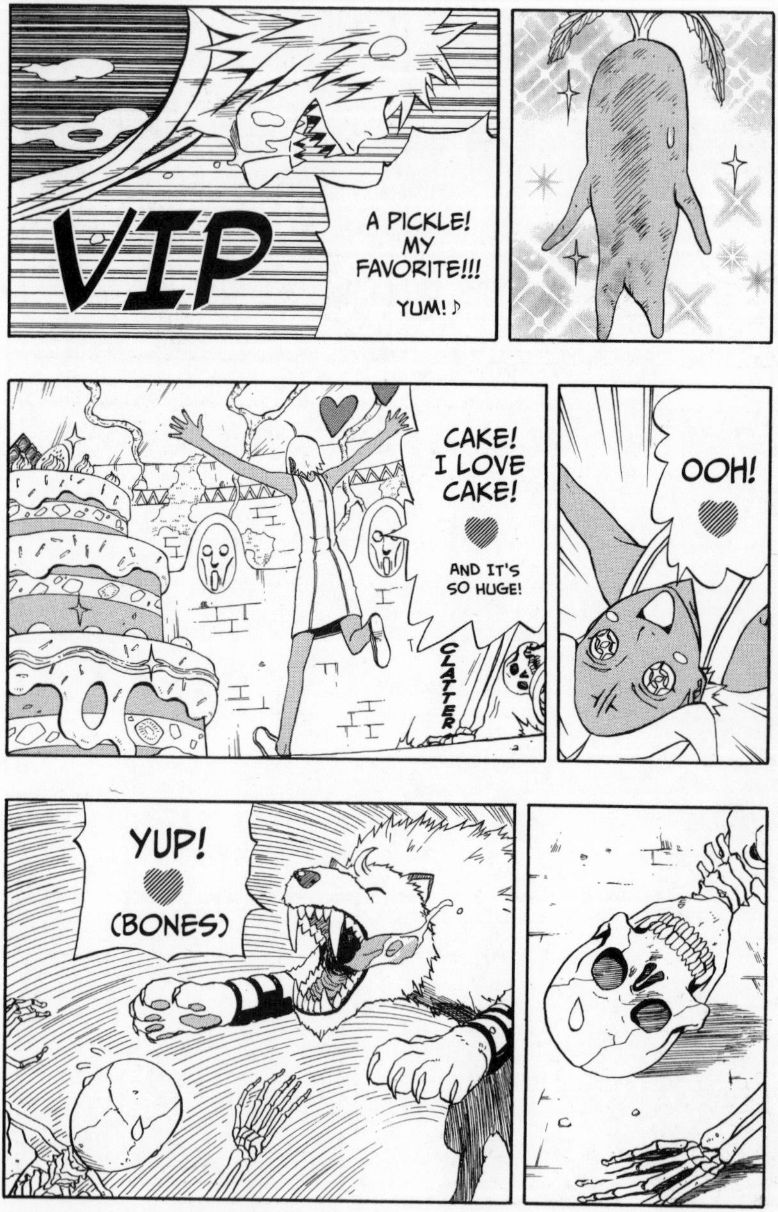
VIP
A PICKLE! MY FAVORITE!!!
YUM! ♪
OOH!
CAKE! I LOVE CAKE!
AND IT'S SO HUGE!
CLATTER
YUP!
(BONES)

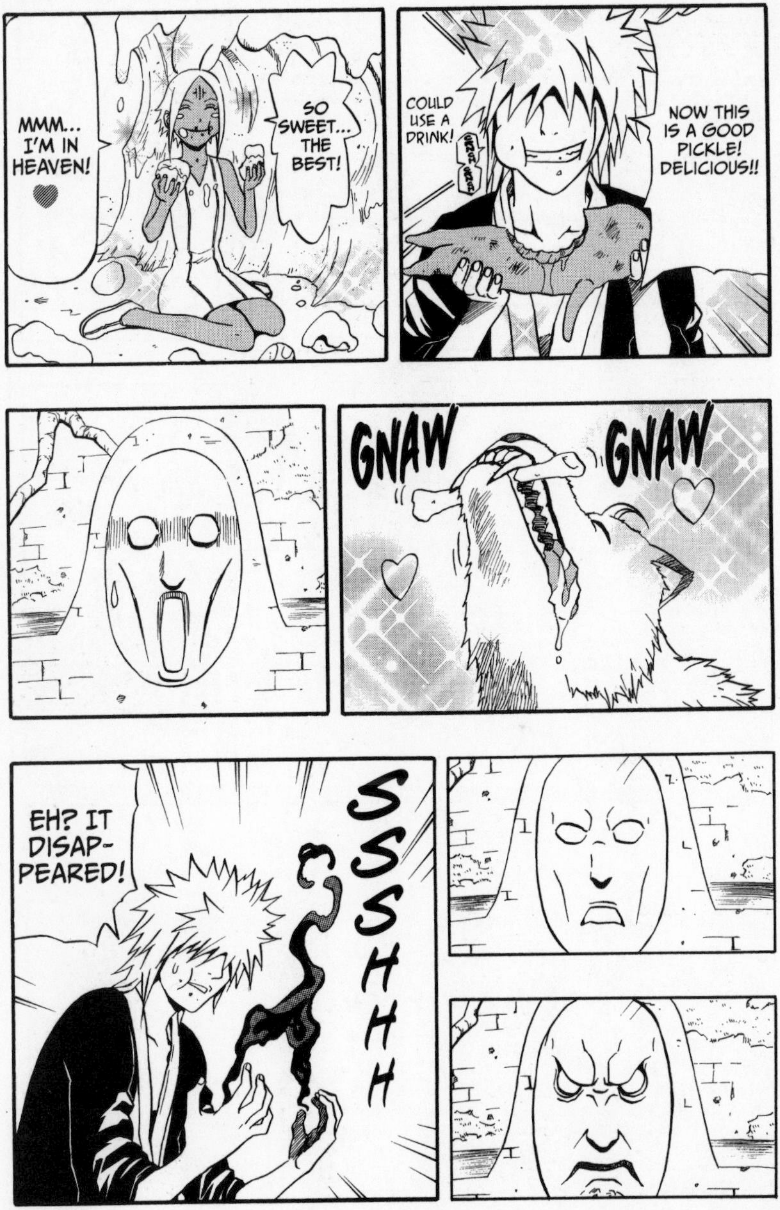
NOW THIS IS A GOOD PICKLE! DELICIOUS!!
COULD USE A DRINK!
SO SWEET... THE BEST!
MMM... I'M IN HEAVEN!
GNAW
GNAW
SSSHHH
EH? IT DISAPPEARED!

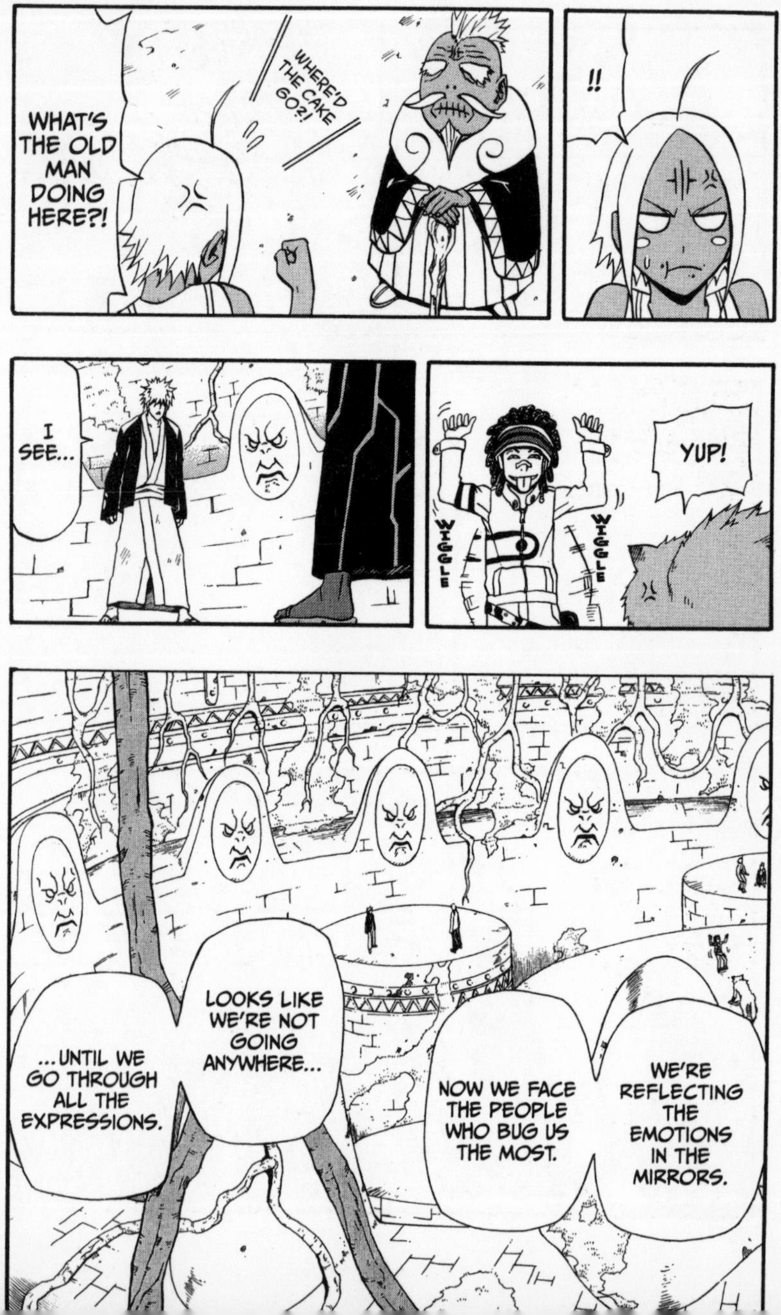
!!
WHERE'D THE CAKE GO?!
WHAT'S THE OLD MAN DOING HERE?!
YUP!
WIGGLE
WIGGLE
I SEE...
WE'RE REFLECTING THE EMOTIONS IN THE MIRRORS.
NOW WE FACE THE PEOPLE WHO BUG US THE MOST.
LOOKS LIKE WE'RE NOT GOING ANYWHERE...
...UNTIL WE GO THROUGH ALL THE EXPRESSIONS.

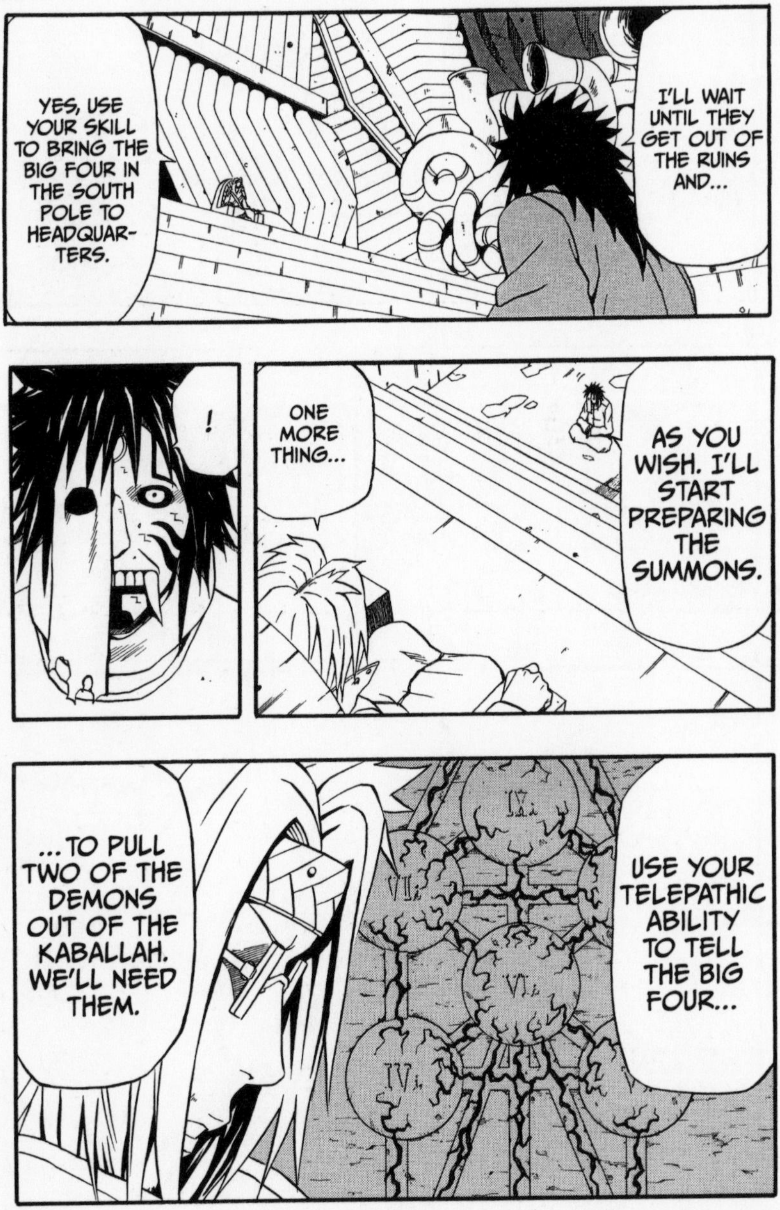
I'LL WAIT UNTIL THEY GET OUT OF THE RUINS AND...
YES, USE YOUR SKILL TO BRING THE BIG FOUR IN THE SOUTH POLE TO HEADQUAR-TERS.
AS YOU WISH. I'LL START PREPARING THE SUMMONS.
ONE MORE THING...
!
USE YOUR TELEPATHIC ABILITY TO TELL THE BIG FOUR...
...TO PULL TWO OF THE DEMONS OUT OF THE KABALLAH. WE'LL NEED THEM.

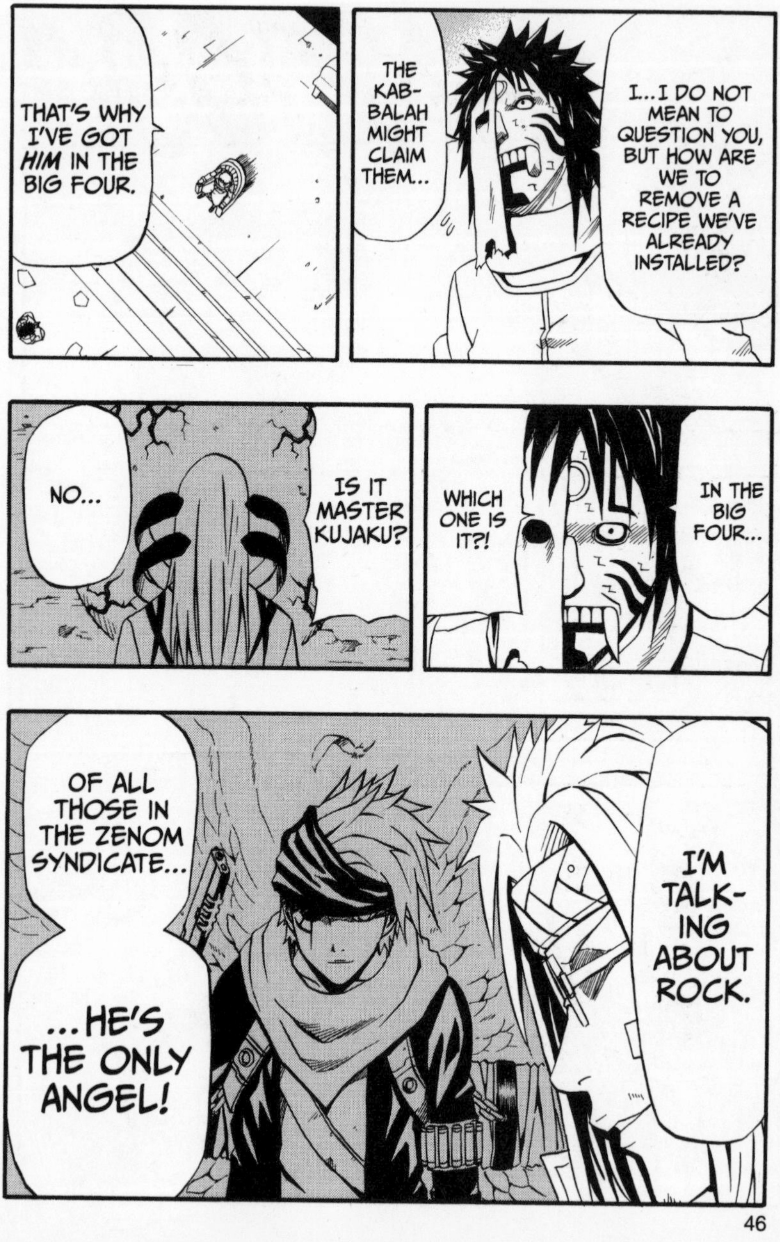

I...I DO NOT MEAN TO QUESTION YOU, BUT HOW ARE WE TO REMOVE A RECIPE WE'VE ALREADY INSTALLED?
THE KAB-BALAH MIGHT CLAIM THEM...
THAT'S WHY I'VE GOT *HIM* IN THE BIG FOUR.
IN THE BIG FOUR...
WHICH ONE IS IT?!
IS IT MASTER KUJAKU?
NO...
I'M TALK-ING ABOUT ROCK.
OF ALL THOSE IN THE ZENOM SYNDICATE...
...HE'S THE ONLY ANGEL!

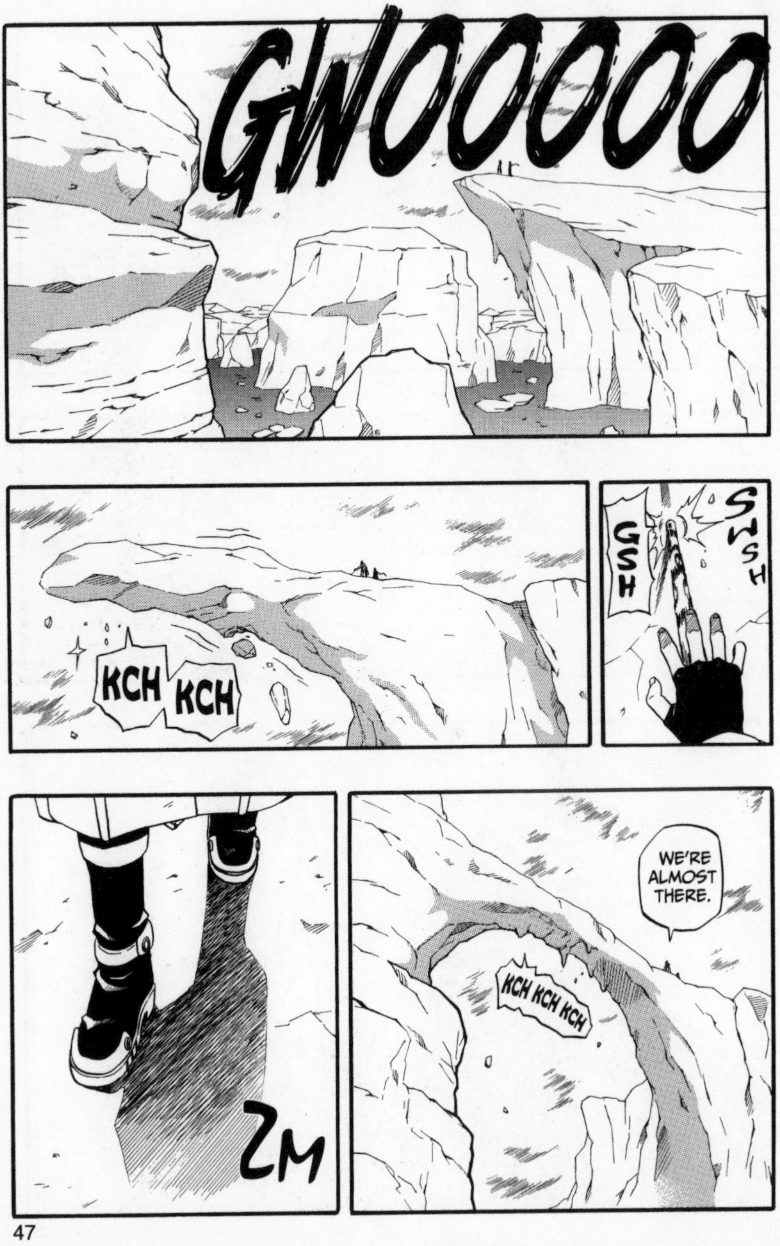
GWOOOOOO
GSH
SWSH
KCH KCH
WE'RE ALMOST THERE.
KCH KCH KCH
ZM

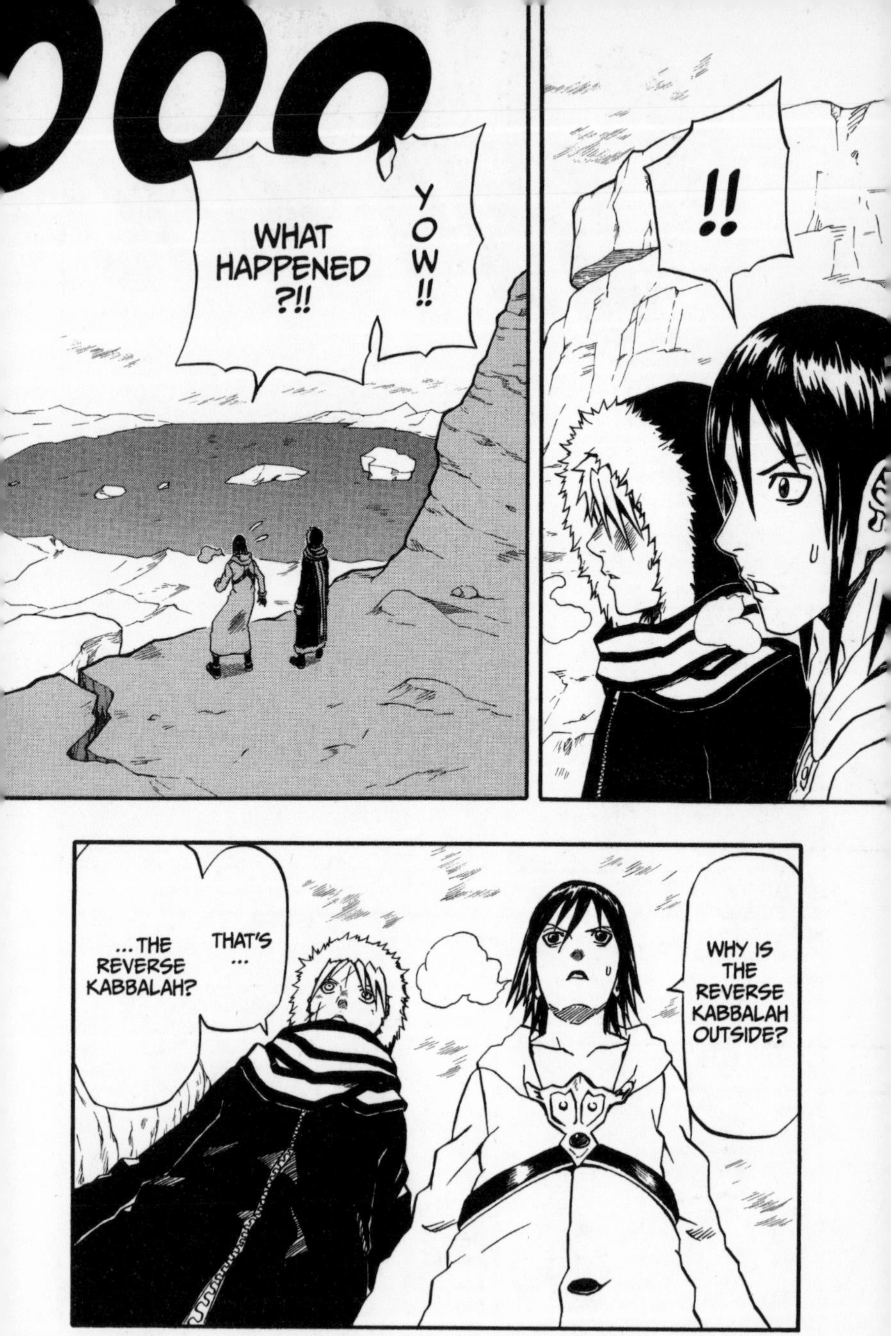
!!
OOOO
YOW!!
WHAT HAPPENED ?!!
WHY IS THE REVERSE KABBALAH OUTSIDE?
THAT'S ...
... THE REVERSE KABBALAH?

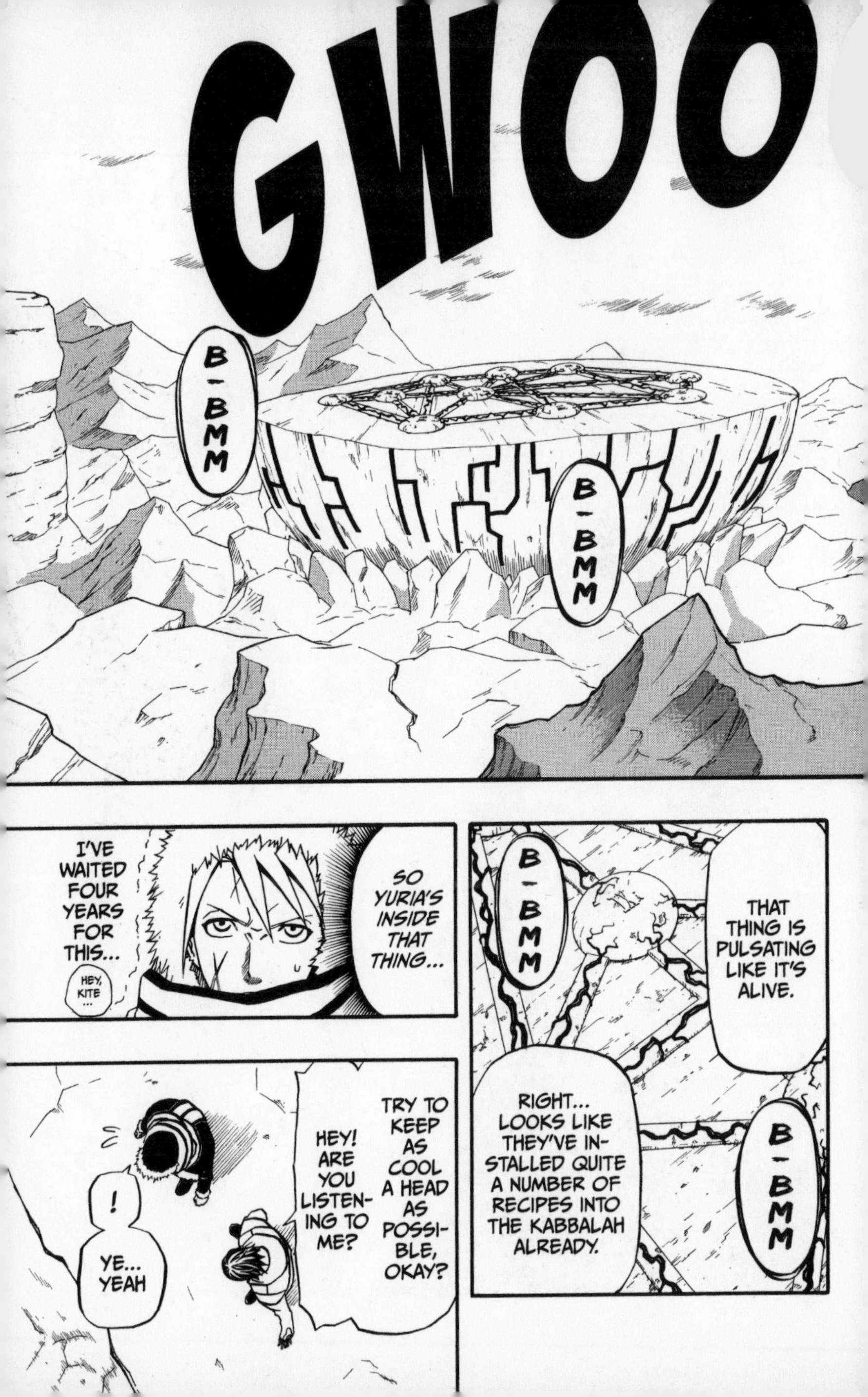
GWOO
B-BMM
B-BMM
THAT THING IS PULSATING LIKE IT'S ALIVE.
B-BMM
RIGHT... LOOKS LIKE THEY'VE IN-STALLED QUITE A NUMBER OF RECIPES INTO THE KABBALAH ALREADY.
B-BMM
SO YURIA'S INSIDE THAT THING...
I'VE WAITED FOUR YEARS FOR THIS...
HEY, KITE...
TRY TO KEEP AS COOL A HEAD AS POSSI-BLE, OKAY?
HEY! ARE YOU LISTEN-ING TO ME?
!
YE... YEAH

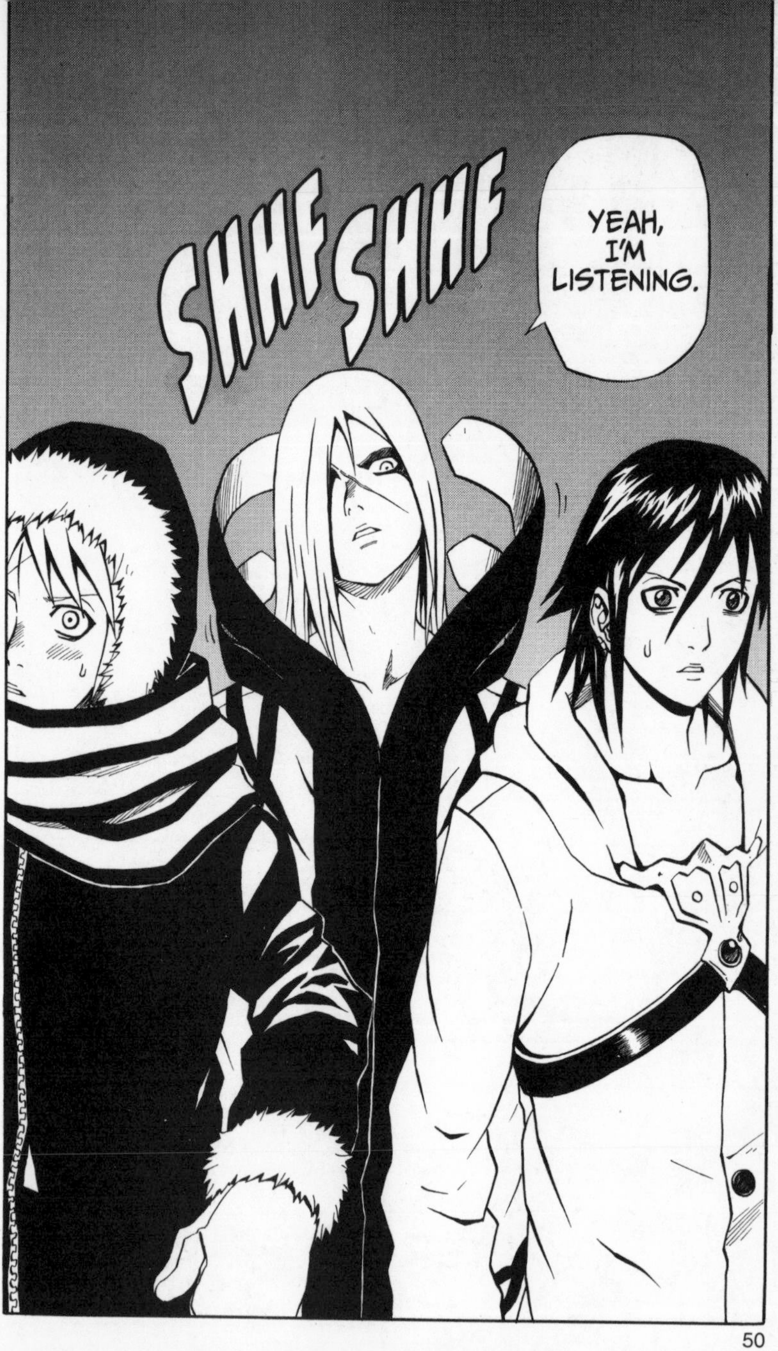
YEAH, I'M LISTENING.
SHHF SHHF

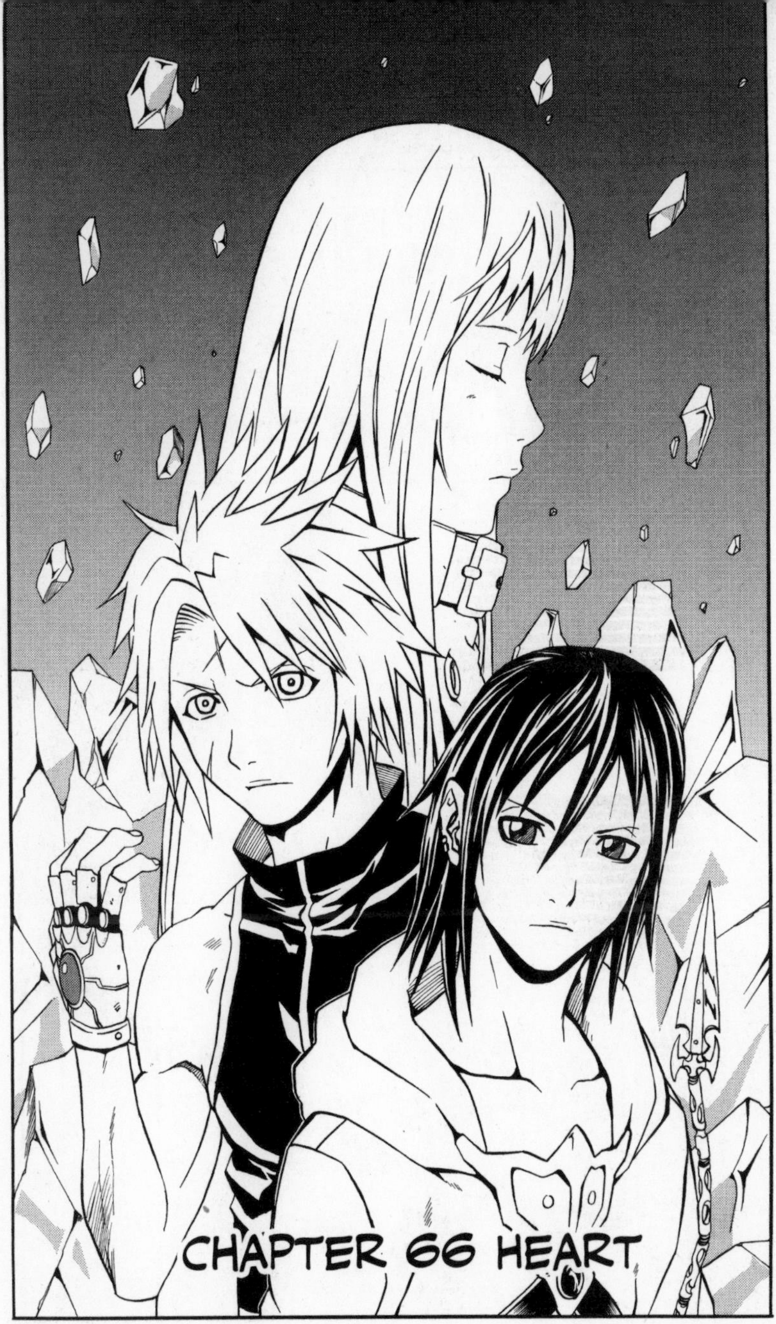
CHAPTER 66 HEART

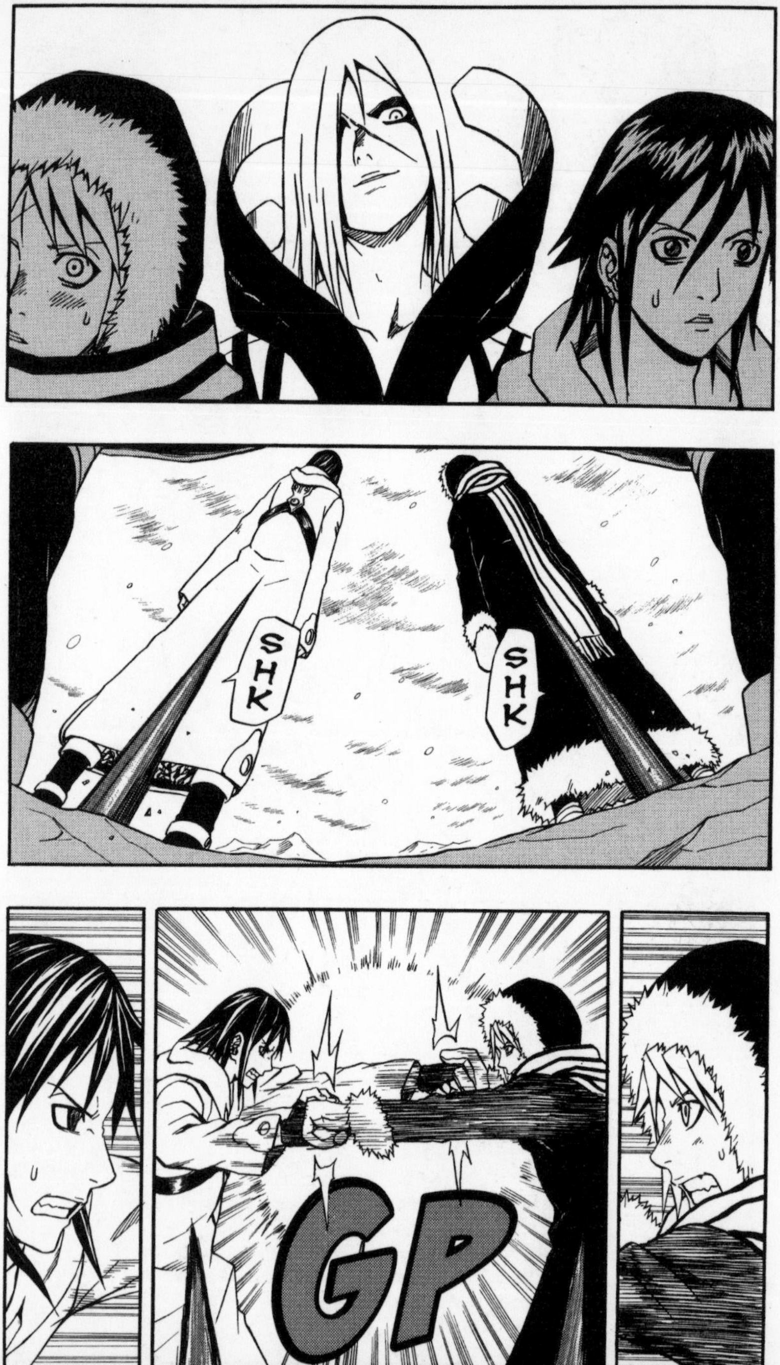
SHK
SHK
GP

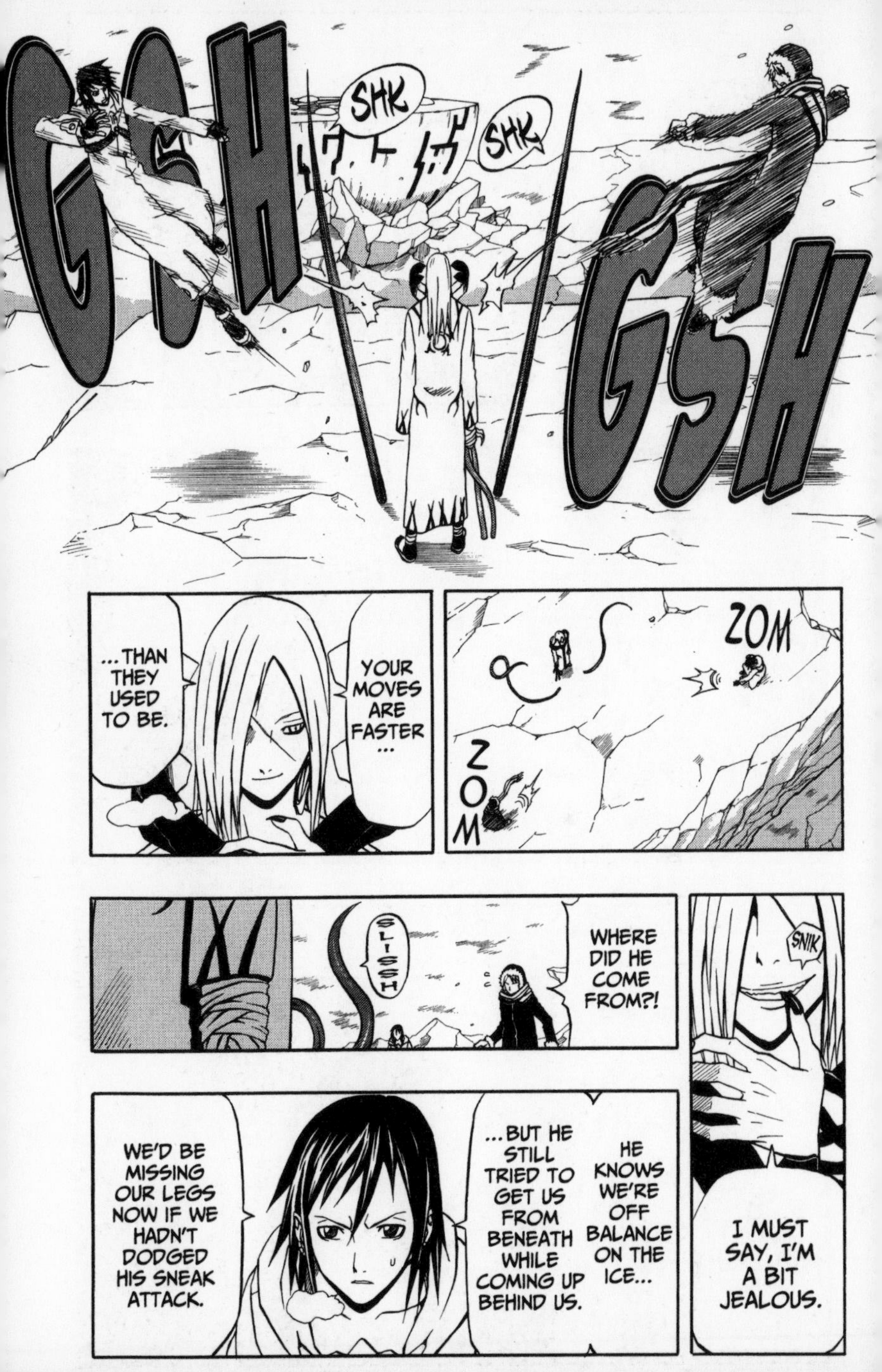
SHK
SHK
GSH
GSH
ZOM
ZOM
YOUR MOVES ARE FASTER...
...THAN THEY USED TO BE.
SNIK
I MUST SAY, I'M A BIT JEALOUS.
WHERE DID HE COME FROM?!
SLISSH
HE KNOWS WE'RE OFF BALANCE ON THE ICE...
...BUT HE STILL TRIED TO GET US FROM BENEATH WHILE COMING UP BEHIND US.
WE'D BE MISSING OUR LEGS NOW IF WE HADN'T DODGED HIS SNEAK ATTACK.

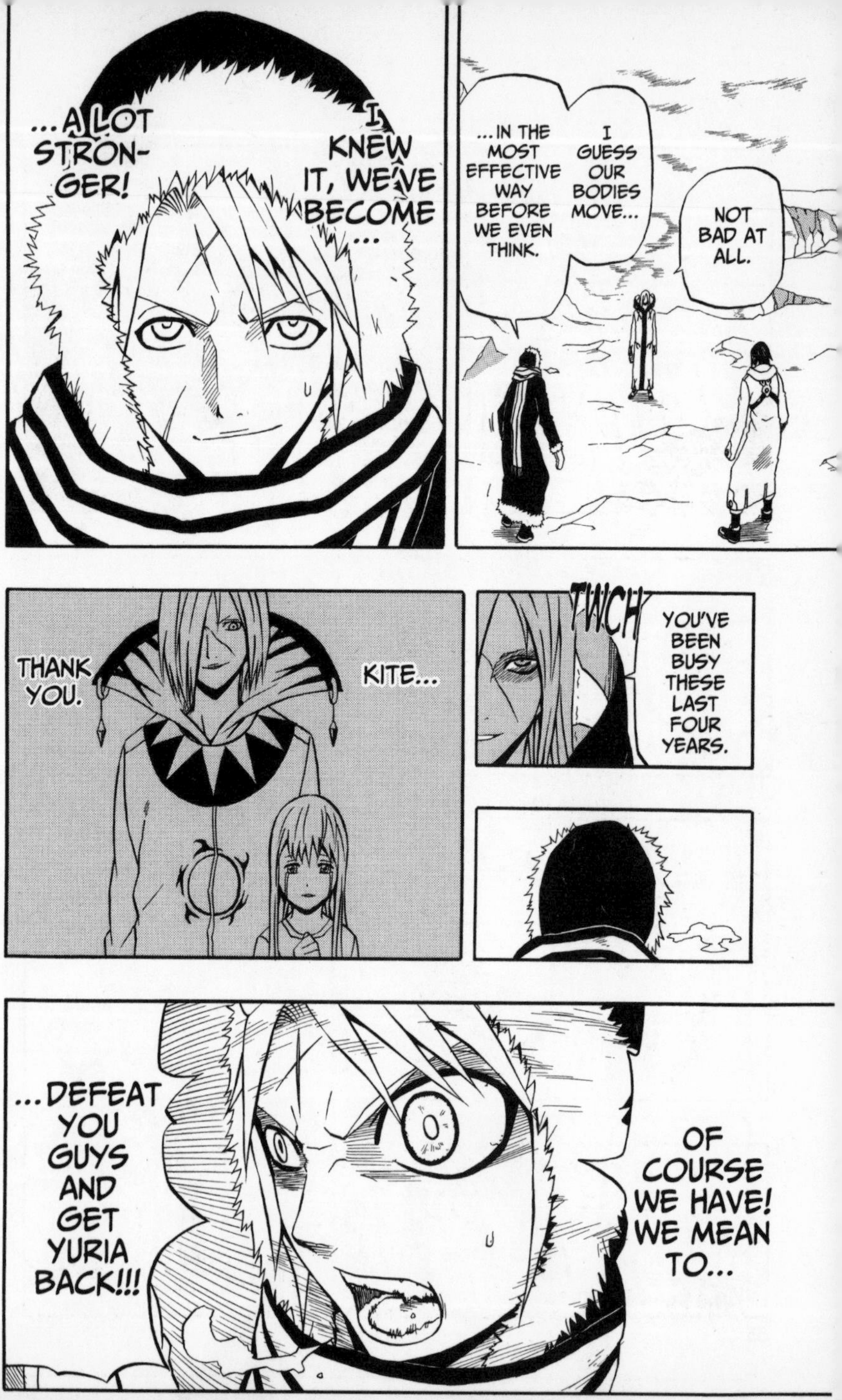
NOT BAD AT ALL.
I GUESS OUR BODIES MOVE...
...IN THE MOST EFFECTIVE WAY BEFORE WE EVEN THINK.
I KNEW IT, WE'VE BECOME...
...A LOT STRONGER!
TWCH
YOU'VE BEEN BUSY THESE LAST FOUR YEARS.
KITE...
THANK YOU.
OF COURSE WE HAVE! WE MEAN TO...
...DEFEAT YOU GUYS AND GET YURIA BACK!!!

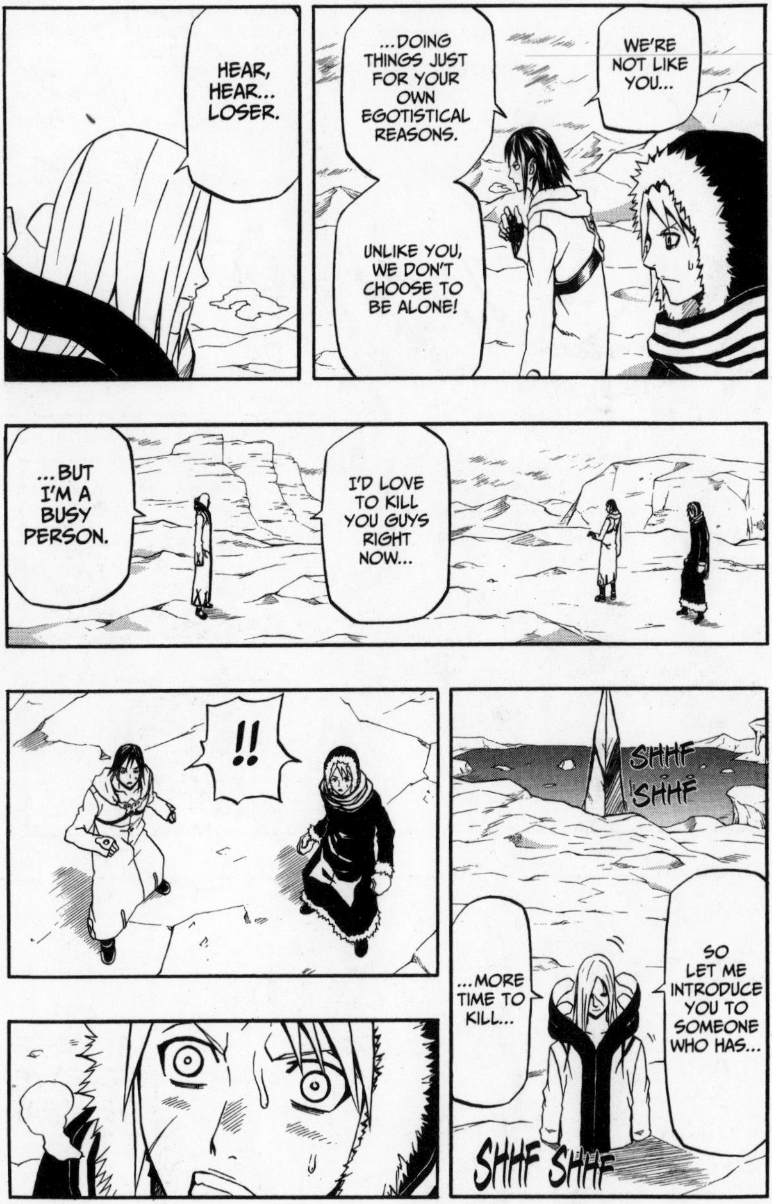
WE'RE NOT LIKE YOU...
...DOING THINGS JUST FOR YOUR OWN EGOTISTICAL REASONS.
UNLIKE YOU, WE DON'T CHOOSE TO BE ALONE!
HEAR, HEAR... LOSER.
I'D LOVE TO KILL YOU GUYS RIGHT NOW...
...BUT I'M A BUSY PERSON.
SHHF SHHF
SO LET ME INTRODUCE YOU TO SOMEONE WHO HAS...
...MORE TIME TO KILL...
SHHF SHHF
!!

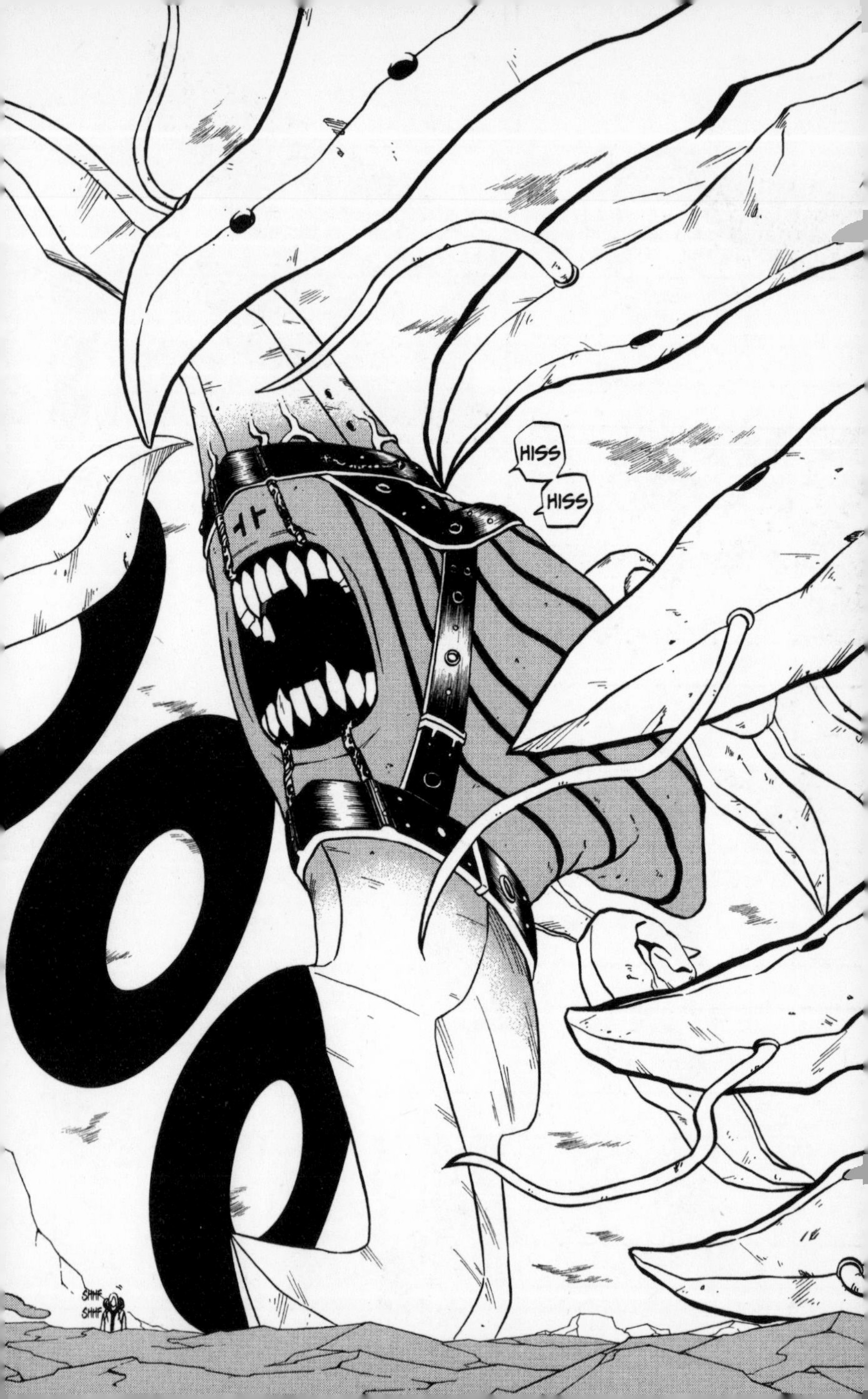
HISS
HISS
SHHF
SHHF

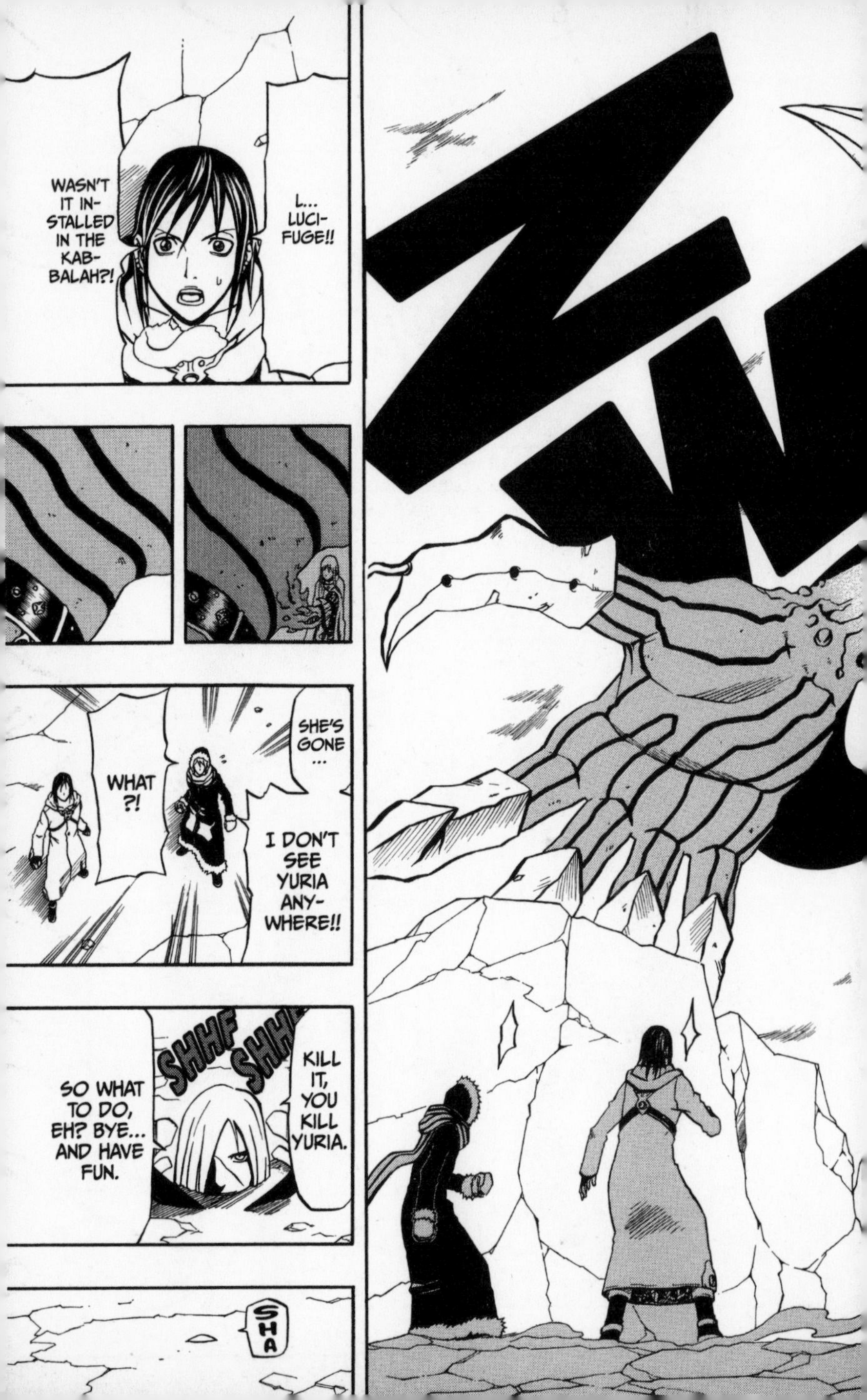
L... LUCIFUGE!!
WASN'T IT INSTALLED IN THE KABBALAH?!
SHE'S GONE...
I DON'T SEE YURIA ANYWHERE!!
WHAT?!
KILL IT, YOU KILL YURIA.
SHHF
SHHF
SO WHAT TO DO, EH? BYE... AND HAVE FUN.
SHA

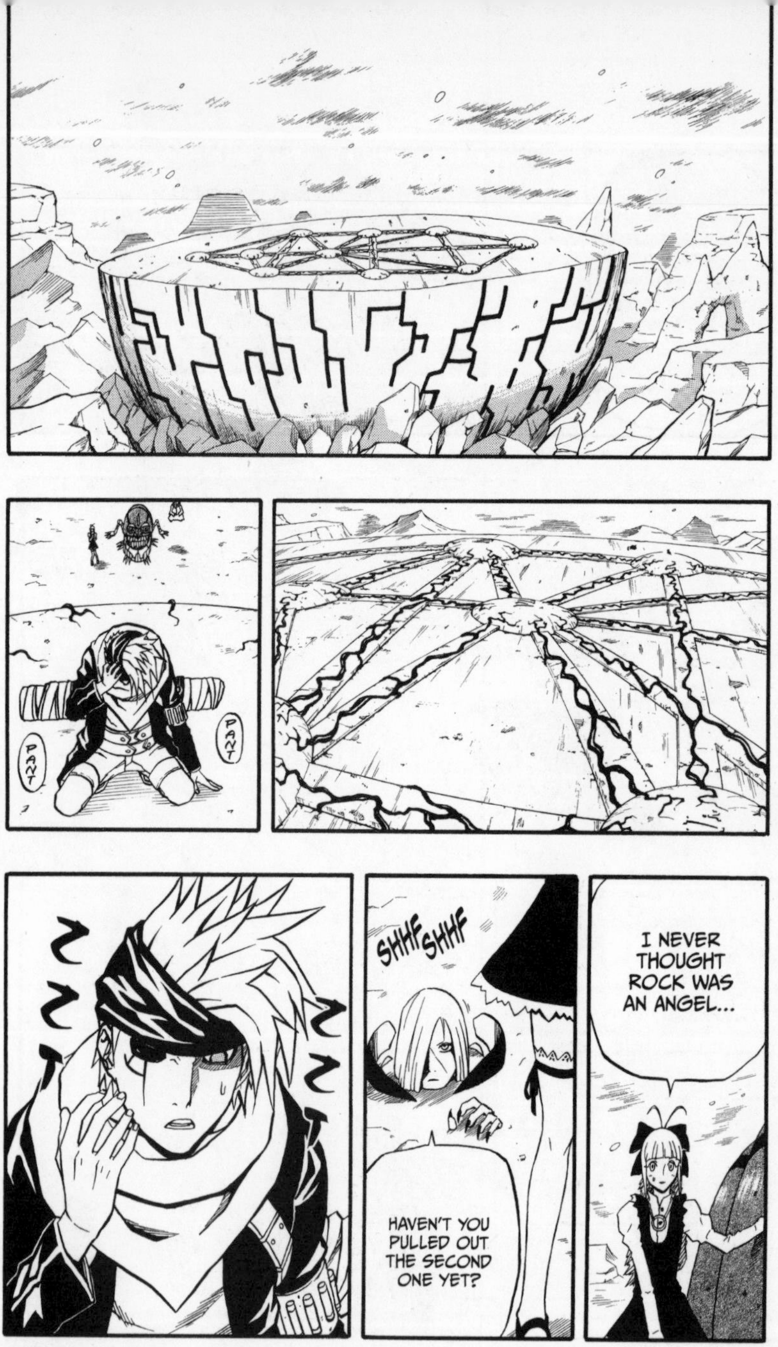
PANT
PANT
I NEVER THOUGHT ROCK WAS AN ANGEL...
SHHF SHHF
HAVEN'T YOU PULLED OUT THE SECOND ONE YET?

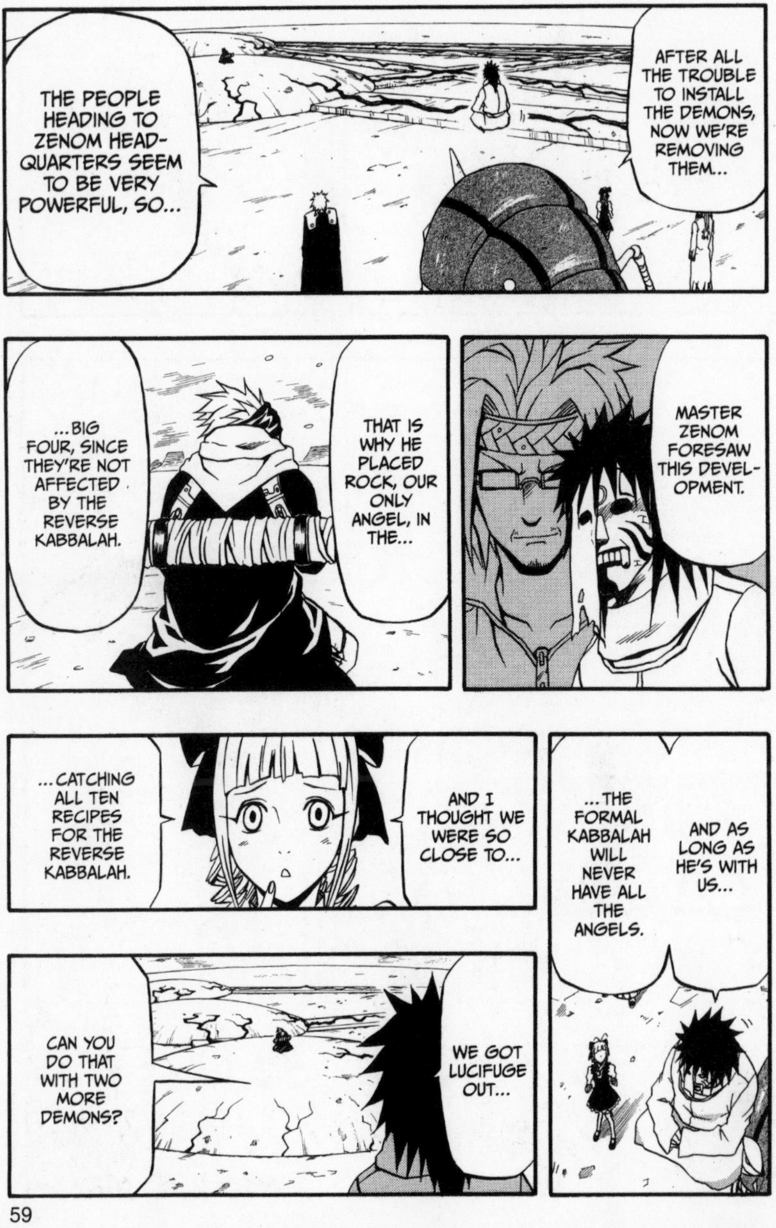
AFTER ALL THE TROUBLE TO INSTALL THE DEMONS, NOW WE'RE REMOVING THEM...
THE PEOPLE HEADING TO ZENOM HEAD-QUARTERS SEEM TO BE VERY POWERFUL, SO...
MASTER ZENOM FORESAW THIS DEVEL-OPMENT.
THAT IS WHY HE PLACED ROCK, OUR ONLY ANGEL, IN THE...
...BIG FOUR, SINCE THEY'RE NOT AFFECTED BY THE REVERSE KABBALAH.
AND AS LONG AS HE'S WITH US...
...THE FORMAL KABBALAH WILL NEVER HAVE ALL THE ANGELS.
AND I THOUGHT WE WERE SO CLOSE TO...
...CATCHING ALL TEN RECIPES FOR THE REVERSE KABBALAH.
WE GOT LUCIFUGE OUT...
CAN YOU DO THAT WITH TWO MORE DEMONS?

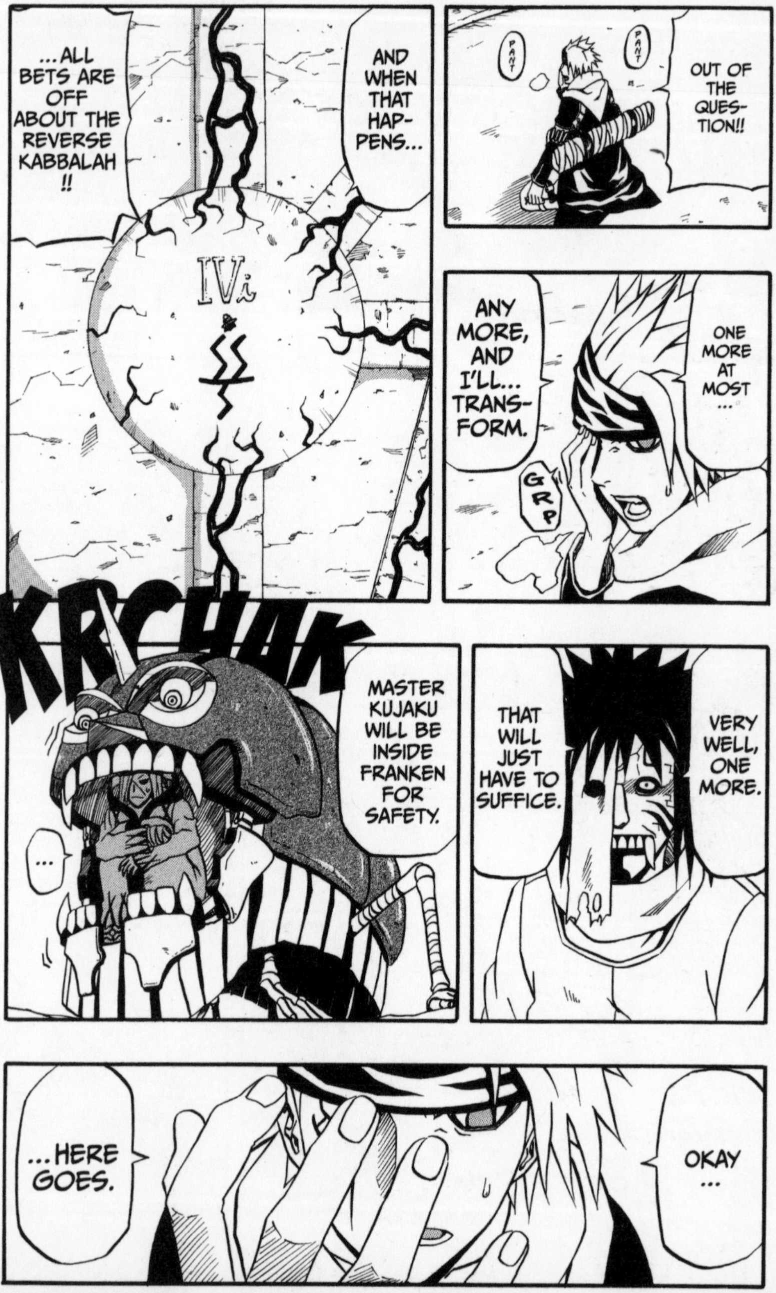
PANT
PANT
OUT OF THE QUES-TION!!
ONE MORE AT MOST...
ANY MORE, AND I'LL... TRANS-FORM.
GRP
AND WHEN THAT HAP-PENS...
...ALL BETS ARE OFF ABOUT THE REVERSE KABBALAH!!
IVi
VERY WELL, ONE MORE.
THAT WILL JUST HAVE TO SUFFICE.
KRCHAK
MASTER KUJAKU WILL BE INSIDE FRANKEN FOR SAFETY.
...
OKAY...
...HERE GOES.

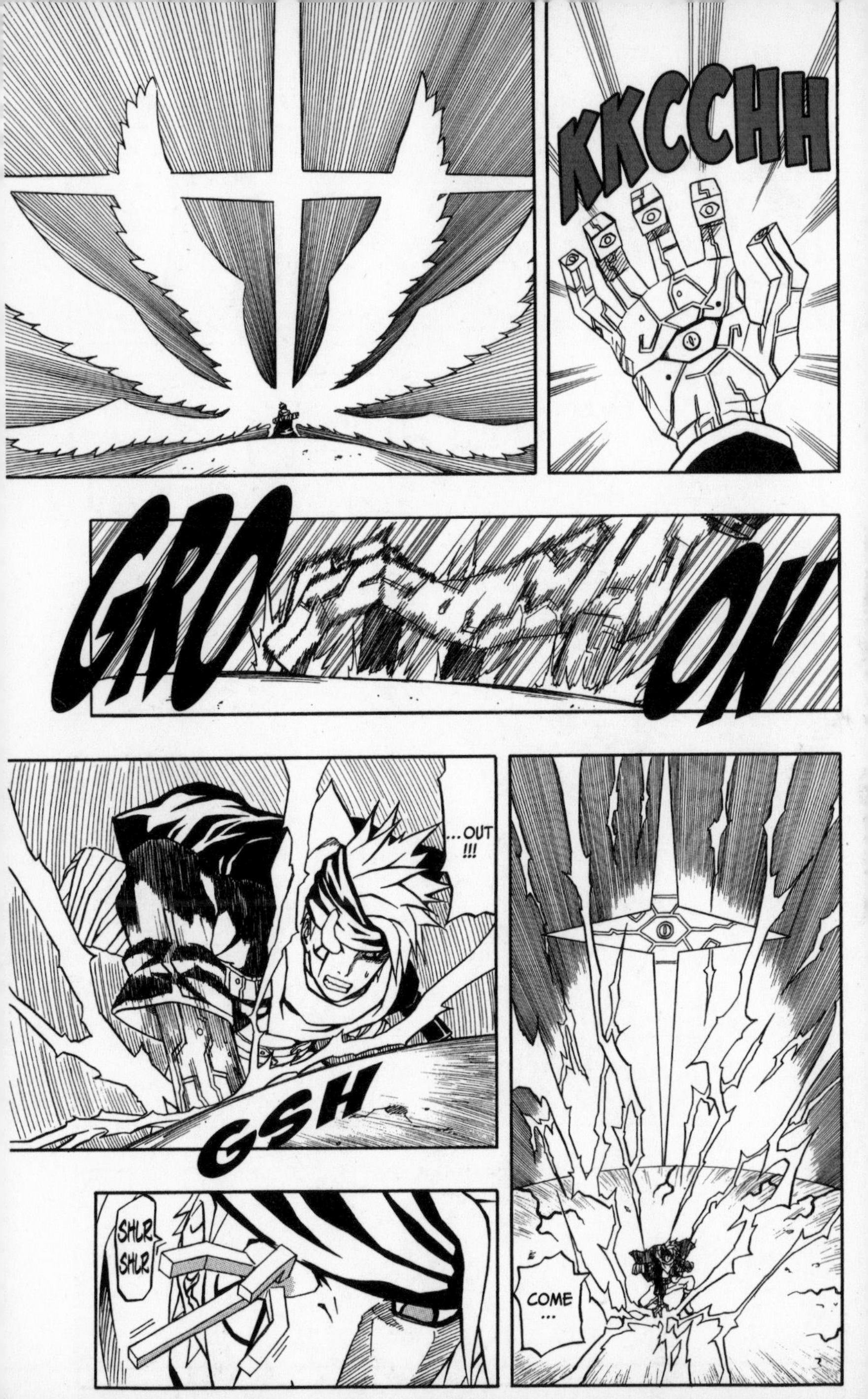
KKCCHH
GRO
ON
COME ...
...OUT !!!
GSH
SHLR SHLR

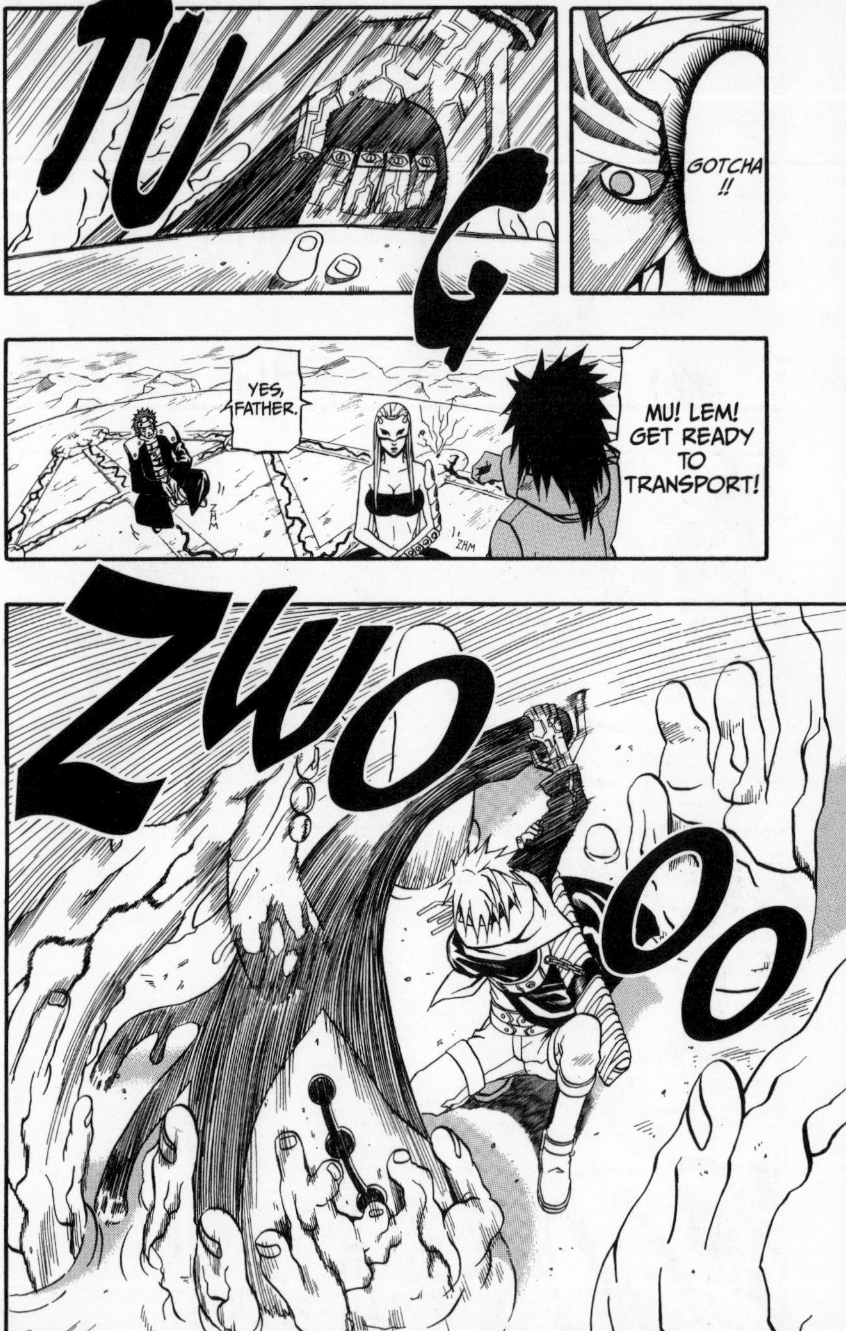
GOTCHA !!
TUG
MU! LEM! GET READY TO TRANSPORT!
YES, FATHER.
ZHM
ZHM
ZWOOO

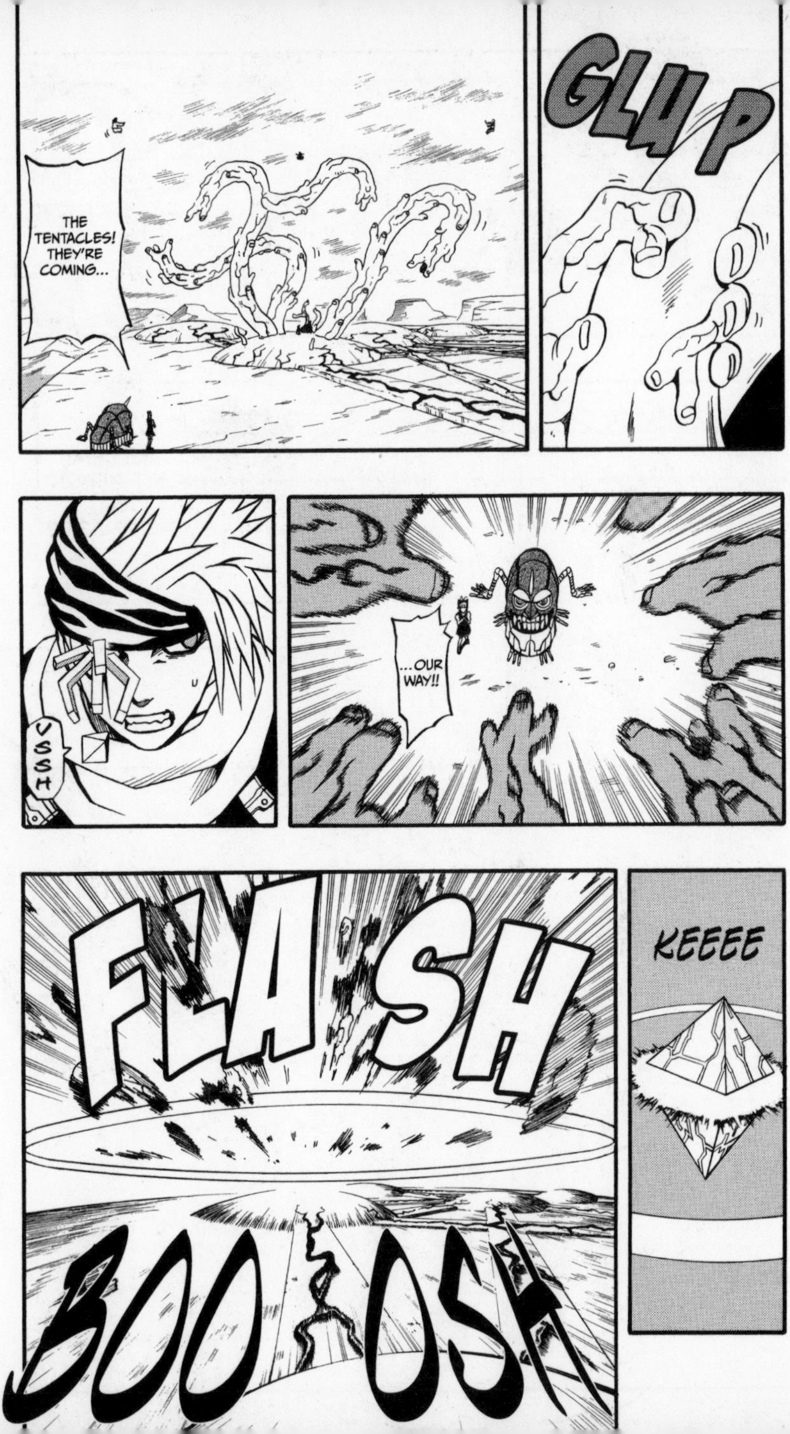
GLUP
THE TENTACLES! THEY'RE COMING...
...OUR WAY!!
VSSH
KEEEE
FLASH
BOOOSH

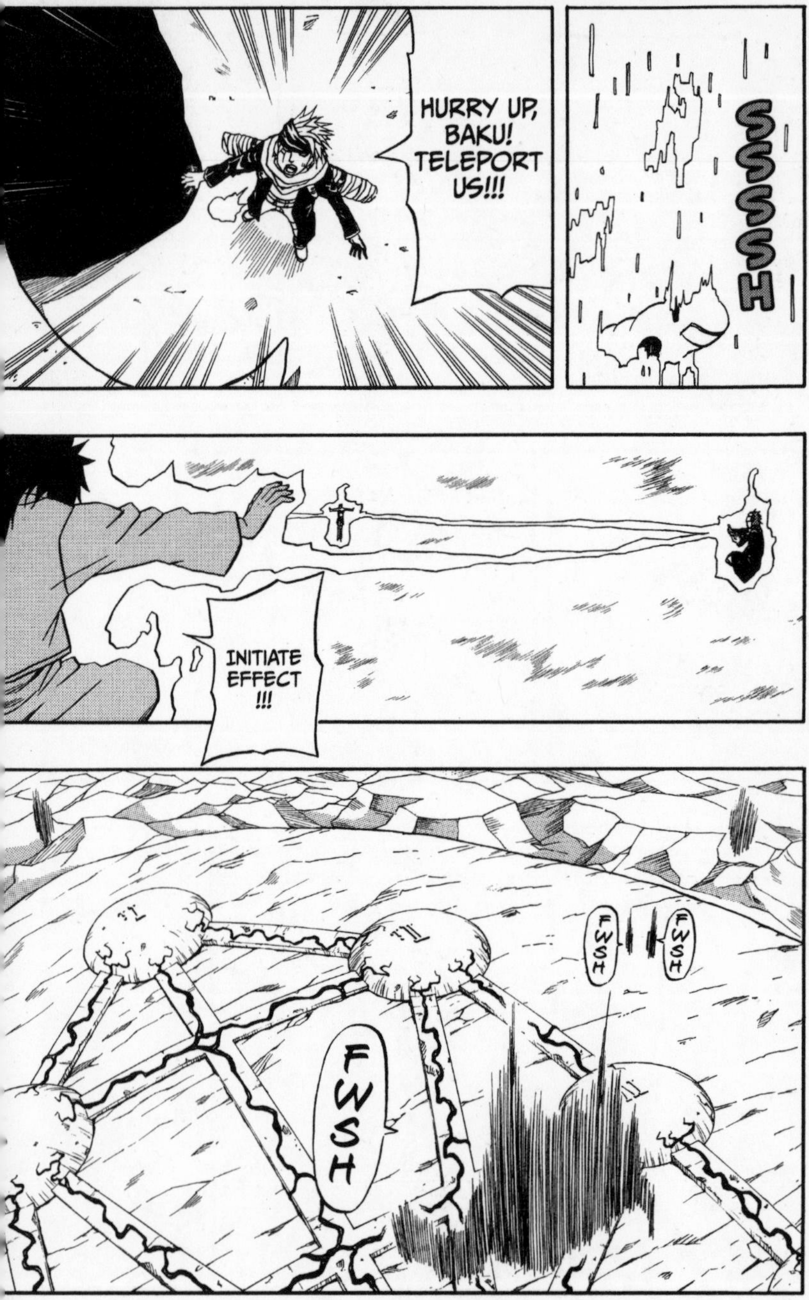
SSSSH
HURRY UP, BAKU! TELEPORT US!!!
INITIATE EFFECT !!!
FWSH
FWSH
FWSH

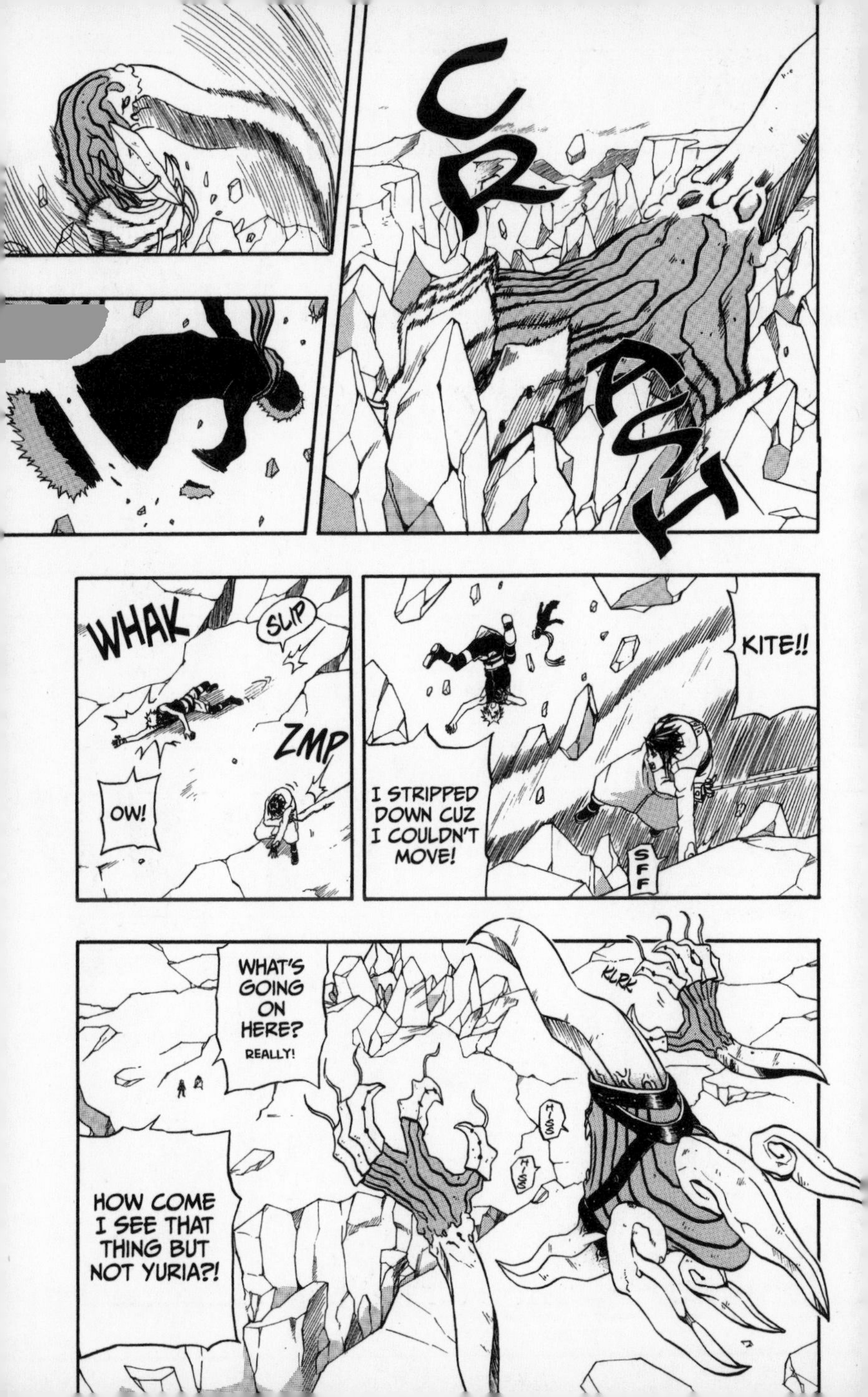
CR
ASH
KITE!!
I STRIPPED DOWN CUZ I COULDN'T MOVE!
SFF
SLIP
WHAK
ZMP
OW!
KURK
WHAT'S GOING ON HERE?
REALLY!
HISS
HISS
HOW COME I SEE THAT THING BUT NOT YURIA?!

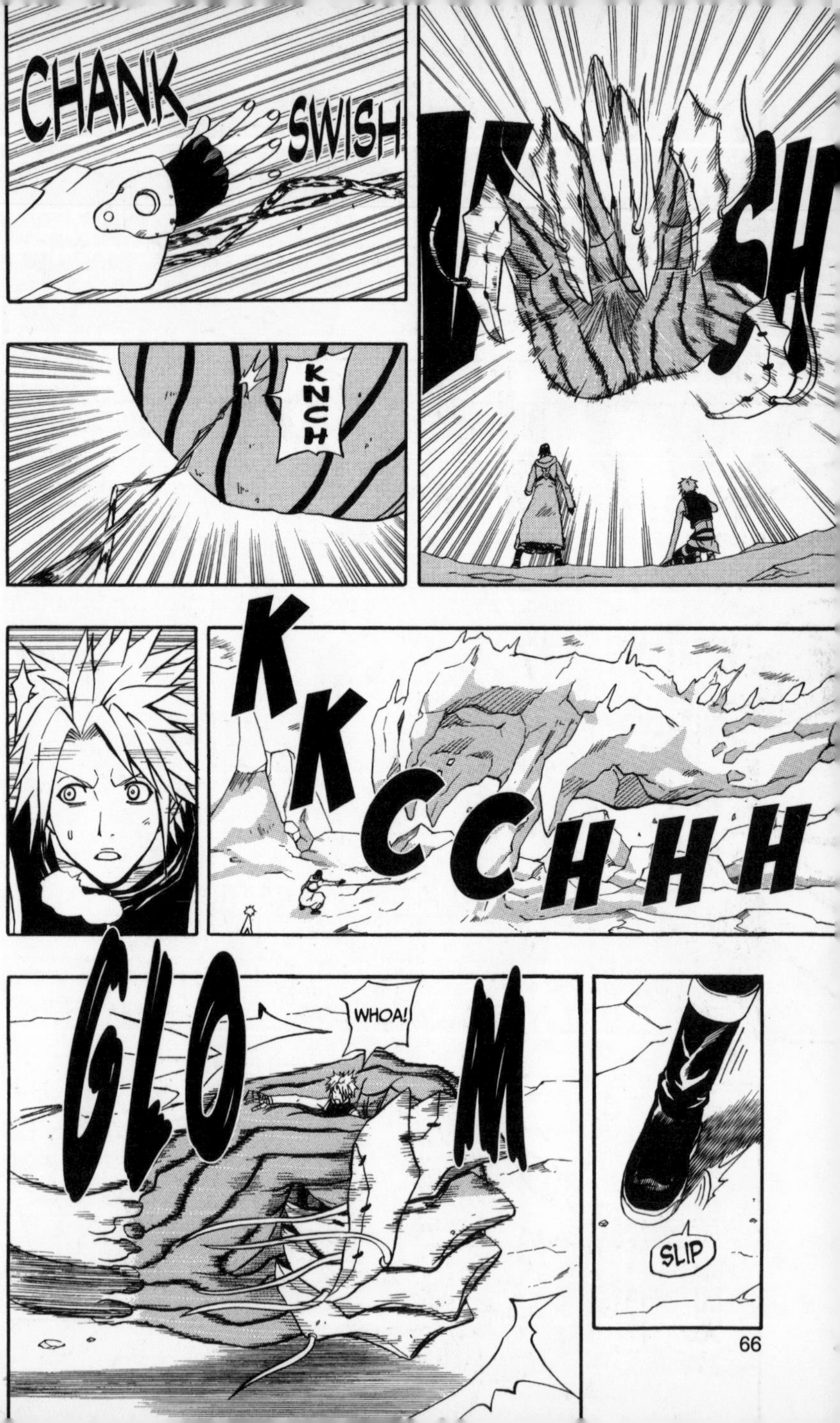
CHANK
SWISH
KNCH
KKCCHHH
SLIP
GLOM
WHOA!

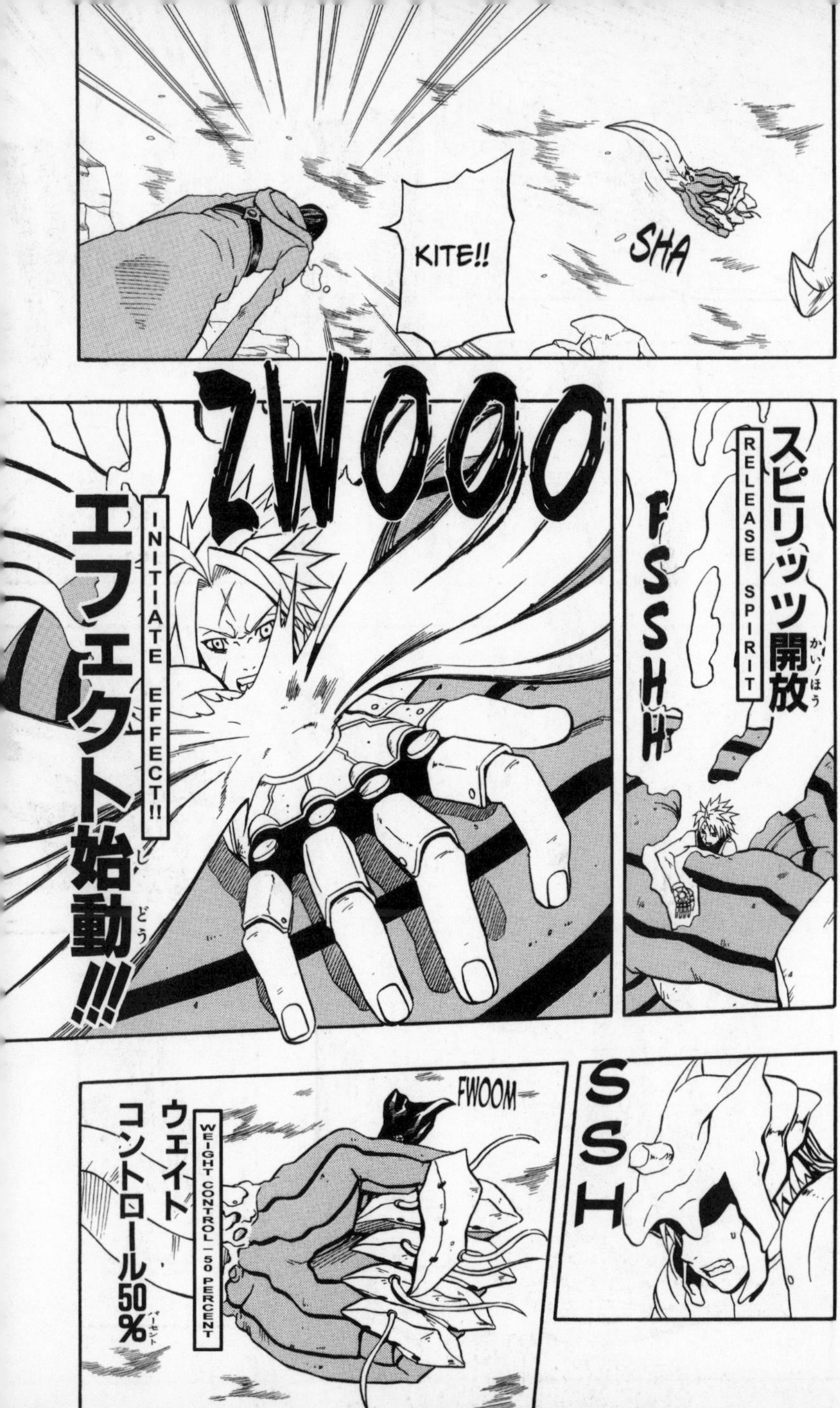
KITE!!
SHA
スピリッツ開放
RELEASE SPIRIT
FSSHH
ZWOOO
エフェクト始動!!!
INITIATE EFFECT!!
SSH
FWOOM
ウェイトコントロール50%
WEIGHT CONTROL – 50 PERCENT

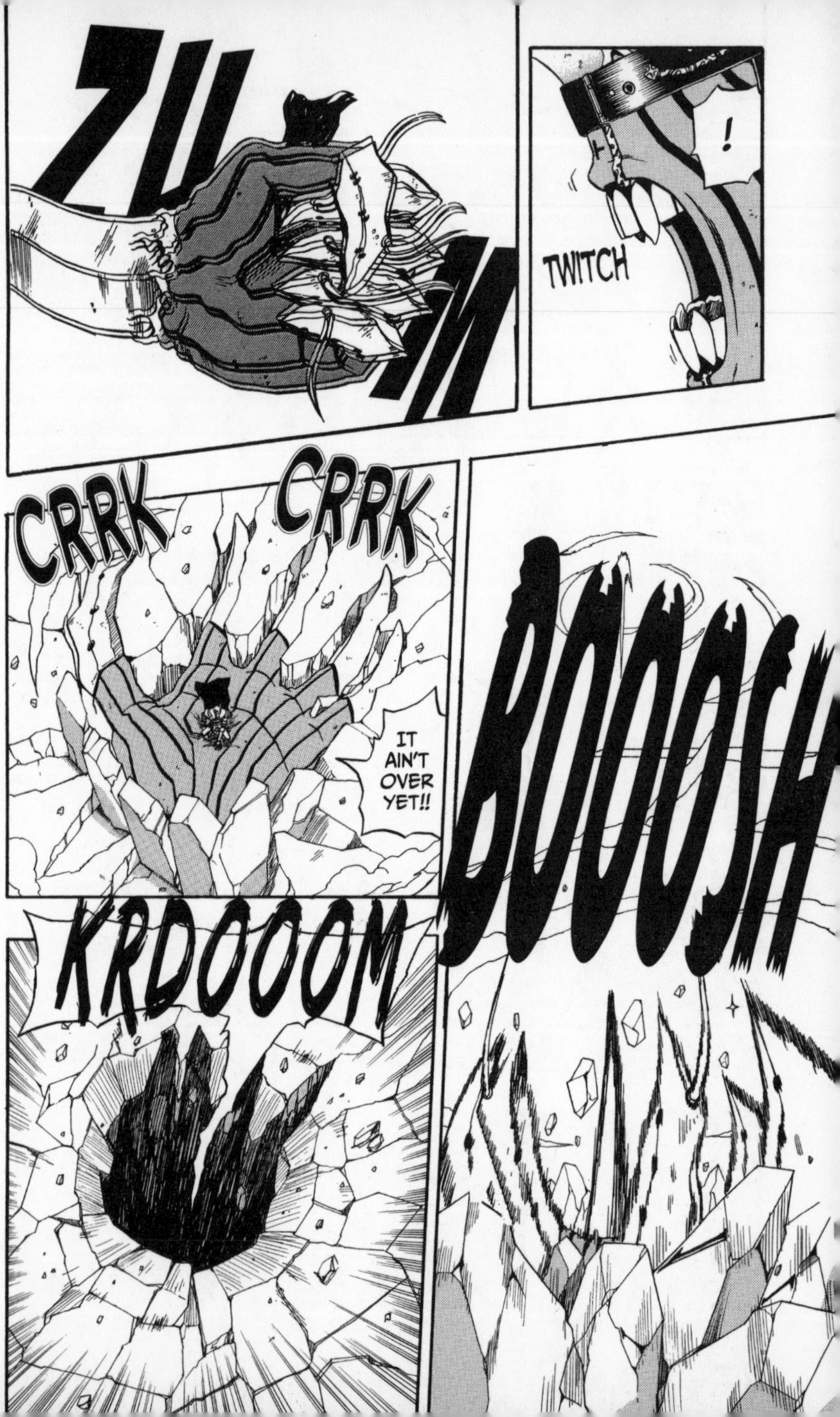
!
TWITCH
ZUM
BOOOSH
CRRK
CRRK
IT AIN'T OVER YET!!
KRDOOOM

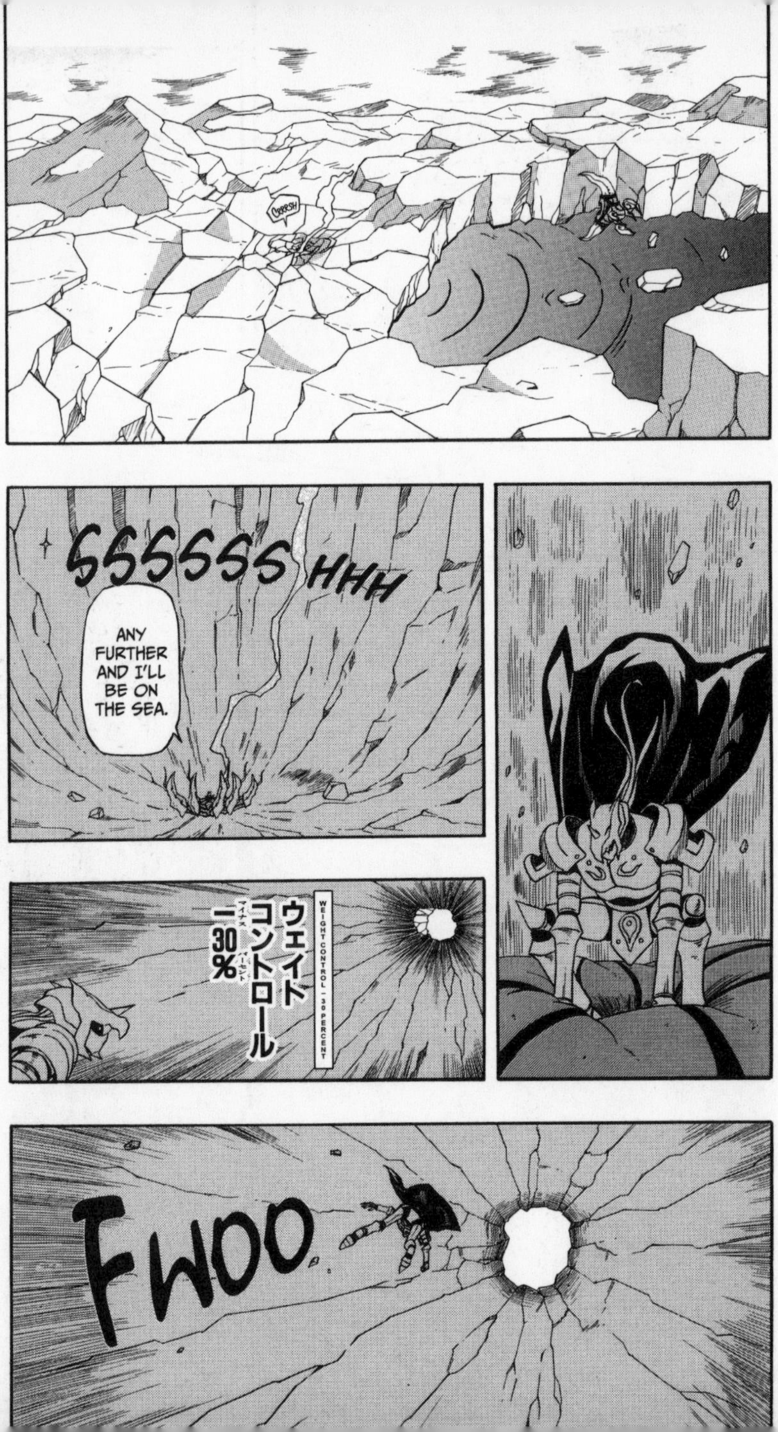
CRRRSH
SSSSSS HHH
ANY FURTHER AND I'LL BE ON THE SEA.
WEIGHT CONTROL – 30 PERCENT
ウェイトコントロール−30%
FWOO.

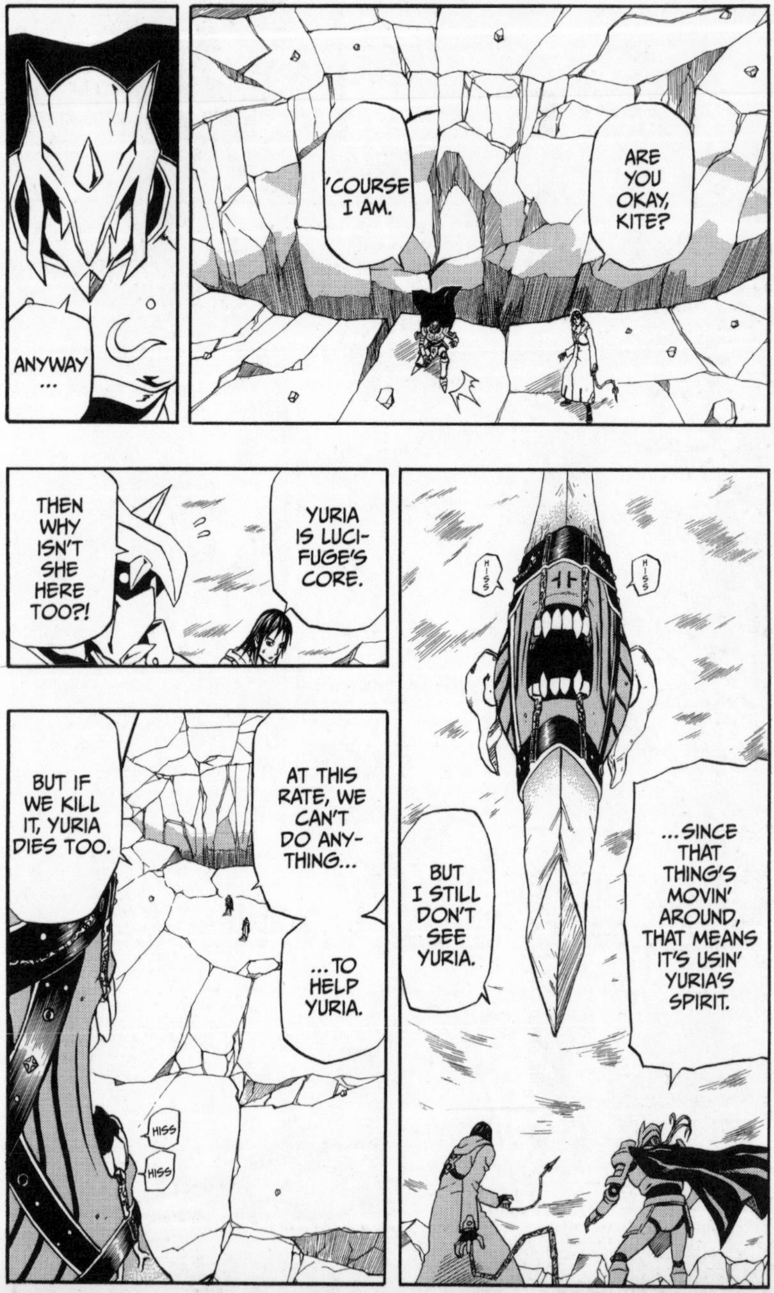
ARE YOU OKAY, KITE?
'COURSE I AM.
ANYWAY ...
HISS
HISS
...SINCE THAT THING'S MOVIN' AROUND, THAT MEANS IT'S USIN' YURIA'S SPIRIT.
BUT I STILL DON'T SEE YURIA.
YURIA IS LUCI-FUGE'S CORE.
THEN WHY ISN'T SHE HERE TOO?!
AT THIS RATE, WE CAN'T DO ANY-THING...
...TO HELP YURIA.
BUT IF WE KILL IT, YURIA DIES TOO.
HISS
HISS

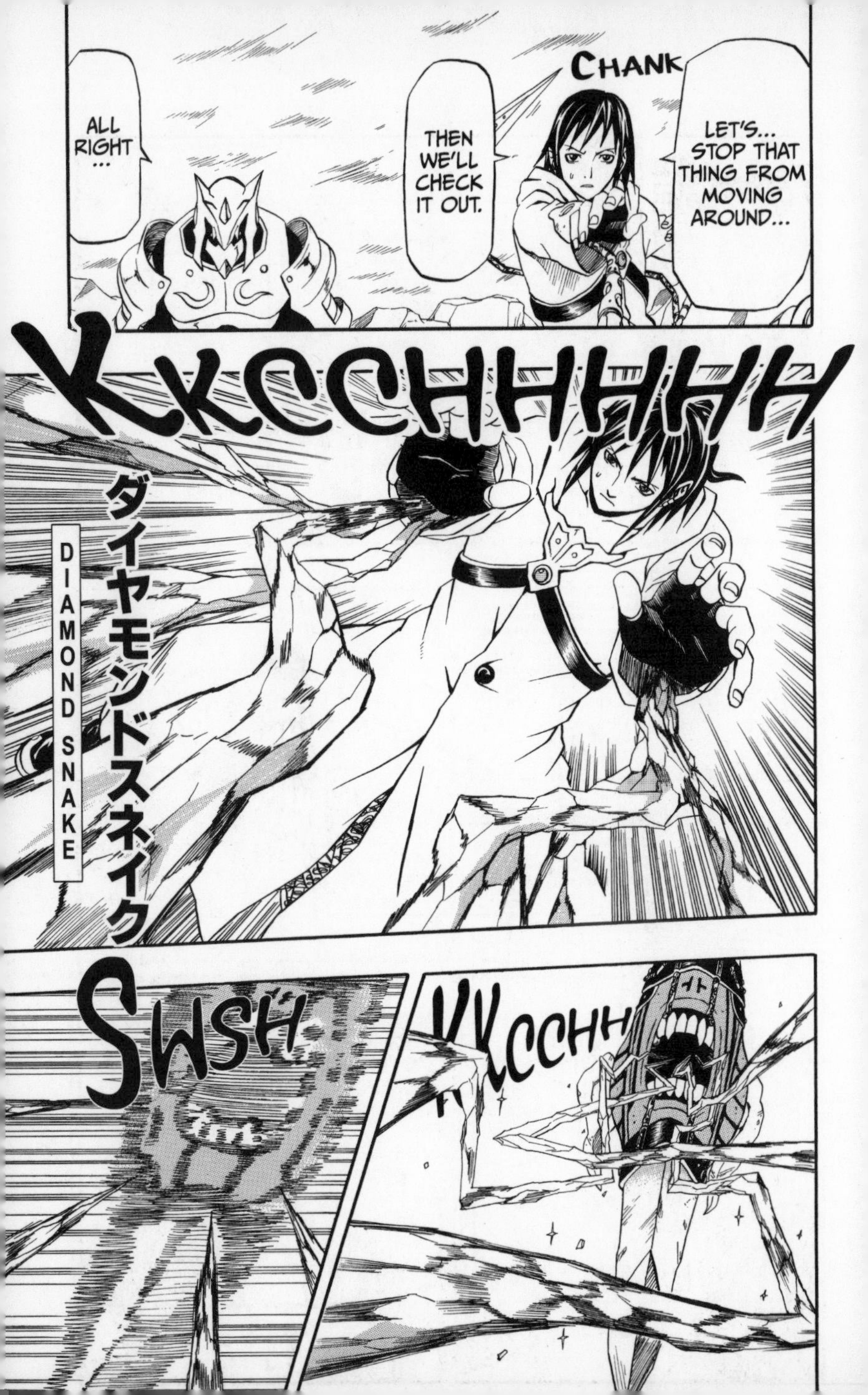
LET'S... STOP THAT THING FROM MOVING AROUND...
CHANK
THEN WE'LL CHECK IT OUT.
ALL RIGHT ...
KKCCHHHHHH
ダイヤモンドスネイク
DIAMOND SNAKE
KKCCHH
SWSH

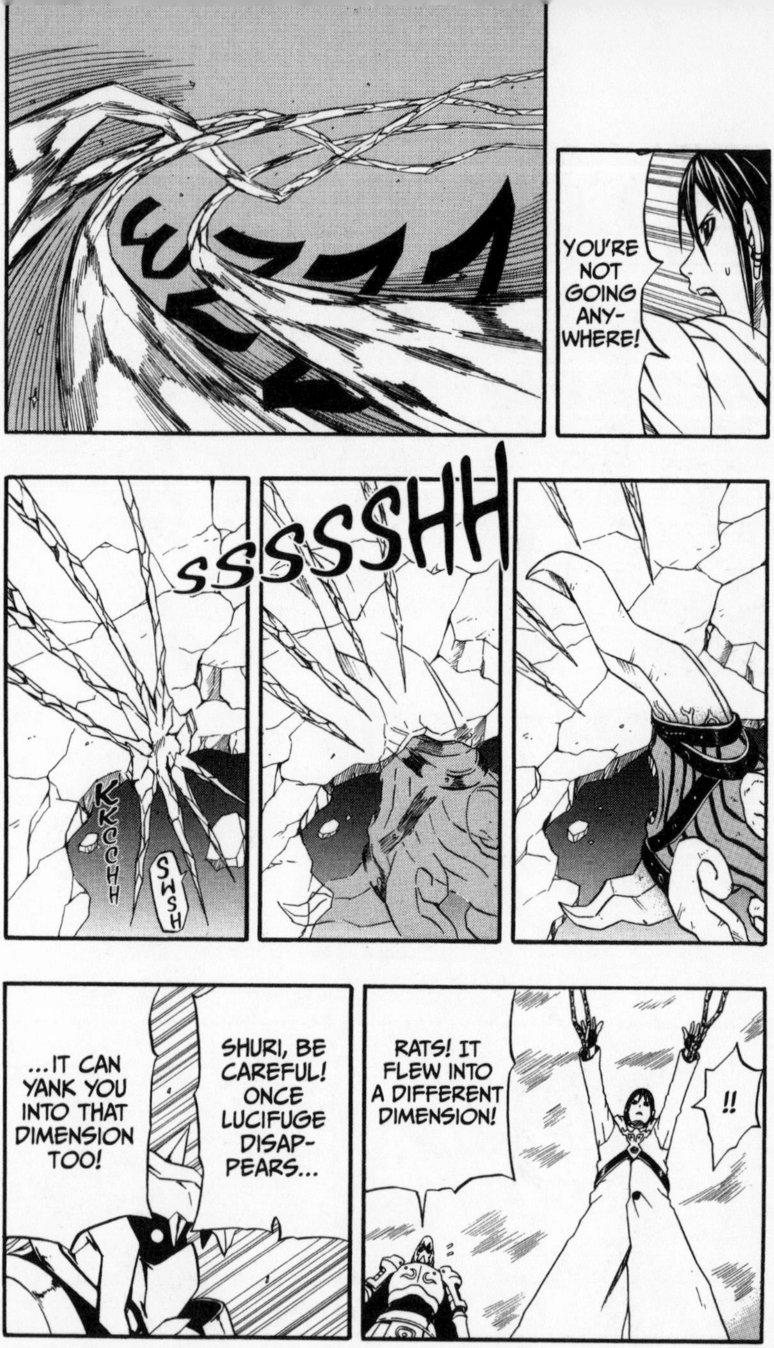
YOU'RE NOT GOING ANY-WHERE!
SSSSSHH
KKCCHH
SWSH
!!
RATS! IT FLEW INTO A DIFFERENT DIMENSION!
SHURI, BE CAREFUL! ONCE LUCIFUGE DISAP-PEARS...
...IT CAN YANK YOU INTO THAT DIMENSION TOO!

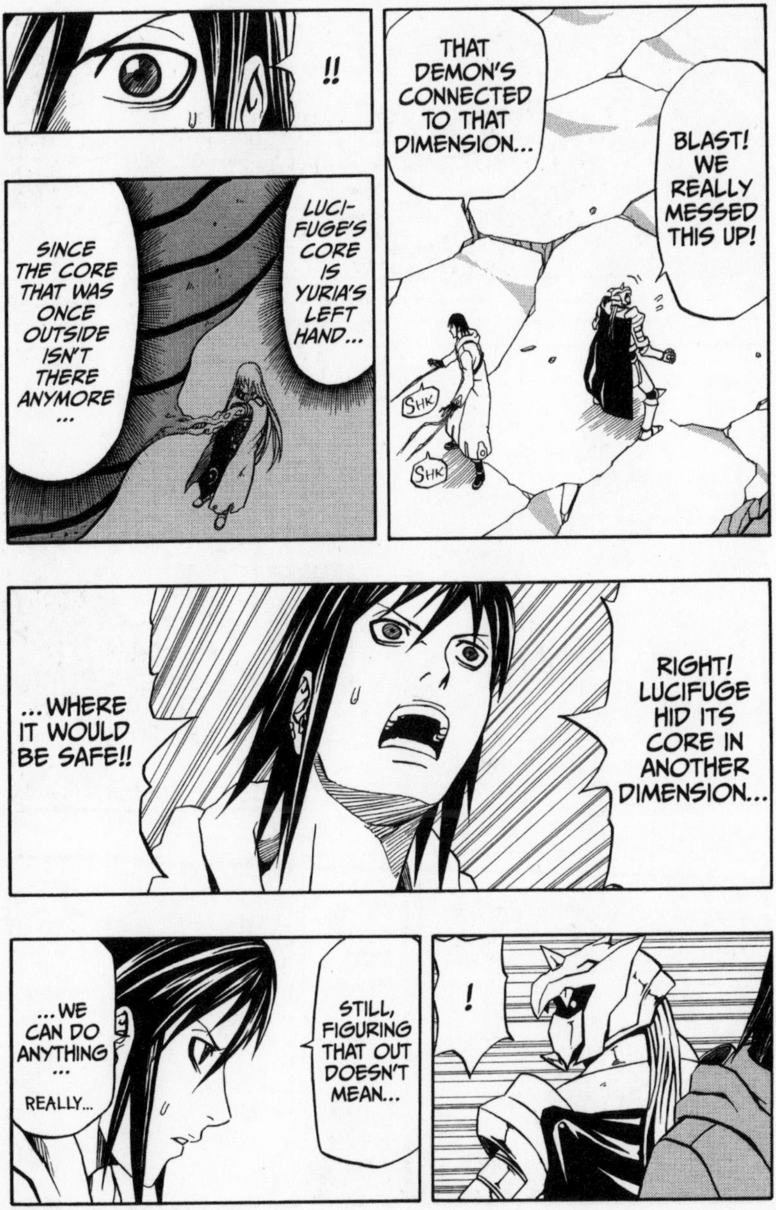
BLAST! WE REALLY MESSED THIS UP!
THAT DEMON'S CONNECTED TO THAT DIMENSION...
SHK
SHK
!!
LUCIFUGE'S CORE IS YURIA'S LEFT HAND...
SINCE THE CORE THAT WAS ONCE OUTSIDE ISN'T THERE ANYMORE...
RIGHT! LUCIFUGE HID ITS CORE IN ANOTHER DIMENSION...
...WHERE IT WOULD BE SAFE!!
!
STILL, FIGURING THAT OUT DOESN'T MEAN...
...WE CAN DO ANYTHING...
REALLY...

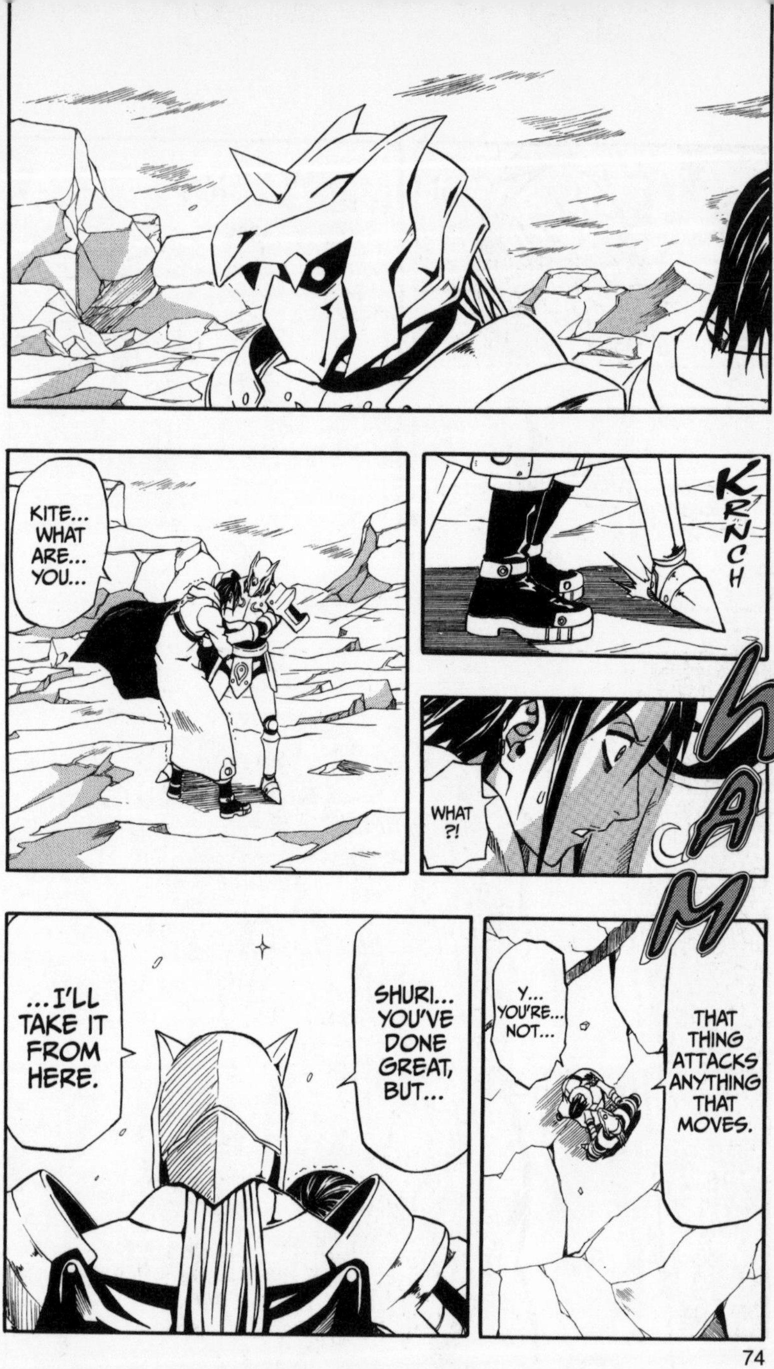
KRNCH
WHAT ?!
WHAM
KITE... WHAT ARE... YOU...
THAT THING ATTACKS ANYTHING THAT MOVES.
Y... YOU'RE... NOT...
SHURI... YOU'VE DONE GREAT, BUT...
...I'LL TAKE IT FROM HERE.

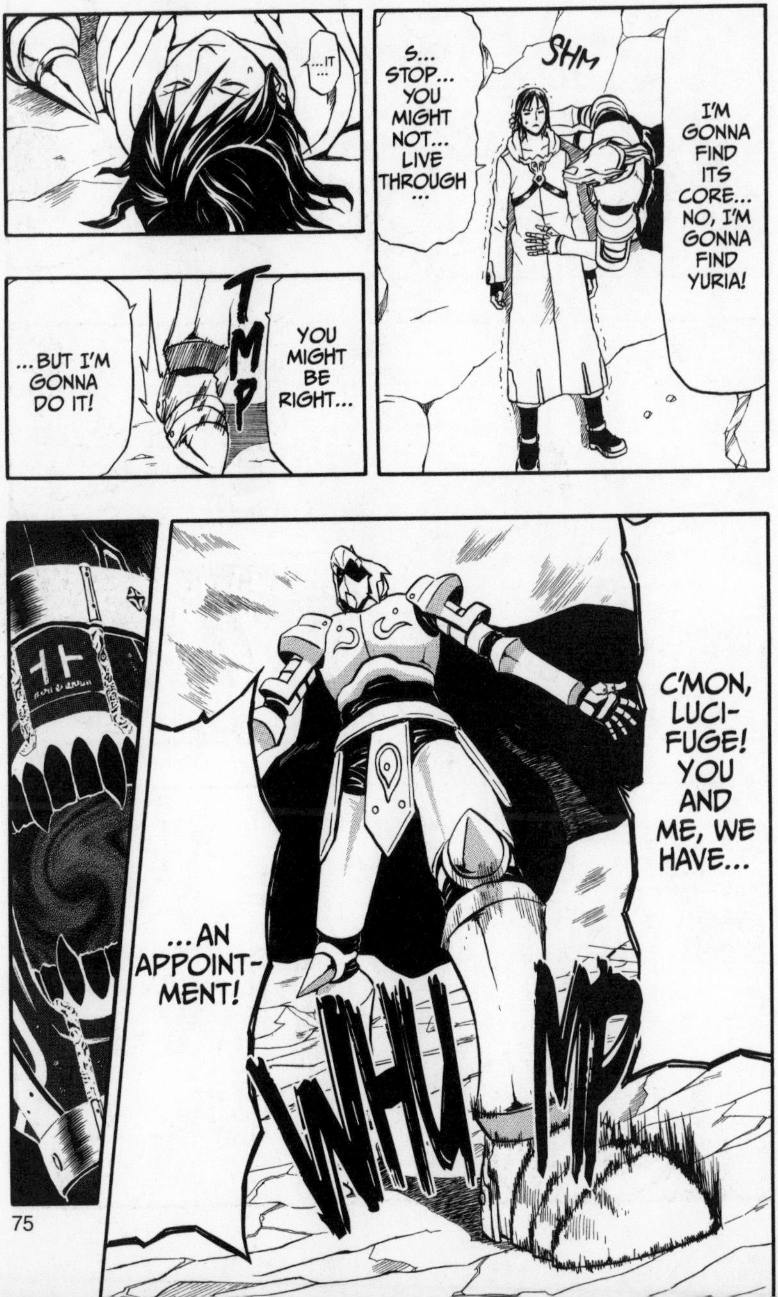
I'M GONNA FIND ITS CORE... NO, I'M GONNA FIND YURIA!
SHM
S... STOP... YOU MIGHT NOT... LIVE THROUGH...
...IT...
YOU MIGHT BE RIGHT...
TMP
...BUT I'M GONNA DO IT!
C'MON, LUCI-FUGE! YOU AND ME, WE HAVE...
...AN APPOINT-MENT!
WHUMP

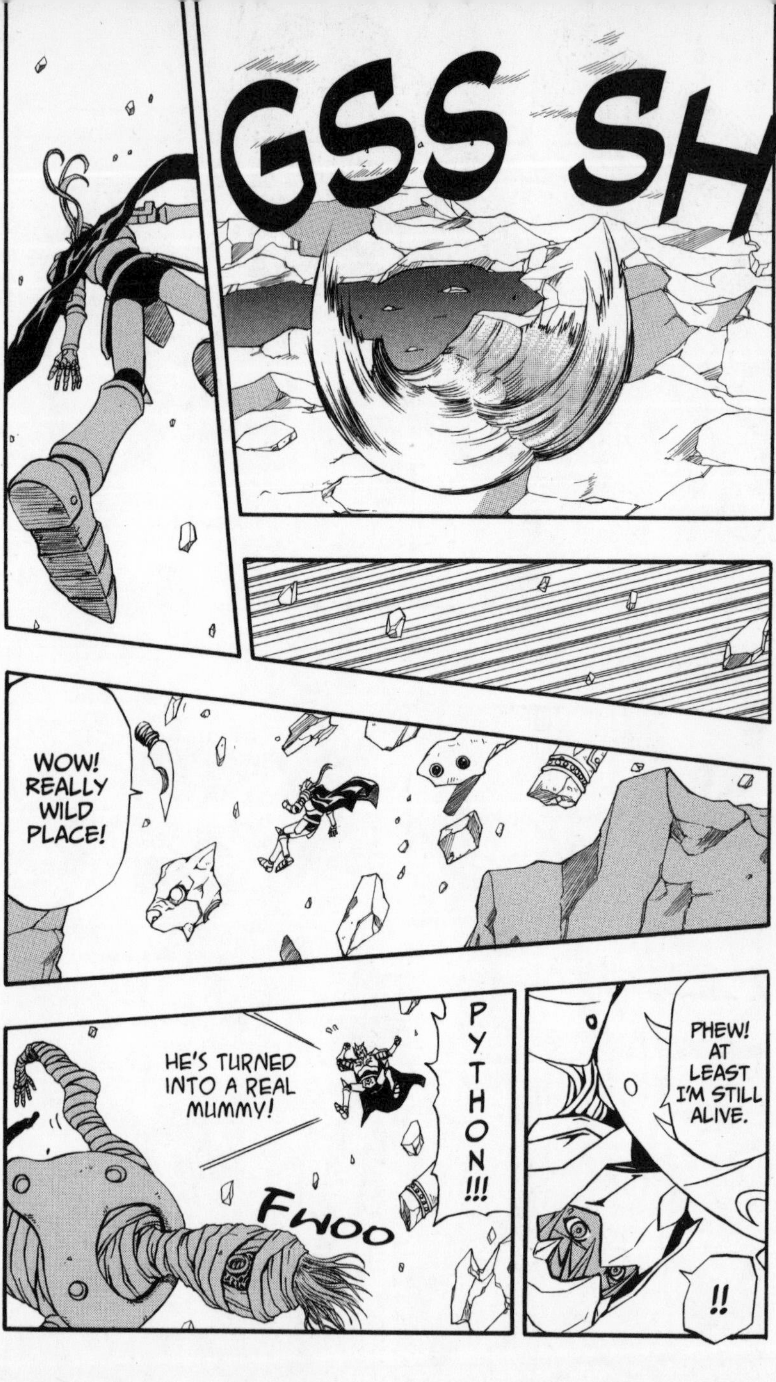
GSS SH
WOW! REALLY WILD PLACE!
PHEW! AT LEAST I'M STILL ALIVE.
!!
PYTHON!!!
HE'S TURNED INTO A REAL MUMMY!
FWOO

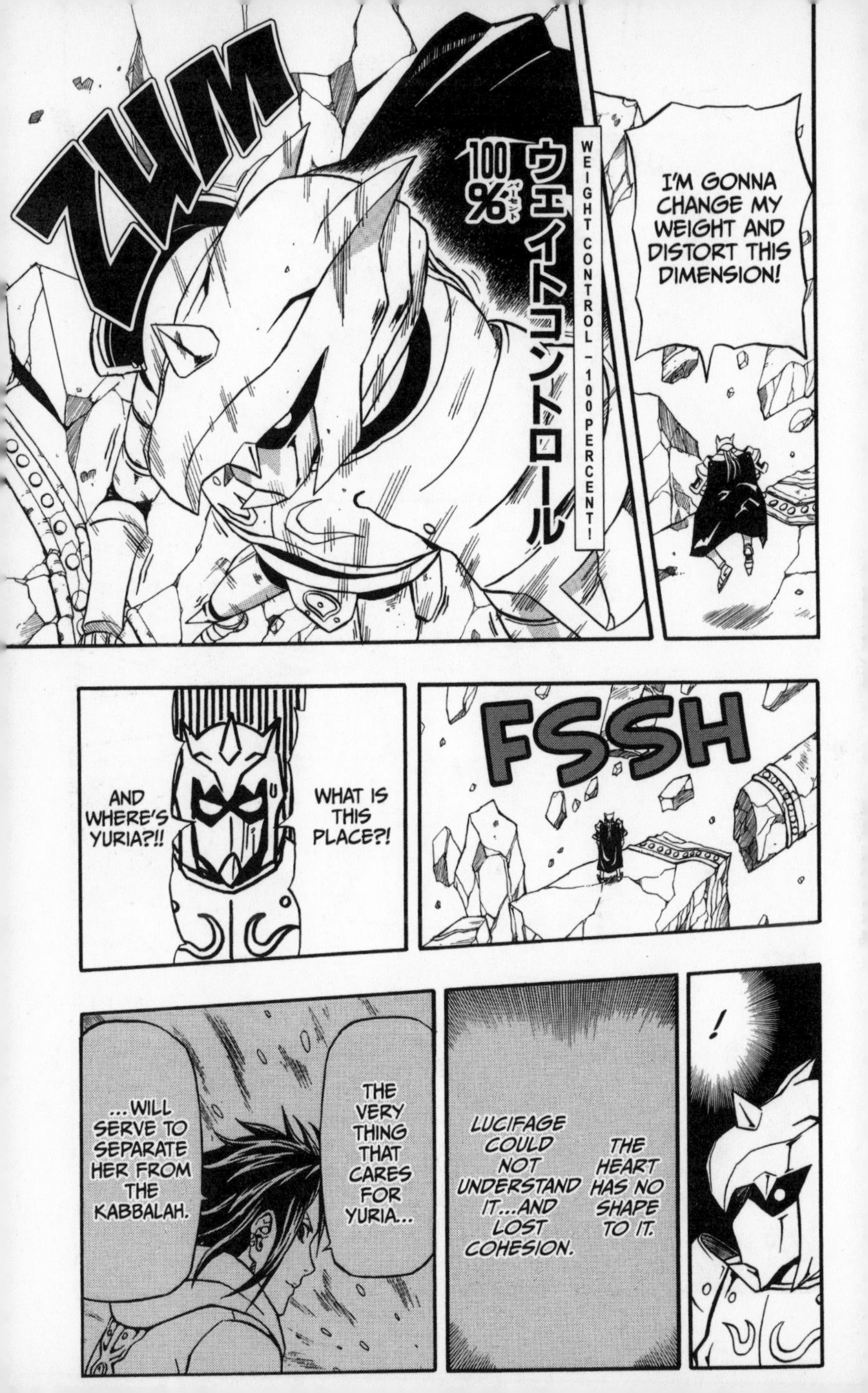
I'M GONNA CHANGE MY WEIGHT AND DISTORT THIS DIMENSION!
WEIGHT CONTROL – 100 PERCENT!
ウェイトコントロール 100%
ZUM
FSSH
WHAT IS THIS PLACE?!
AND WHERE'S YURIA?!!
!
THE HEART HAS NO SHAPE TO IT.
LUCIFAGE COULD NOT UNDERSTAND IT...AND LOST COHESION.
THE VERY THING THAT CARES FOR YURIA...
...WILL SERVE TO SEPARATE HER FROM THE KABBALAH.

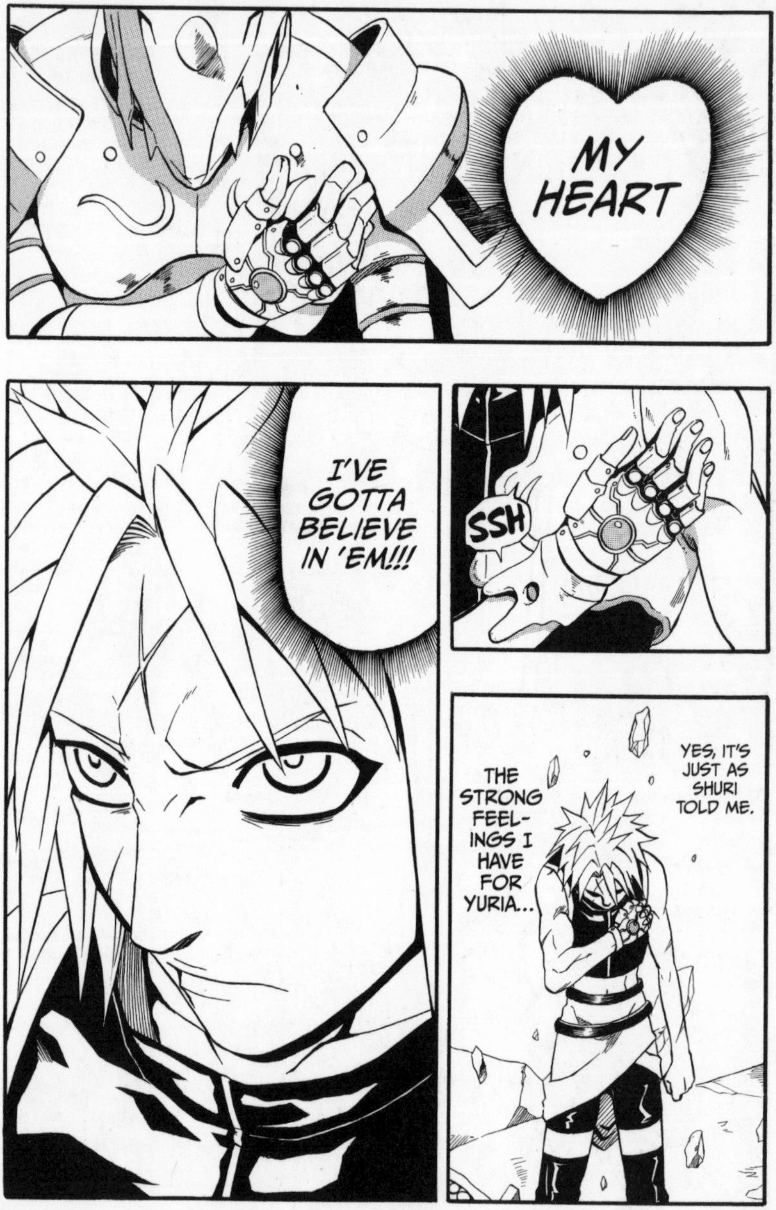
MY HEART
SSH
I'VE GOTTA BELIEVE IN 'EM!!!
YES, IT'S JUST AS SHURI TOLD ME.
THE STRONG FEEL-INGS I HAVE FOR YURIA...

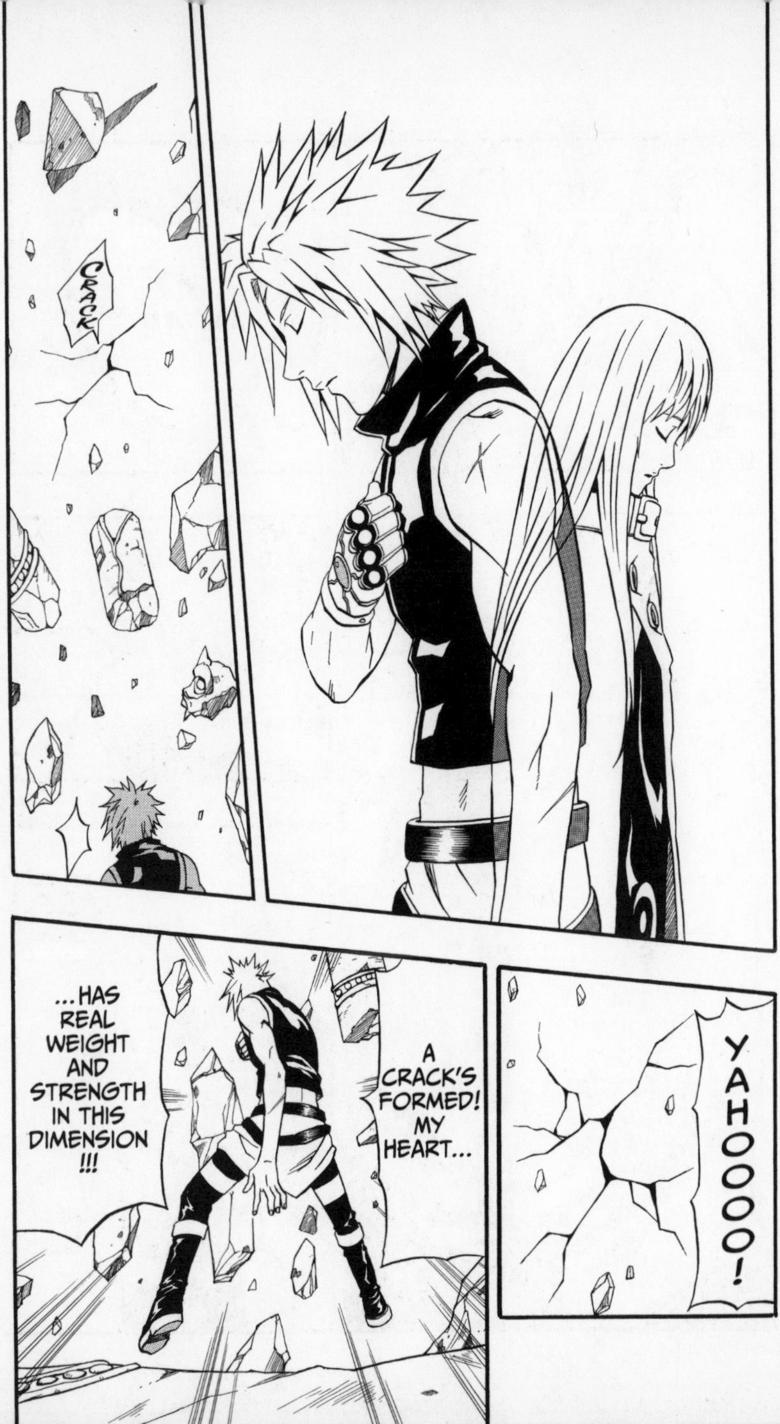
CRACK
YAHOOOOO!
A CRACK'S FORMED! MY HEART...
...HAS REAL WEIGHT AND STRENGTH IN THIS DIMENSION!!!

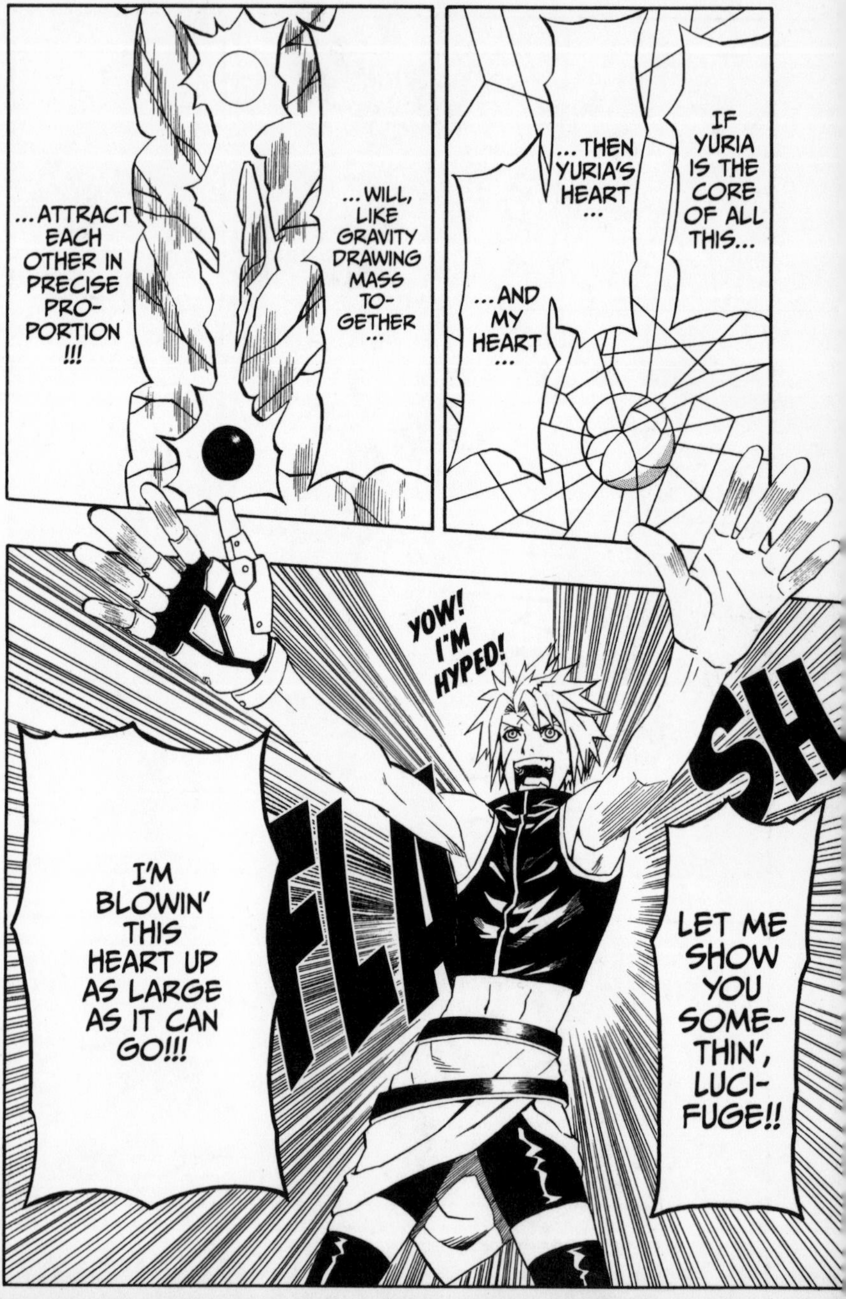
IF YURIA IS THE CORE OF ALL THIS...
...THEN YURIA'S HEART ...
...AND MY HEART ...
...WILL, LIKE GRAVITY DRAWING MASS TO-GETHER ...
...ATTRACT EACH OTHER IN PRECISE PRO-PORTION !!!
LET ME SHOW YOU SOME-THIN', LUCI-FUGE!!
YOW! I'M HYPED!
SH
FLA
I'M BLOWIN' THIS HEART UP AS LARGE AS IT CAN GO!!!

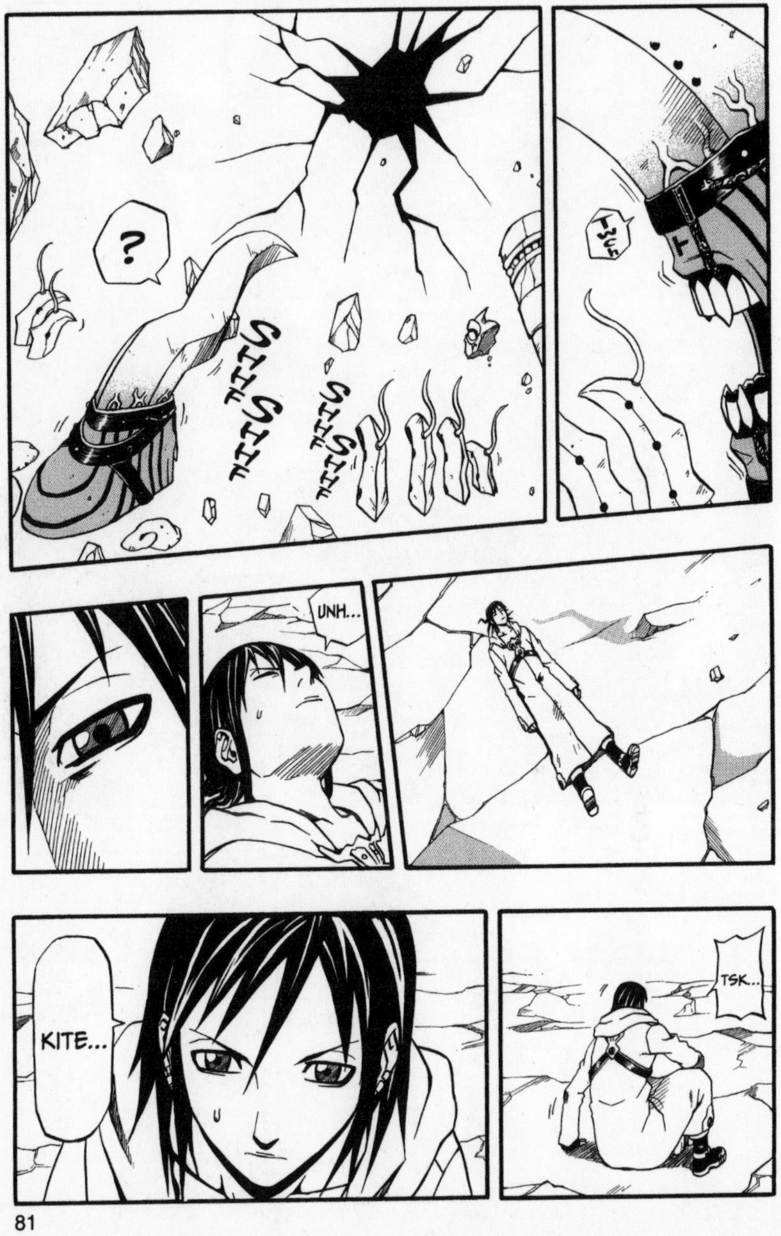
TWCh
?
SHHF SHHF
SHHF SHHF
UNH...
TSK...
KITE...

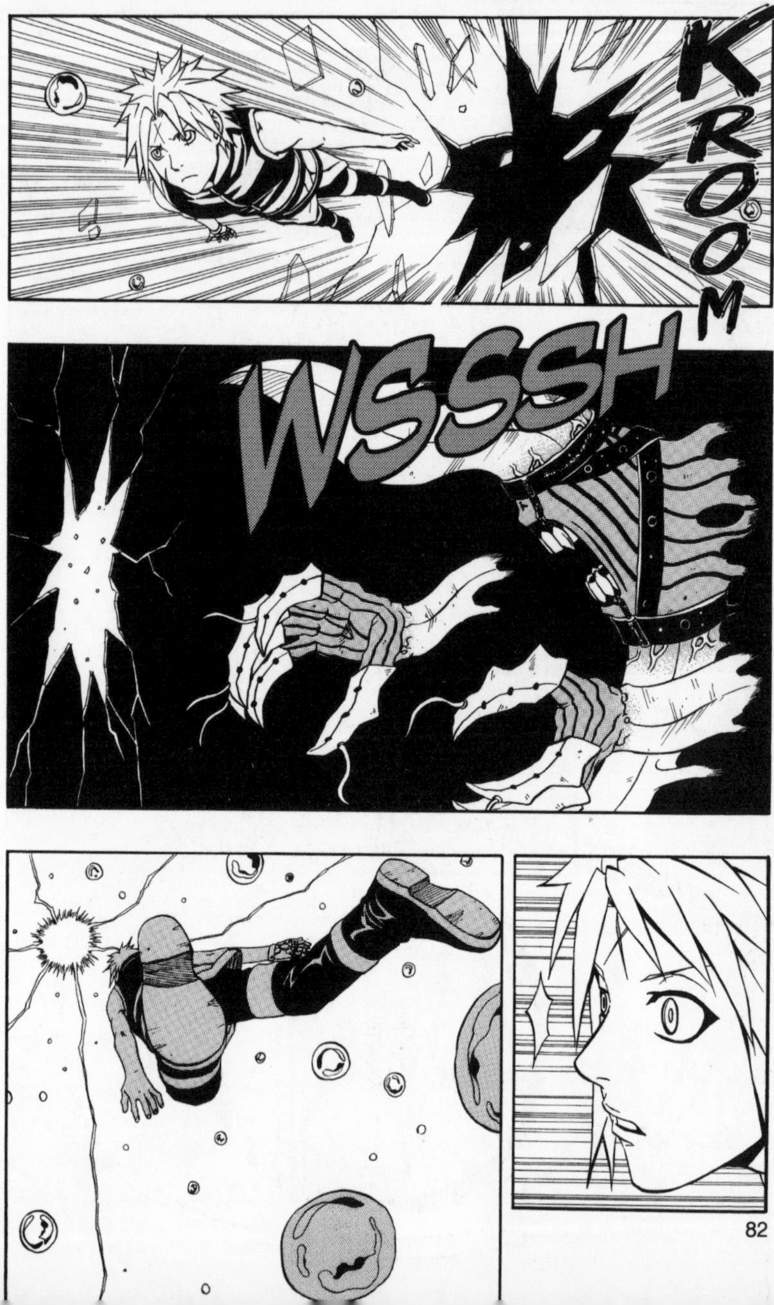
KROOM
WSSSH

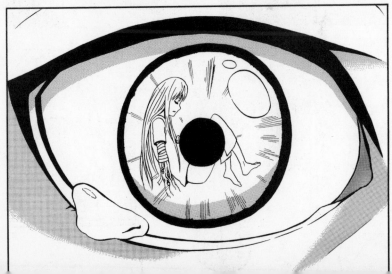

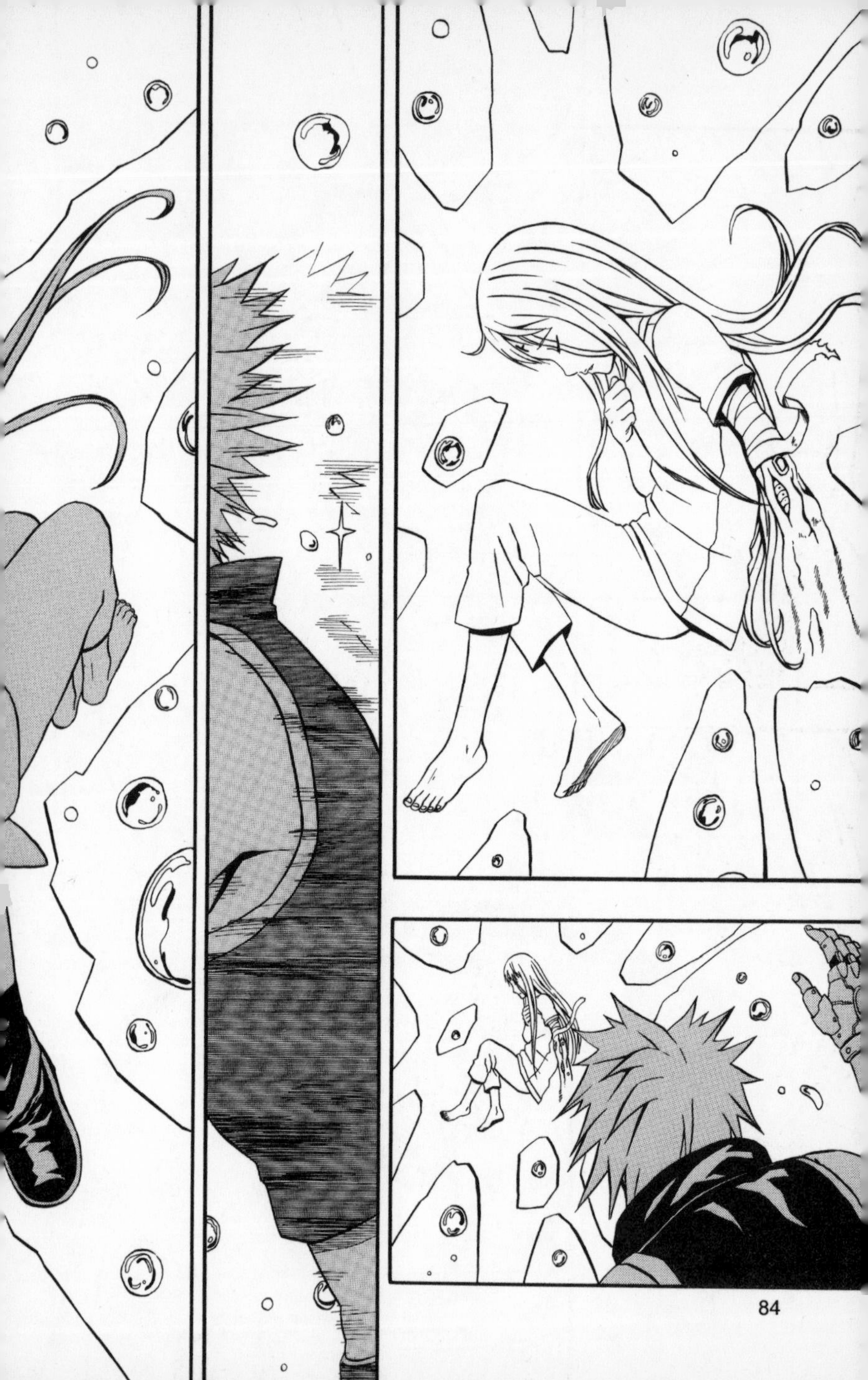

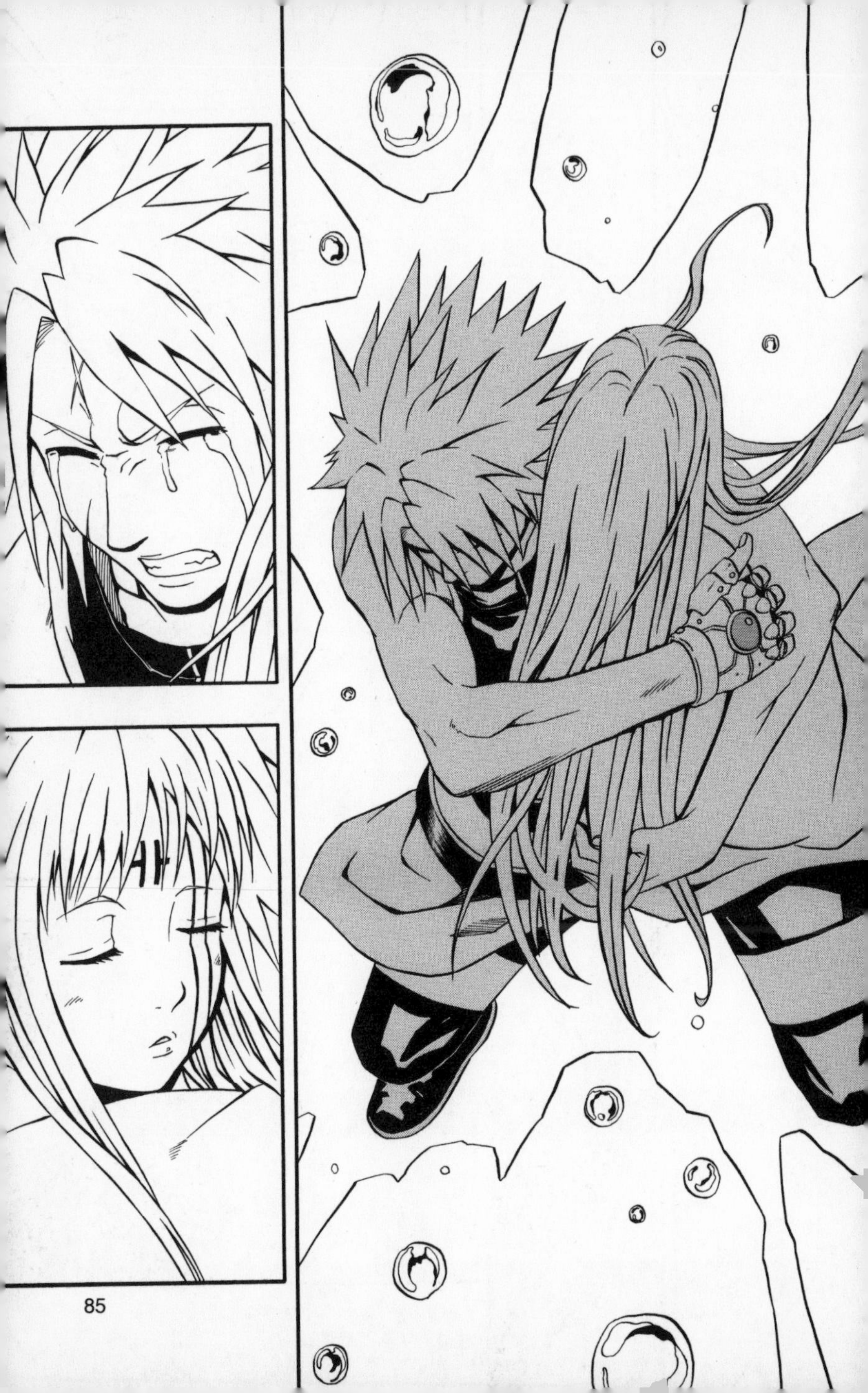

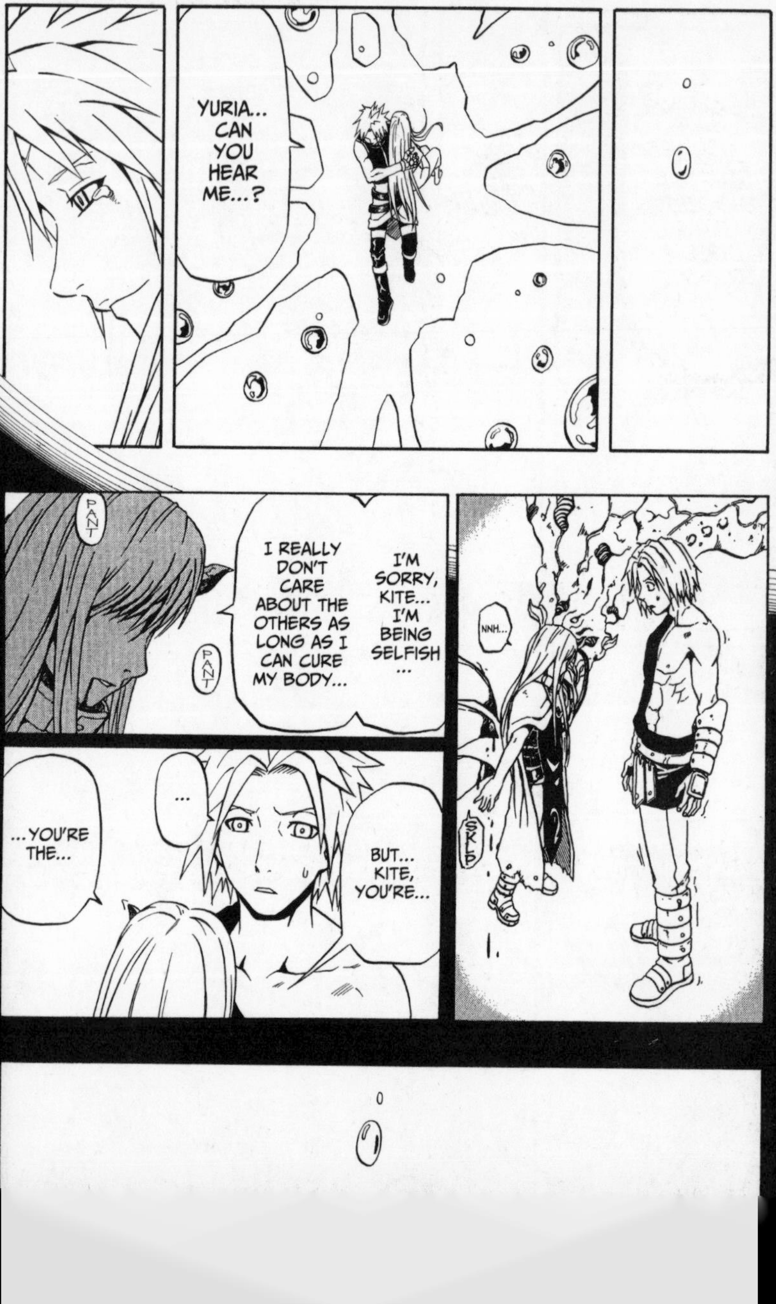
YURIA... CAN YOU HEAR ME...?
NNH...
SKLP
I'M SORRY, KITE... I'M BEING SELFISH...
I REALLY DON'T CARE ABOUT THE OTHERS AS LONG AS I CAN CURE MY BODY...
PANT
PANT
BUT... KITE, YOU'RE...
...
...YOU'RE THE...

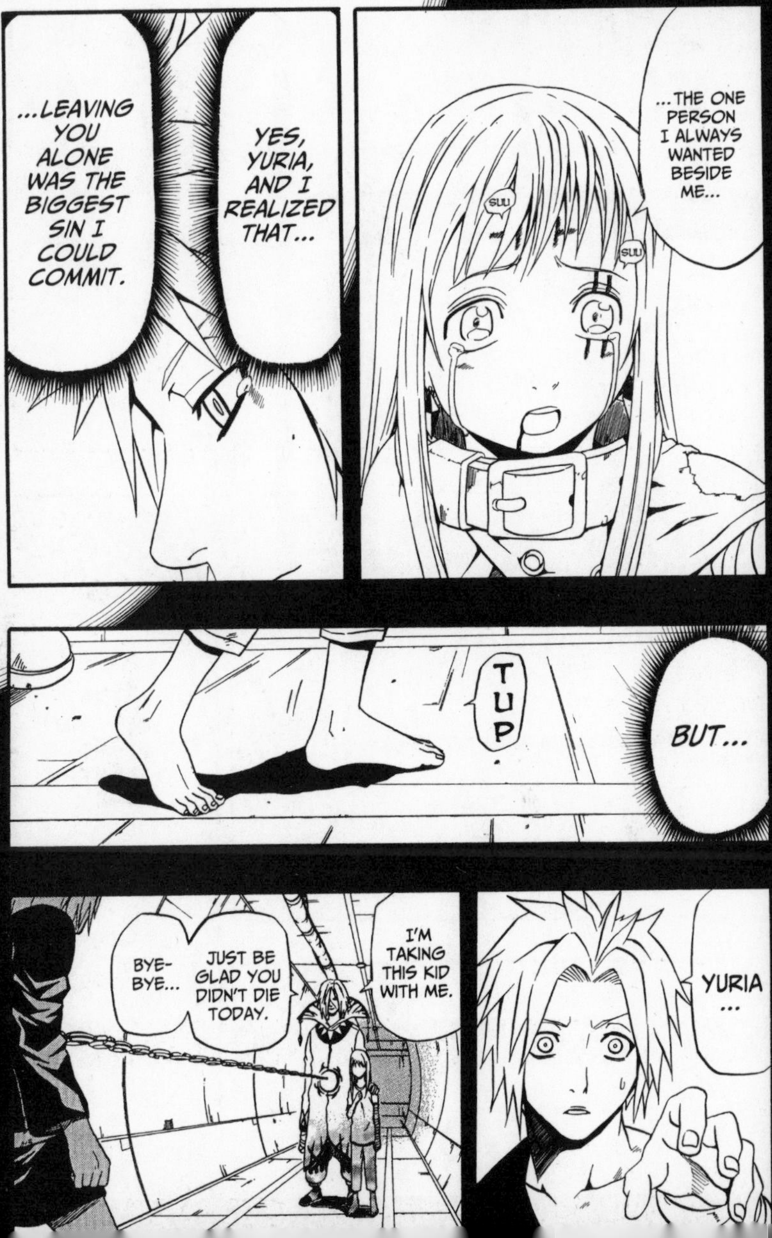
...THE ONE PERSON I ALWAYS WANTED BESIDE ME...
SUU
SUU
YES, YURIA, AND I REALIZED THAT...
...LEAVING YOU ALONE WAS THE BIGGEST SIN I COULD COMMIT.
BUT...
TUP
YURIA ...
I'M TAKING THIS KID WITH ME.
JUST BE GLAD YOU DIDN'T DIE TODAY.
BYE-BYE...

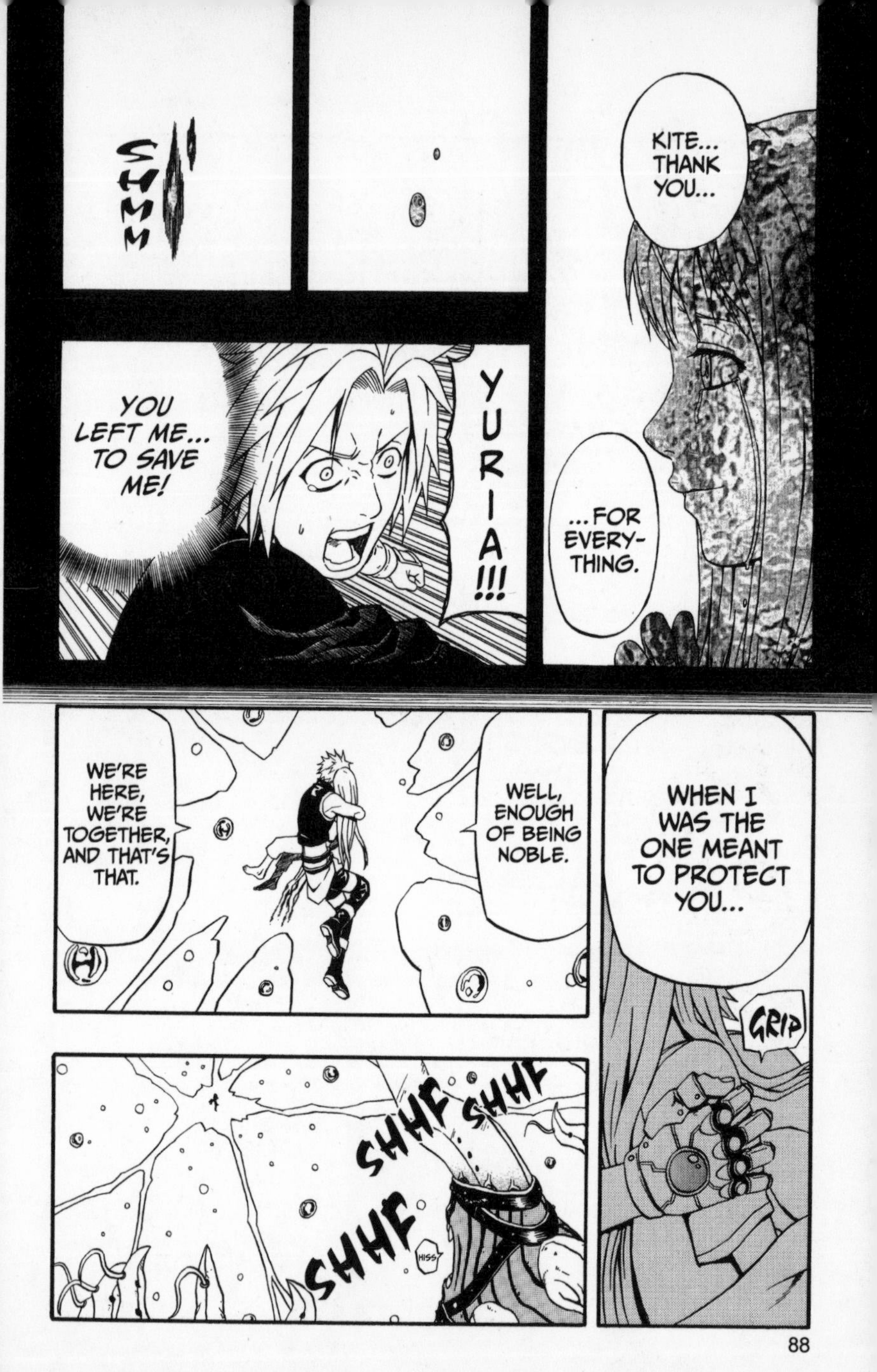
KITE... THANK YOU...
...FOR EVERY-THING.
SHMM
YURIA!!!
YOU LEFT ME... TO SAVE ME!
WHEN I WAS THE ONE MEANT TO PROTECT YOU...
GRIP
WELL, ENOUGH OF BEING NOBLE.
WE'RE HERE, WE'RE TOGETHER, AND THAT'S THAT.
SHHF SHHF
SHHF
HISS

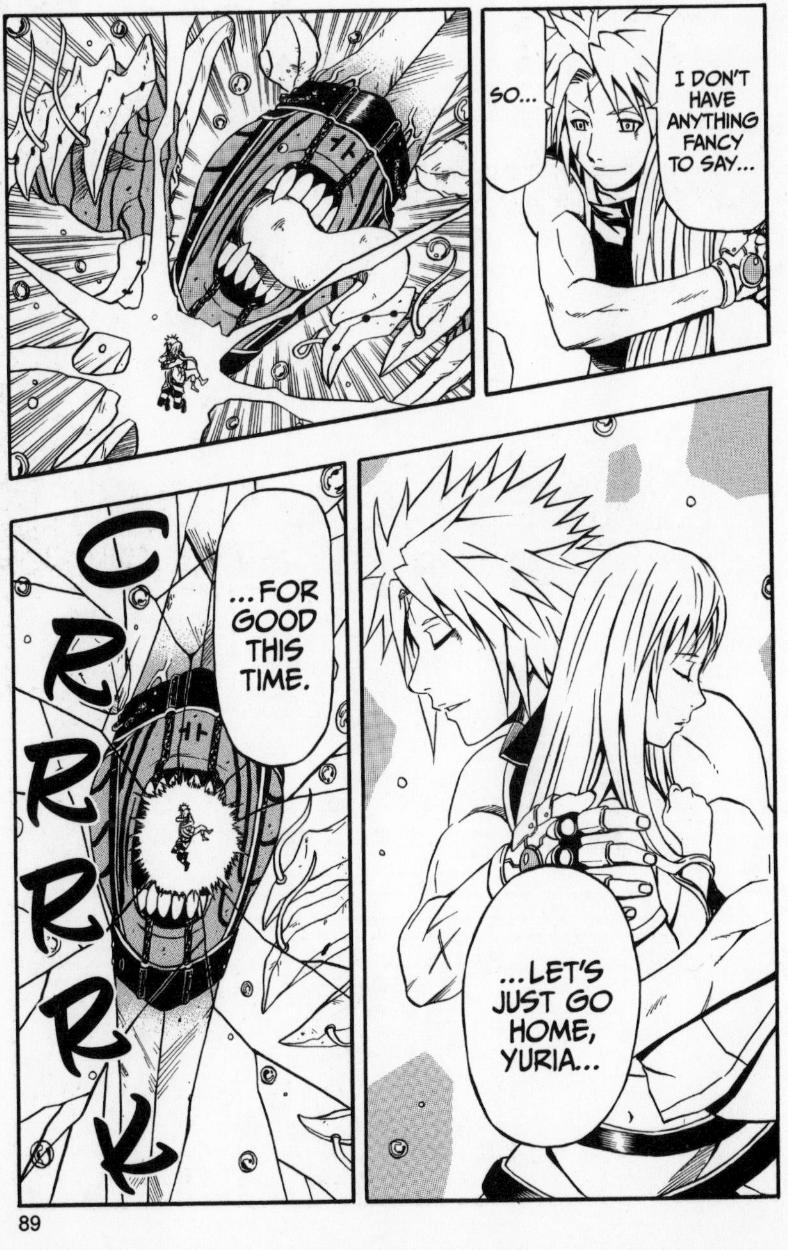
I DON'T HAVE ANYTHING FANCY TO SAY...
SO...
...LET'S JUST GO HOME, YURIA...
...FOR GOOD THIS TIME.
CRRRRRK

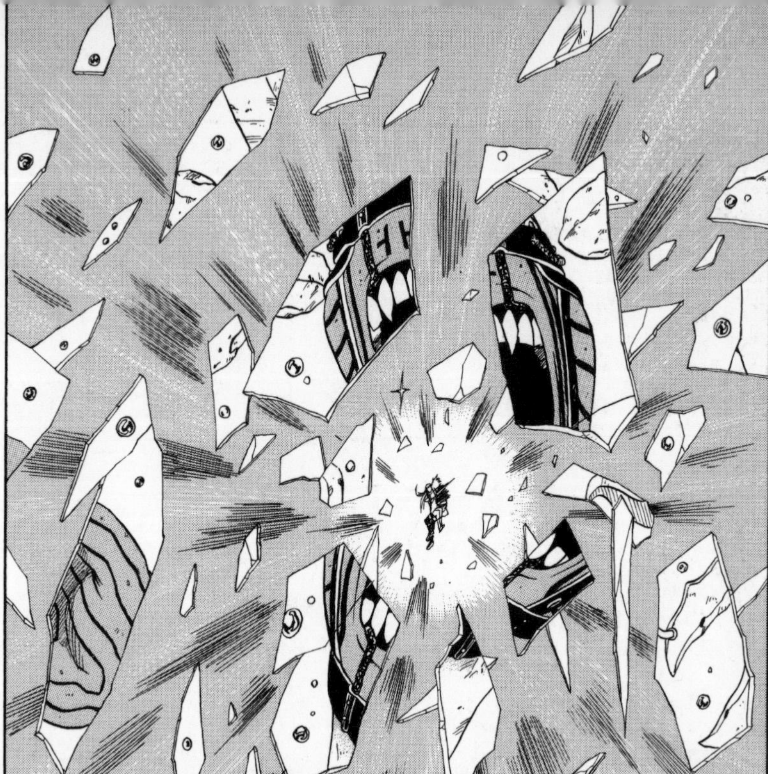

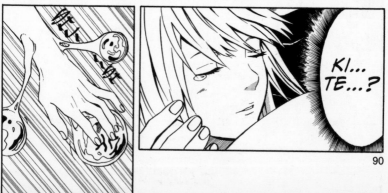

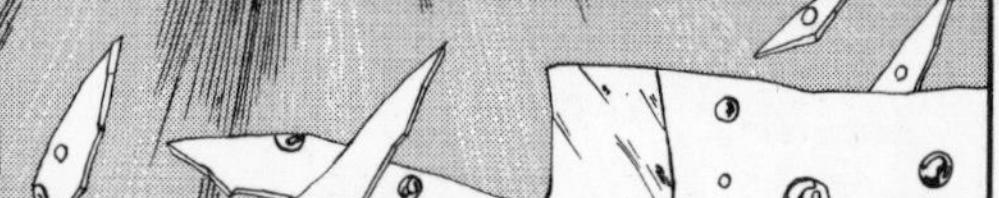
KI... TE...?

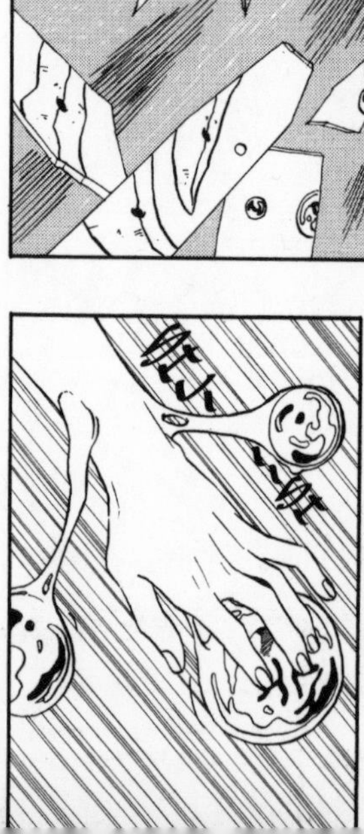

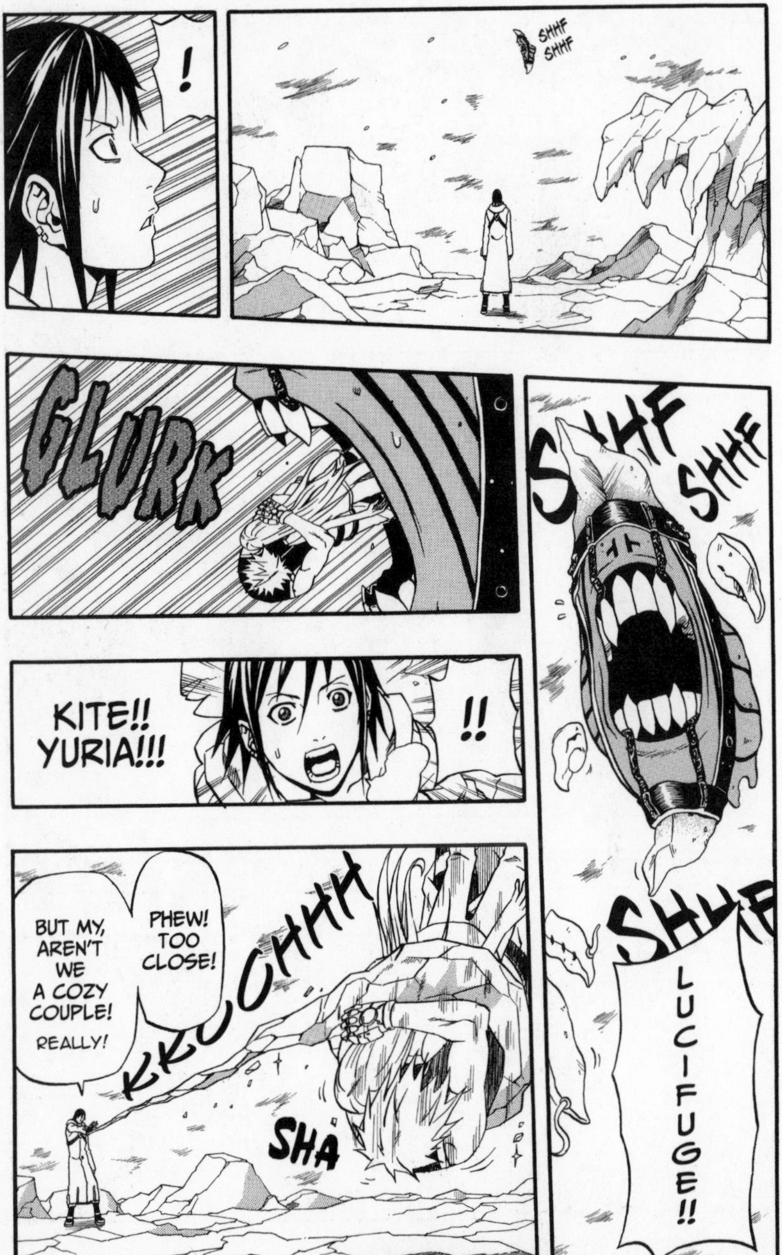
SHHF SHHF
!
SHHF
SHHF
SHHF
LUCIFUGE!!
GLURK
!!
KITE!! YURIA!!!
PHEW! TOO CLOSE!
BUT MY, AREN'T WE A COZY COUPLE!
REALLY!
KKCCHHH
SHA

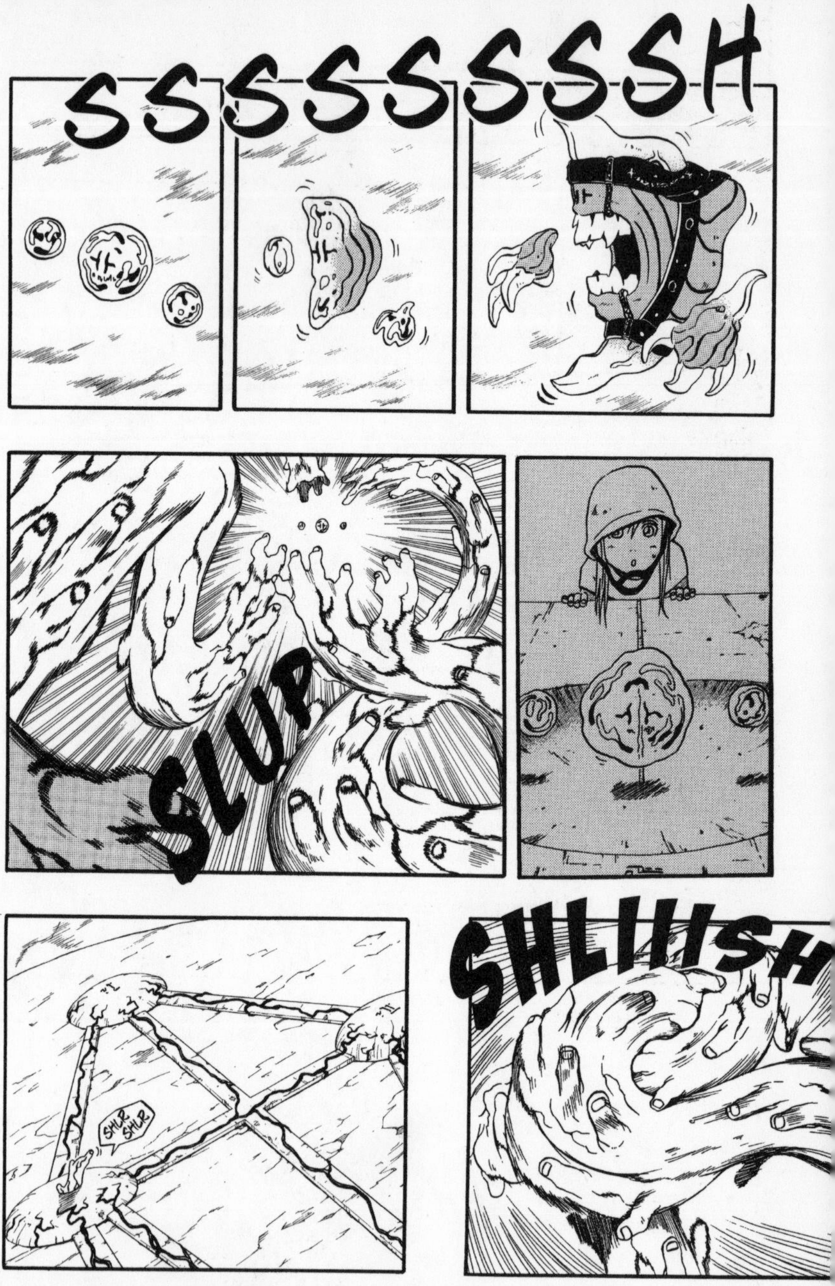
SSSSSSSSSH
SLUP
SHLIIISH
SHLR SHLR

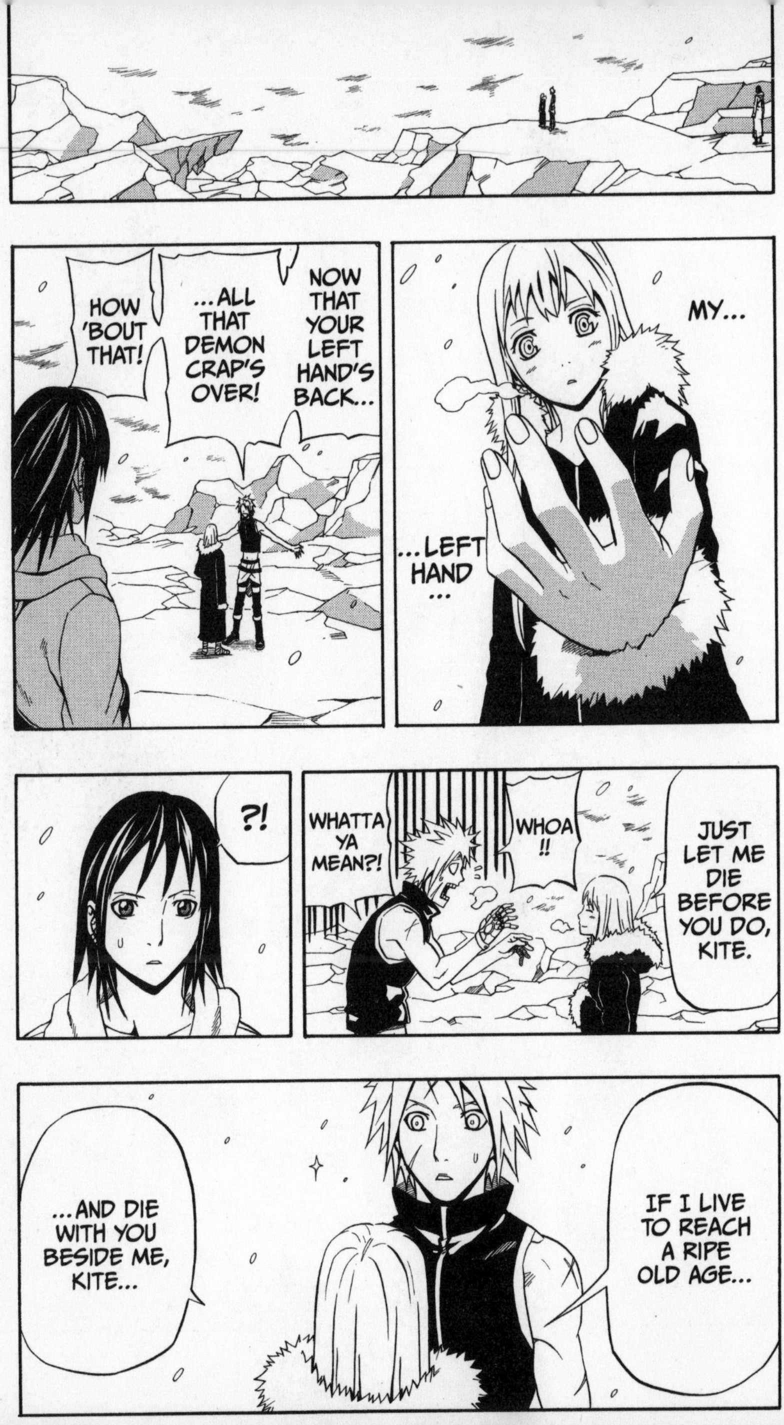
MY...
...LEFT HAND ...
NOW THAT YOUR LEFT HAND'S BACK...
...ALL THAT DEMON CRAP'S OVER!
HOW 'BOUT THAT!
JUST LET ME DIE BEFORE YOU DO, KITE.
WHOA !!
WHATTA YA MEAN?!
?!
IF I LIVE TO REACH A RIPE OLD AGE...
...AND DIE WITH YOU BESIDE ME, KITE...

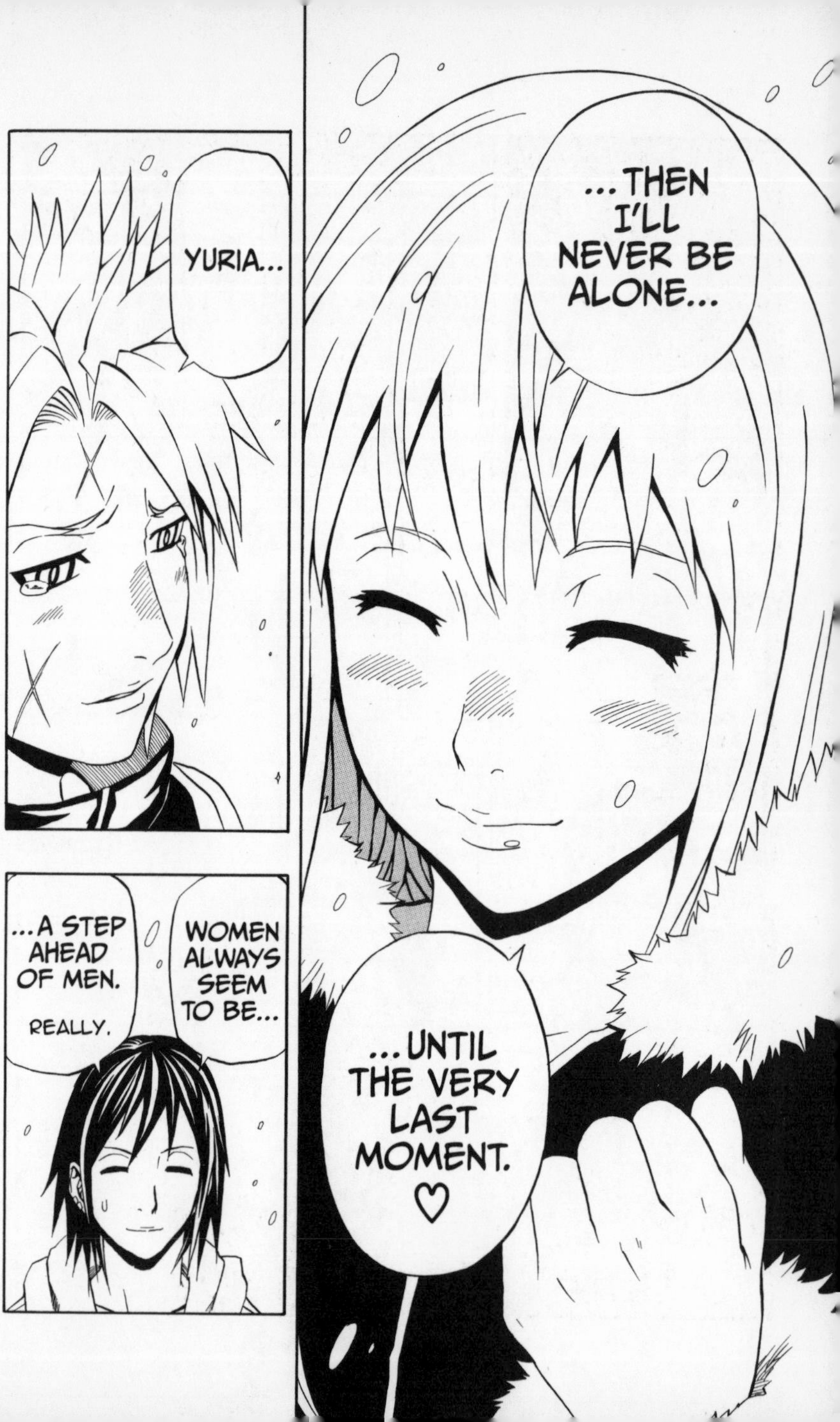
...THEN I'LL NEVER BE ALONE...
...UNTIL THE VERY LAST MOMENT. ♡
YURIA...
WOMEN ALWAYS SEEM TO BE...
...A STEP AHEAD OF MEN.
REALLY.

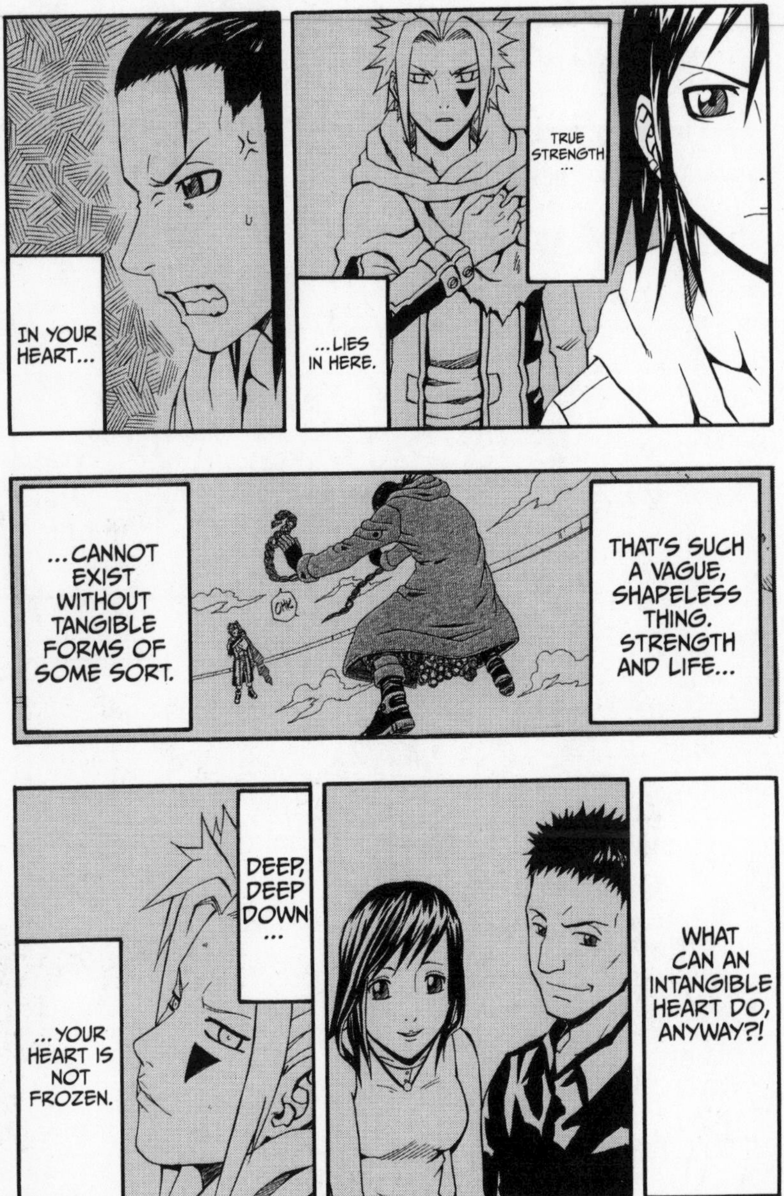
TRUE STRENGTH...
...LIES IN HERE.
IN YOUR HEART...
THAT'S SUCH A VAGUE, SHAPELESS THING. STRENGTH AND LIFE...
...CANNOT EXIST WITHOUT TANGIBLE FORMS OF SOME SORT.
WHAT CAN AN INTANGIBLE HEART DO, ANYWAY?!
DEEP, DEEP DOWN...
...YOUR HEART IS NOT FROZEN.

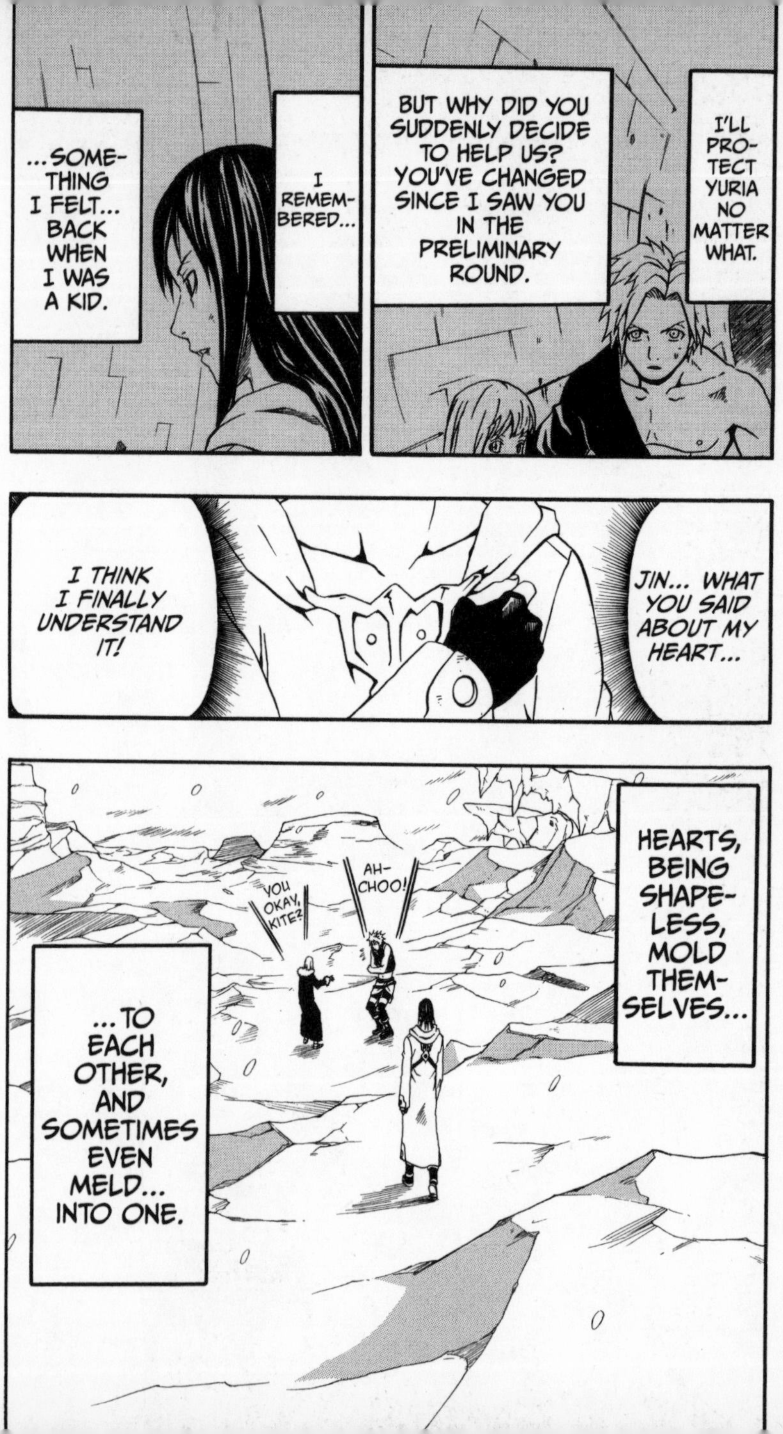
I'LL PROTECT YURIA NO MATTER WHAT.
BUT WHY DID YOU SUDDENLY DECIDE TO HELP US? YOU'VE CHANGED SINCE I SAW YOU IN THE PRELIMINARY ROUND.
I REMEMBERED...
...SOMETHING I FELT... BACK WHEN I WAS A KID.
JIN... WHAT YOU SAID ABOUT MY HEART...
I THINK I FINALLY UNDERSTAND IT!
HEARTS, BEING SHAPELESS, MOLD THEMSELVES...
AH-CHOO!
YOU OKAY, KITE?
...TO EACH OTHER, AND SOMETIMES EVEN MELD... INTO ONE.

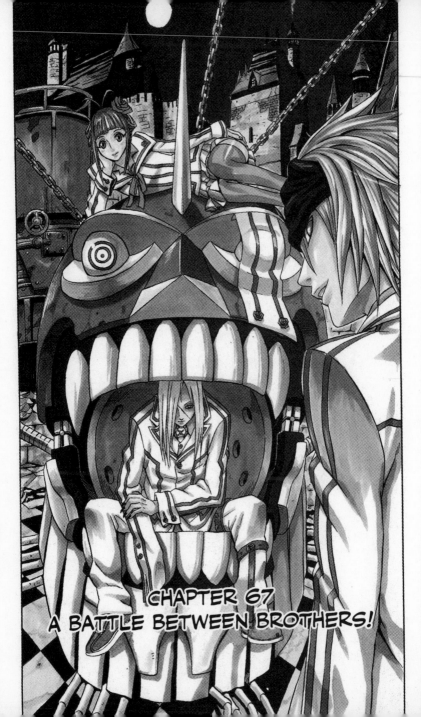

CHAPTER 67
A BATTLE BETWEEN BROTHERS!

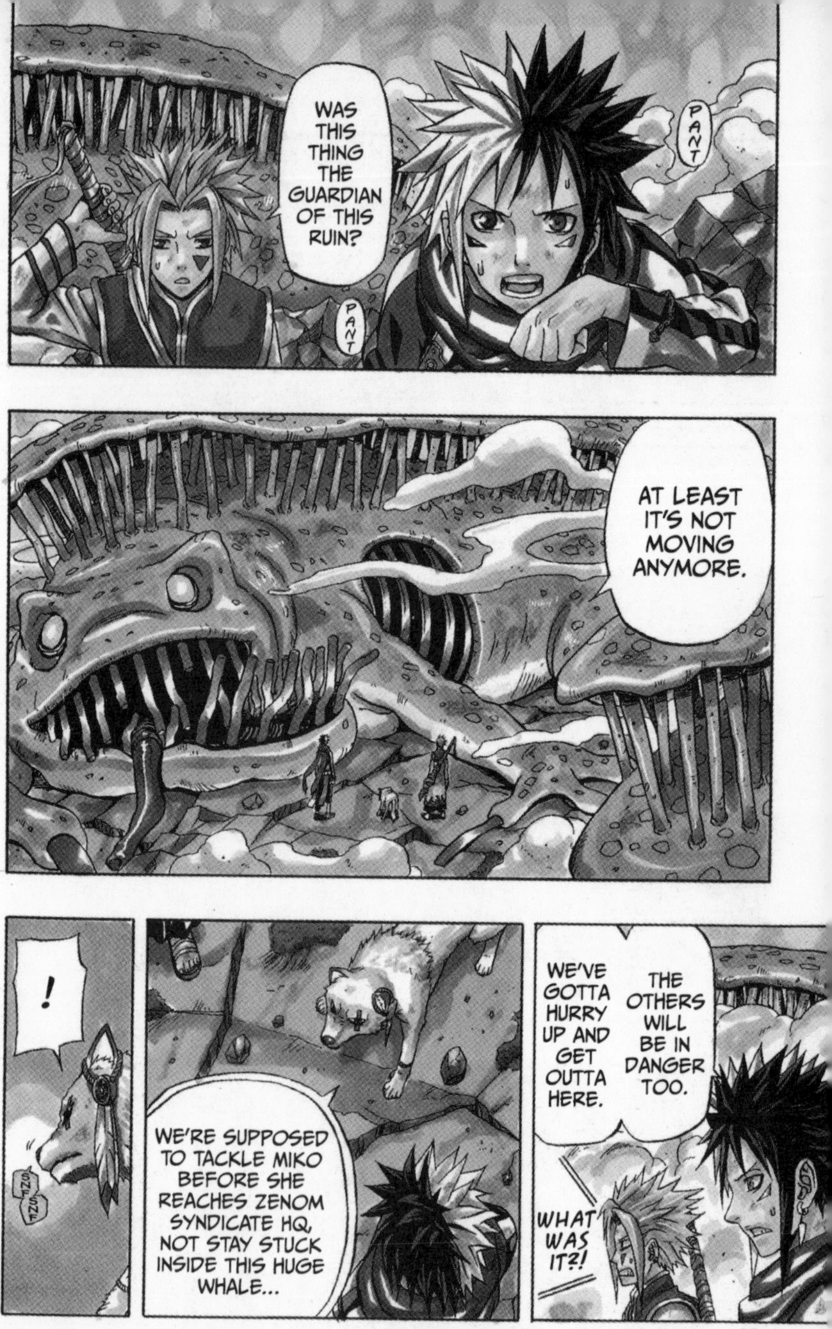
PANT
WAS THIS THING THE GUARDIAN OF THIS RUIN?
PANT
AT LEAST IT'S NOT MOVING ANYMORE.
THE OTHERS WILL BE IN DANGER TOO.
WE'VE GOTTA HURRY UP AND GET OUTTA HERE.
WHAT WAS IT?!
WE'RE SUPPOSED TO TACKLE MIKO BEFORE SHE REACHES ZENOM SYNDICATE HQ, NOT STAY STUCK INSIDE THIS HUGE WHALE...
!
SNF SNF

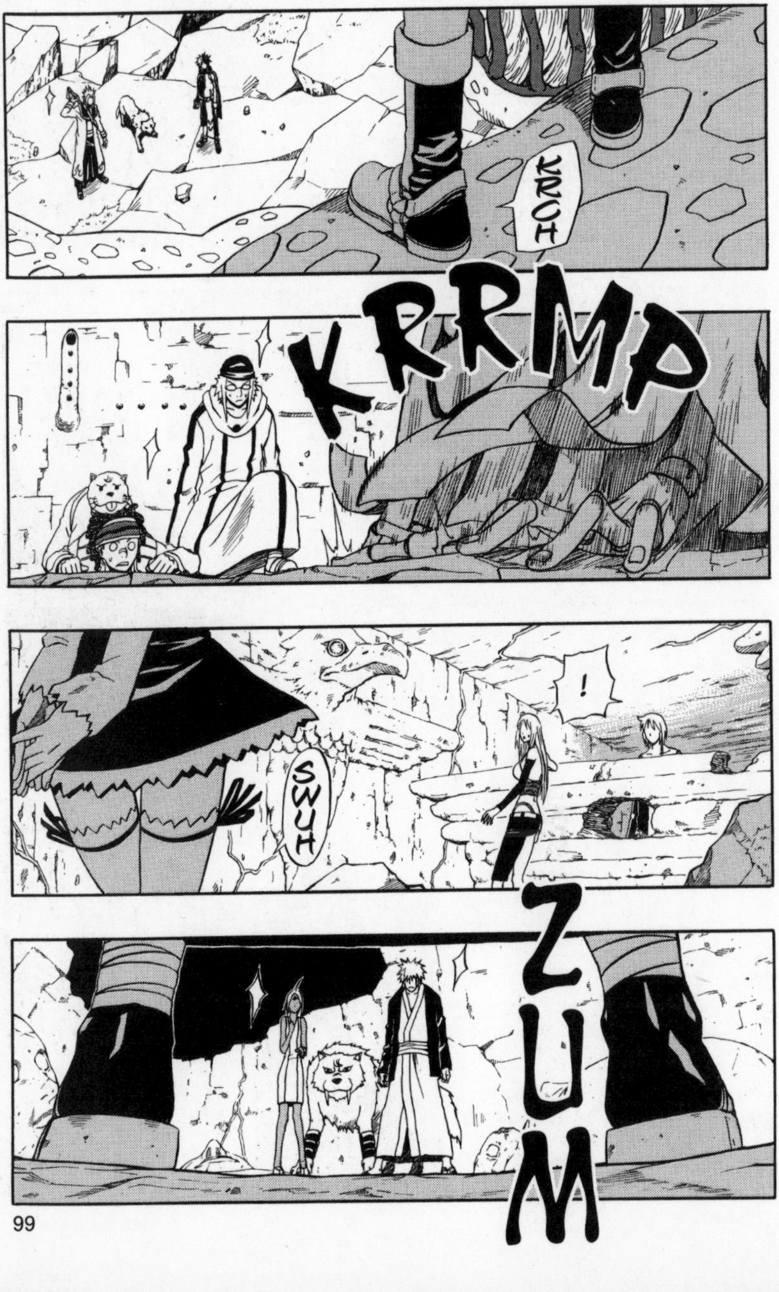
KROCH
KRRMP
!
SWUH
ZUM

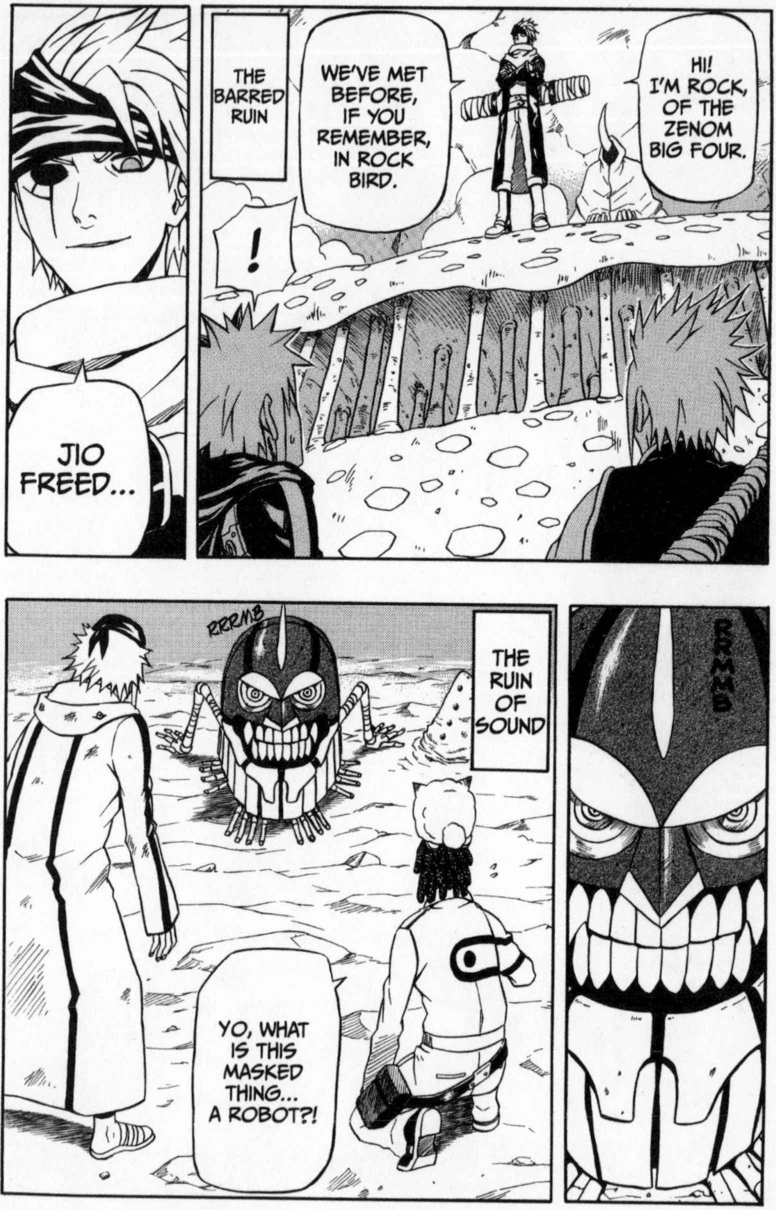
JIO FREED...
THE BARRED RUIN
HI! I'M ROCK, OF THE ZENOM BIG FOUR.
WE'VE MET BEFORE, IF YOU REMEMBER, IN ROCK BIRD.
!
THE RUIN OF SOUND
RRRMB
YO, WHAT IS THIS MASKED THING... A ROBOT?!
RRRMB

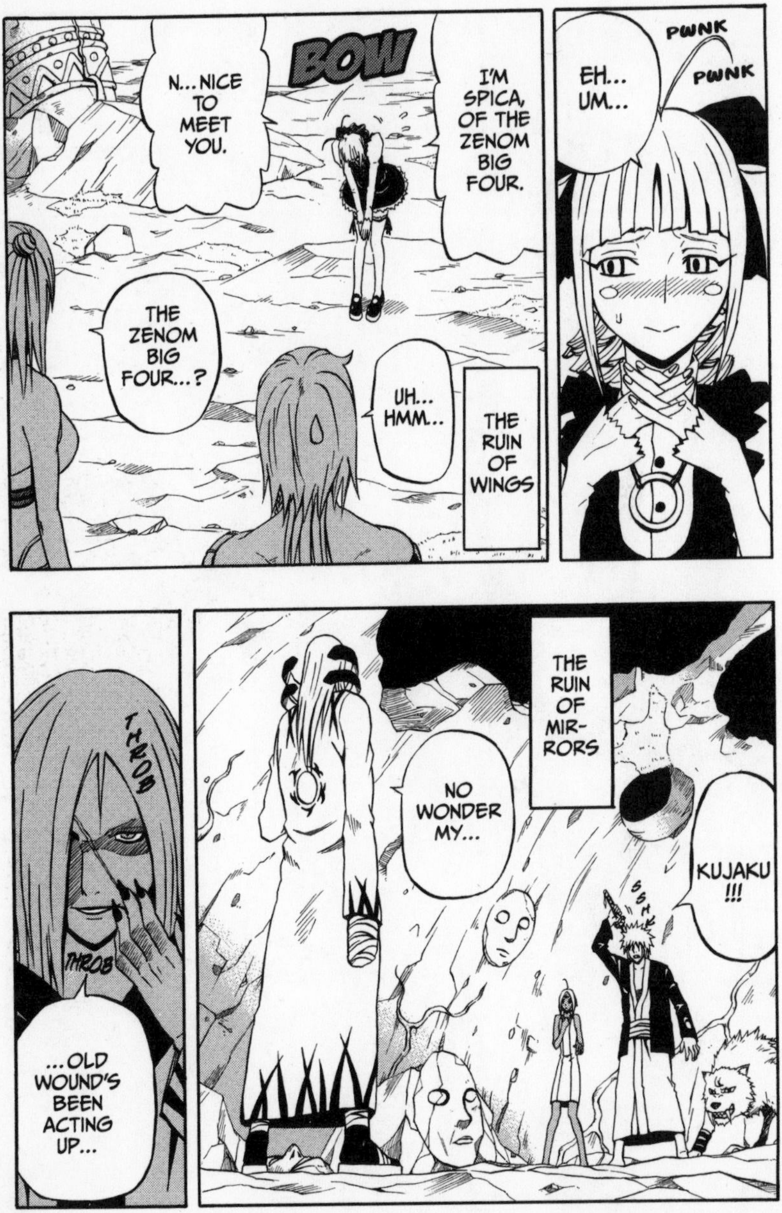
PWNK
PWNK
EH... UM...
I'M SPICA, OF THE ZENOM BIG FOUR.
BOW
N...NICE TO MEET YOU.
THE RUIN OF WINGS
UH... HMM...
THE ZENOM BIG FOUR...?
THE RUIN OF MIR-RORS
KUJAKU!!!
SSH
NO WONDER MY...
THROB
THROB
...OLD WOUND'S BEEN ACTING UP...

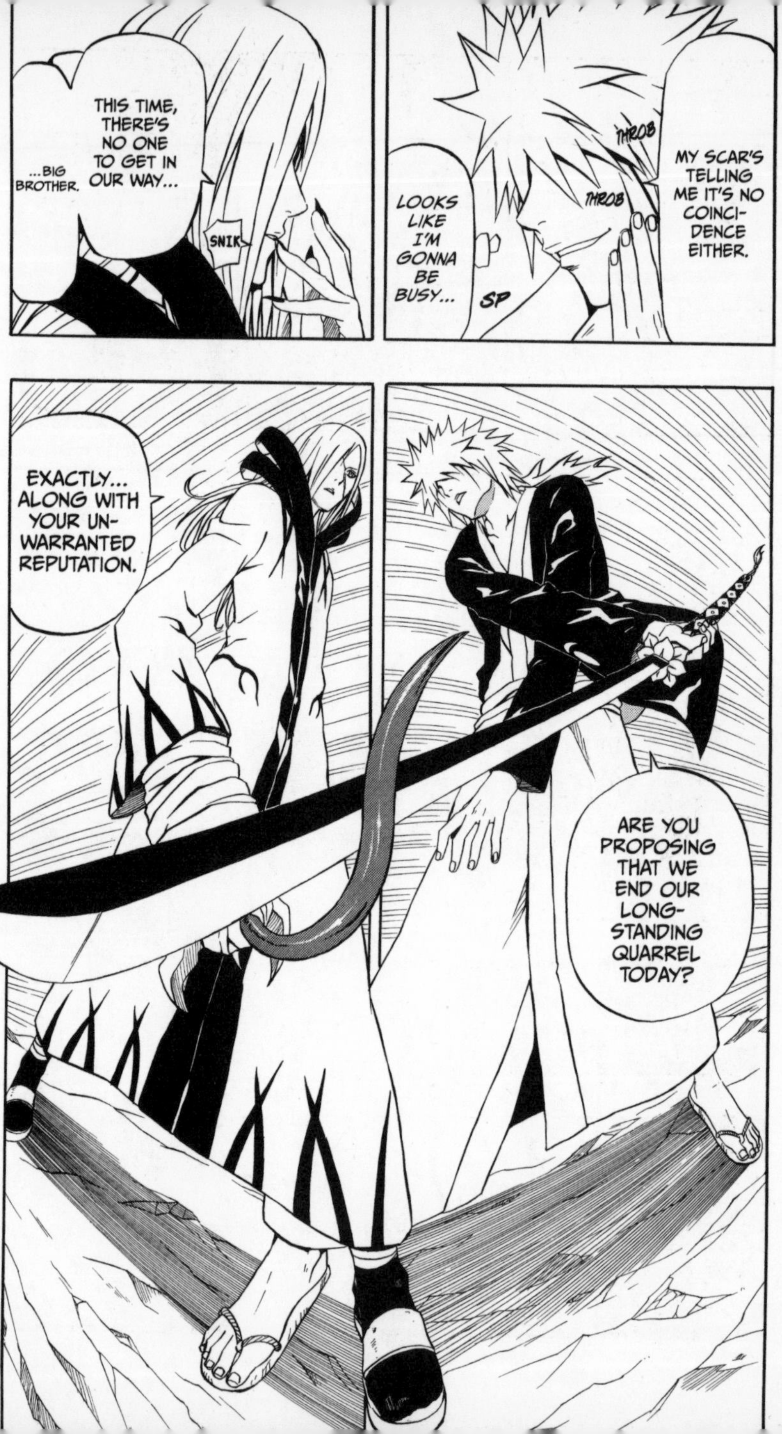
THROB
MY SCAR'S TELLING ME IT'S NO COINCIDENCE EITHER.
THROB
LOOKS LIKE I'M GONNA BE BUSY...
SP
THIS TIME, THERE'S NO ONE TO GET IN OUR WAY...
...BIG BROTHER.
SNIK
ARE YOU PROPOSING THAT WE END OUR LONG-STANDING QUARREL TODAY?
EXACTLY... ALONG WITH YOUR UNWARRANTED REPUTATION.

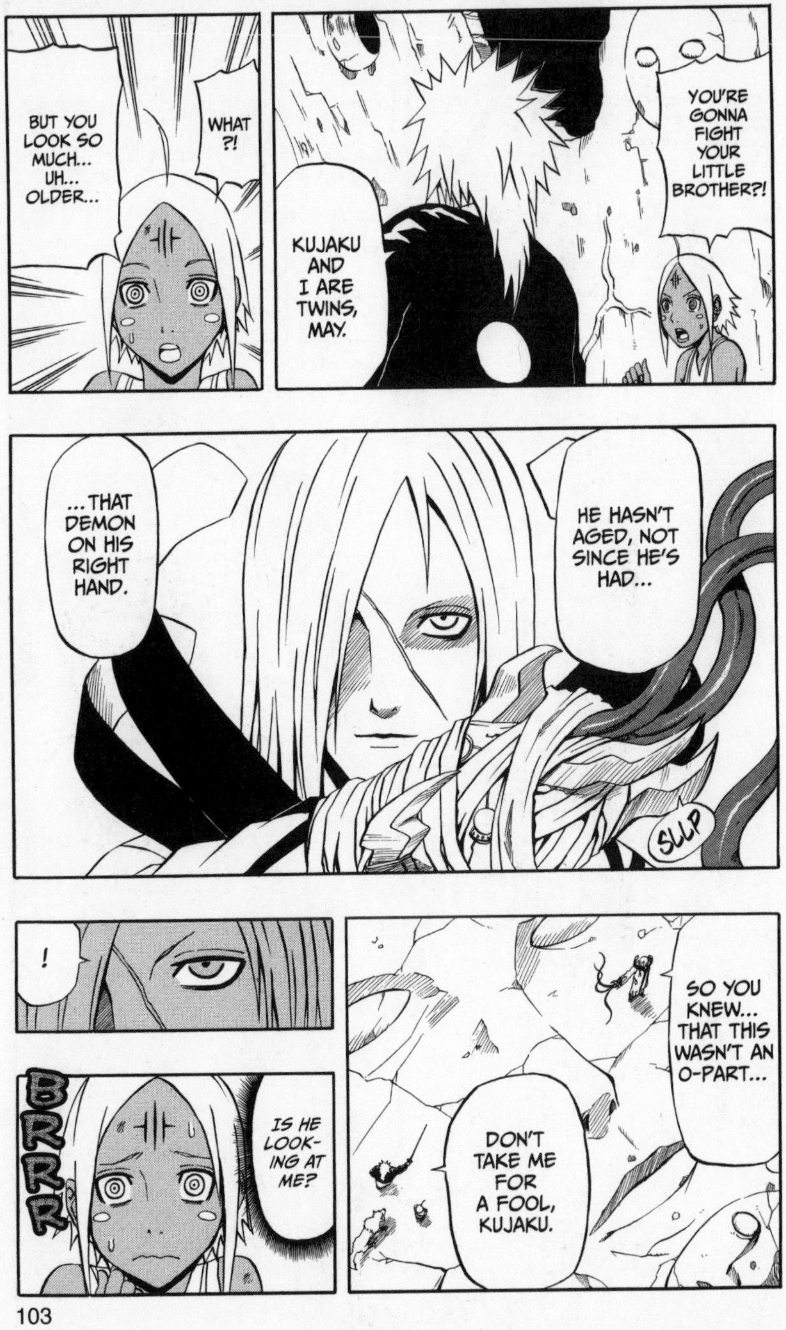
YOU'RE GONNA FIGHT YOUR LITTLE BROTHER?!
KUJAKU AND I ARE TWINS, MAY.
WHAT?!
BUT YOU LOOK SO MUCH... UH... OLDER...
HE HASN'T AGED, NOT SINCE HE'S HAD...
...THAT DEMON ON HIS RIGHT HAND.
SLLP
SO YOU KNEW... THAT THIS WASN'T AN O-PART...
DON'T TAKE ME FOR A FOOL, KUJAKU.
!
BRRR
IS HE LOOKING AT ME?

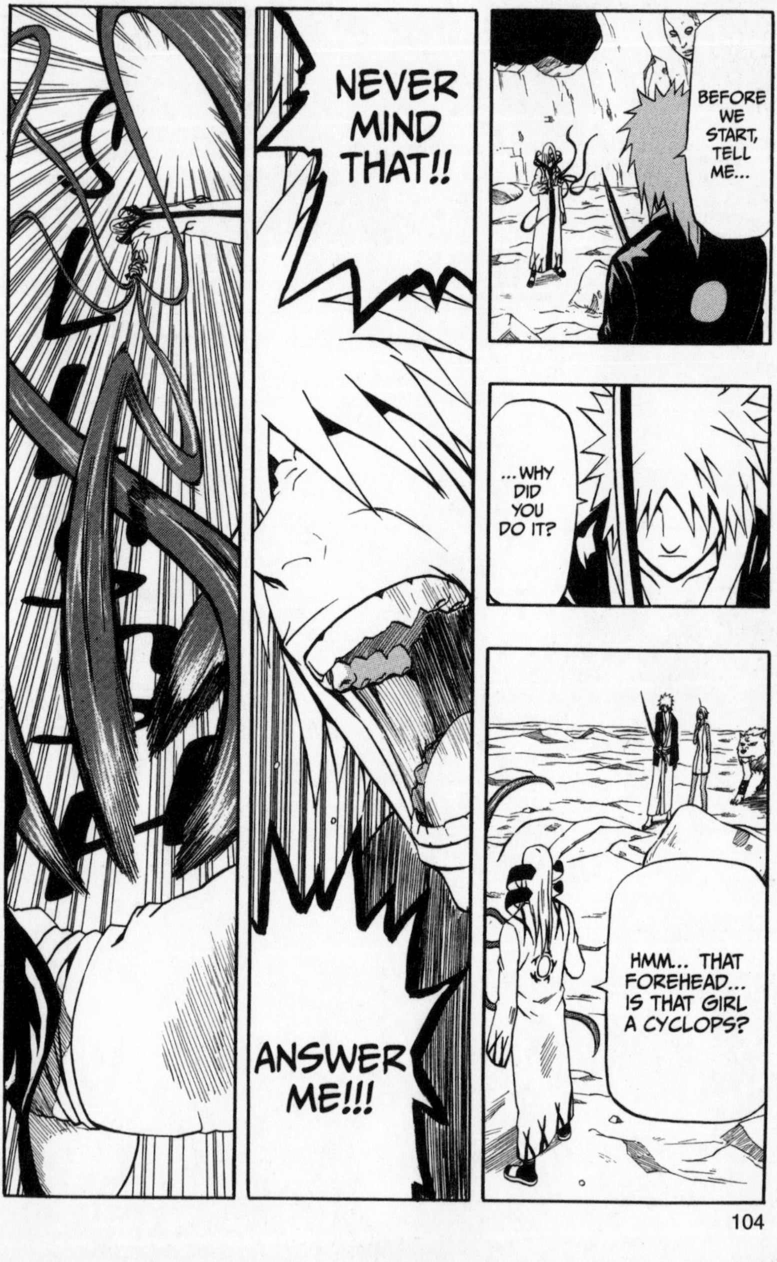
BEFORE WE START, TELL ME...
...WHY DID YOU DO IT?
HMM... THAT FOREHEAD... IS THAT GIRL A CYCLOPS?
NEVER MIND THAT!!
ANSWER ME!!!

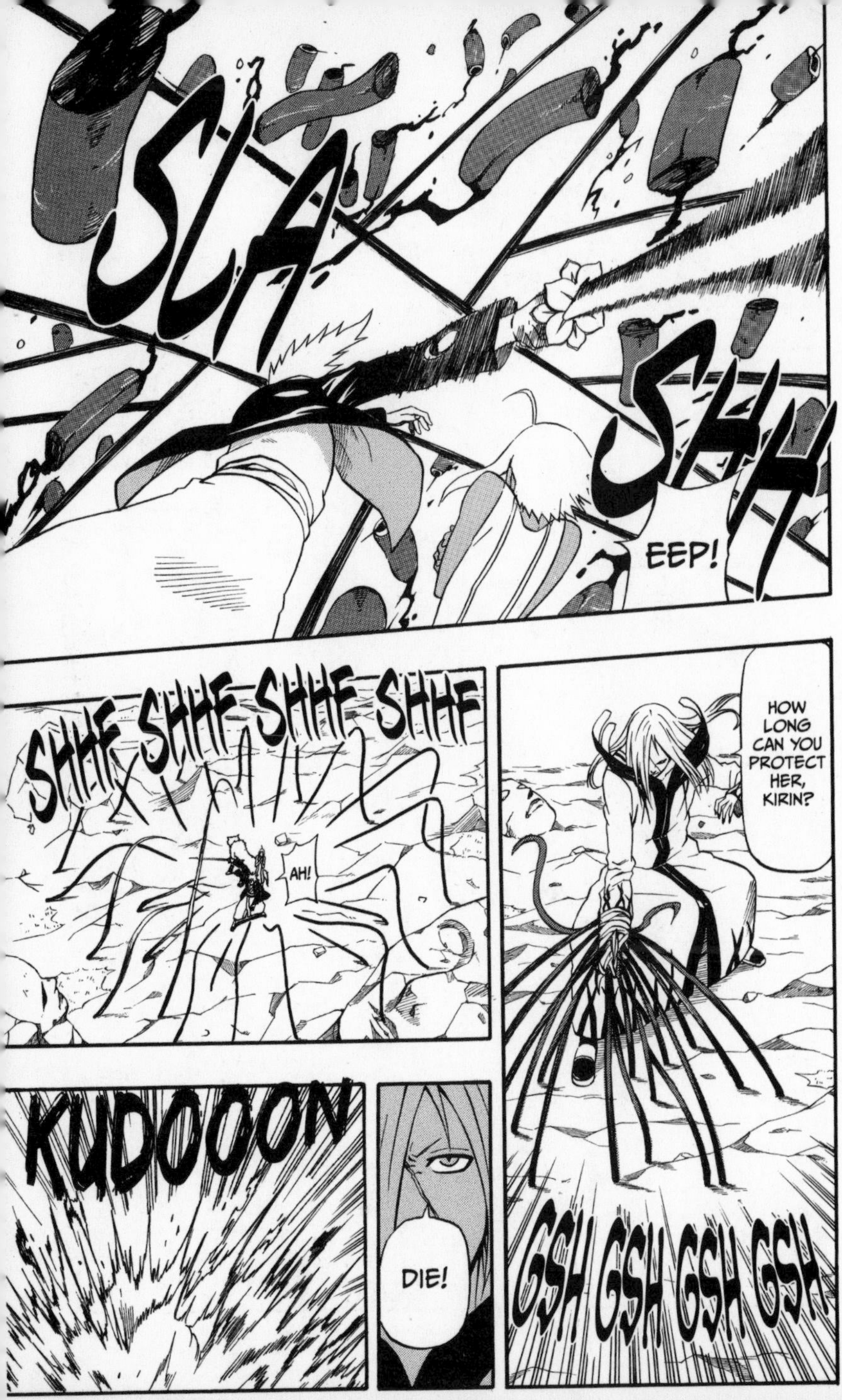
SLA
SHH
EEP!
HOW LONG CAN YOU PROTECT HER, KIRIN?
GSH GSH GSH GSH
SHHF SHHF SHHF SHHF
AH!
DIE!
KUDOOOON

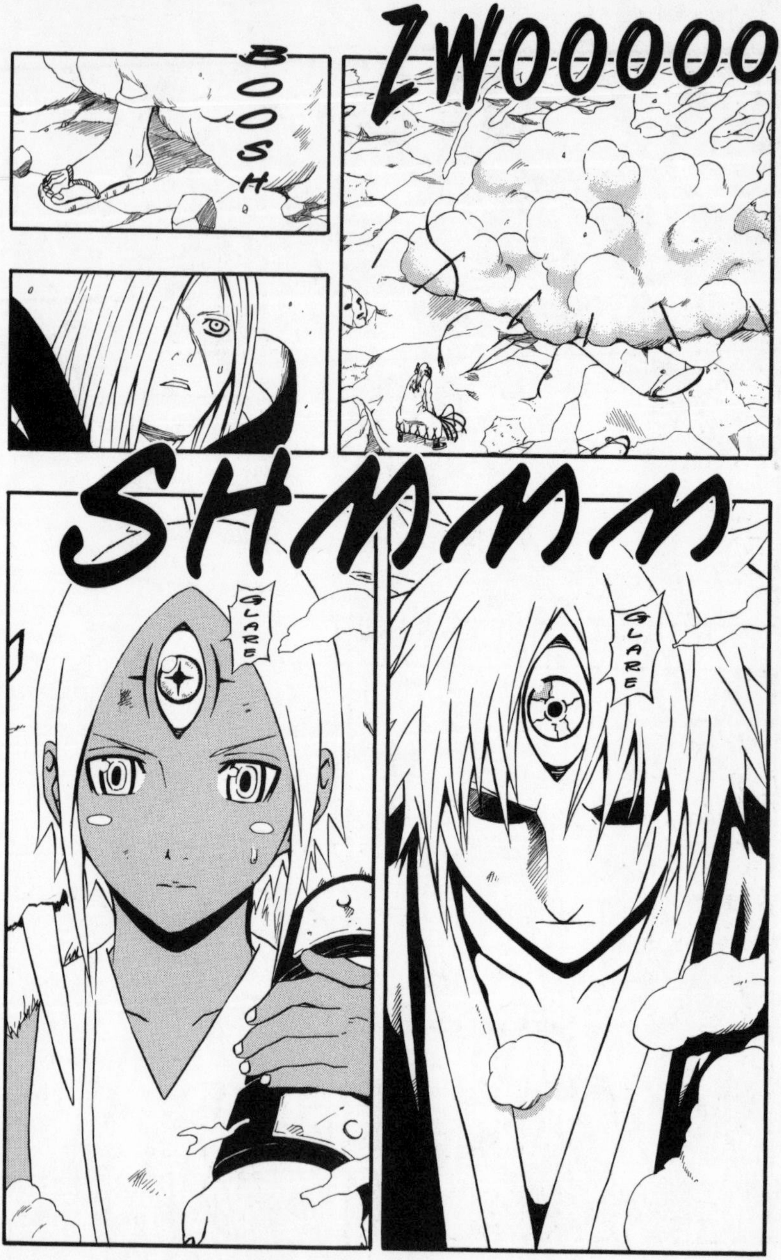
ZWOOOOO
BOOOSH
SHMMM
GLARE
GLARE

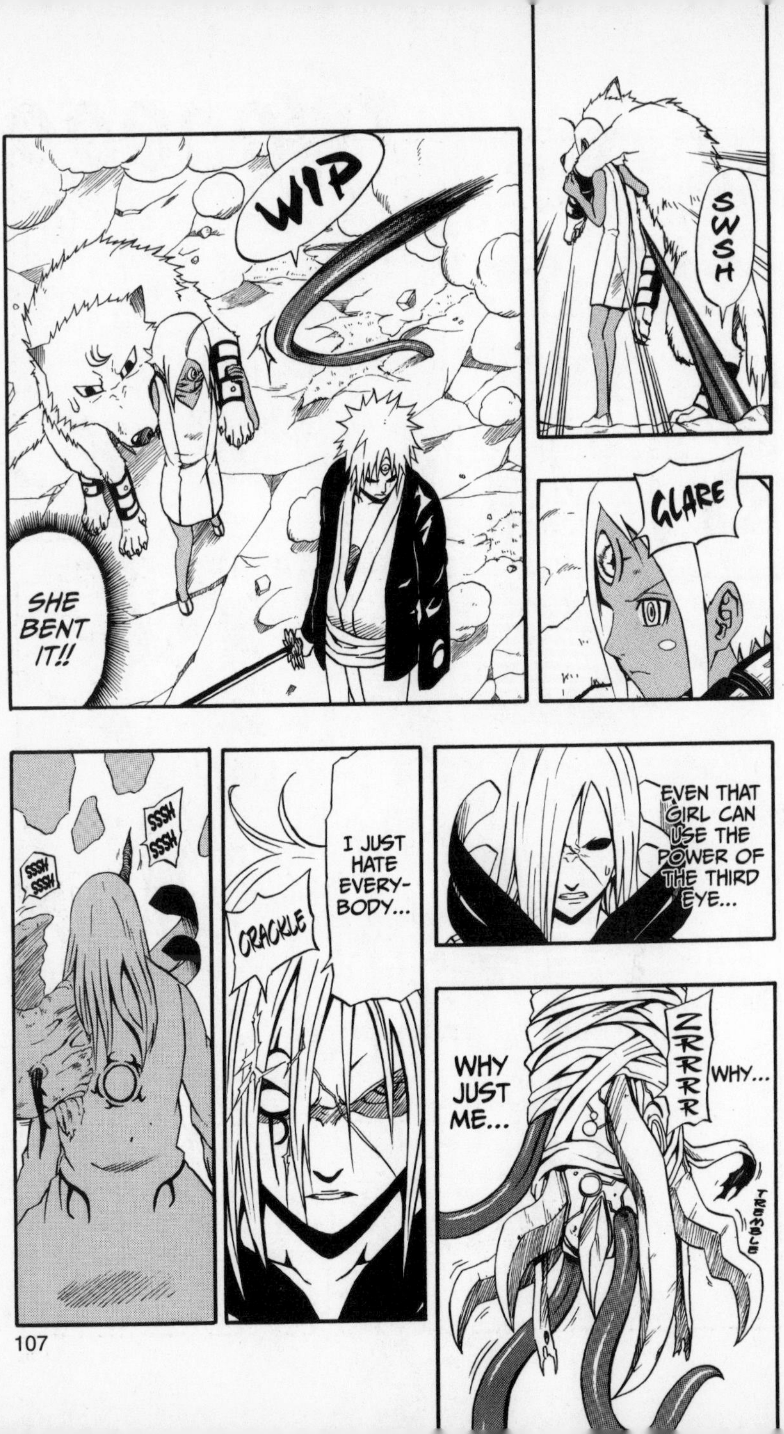
SWSH
GLARE
WIP
SHE BENT IT!!
EVEN THAT GIRL CAN USE THE POWER OF THE THIRD EYE...
WHY...
ZRRRR
WHY JUST ME...
TREMBLE
I JUST HATE EVERY-BODY...
CRACKLE
SSSH SSSH
SSSH SSSH

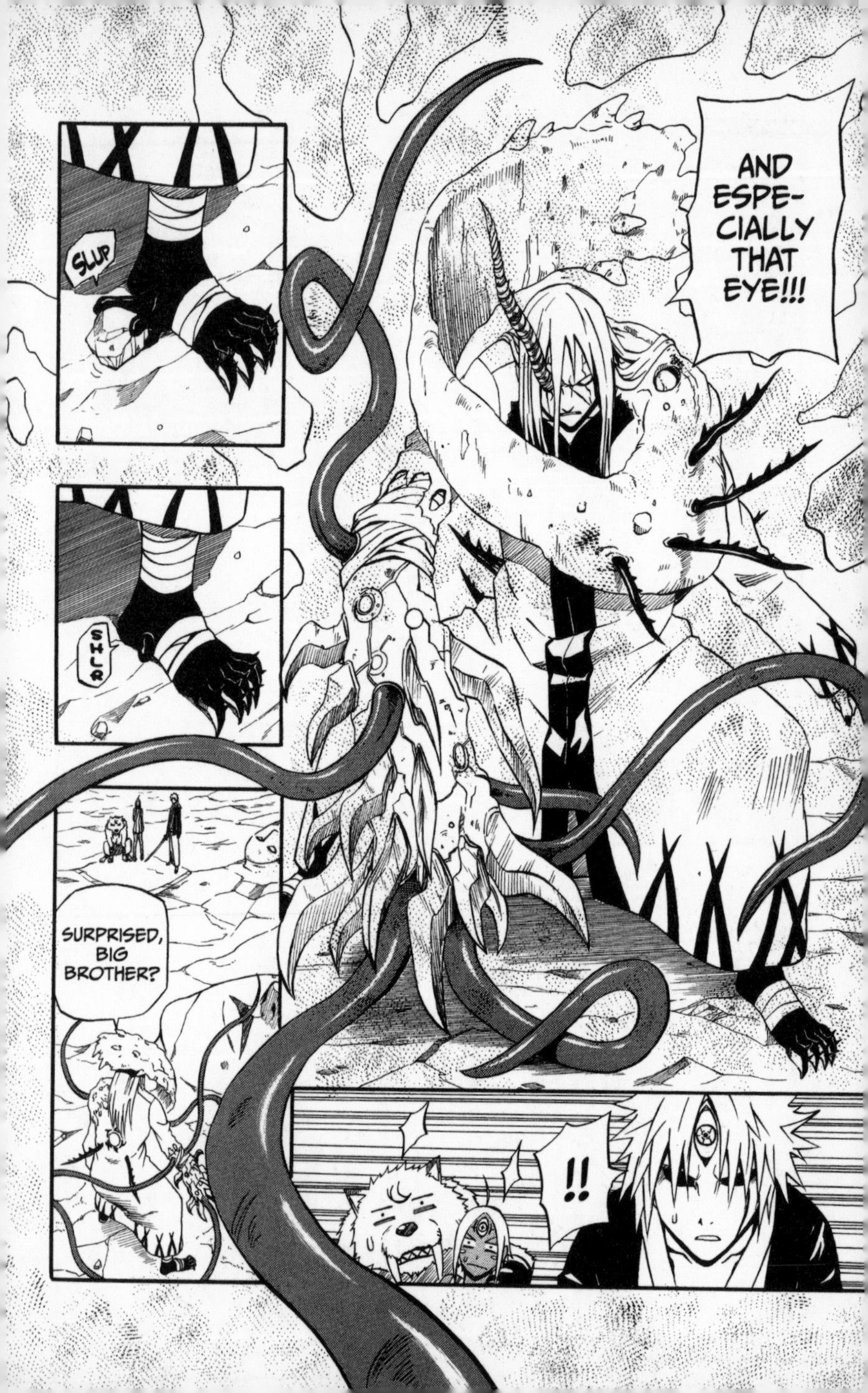
AND ESPE-CIALLY THAT EYE!!!
!!
SLUP
SHLR
SURPRISED, BIG BROTHER?

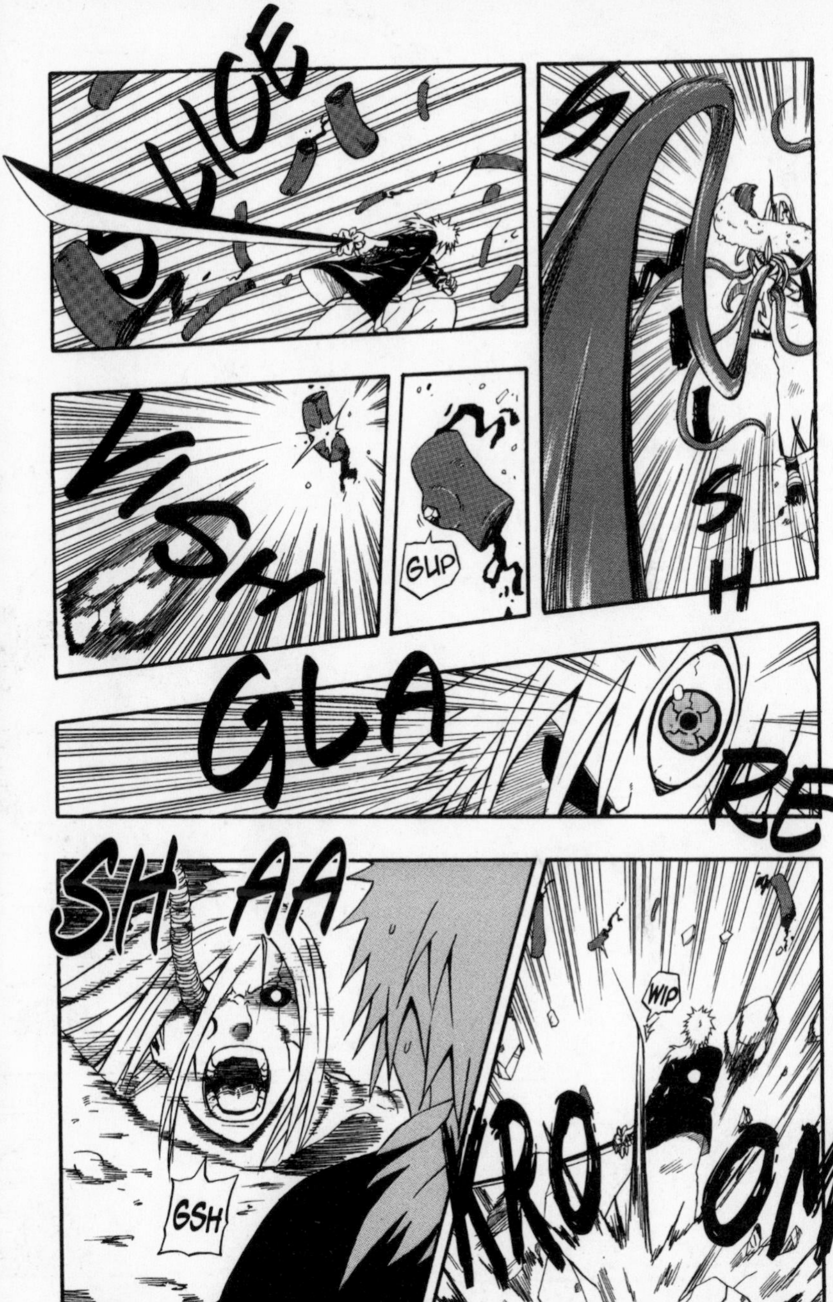
SWISH
SLICE
GUP
VISH
GLARE
WIP
KRO OM
SH AA
GSH

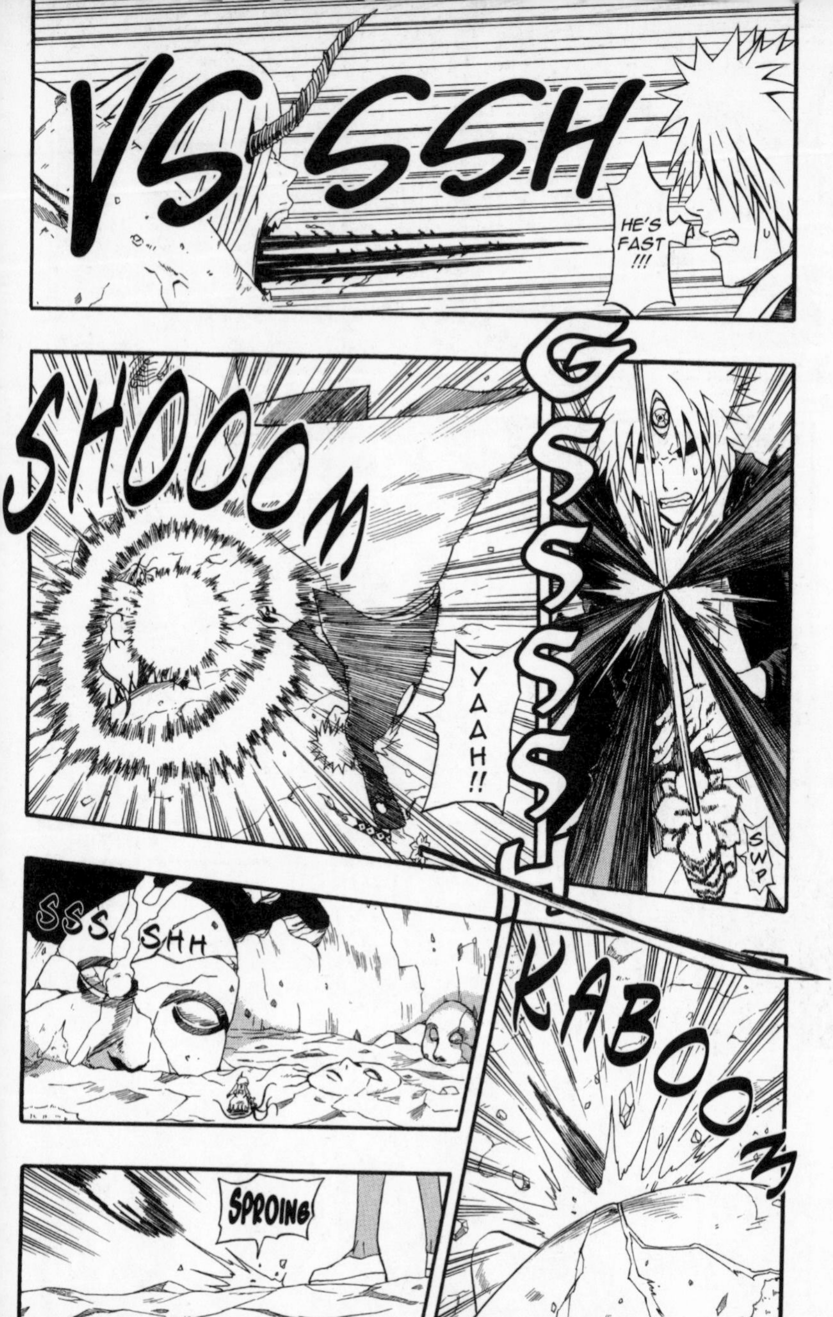
VSSSH
HE'S FAST!!!
GSSSSH
SWP
SHOOOM
YAAAH!!
KABOOOM
SSS SHH
SPROING

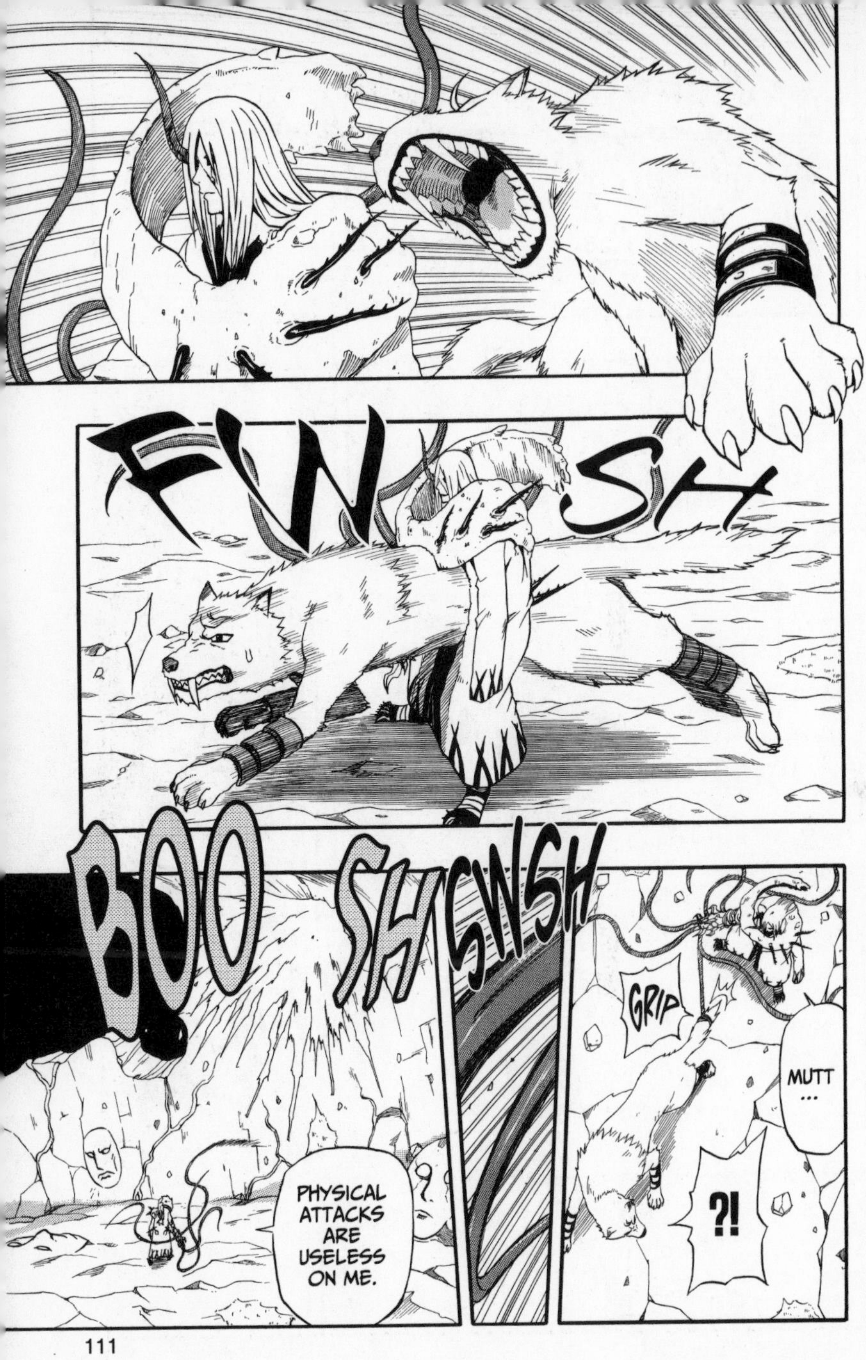
FWSH
GRIP
MUTT...
?!
SWSH
BOOSH
PHYSICAL ATTACKS ARE USELESS ON ME.

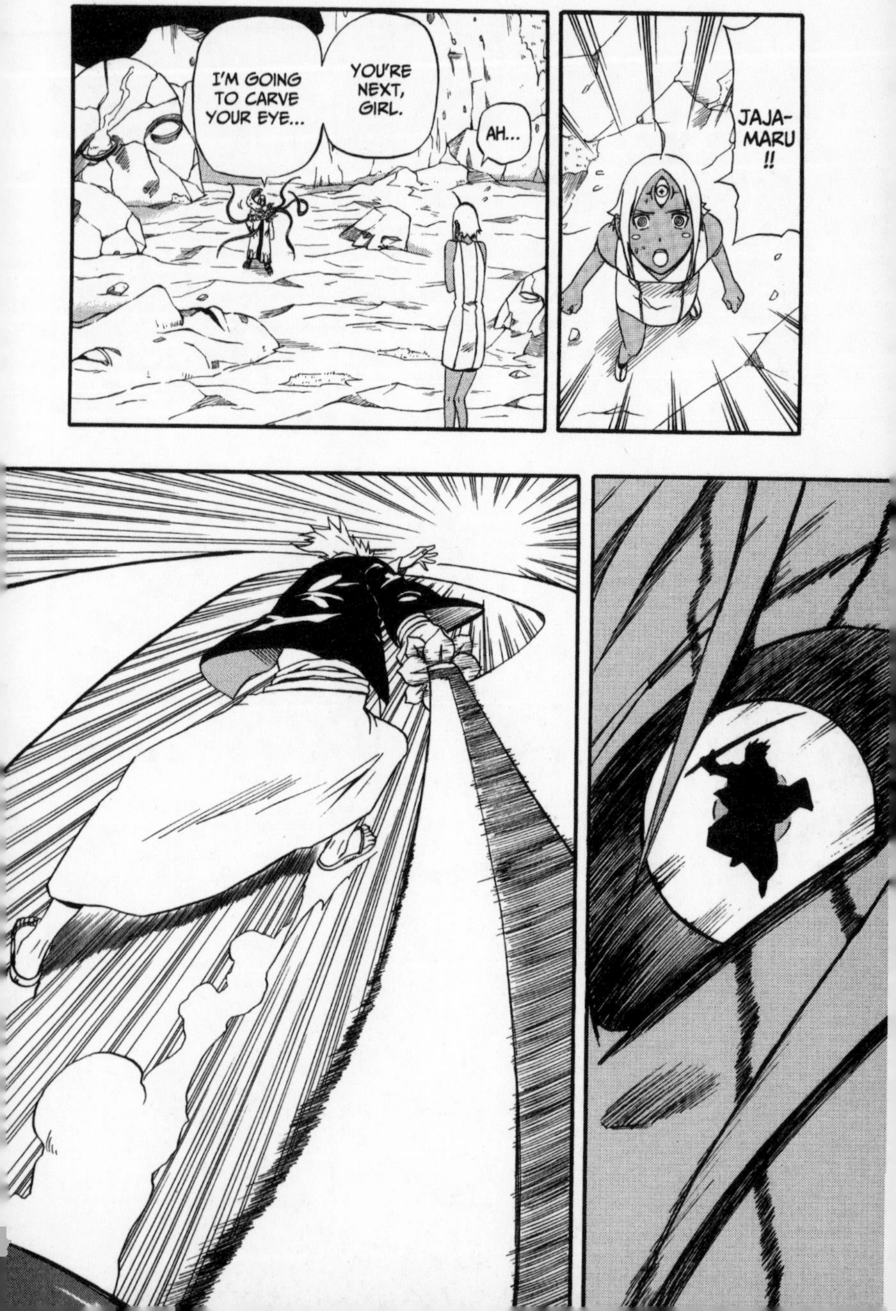
JAJA-MARU!!
YOU'RE NEXT, GIRL.
I'M GOING TO CARVE YOUR EYE...
AH...

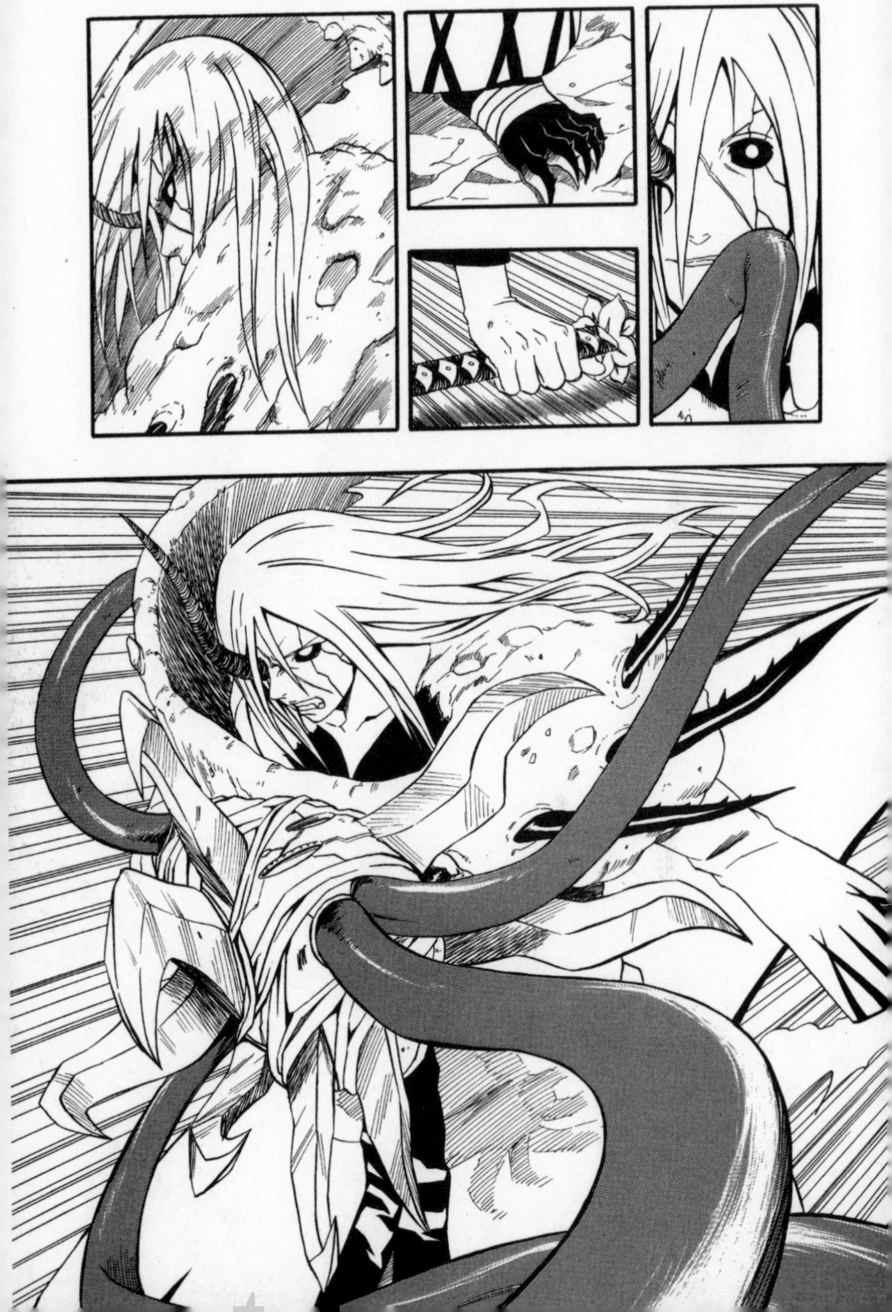

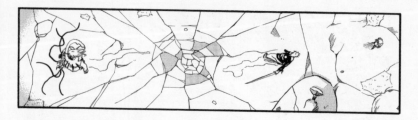

KIRIN
!!

SPUB

PLIP

IS THAT THE BEST YOU CAN DO, KIRIN? DIDN'T I SAY...

...PHYSICAL ATTACKS ARE USELESS ON...

HA HA HA HA !!

HA HA...

HA HA HA HA...

114

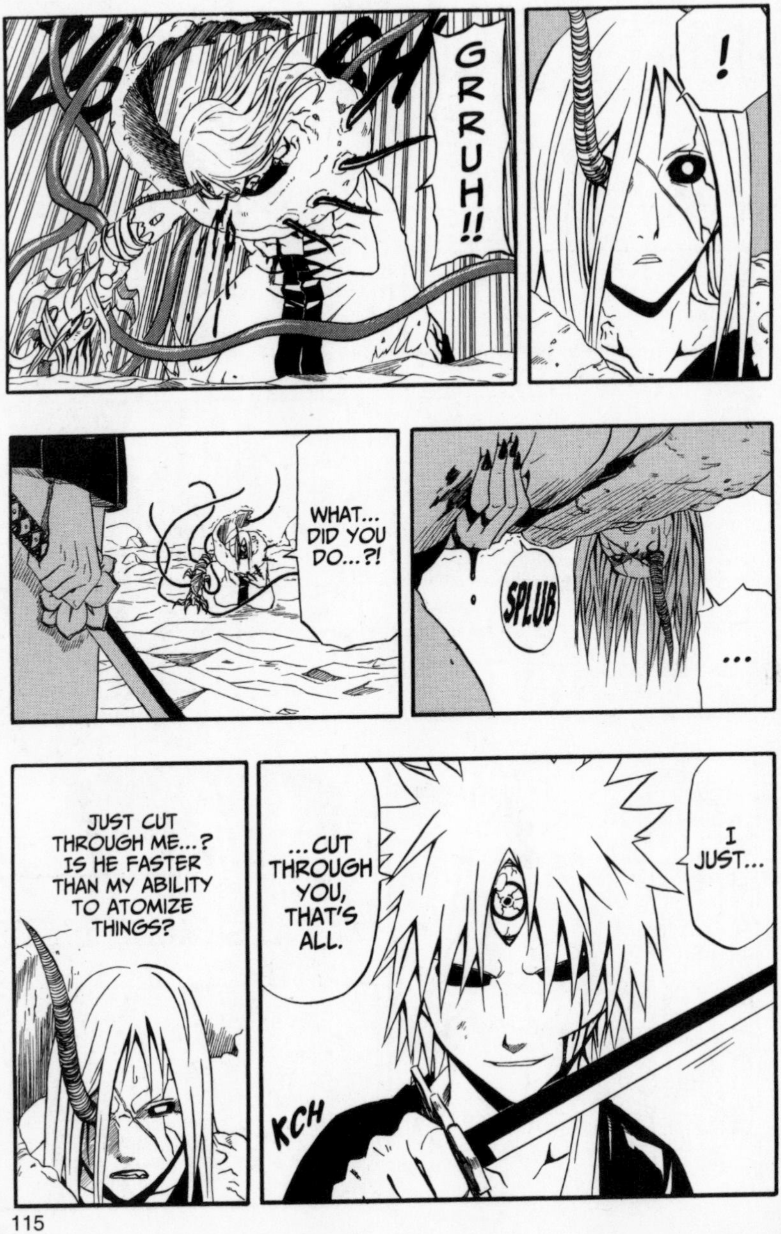
!
GRRUH!!
SPLUB
...
WHAT... DID YOU DO...?!
I JUST...
...CUT THROUGH YOU, THAT'S ALL.
KCH
JUST CUT THROUGH ME...? IS HE FASTER THAN MY ABILITY TO ATOMIZE THINGS?

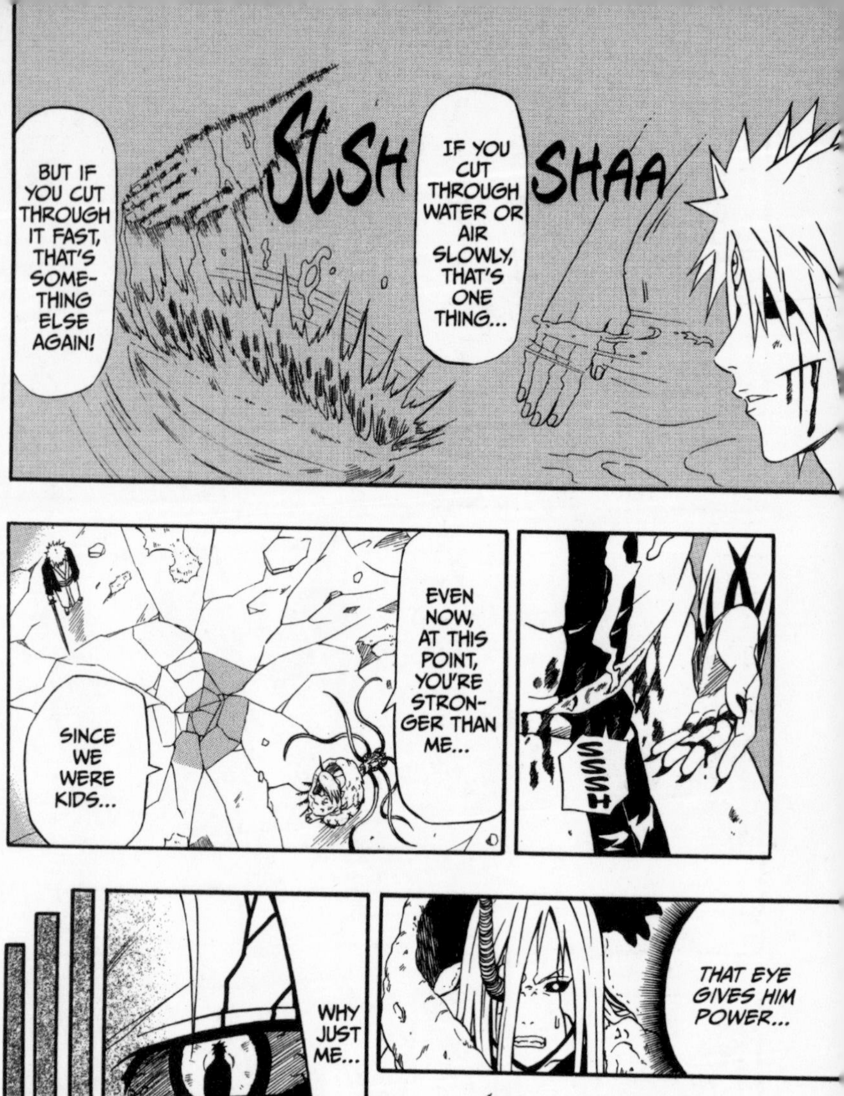
SHAA
IF YOU CUT THROUGH WATER OR AIR SLOWLY, THAT'S ONE THING...
SLSH
BUT IF YOU CUT THROUGH IT FAST, THAT'S SOME-THING ELSE AGAIN!
SSSH
EVEN NOW, AT THIS POINT, YOU'RE STRON-GER THAN ME...
SINCE WE WERE KIDS...
THAT EYE GIVES HIM POWER...
THAT THIRD EYE I NEVER HAD...
WHY JUST ME...

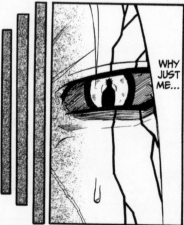

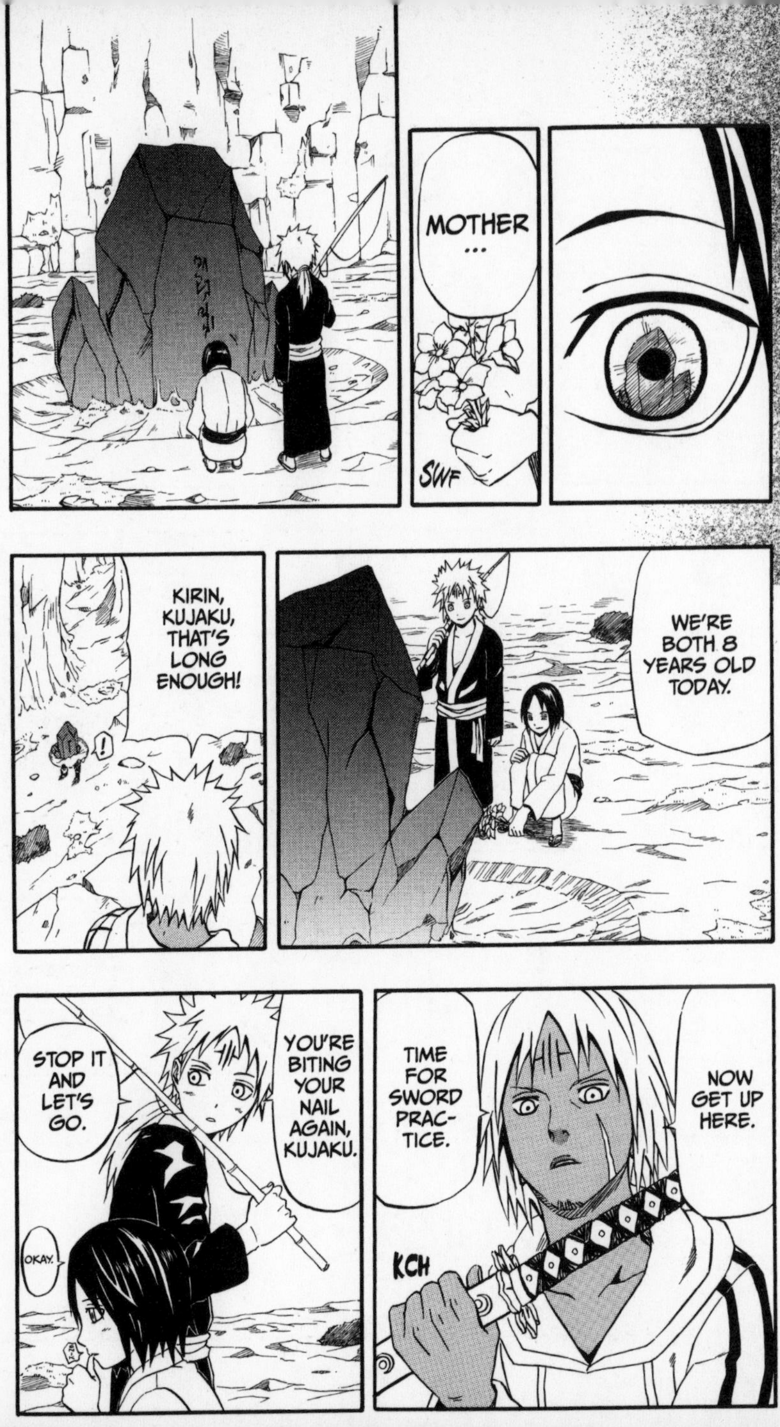
MOTHER ...
SWF
WE'RE BOTH 8 YEARS OLD TODAY.
KIRIN, KUJAKU, THAT'S LONG ENOUGH!
!
NOW GET UP HERE.
TIME FOR SWORD PRAC-TICE.
KCH
YOU'RE BITING YOUR NAIL AGAIN, KUJAKU.
STOP IT AND LET'S GO.
OKAY.

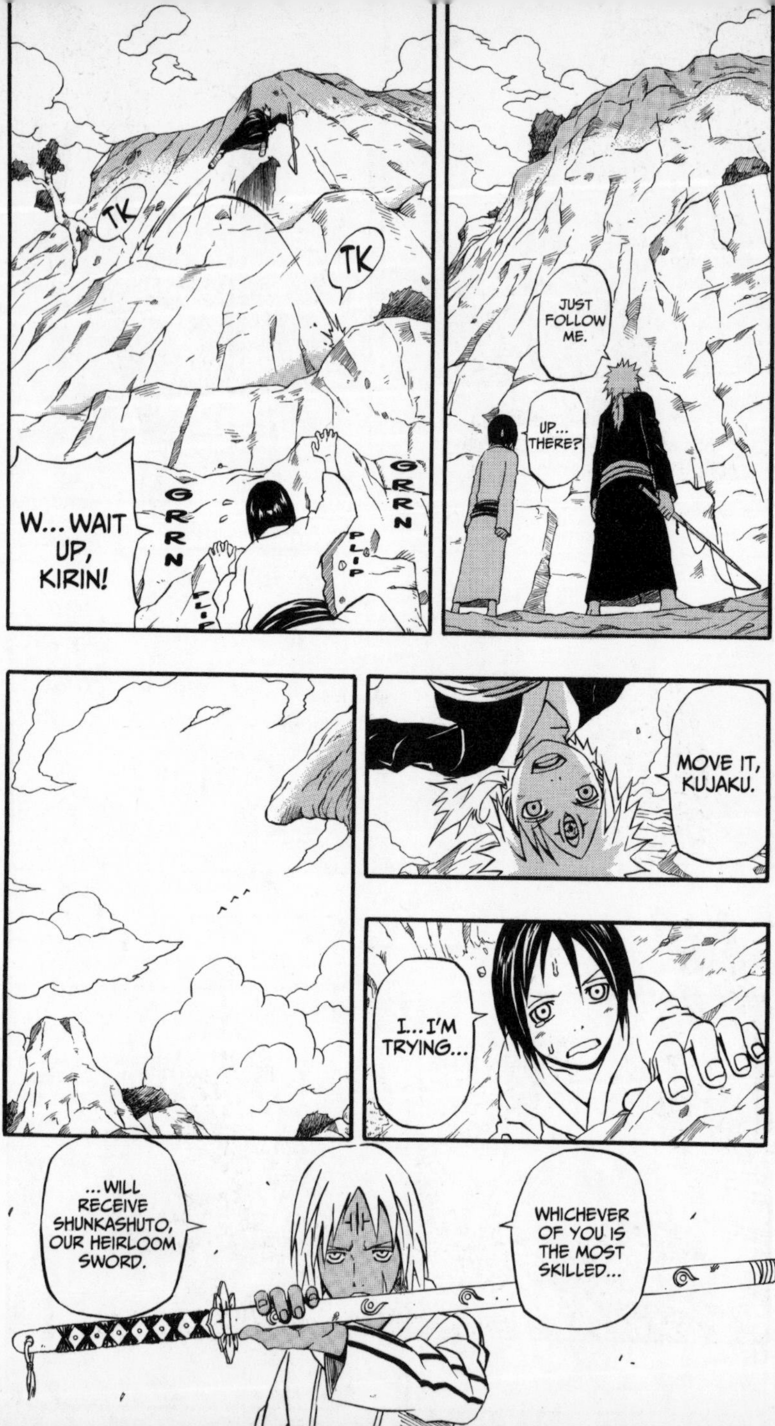
JUST FOLLOW ME.
UP... THERE?
TK
TK
GRRN
GRRN
PLIP
PLIP
W... WAIT UP, KIRIN!
MOVE IT, KUJAKU.
I... I'M TRYING...
WHICHEVER OF YOU IS THE MOST SKILLED...
...WILL RECEIVE SHUNKASHUTO, OUR HEIRLOOM SWORD.

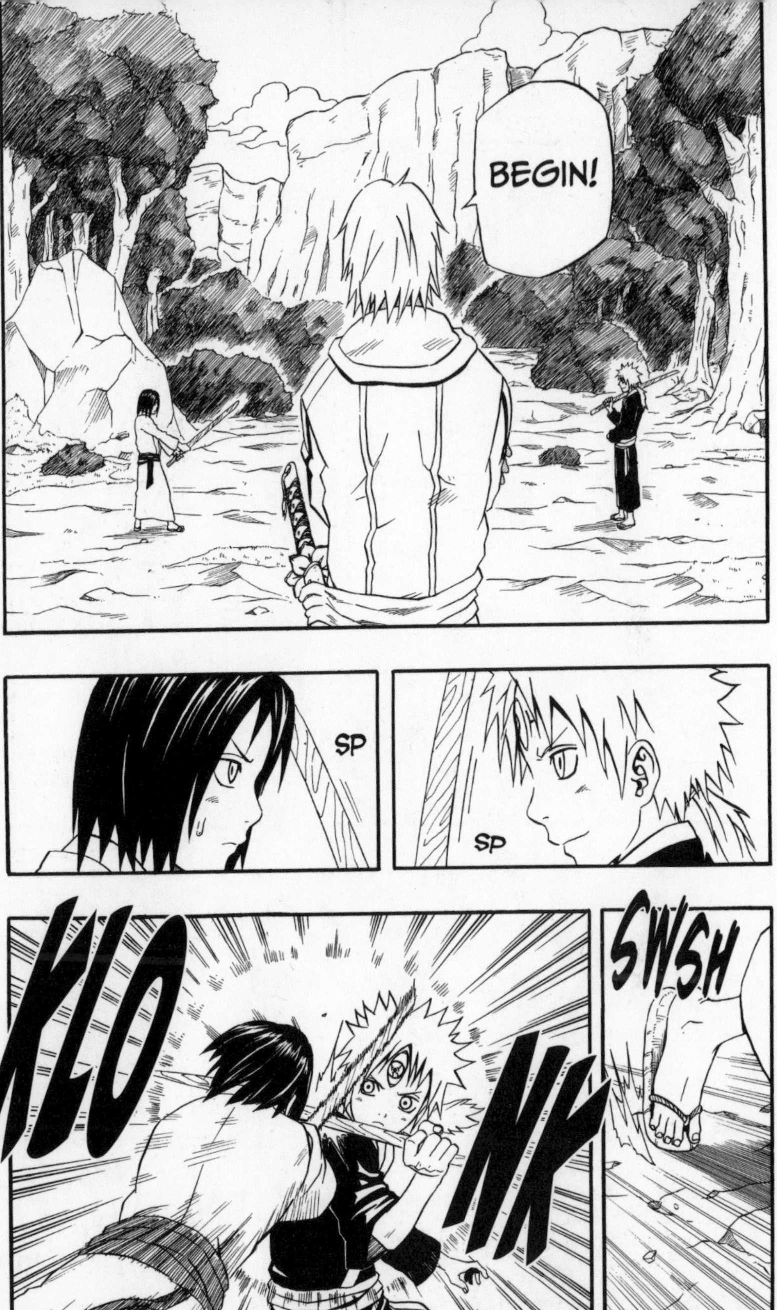

BEGIN!
SP
SP
SWSH
KLO
NK

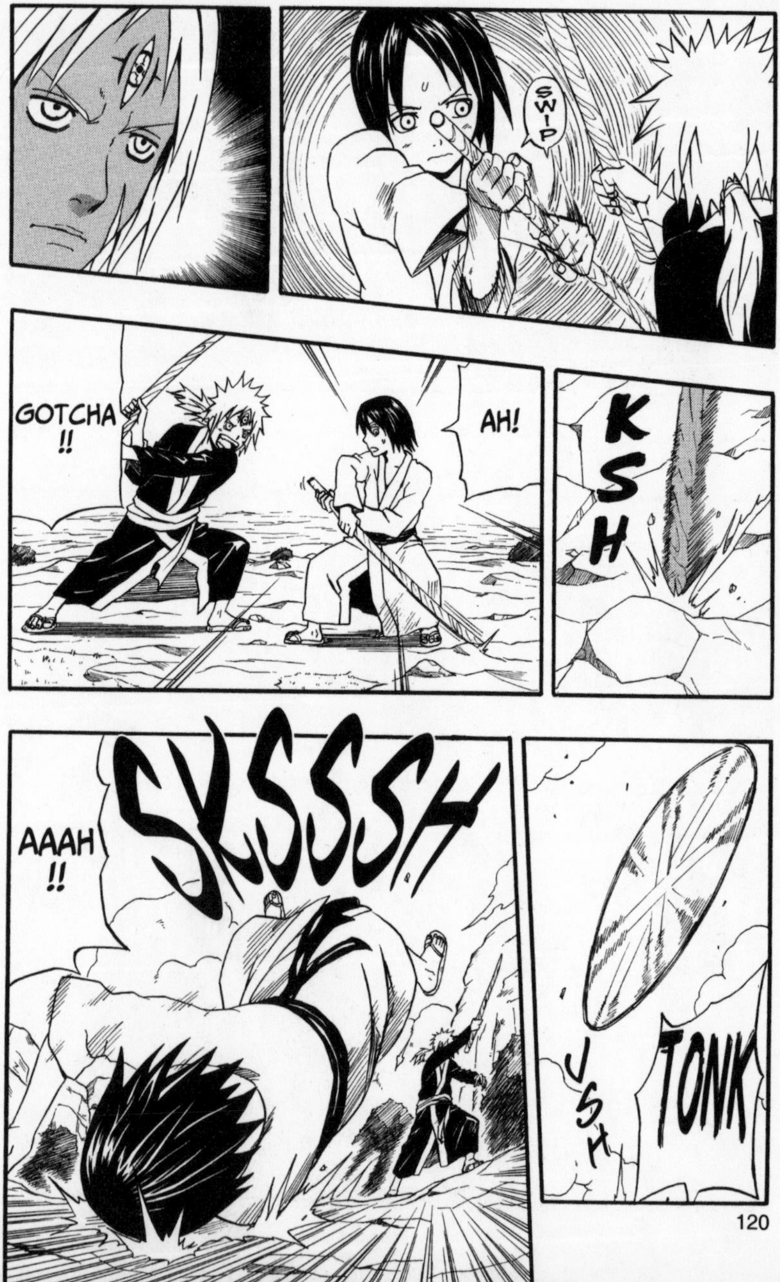
SWIP
KSH
AH!
GOTCHA!!
TONK
JSH
SKSSSH
AAAH!!

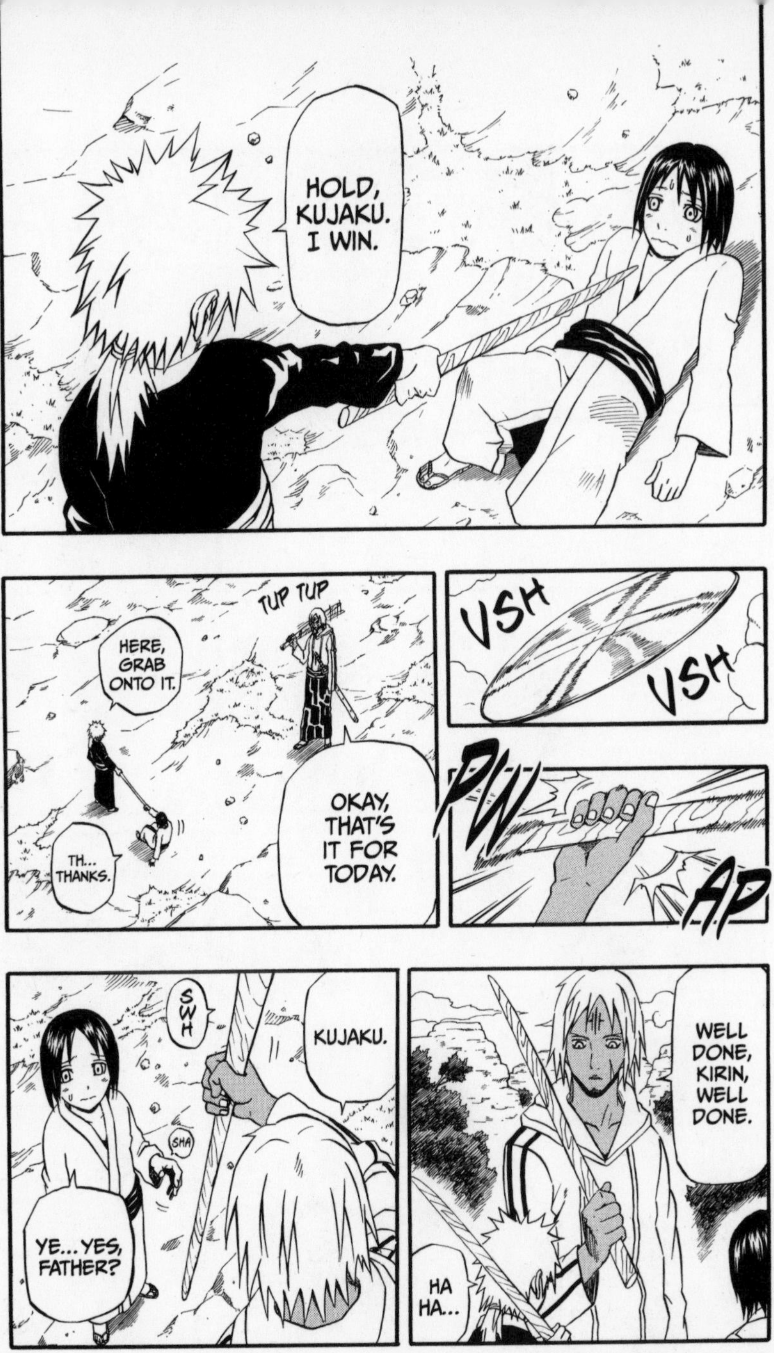
HOLD, KUJAKU. I WIN.
VSH
VSH
PW
AP
TUP TUP
HERE, GRAB ONTO IT.
OKAY, THAT'S IT FOR TODAY.
TH... THANKS.
WELL DONE, KIRIN, WELL DONE.
HA HA...
KUJAKU.
SWH
SHA
YE... YES, FATHER?

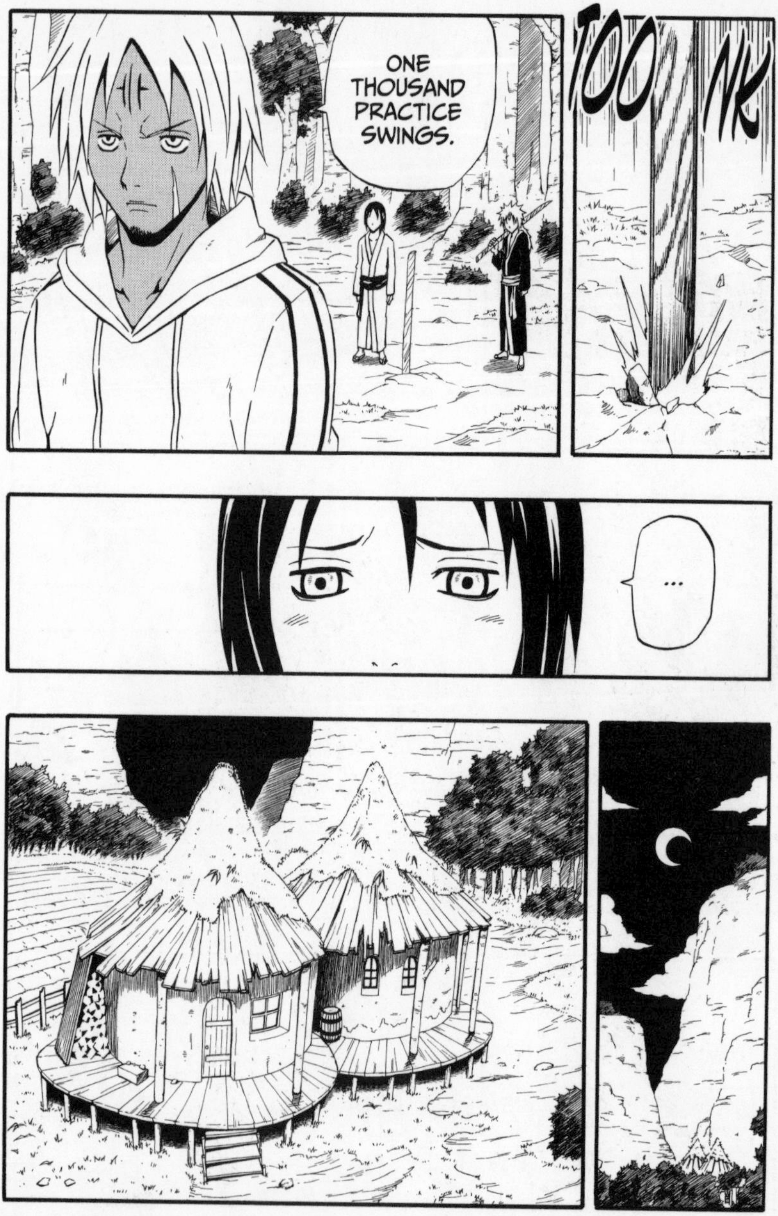
TOONK
ONE THOUSAND PRACTICE SWINGS.
...

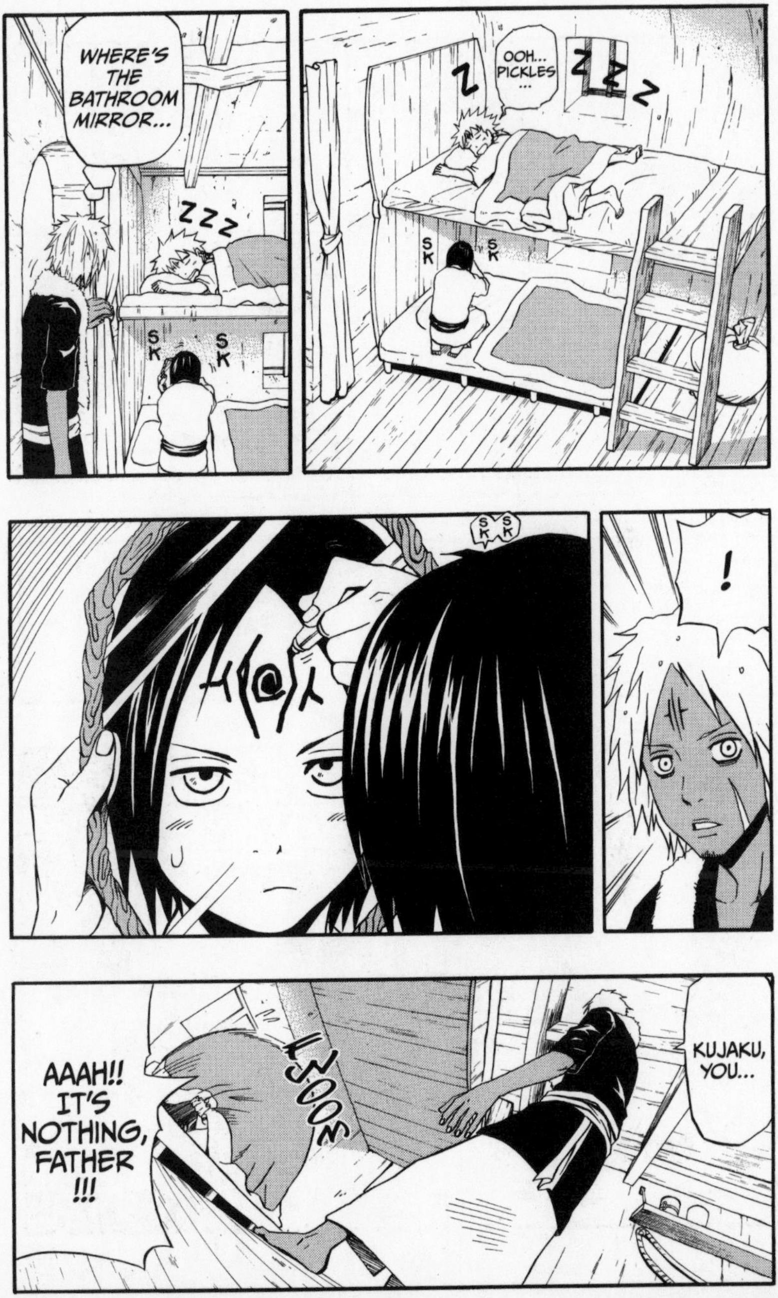
OOH... PICKLES...
Z Z Z Z
SK SK
WHERE'S THE BATHROOM MIRROR...
ZZZ
SK SK
!
SK SK
KUJAKU, YOU...
FWOON
AAAH!! IT'S NOTHING, FATHER!!!

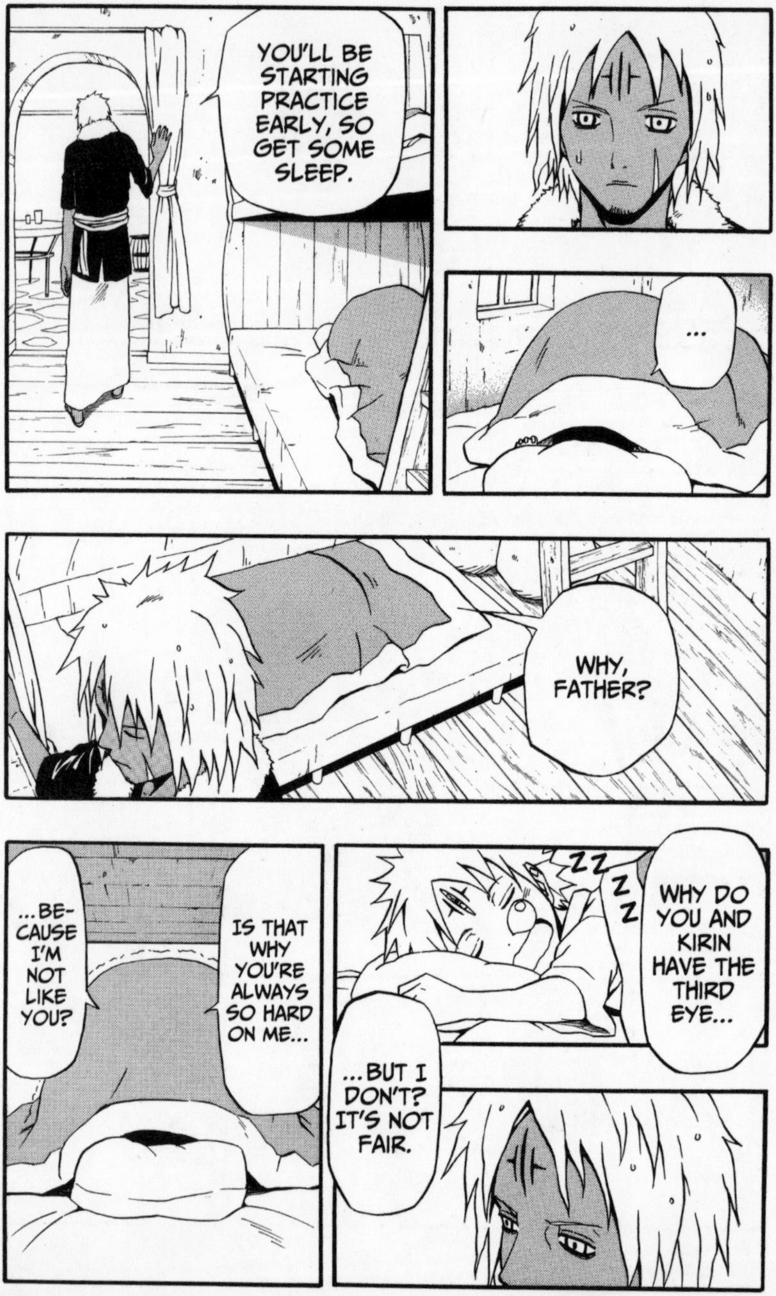
...
YOU'LL BE STARTING PRACTICE EARLY, SO GET SOME SLEEP.
WHY, FATHER?
ZZZ
WHY DO YOU AND KIRIN HAVE THE THIRD EYE...
...BUT I DON'T? IT'S NOT FAIR.
IS THAT WHY YOU'RE ALWAYS SO HARD ON ME...
...BE-CAUSE I'M NOT LIKE YOU?

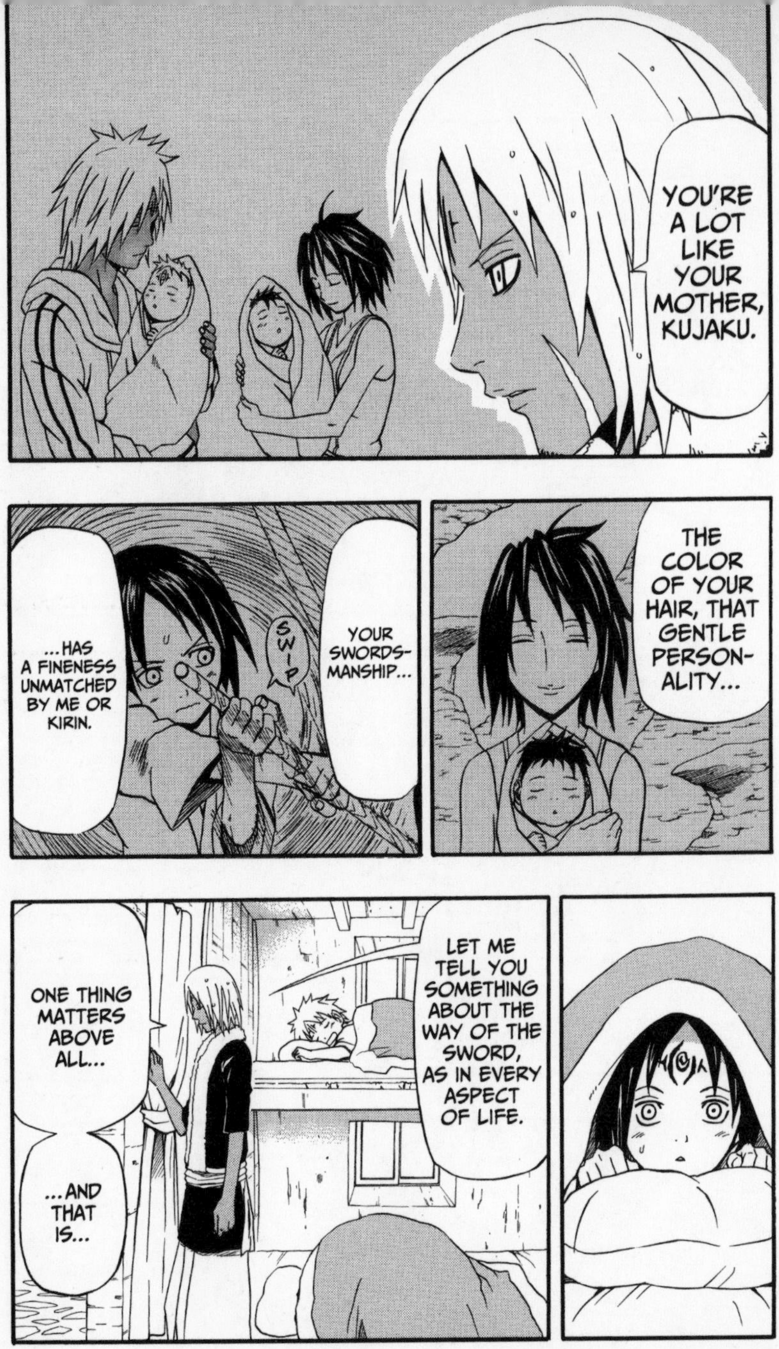
YOU'RE A LOT LIKE YOUR MOTHER, KUJAKU.
THE COLOR OF YOUR HAIR, THAT GENTLE PERSONALITY...
YOUR SWORDSMANSHIP...
SWIP
...HAS A FINENESS UNMATCHED BY ME OR KIRIN.
LET ME TELL YOU SOMETHING ABOUT THE WAY OF THE SWORD, AS IN EVERY ASPECT OF LIFE.
ONE THING MATTERS ABOVE ALL...
...AND THAT IS...

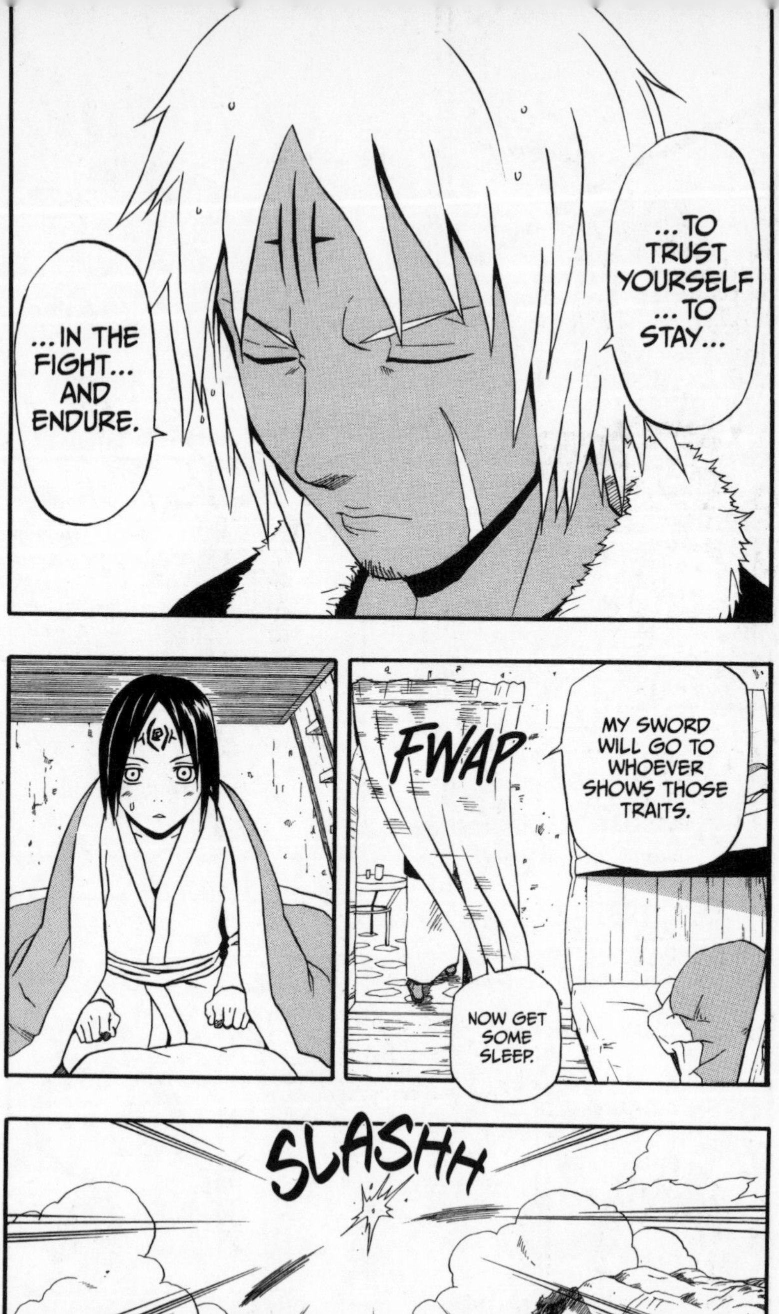
...TO TRUST YOURSELF ...TO STAY...
...IN THE FIGHT... AND ENDURE.
MY SWORD WILL GO TO WHOEVER SHOWS THOSE TRAITS.
FWAP
NOW GET SOME SLEEP.
SLASHH

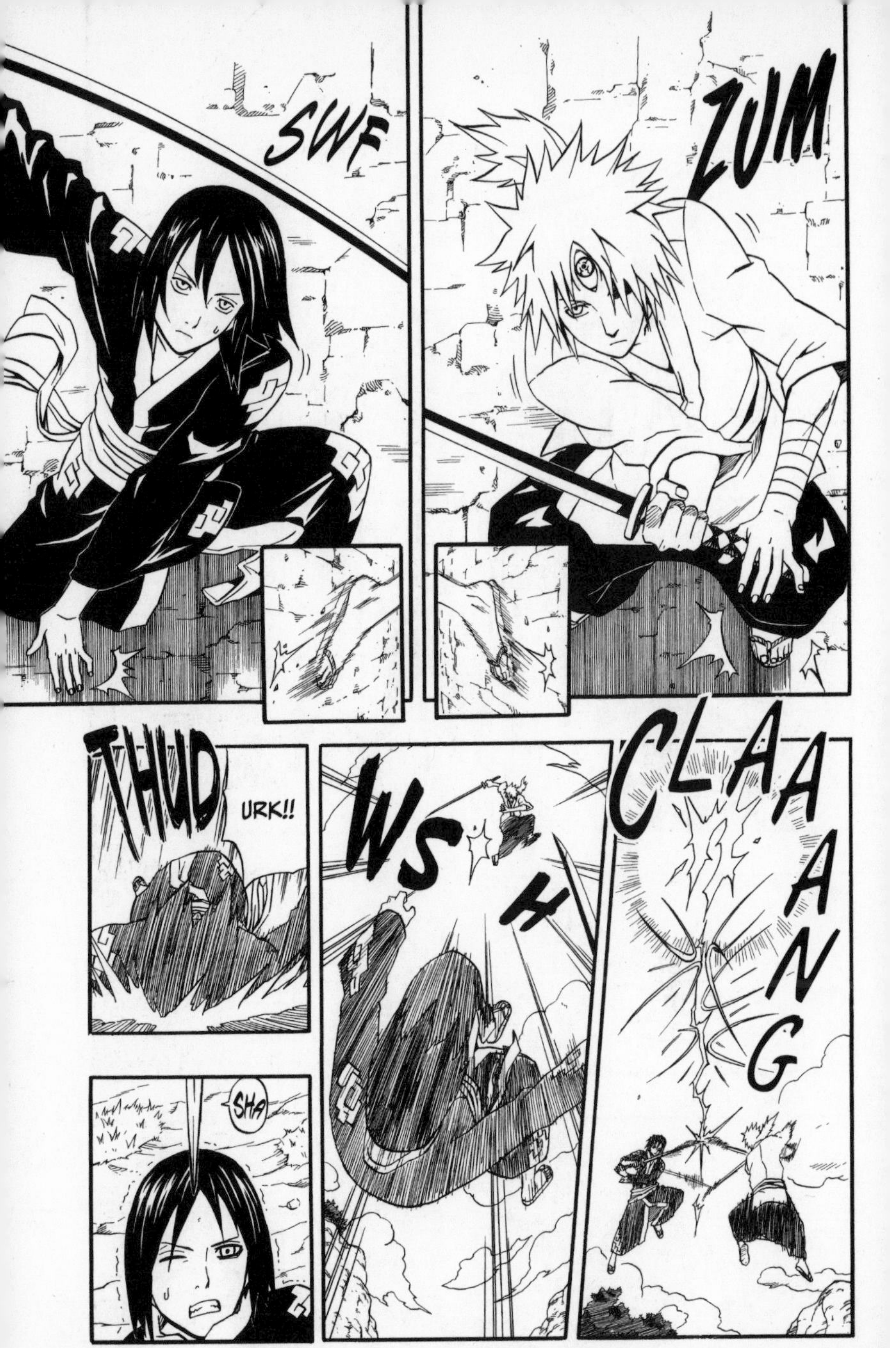
ZUM
SWF
CLAAANG
WSH
THUD
URK!!
SHA

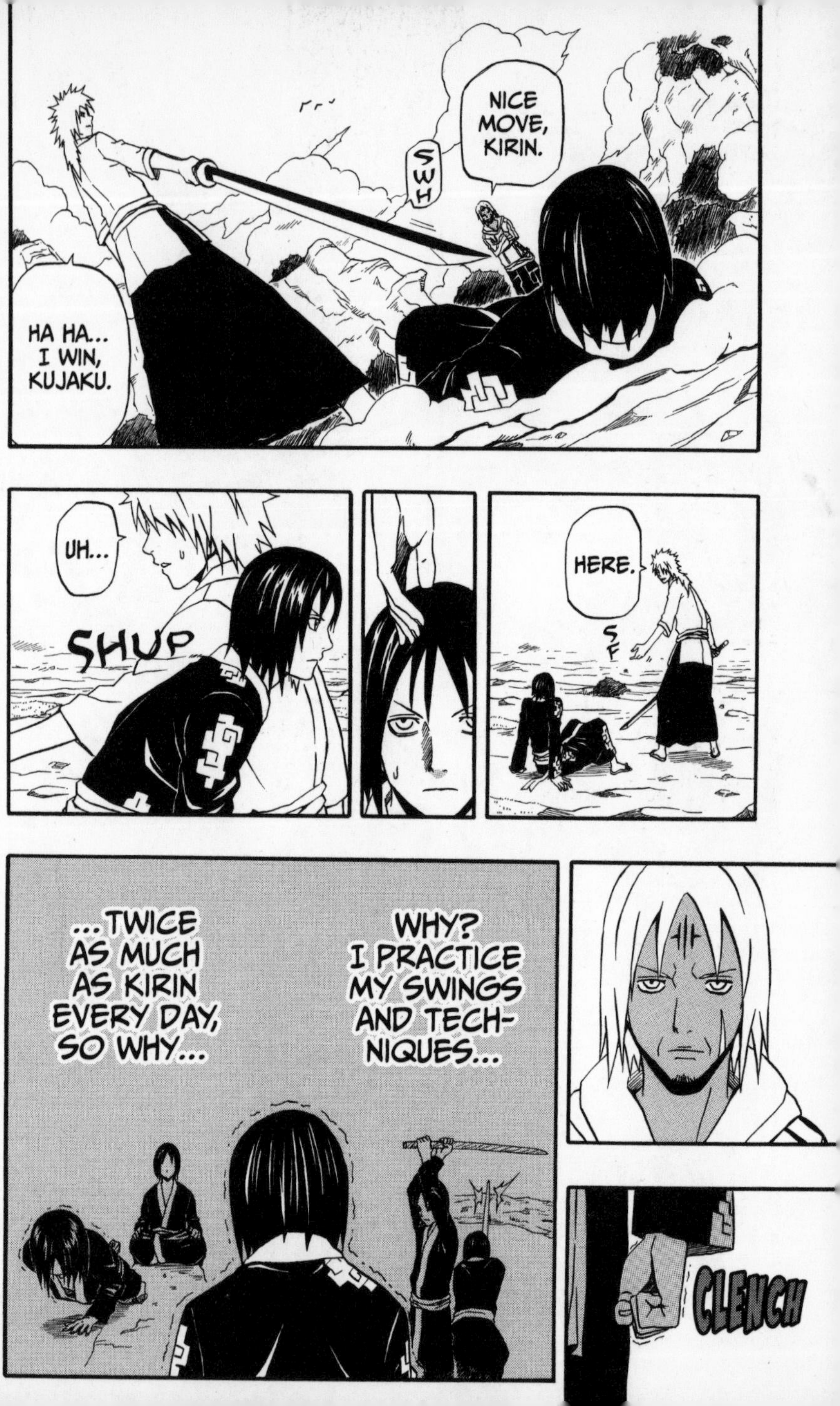
NICE MOVE, KIRIN.
SWH
HA HA... I WIN, KUJAKU.
HERE.
SF
UH...
SHUP
WHY? I PRACTICE MY SWINGS AND TECH- NIQUES...
...TWICE AS MUCH AS KIRIN EVERY DAY, SO WHY...
CLENCH

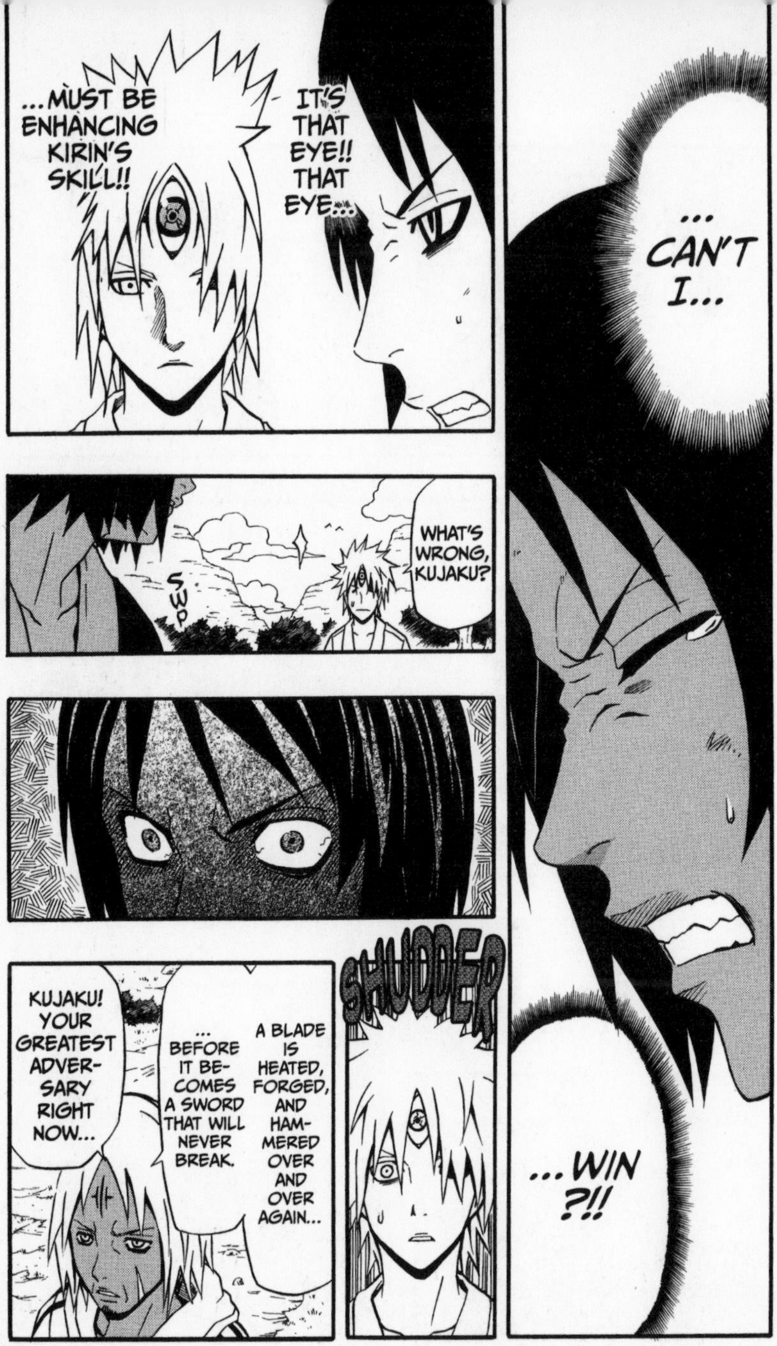
...CAN'T I...
...WIN ?!!
IT'S THAT EYE!! THAT EYE...
...MUST BE ENHANCING KIRIN'S SKILL!!
WHAT'S WRONG, KUJAKU?
SWP
SHUDDER
A BLADE IS HEATED, FORGED, AND HAMMERED OVER AND OVER AGAIN...
...BEFORE IT BECOMES A SWORD THAT WILL NEVER BREAK.
KUJAKU! YOUR GREATEST ADVERSARY RIGHT NOW...

...IS IMPATIENCE.
SNIK
SNIK
YOU ONLY PAY ATTENTION TO KIRIN!
AND ALL YOU DO IS COMPLAIN ABOUT ME!
I'VE DONE EVERYTHING YOU'VE SAID! ARE YOU TELLING ME THAT'S STILL NOT ENOUGH?!!
WELL, I'M NOT GONNA LISTEN TO YOU ANYMORE!!
SWSH
KUJAKU!!!
LEAVE HIM ALONE!!

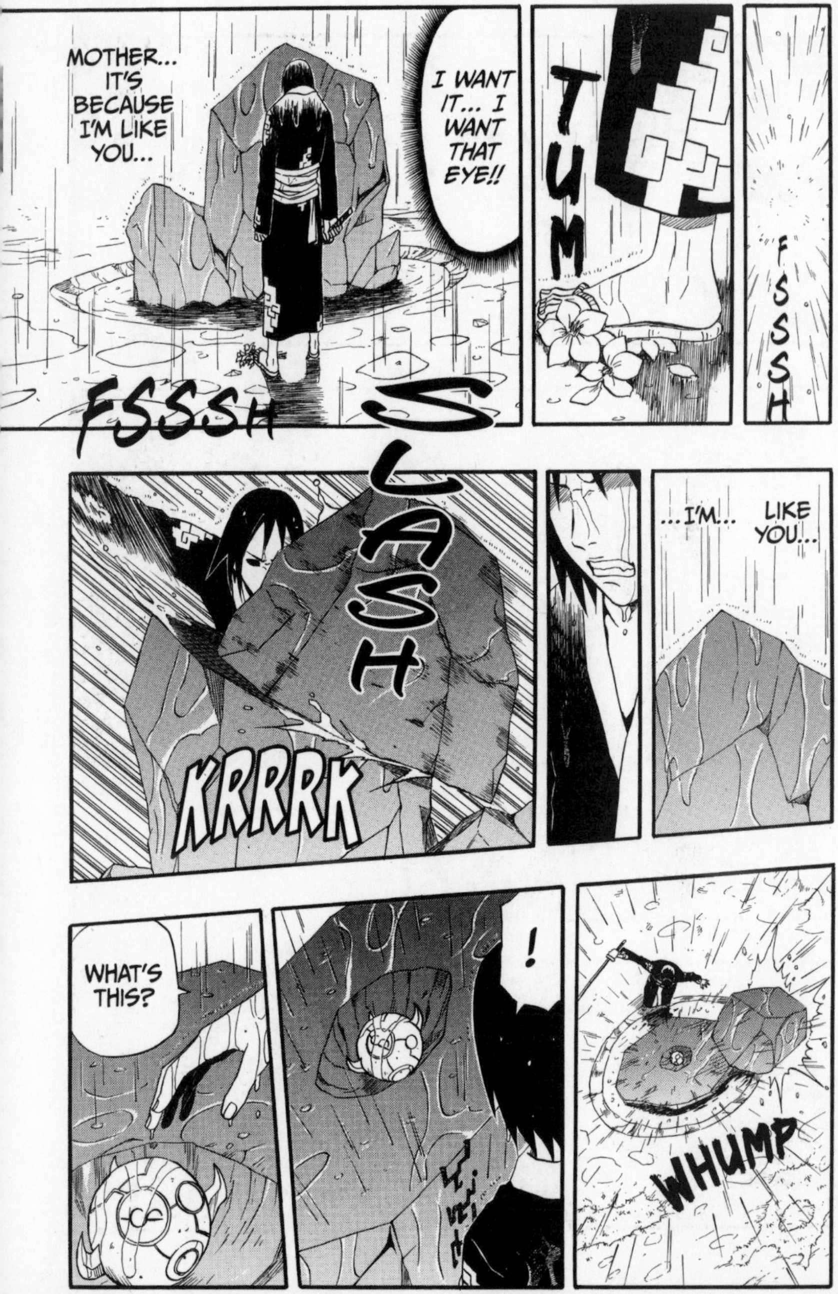
FSSSH
TUM
I WANT IT... I WANT THAT EYE!!
MOTHER... IT'S BECAUSE I'M LIKE YOU...
FSSSH
...I'M... LIKE YOU...
SLASH
KRRRK
WHUMP
!
WHAT'S THIS?

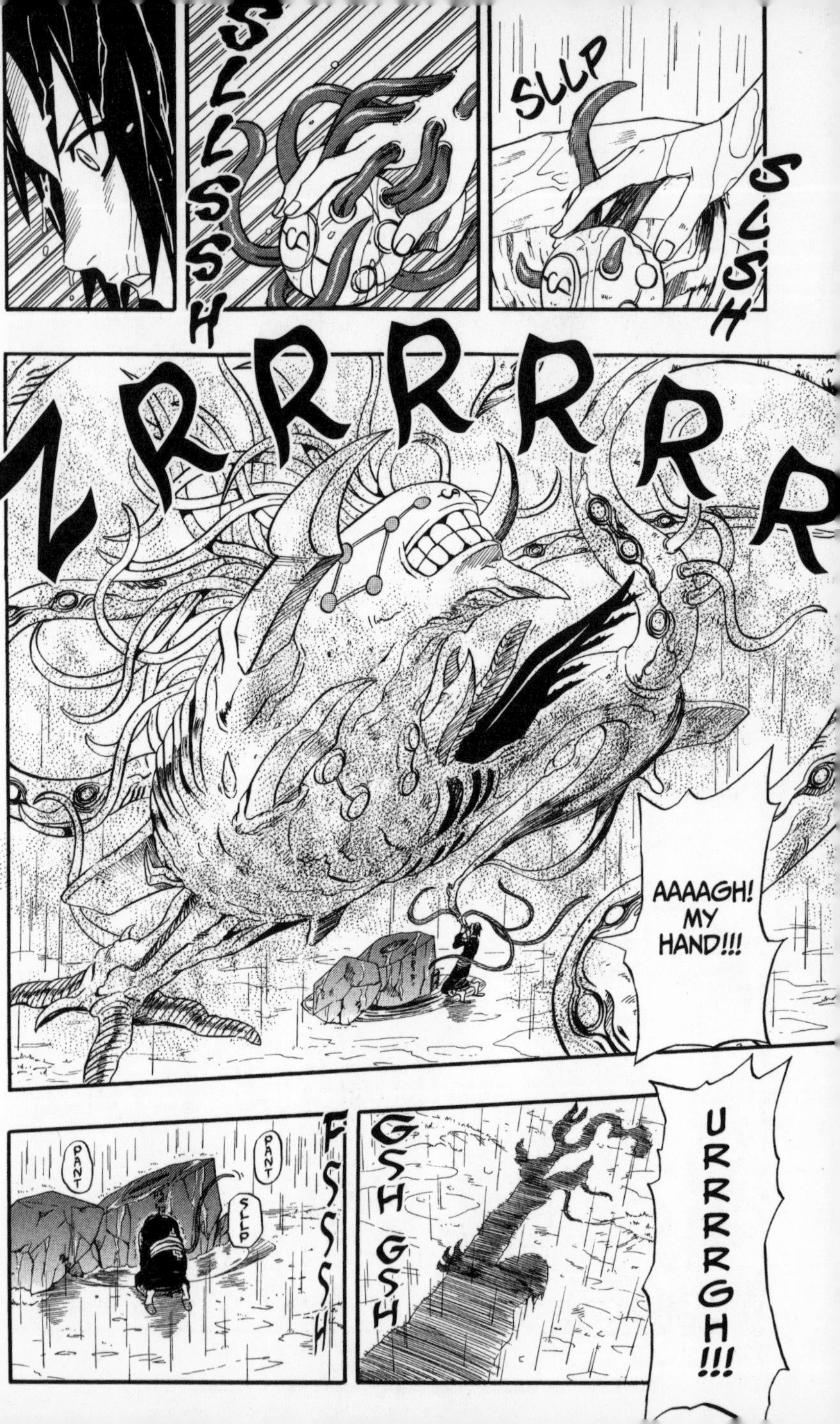
SLLP
SLSH
SLLSSH
ZRRRRRR
AAAAGH! MY HAND!!!
URRRRGH!!!
GSH GSH
FSSSH
PANT
PANT
SLLP

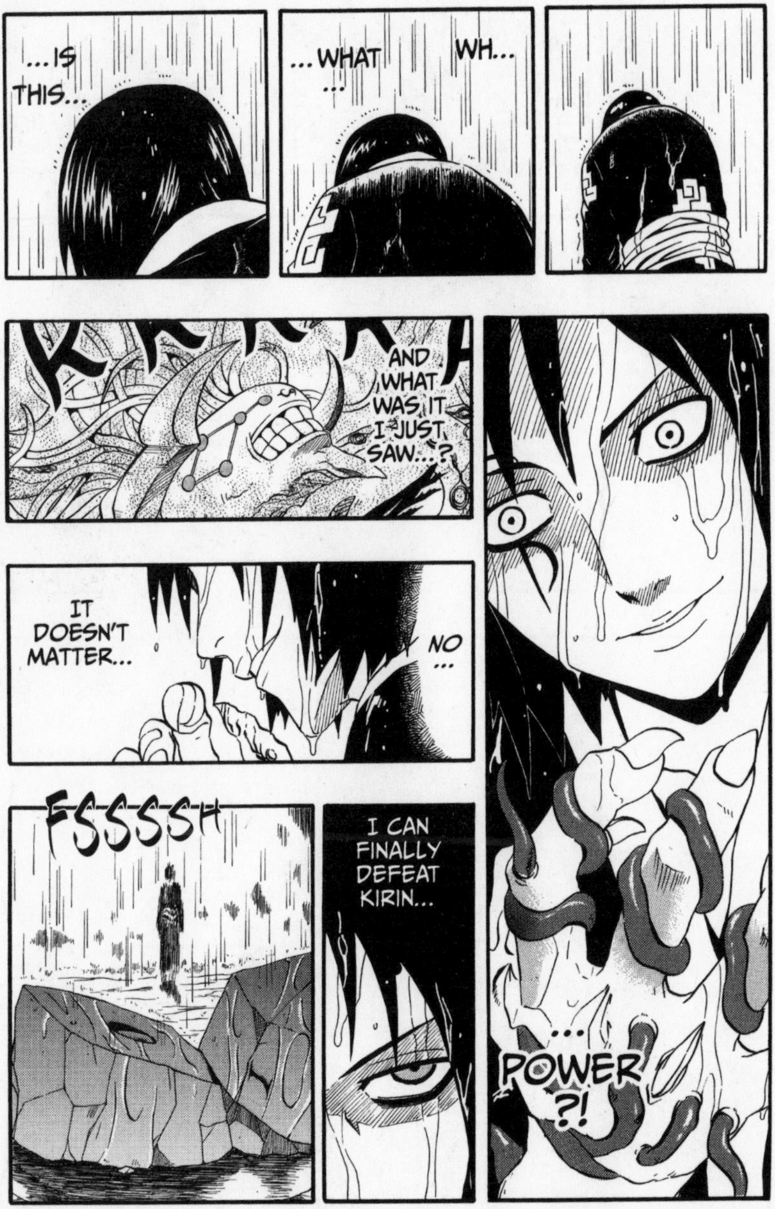
WH...
...WHAT ...
...IS THIS...
...POWER ?!
AND WHAT WAS IT I JUST SAW...?
NO ...
IT DOESN'T MATTER...
I CAN FINALLY DEFEAT KIRIN...
FSSSSH

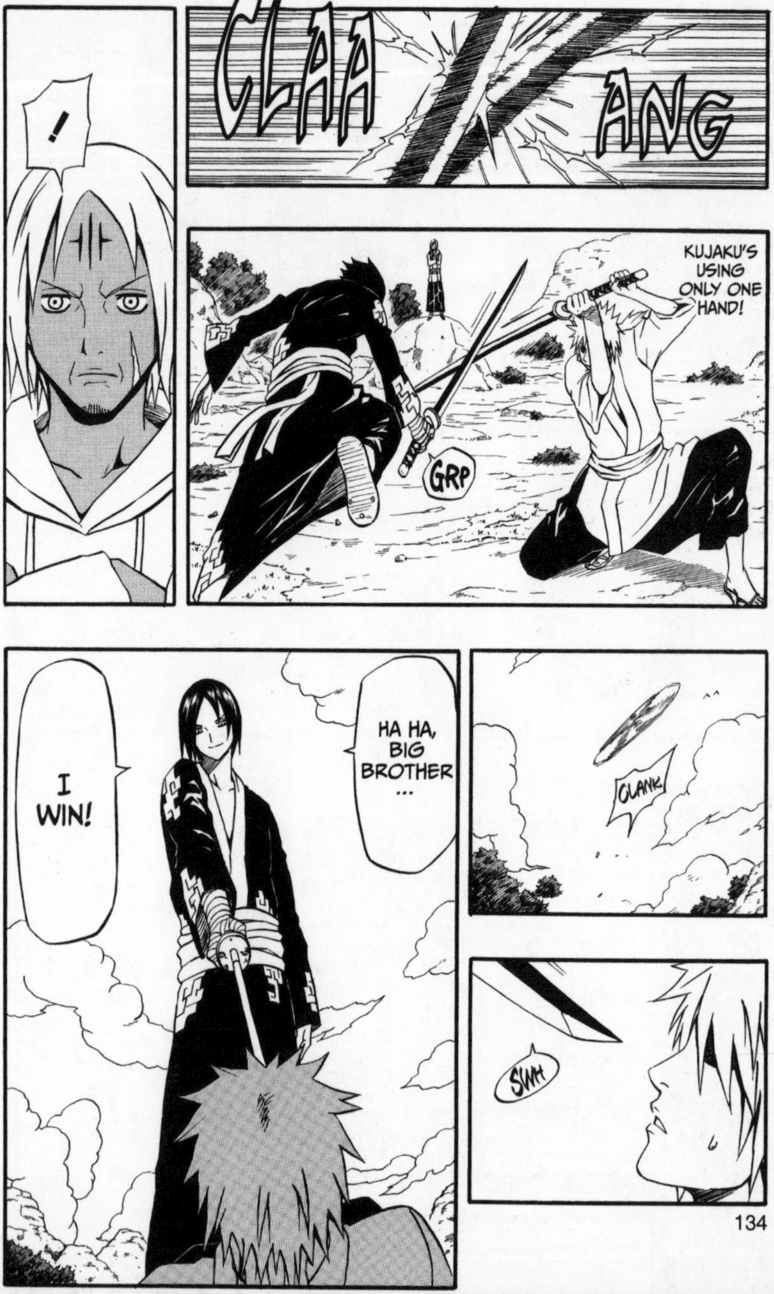
CLAA ANG
KUJAKU'S USING ONLY ONE HAND!
GRP
!
CLANK
SWH
HA HA, BIG BROTHER ...
I WIN!

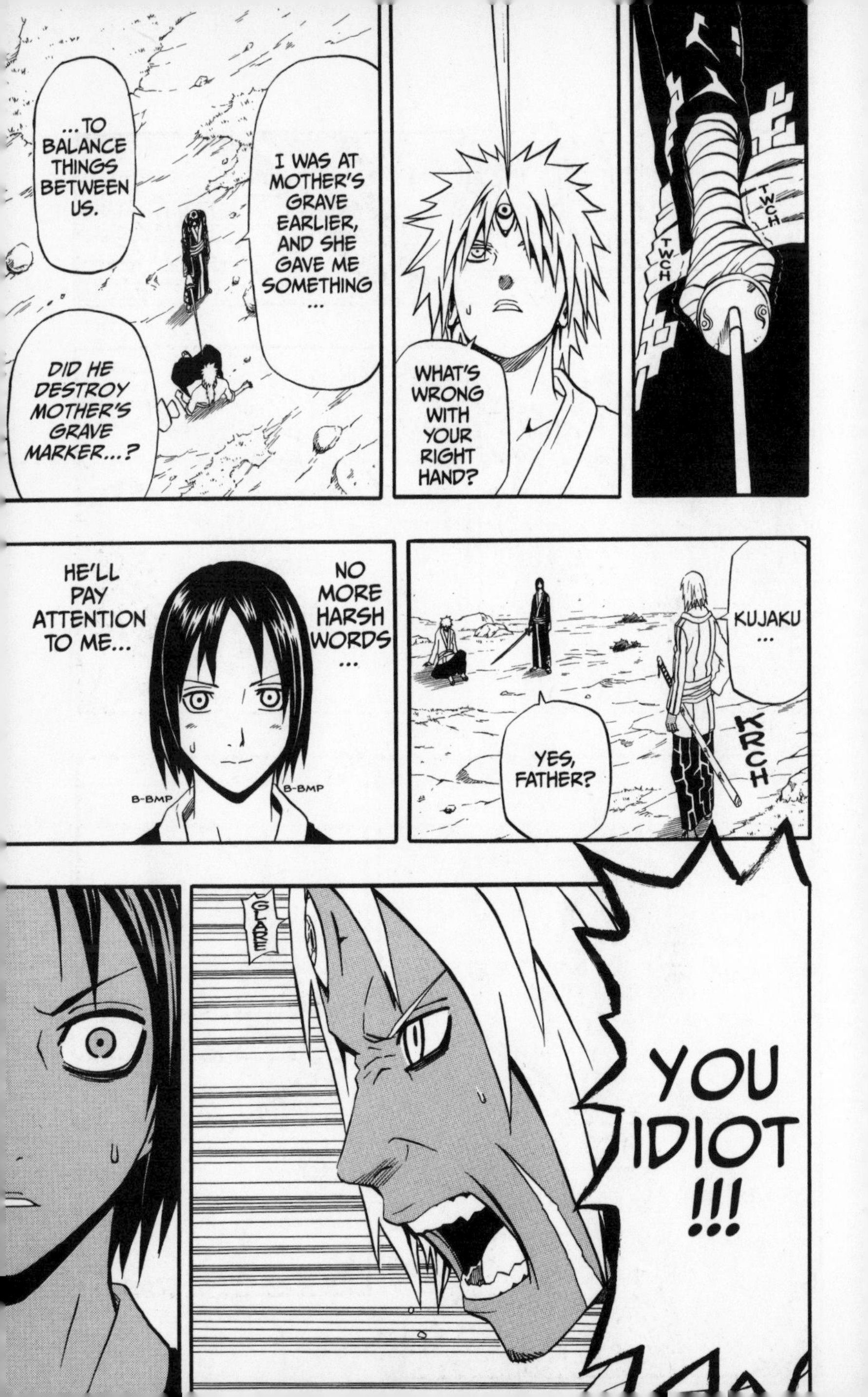
TWCH
TWCH
WHAT'S WRONG WITH YOUR RIGHT HAND?
I WAS AT MOTHER'S GRAVE EARLIER, AND SHE GAVE ME SOMETHING...
...TO BALANCE THINGS BETWEEN US.
DID HE DESTROY MOTHER'S GRAVE MARKER...?
KUJAKU...
KRCH
YES, FATHER?
NO MORE HARSH WORDS...
HE'LL PAY ATTENTION TO ME...
B-BMP
B-BMP
YOU IDIOT!!!
GLARE

WHAT HAPPENED TO YOUR GENTLE, FLOWING SWORD?!

YOU NOW WIELD IT WITH A HARD HAND!!

WHY...

NOTHING?!!

HAVE YOU LEARNED NOTHING, KUJAKU?!

...DONE WELL...?

...I'VE...

...WON'T HE TELL ME...

WHY...

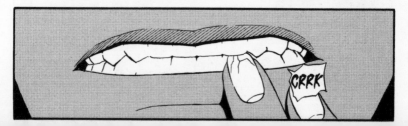

CRRK

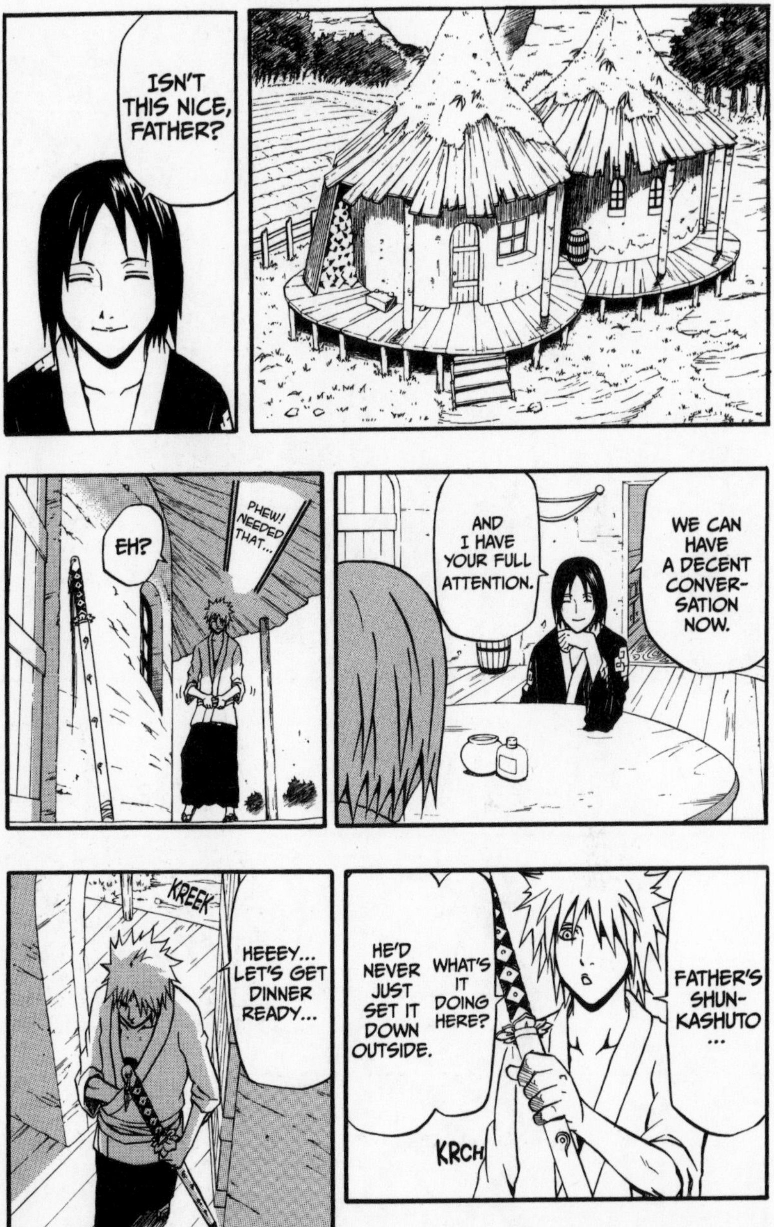
ISN'T THIS NICE, FATHER?
WE CAN HAVE A DECENT CONVERSATION NOW.
AND I HAVE YOUR FULL ATTENTION.
PHEW! NEEDED THAT...
EH?
FATHER'S SHUN-KASHUTO ...
WHAT'S IT DOING HERE?
HE'D NEVER JUST SET IT DOWN OUTSIDE.
KRCH
KREEK
HEEEY... LET'S GET DINNER READY...

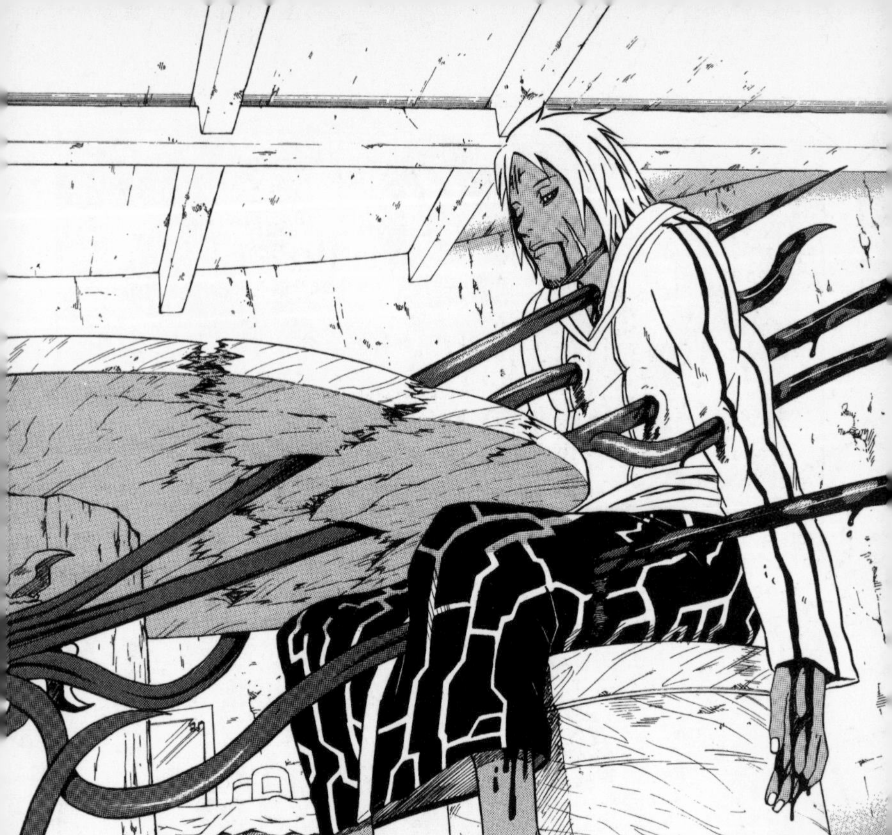
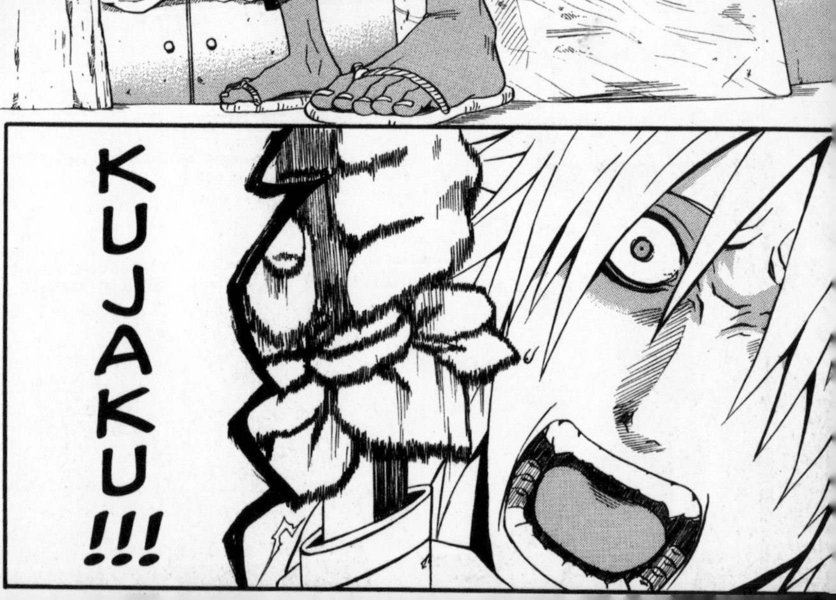
KUJAKU!!!

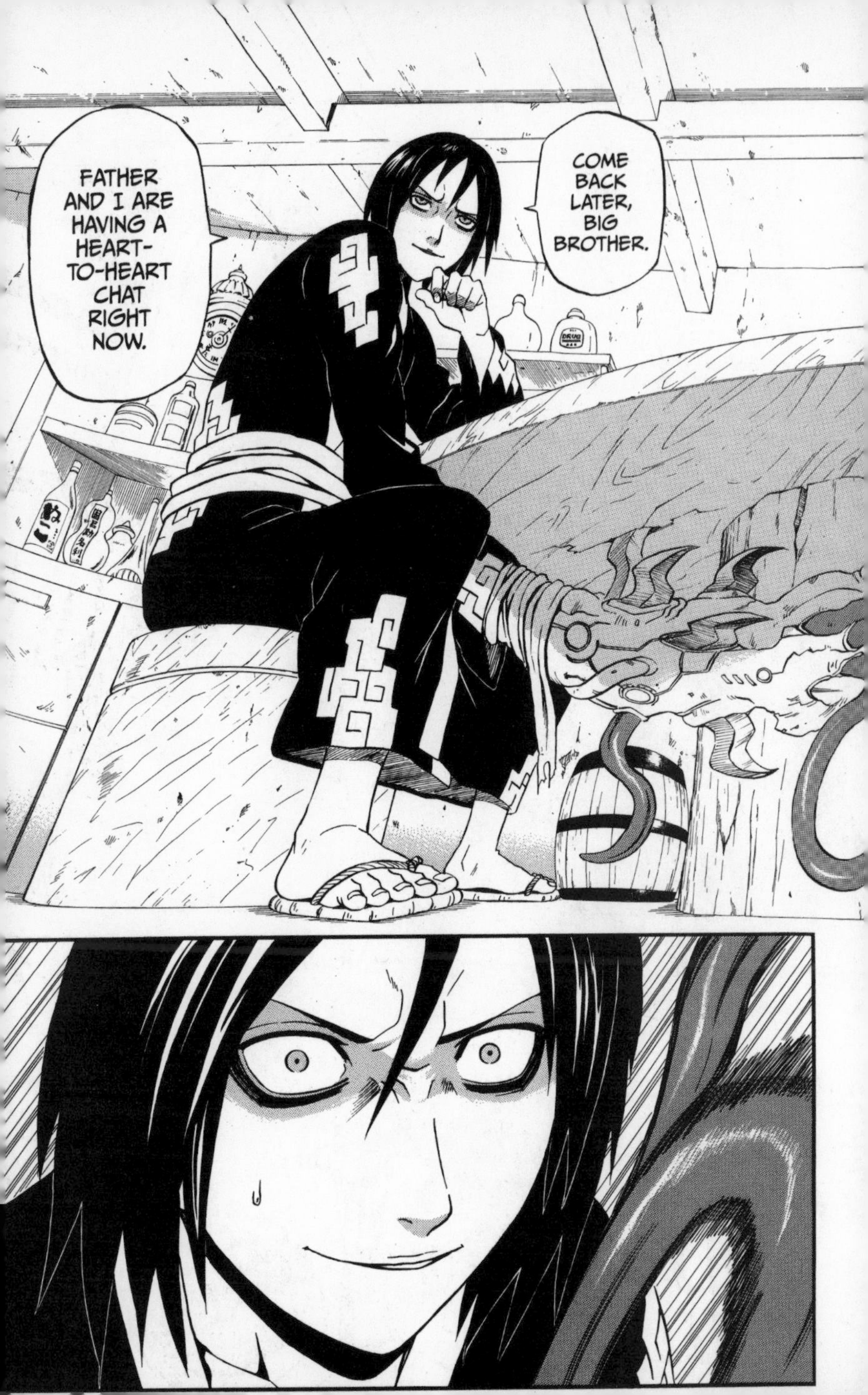
COME BACK LATER, BIG BROTHER.
FATHER AND I ARE HAVING A HEART-TO-HEART CHAT RIGHT NOW.

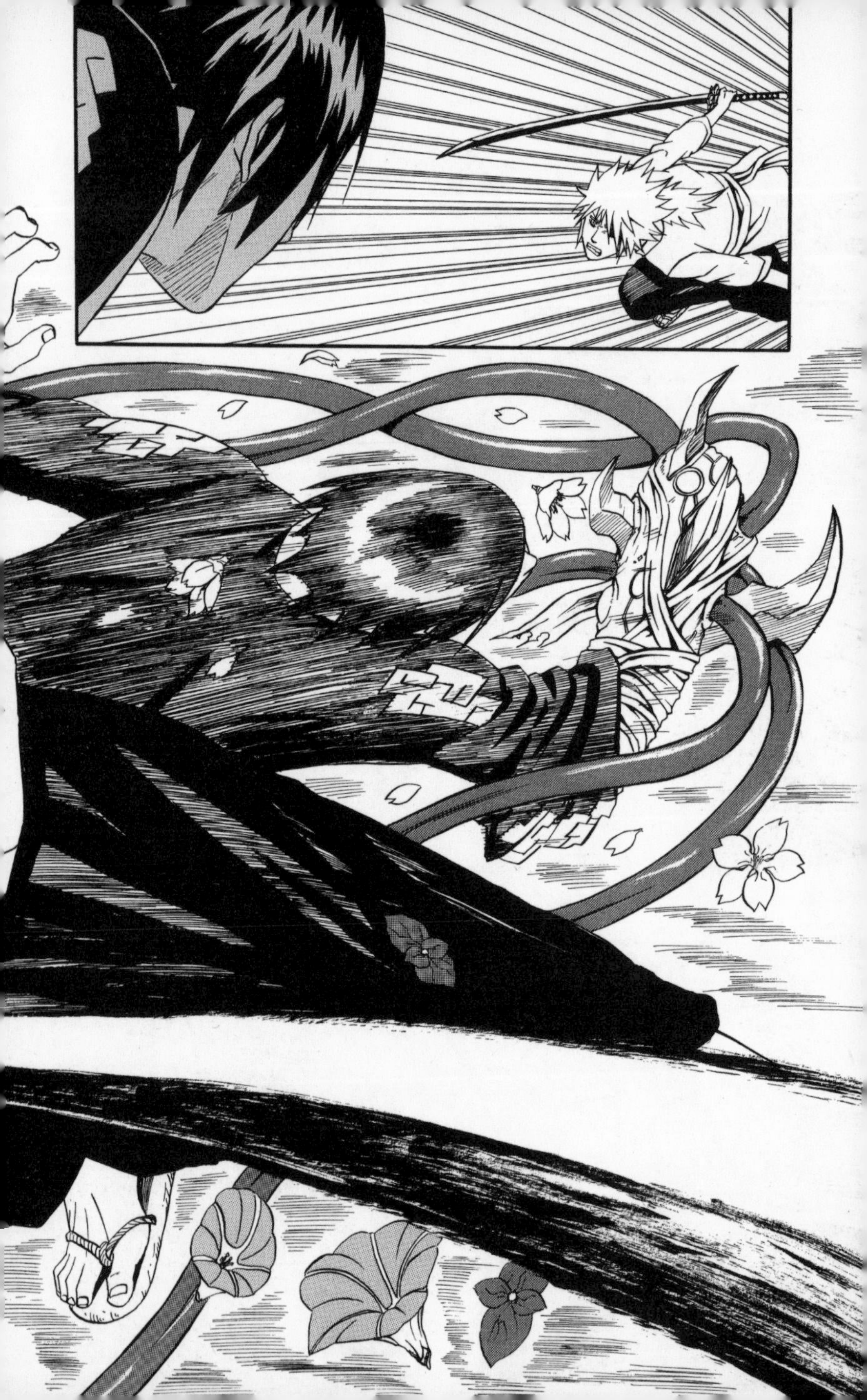

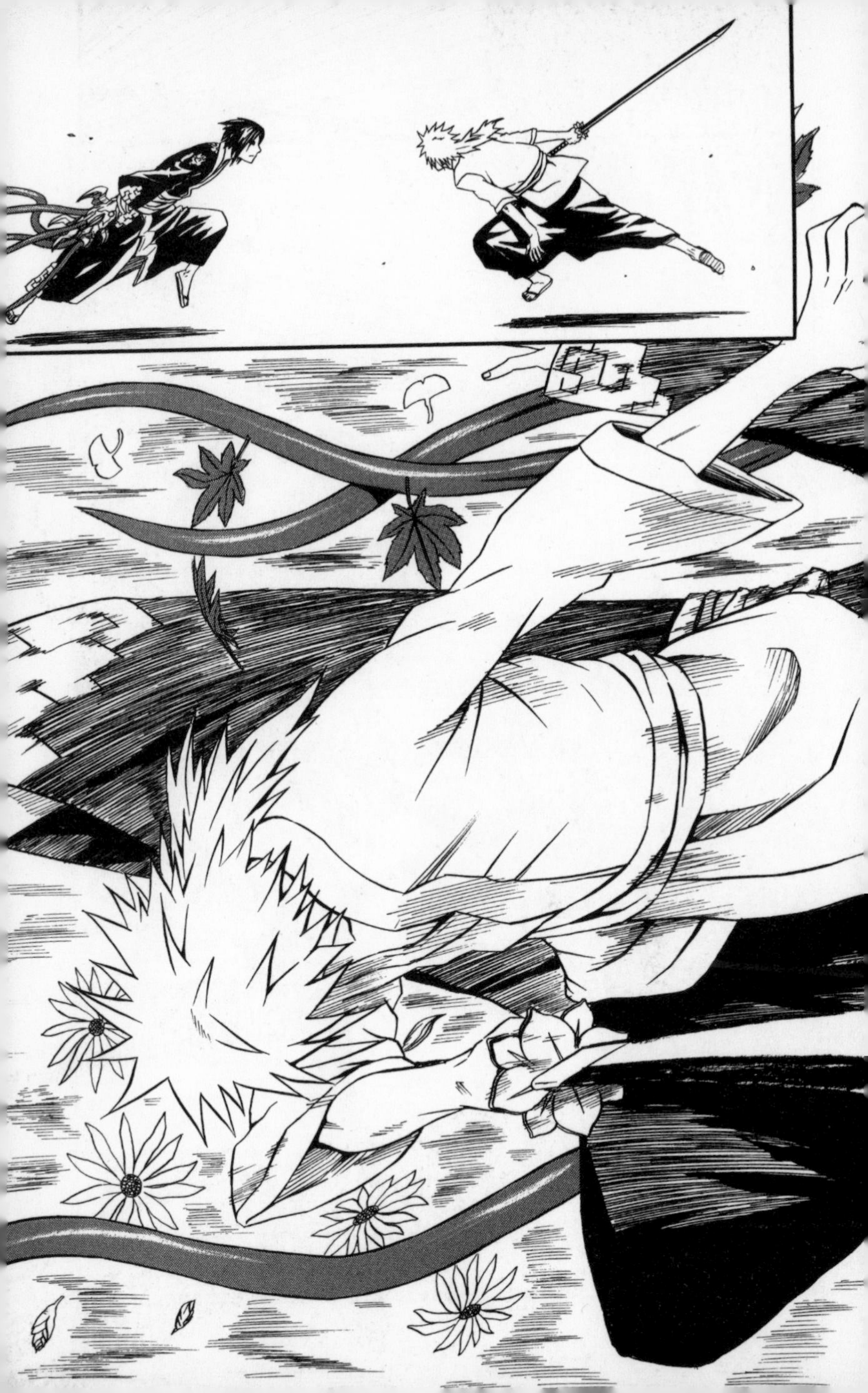

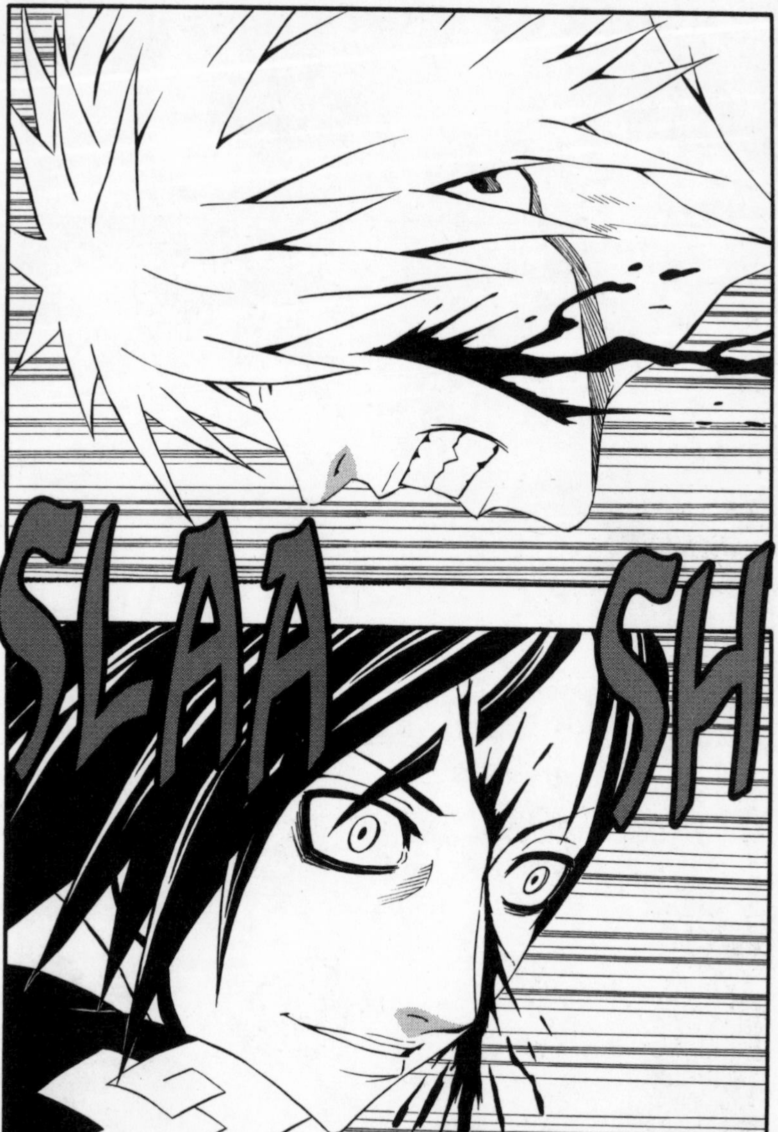
SLAA SH

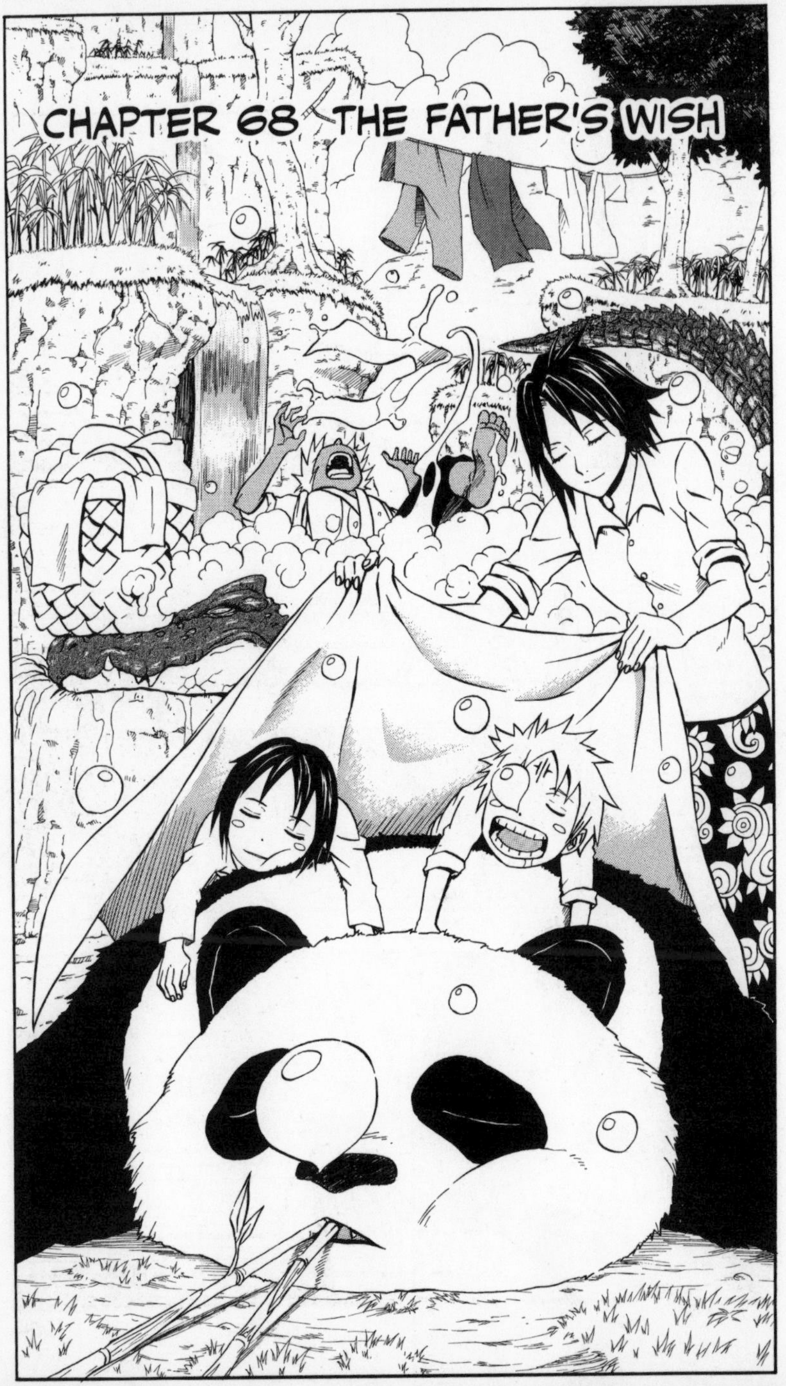
CHAPTER 68 THE FATHER'S WISH

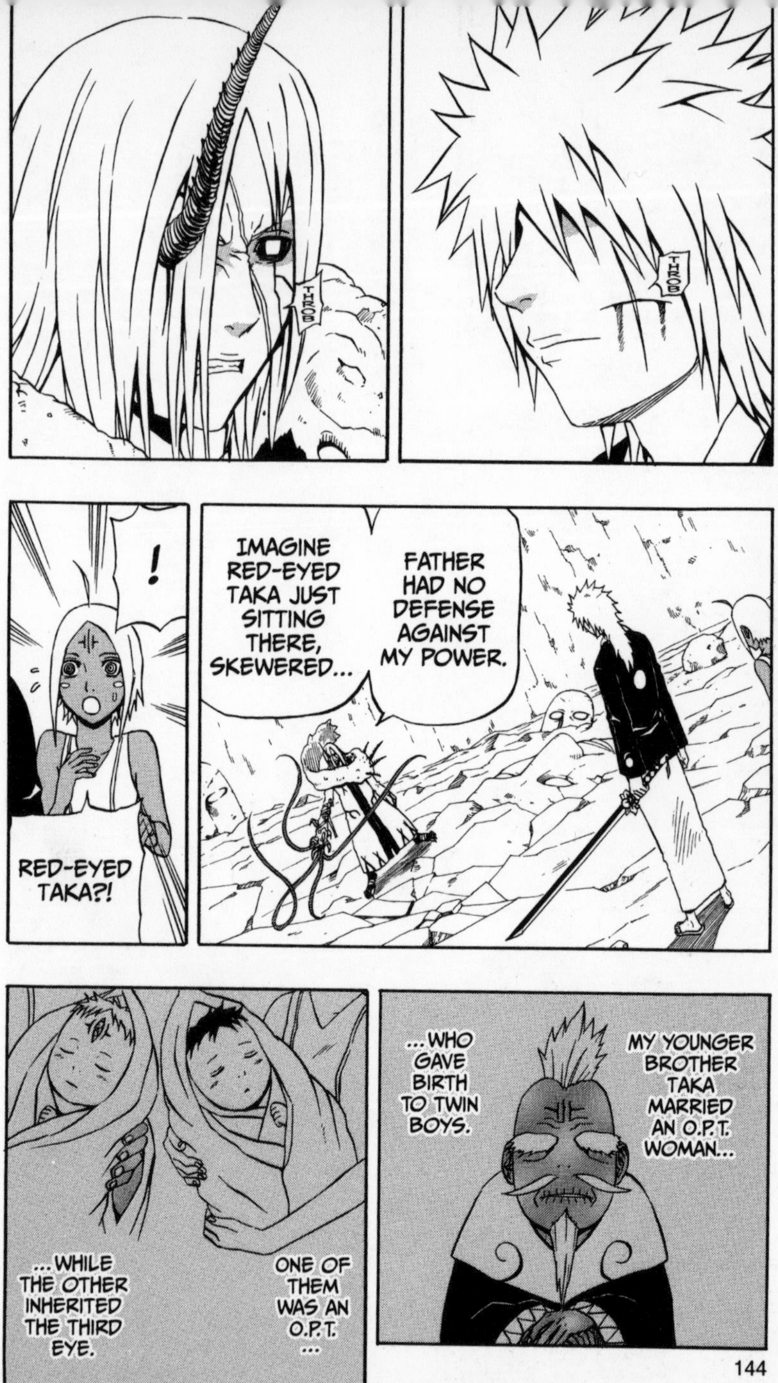
THROB
THROB
FATHER HAD NO DEFENSE AGAINST MY POWER.
IMAGINE RED-EYED TAKA JUST SITTING THERE, SKEWERED...
!
RED-EYED TAKA?!
MY YOUNGER BROTHER TAKA MARRIED AN O.P.T. WOMAN...
...WHO GAVE BIRTH TO TWIN BOYS.
ONE OF THEM WAS AN O.P.T. ...
...WHILE THE OTHER INHERITED THE THIRD EYE.

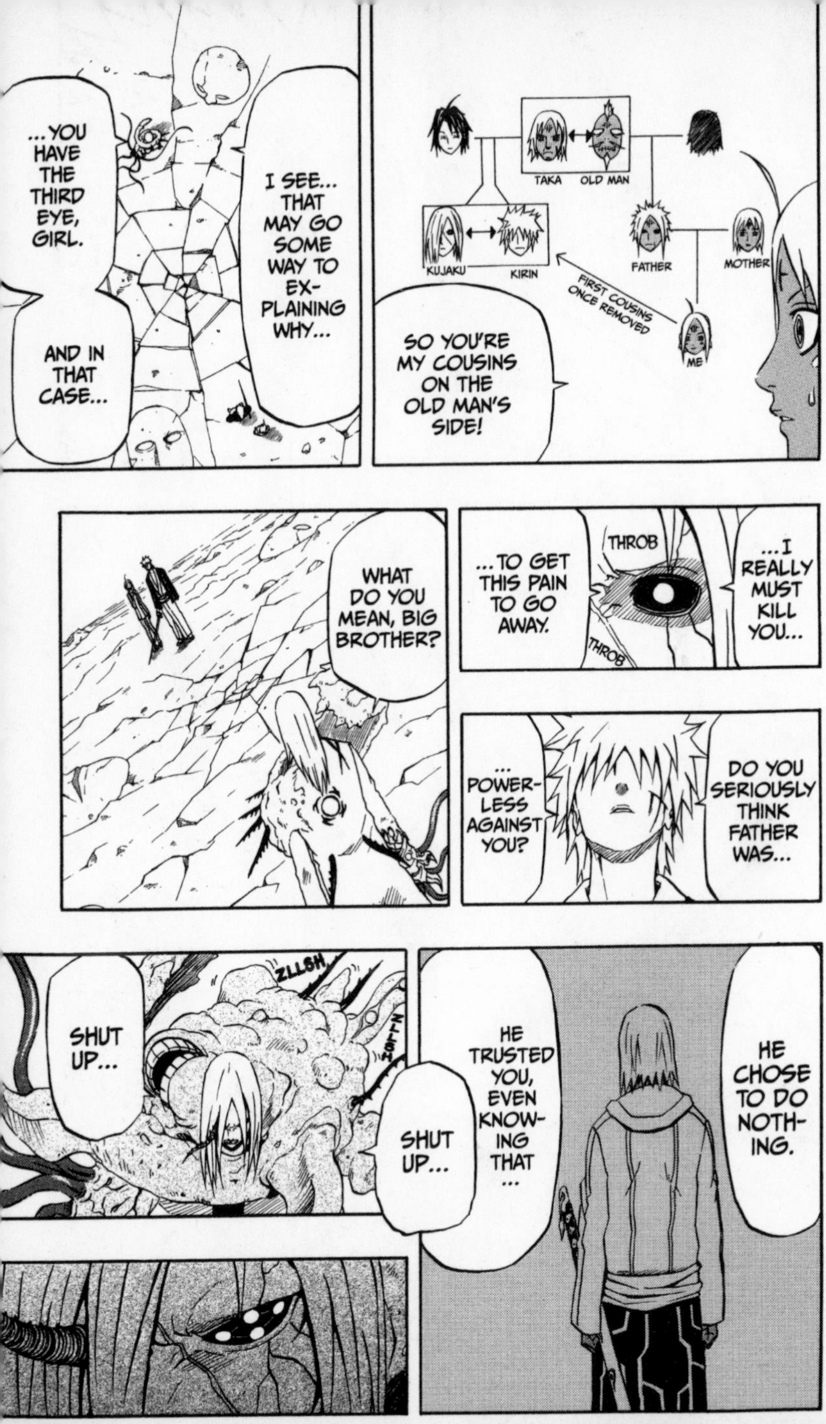
TAKA
OLD MAN
KUJAKU
KIRIN
FATHER
MOTHER
FIRST COUSINS ONCE REMOVED
ME
SO YOU'RE MY COUSINS ON THE OLD MAN'S SIDE!
I SEE... THAT MAY GO SOME WAY TO EX-PLAINING WHY...
...YOU HAVE THE THIRD EYE, GIRL.
AND IN THAT CASE...
...I REALLY MUST KILL YOU...
THROB
THROB
...TO GET THIS PAIN TO GO AWAY.
DO YOU SERIOUSLY THINK FATHER WAS...
...POWER-LESS AGAINST YOU?
WHAT DO YOU MEAN, BIG BROTHER?
HE CHOSE TO DO NOTH-ING.
HE TRUSTED YOU, EVEN KNOW-ING THAT...
ZLLSH
ZLLSH
SHUT UP...
SHUT UP...

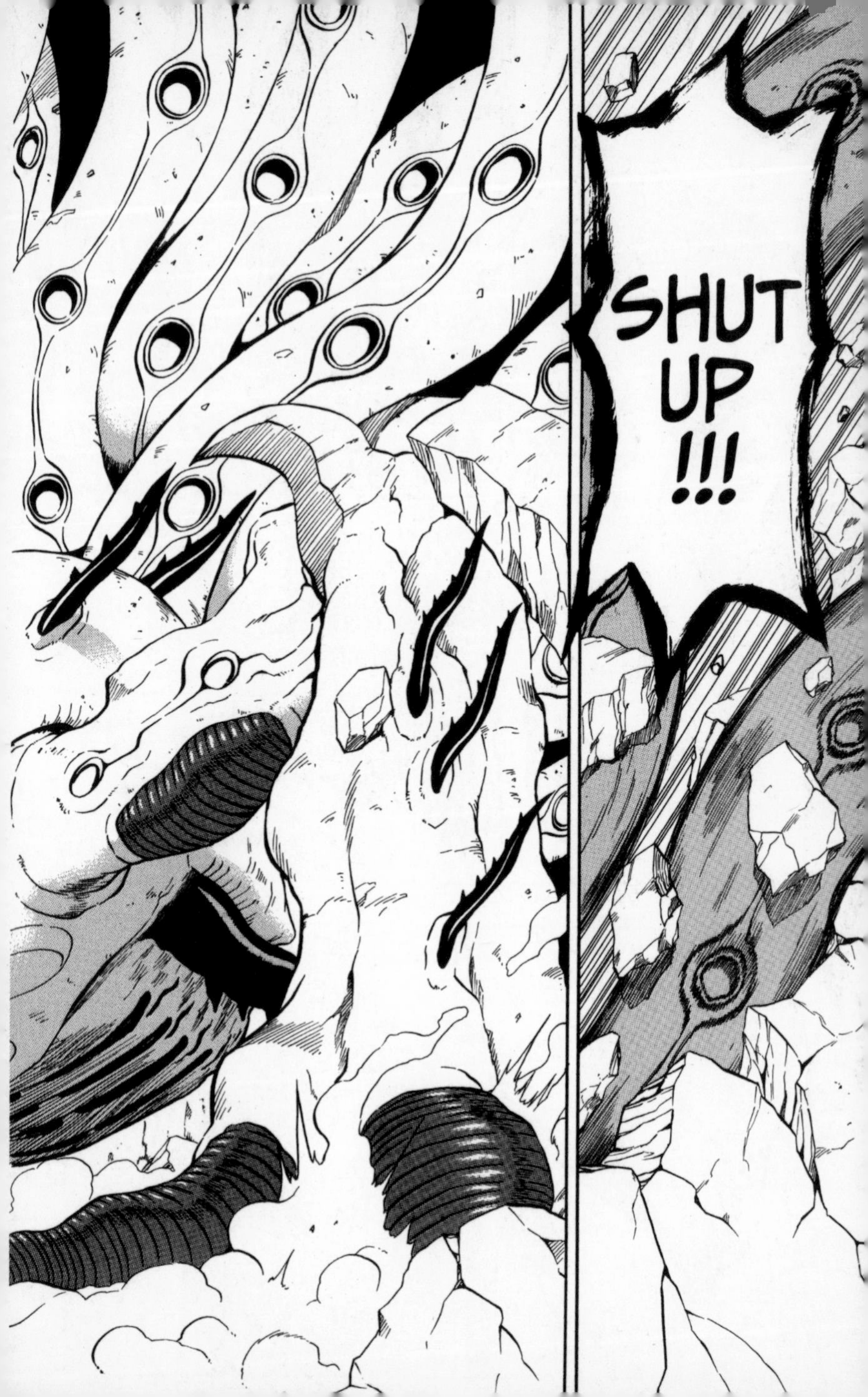
SHUT UP !!!

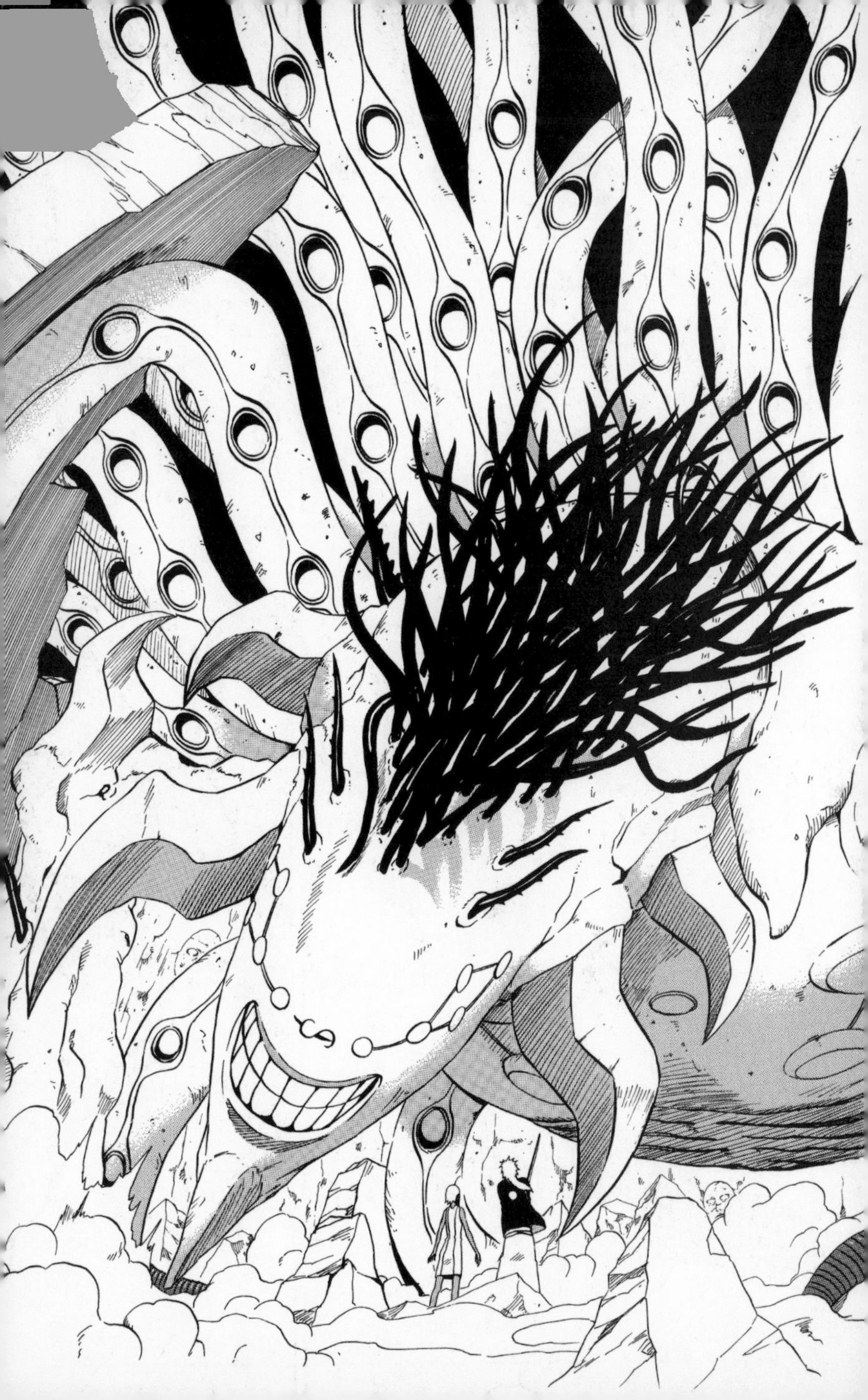

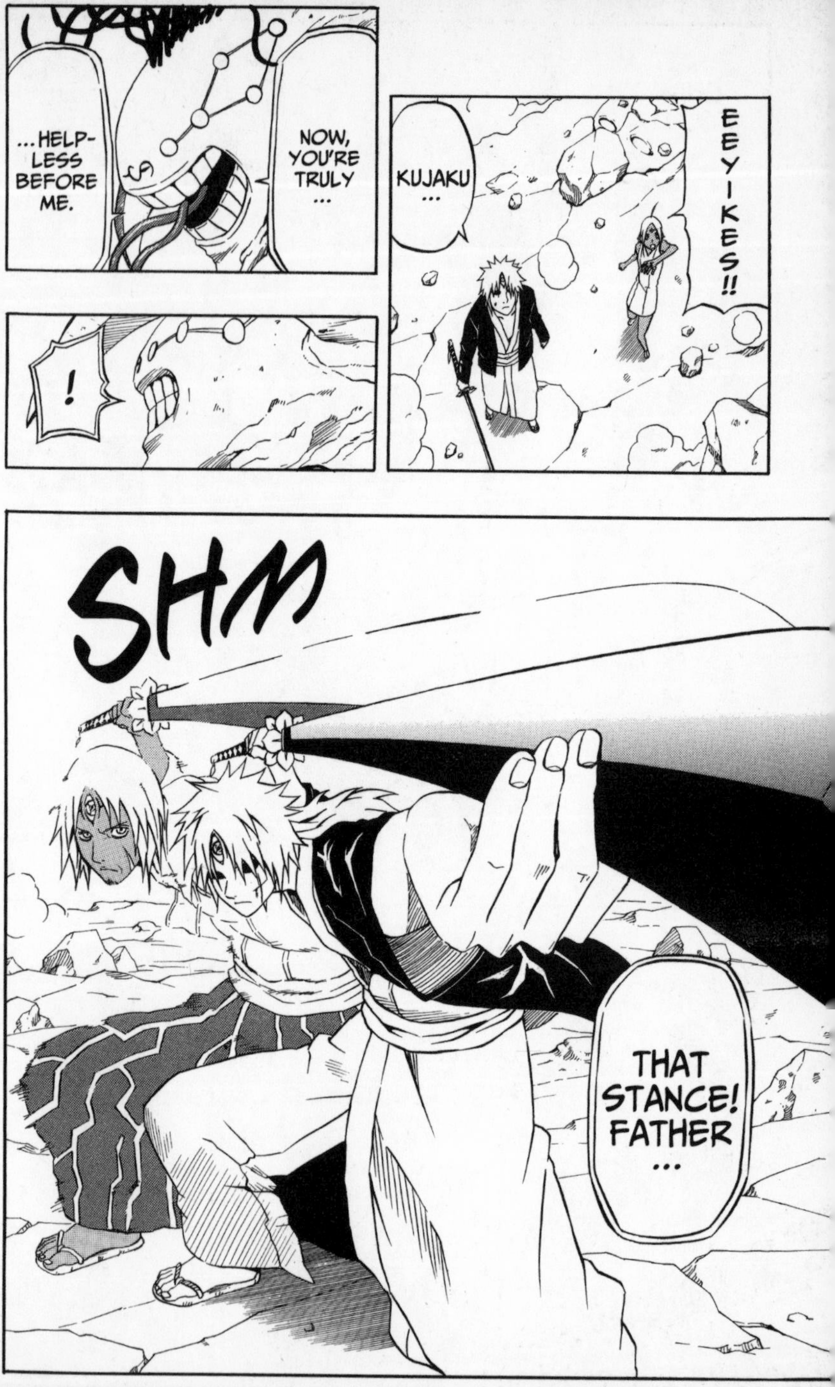
KUJAKU ...
EEYIKES!!
NOW, YOU'RE TRULY ...
...HELP-LESS BEFORE ME.
!
SHM
THAT STANCE! FATHER ...

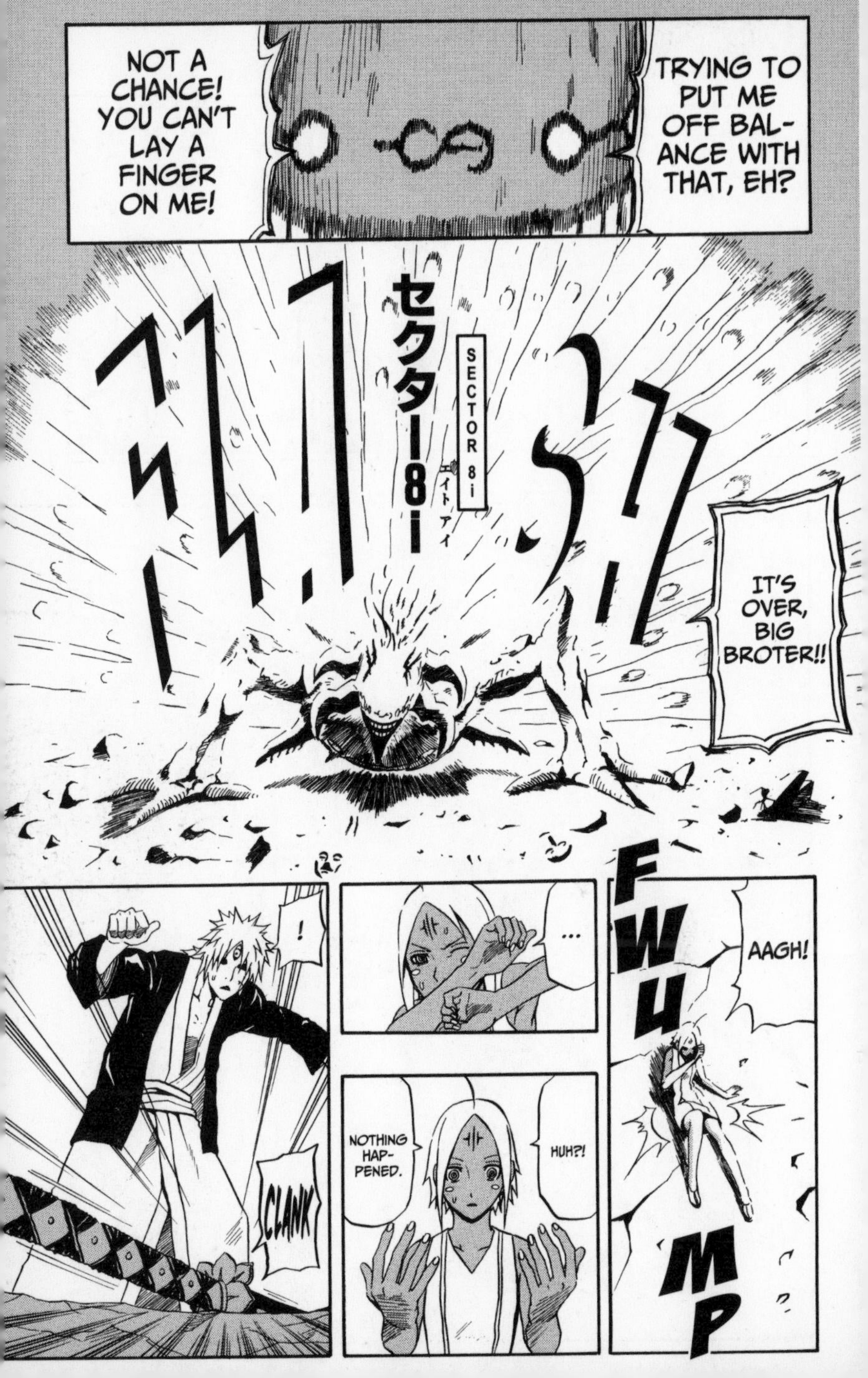
TRYING TO PUT ME OFF BAL-ANCE WITH THAT, EH?
NOT A CHANCE! YOU CAN'T LAY A FINGER ON ME!
セクター8i
エイトアイ
SECTOR 8i
IT'S OVER, BIG BROTER!!
FWUMP
AAGH!
...
HUH?!
NOTHING HAP-PENED.
!
CLANK

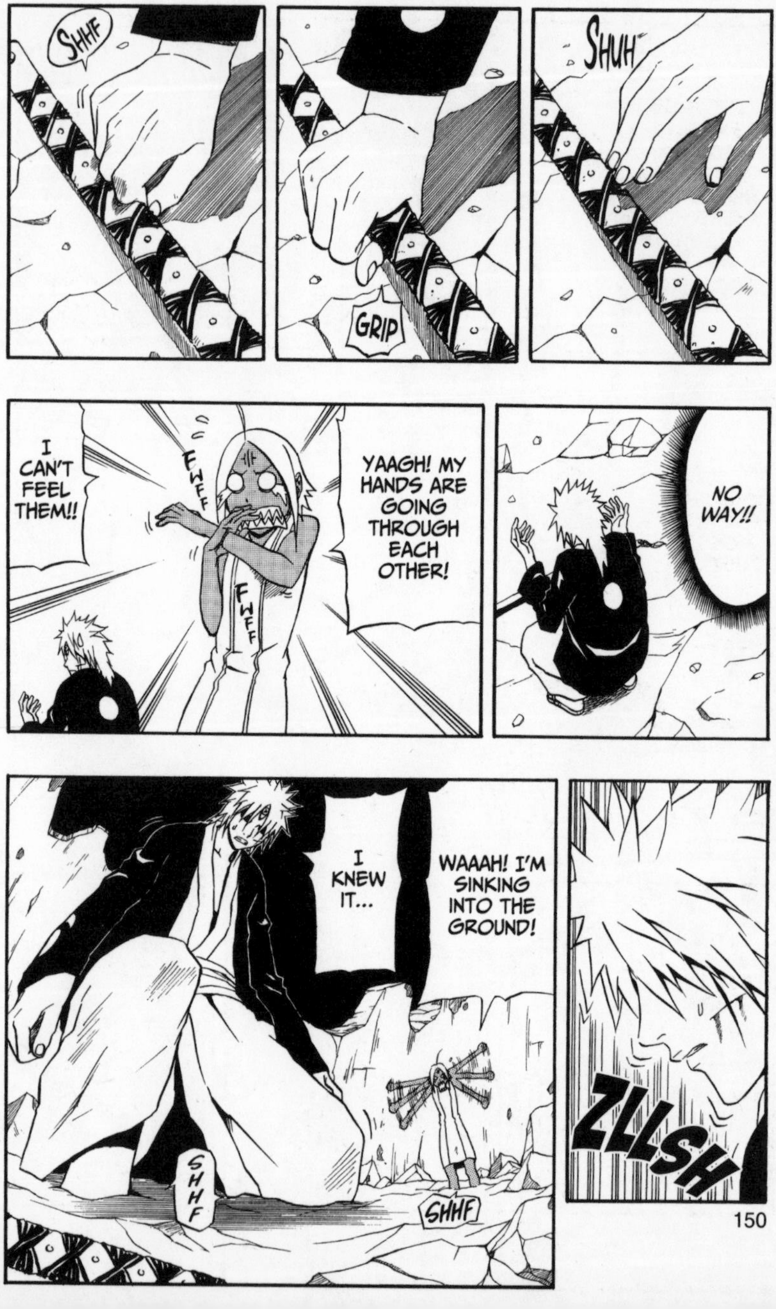
SHUH
GRIP
SHHF
NO WAY!!
YAAGH! MY HANDS ARE GOING THROUGH EACH OTHER!
FWFF
FWFF
I CAN'T FEEL THEM!!
ZLISH
WAAAH! I'M SINKING INTO THE GROUND!
I KNEW IT...
SHHF
SHHF

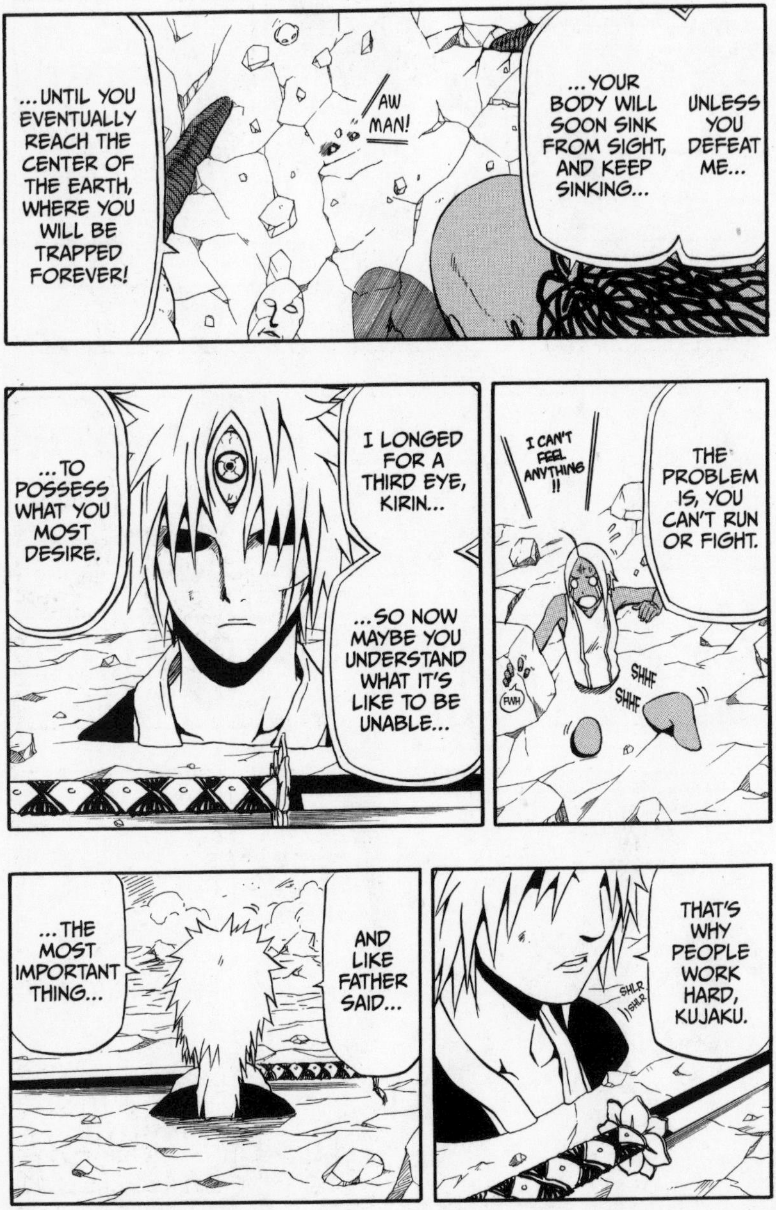
UNLESS YOU DEFEAT ME...
...YOUR BODY WILL SOON SINK FROM SIGHT, AND KEEP SINKING...
AW MAN!
...UNTIL YOU EVENTUALLY REACH THE CENTER OF THE EARTH, WHERE YOU WILL BE TRAPPED FOREVER!
THE PROBLEM IS, YOU CAN'T RUN OR FIGHT.
I CAN'T FEEL ANYTHING !!
SHHF
SHHF
FWH
I LONGED FOR A THIRD EYE, KIRIN...
...SO NOW MAYBE YOU UNDERSTAND WHAT IT'S LIKE TO BE UNABLE...
...TO POSSESS WHAT YOU MOST DESIRE.
THAT'S WHY PEOPLE WORK HARD, KUJAKU.
SHLR
SHLR
AND LIKE FATHER SAID...
...THE MOST IMPORTANT THING...

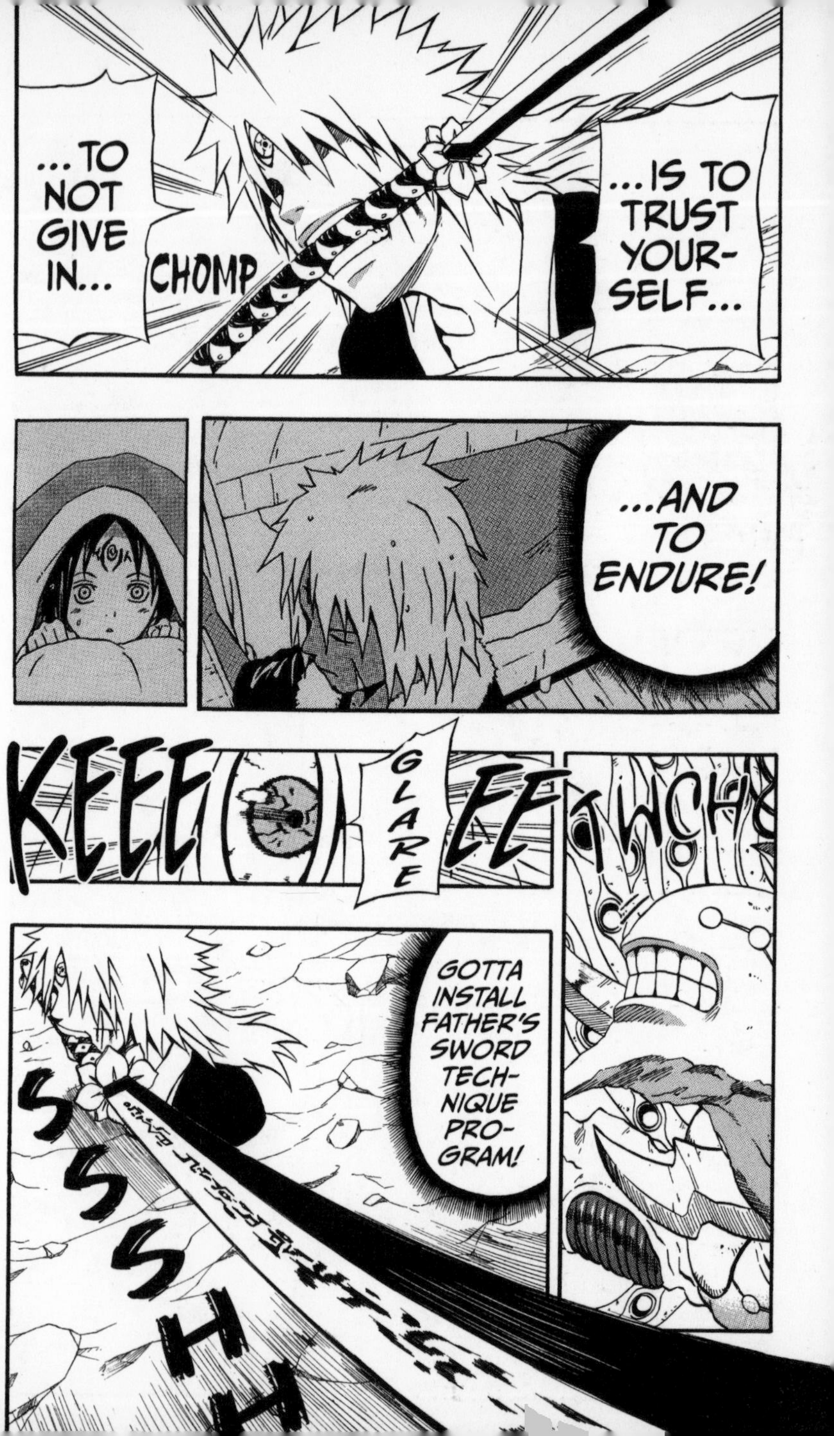

...IS TO TRUST YOUR-SELF...
CHOMP
...TO NOT GIVE IN...
...AND TO ENDURE!
TWCH
KEEEEE
GLARE
GOTTA INSTALL FATHER'S SWORD TECH-NIQUE PRO-GRAM!
SSSHH

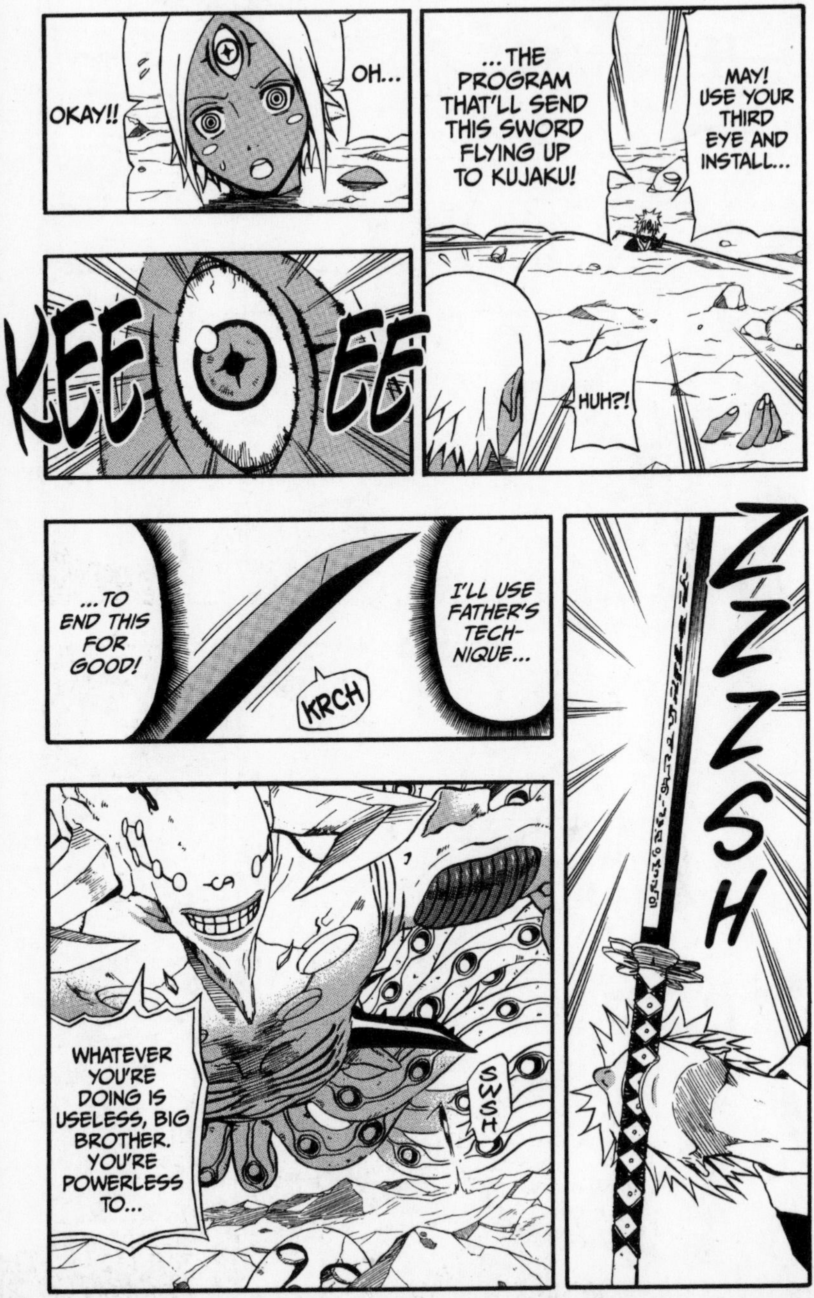
MAY! USE YOUR THIRD EYE AND INSTALL...
...THE PROGRAM THAT'LL SEND THIS SWORD FLYING UP TO KUJAKU!
HUH?!
OH...
OKAY!!
KEE-EE
ZZZSH
I'LL USE FATHER'S TECH-NIQUE...
KRCH
...TO END THIS FOR GOOD!
WHATEVER YOU'RE DOING IS USELESS, BIG BROTHER. YOU'RE POWERLESS TO...
SWSH

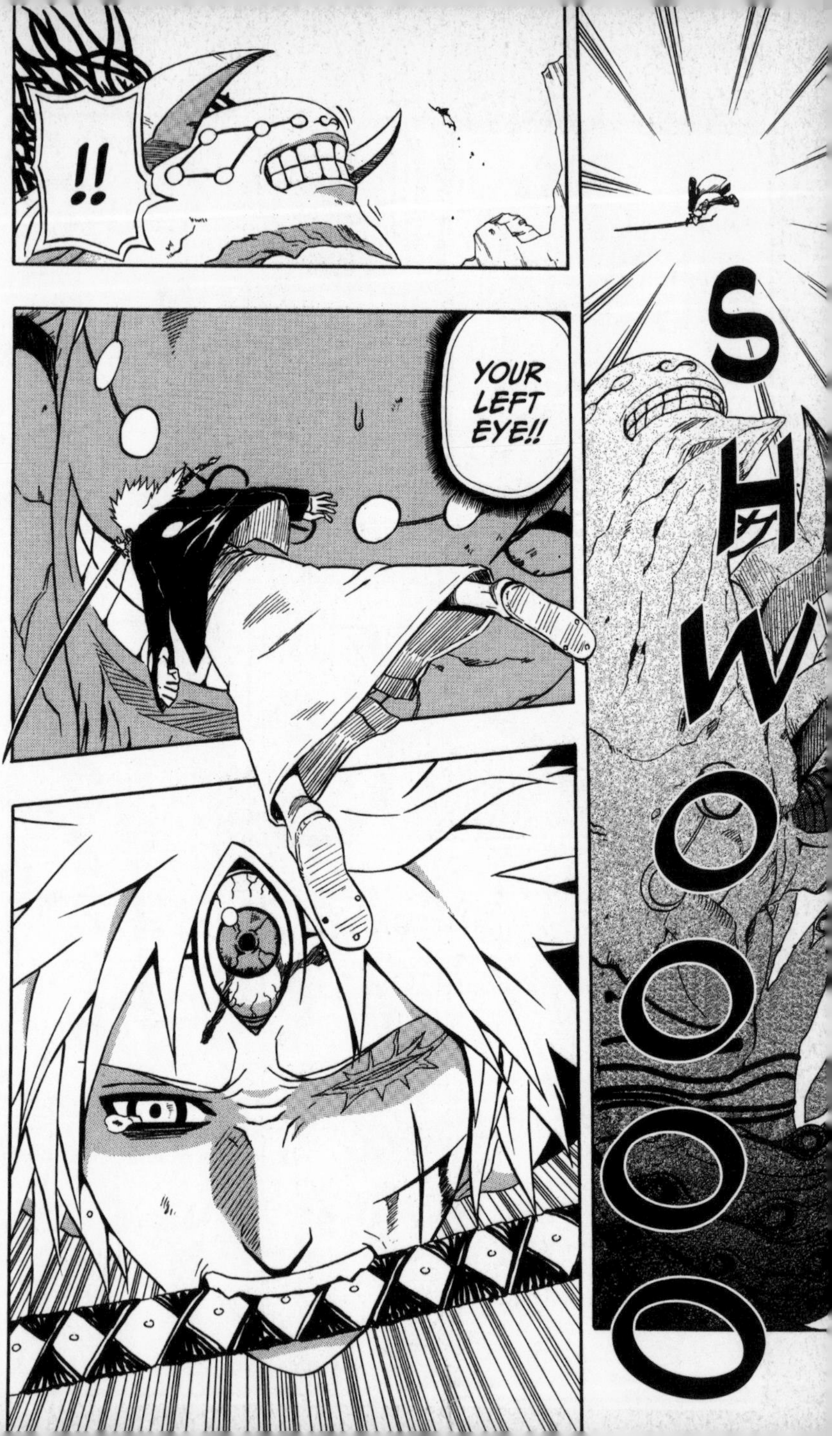
SHWOOOO
!!
YOUR LEFT EYE!!

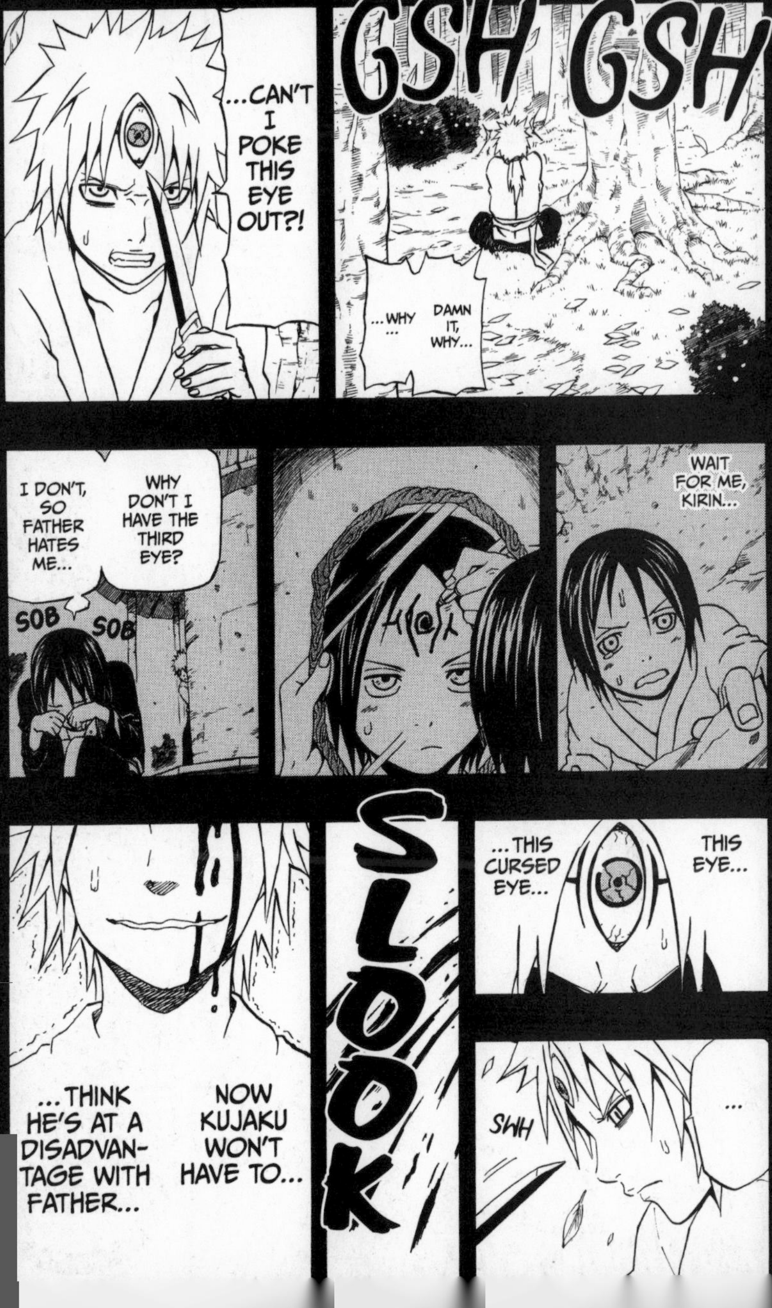
GSH GSH
DAMN IT, WHY...
...WHY...
...CAN'T I POKE THIS EYE OUT?!
WAIT FOR ME, KIRIN...
WHY DON'T I HAVE THE THIRD EYE?
I DON'T, SO FATHER HATES ME...
SOB SOB
THIS EYE...
...THIS CURSED EYE...
...
SWH
SLOOK
NOW KUJAKU WON'T HAVE TO...
...THINK HE'S AT A DISADVANTAGE WITH FATHER...

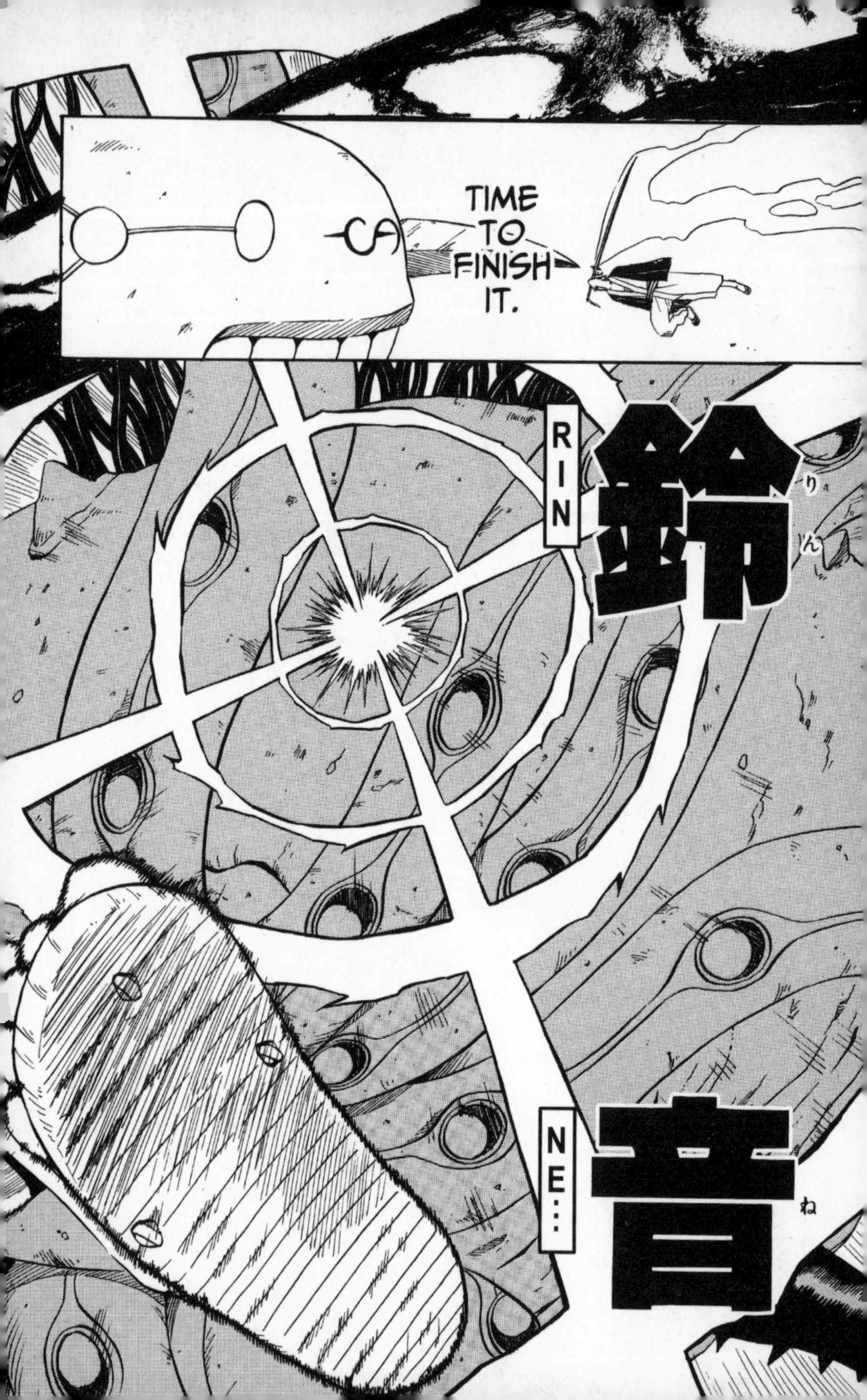
TIME TO FINISH IT.
RIN
鈴
りん
NE...
音
ね

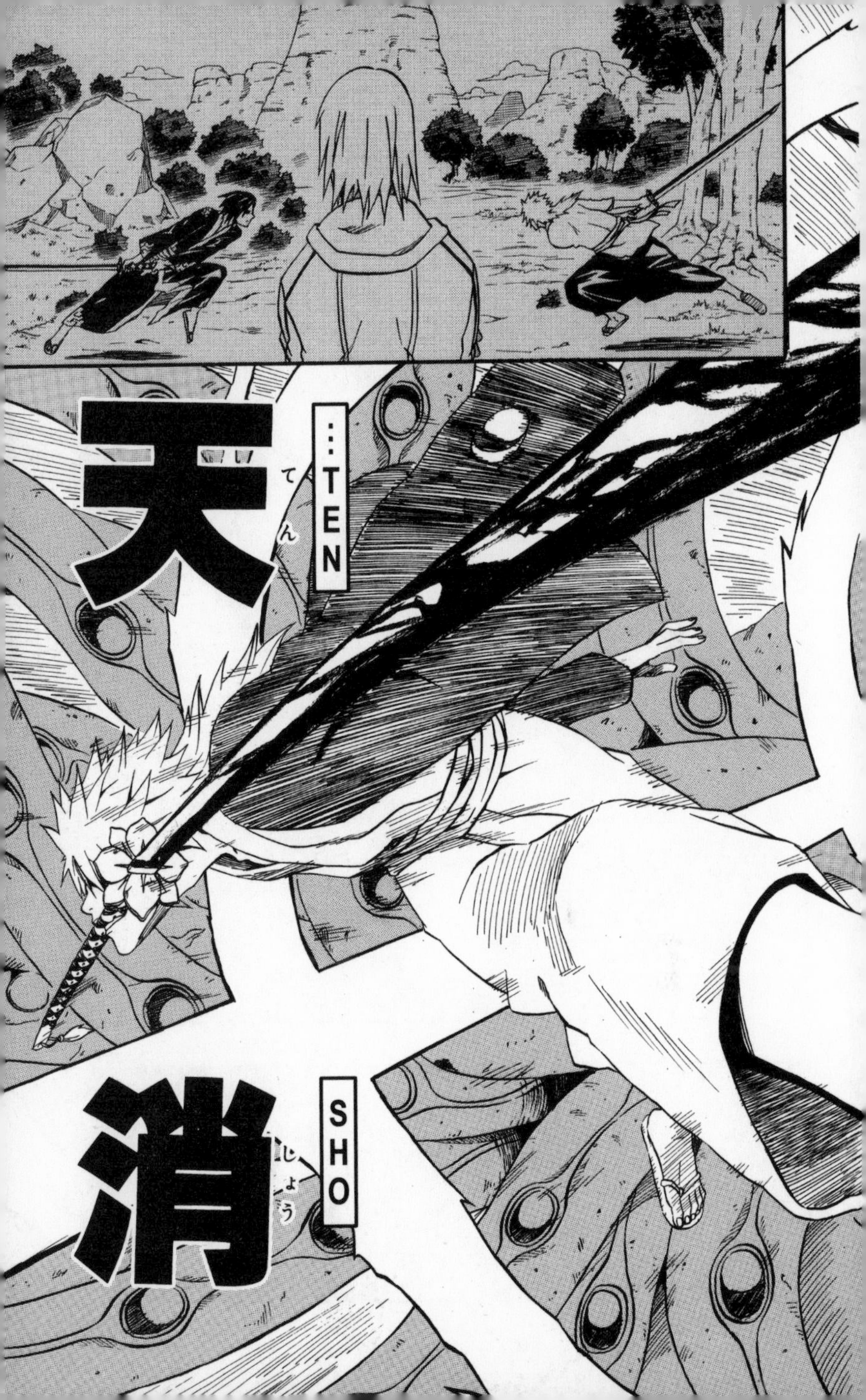

天
てん
...TEN
消
しょう
SHO

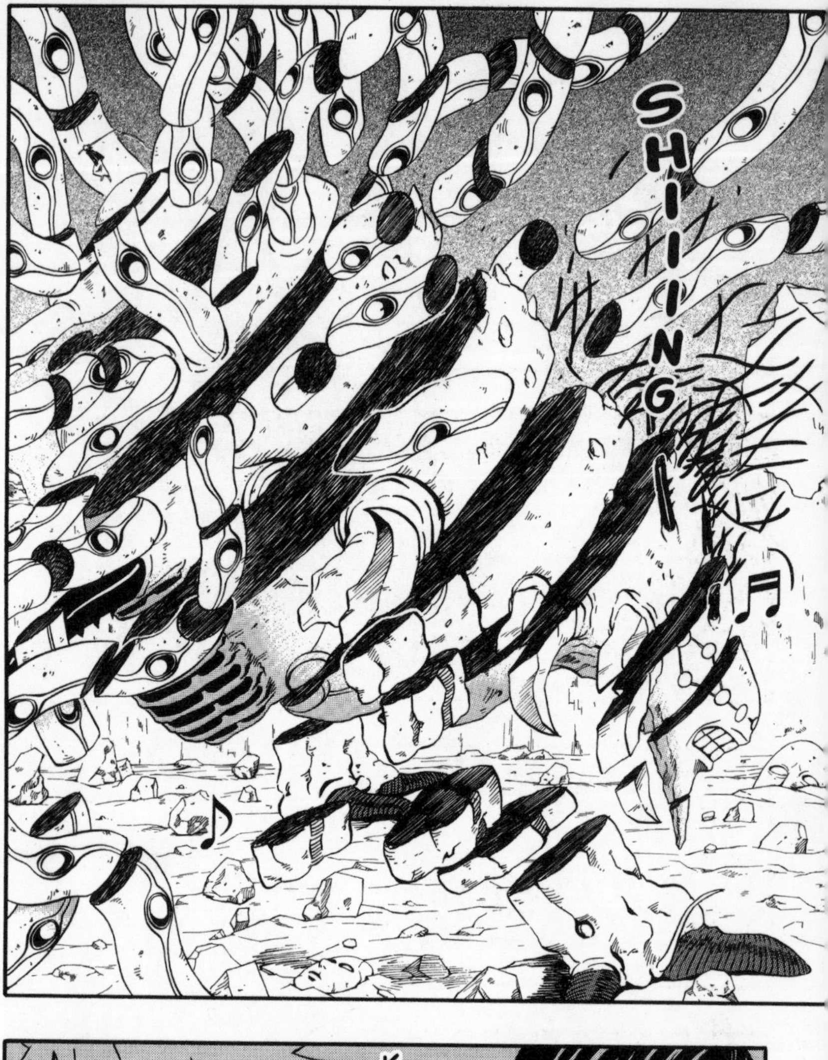
SHIIING
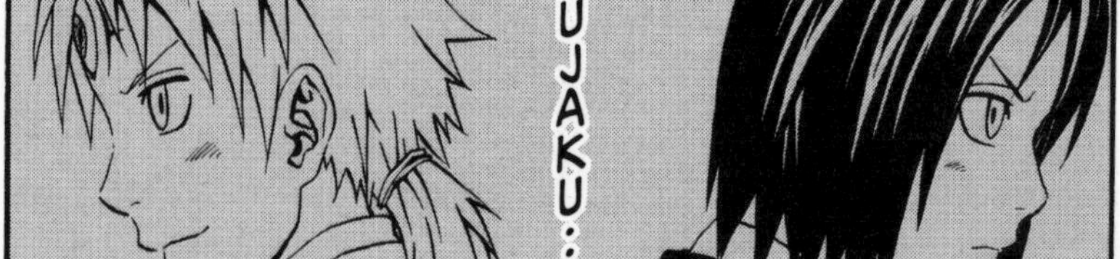
KUJAKU...

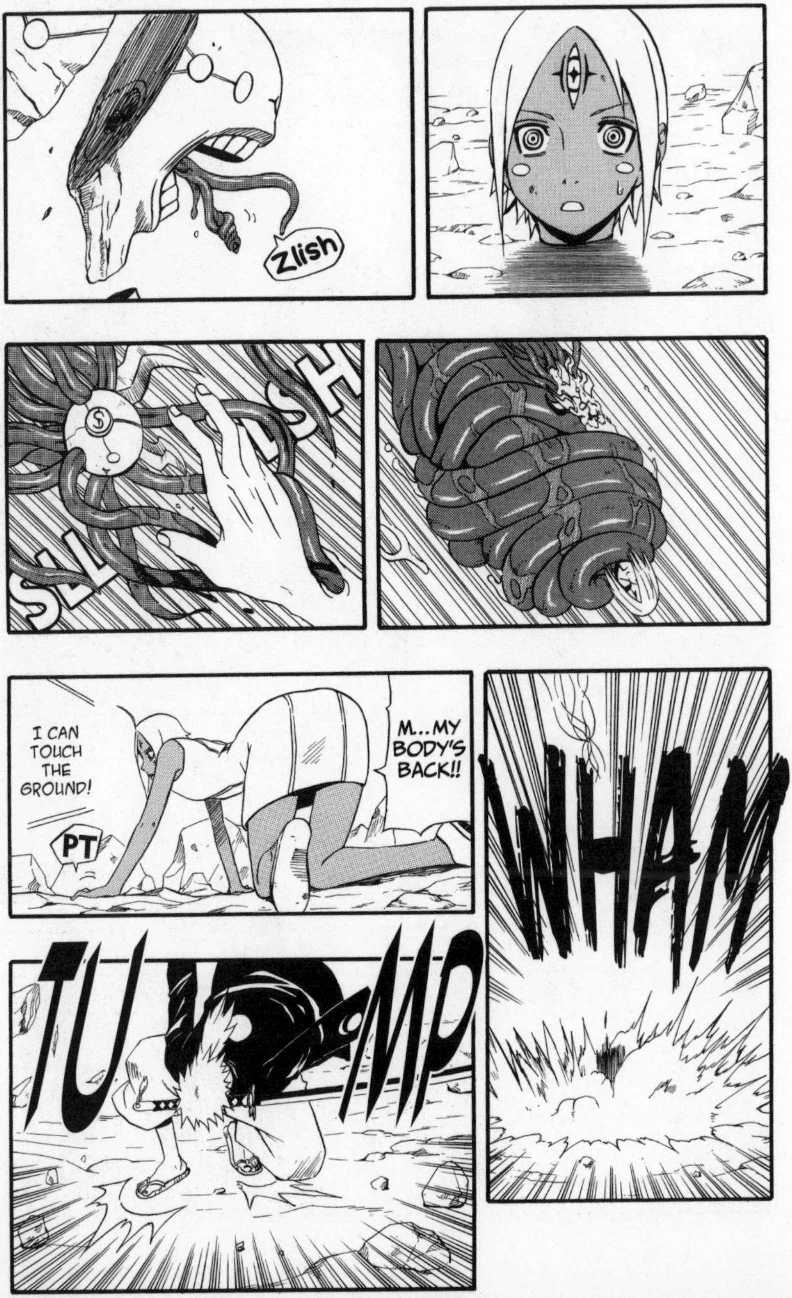
Zlish
WHAM
M...MY BODY'S BACK!!
I CAN TOUCH THE GROUND!
PT

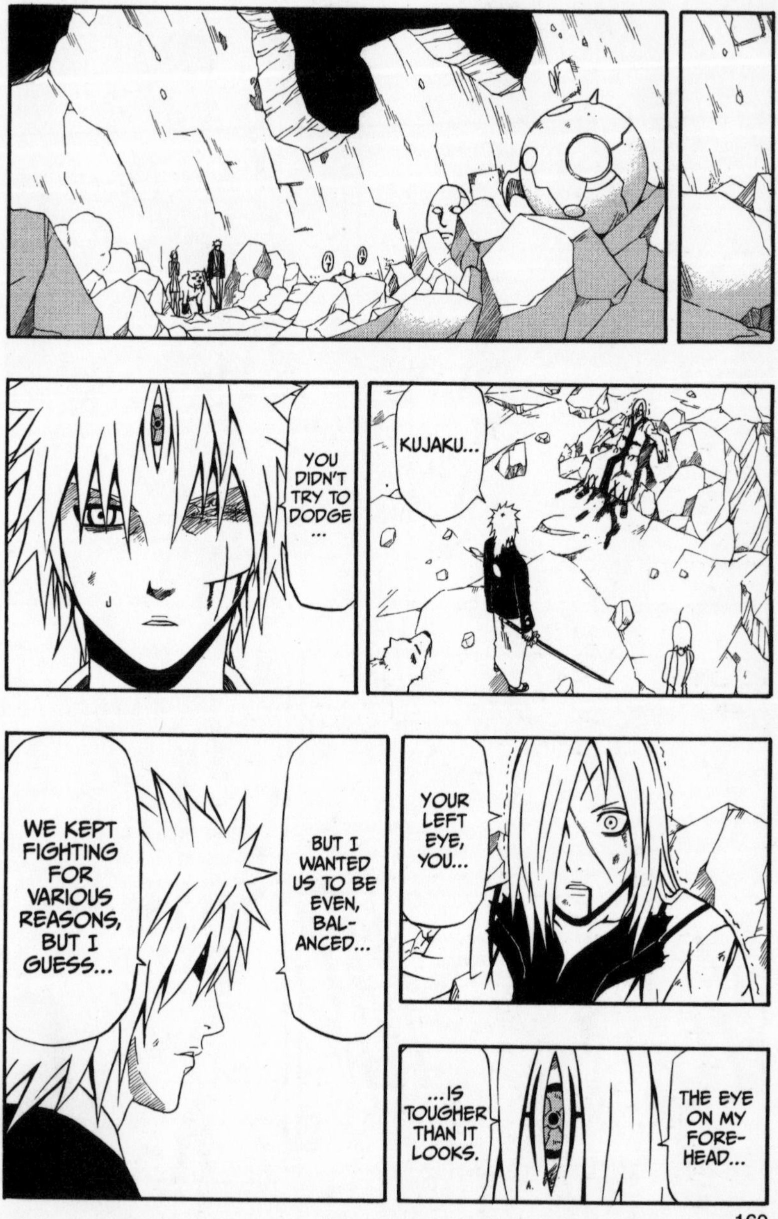
KUJAKU...
YOU DIDN'T TRY TO DODGE...
YOUR LEFT EYE, YOU...
THE EYE ON MY FORE-HEAD...
...IS TOUGHER THAN IT LOOKS.
BUT I WANTED US TO BE EVEN, BAL-ANCED...
WE KEPT FIGHTING FOR VARIOUS REASONS, BUT I GUESS...

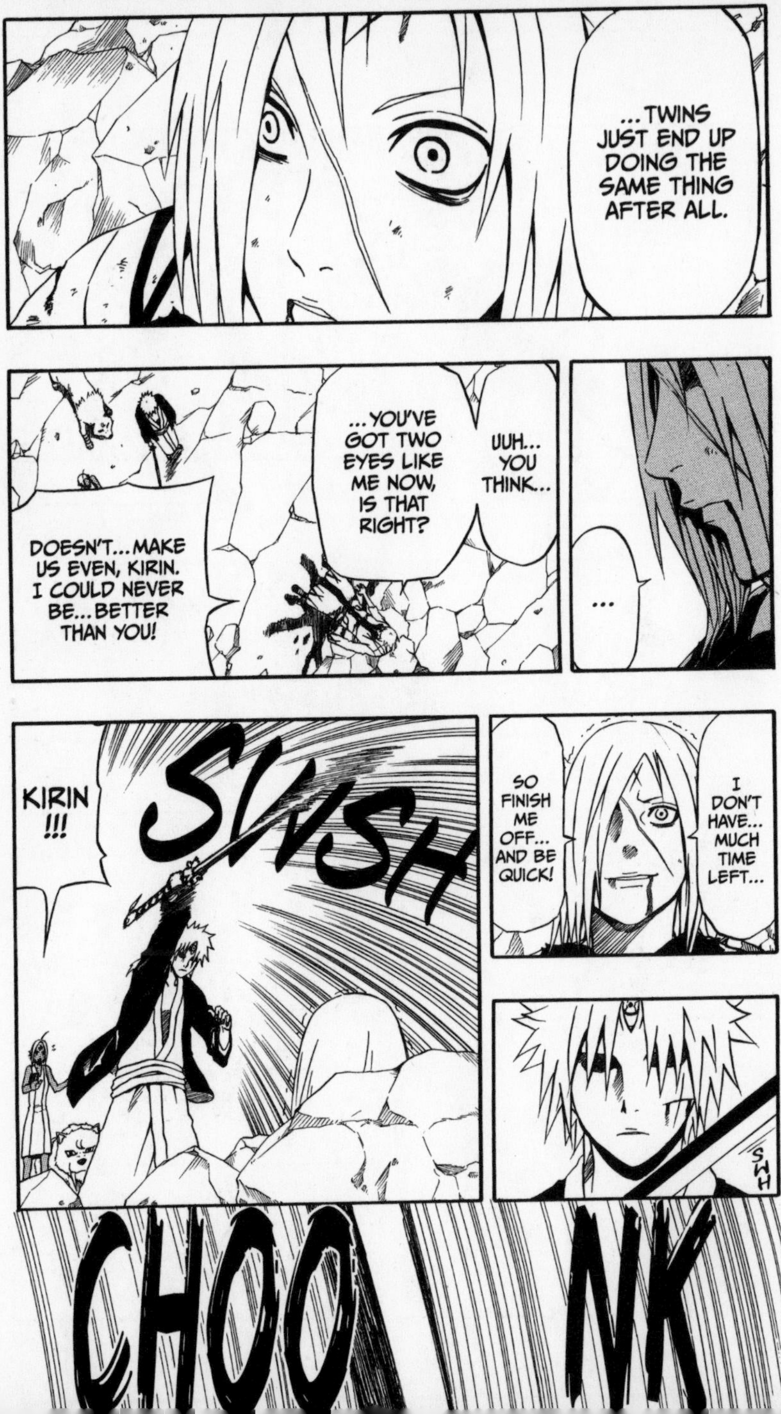
...TWINS JUST END UP DOING THE SAME THING AFTER ALL.
...
UUH... YOU THINK...
...YOU'VE GOT TWO EYES LIKE ME NOW, IS THAT RIGHT?
DOESN'T...MAKE US EVEN, KIRIN. I COULD NEVER BE...BETTER THAN YOU!
I DON'T HAVE... MUCH TIME LEFT...
SO FINISH ME OFF... AND BE QUICK!
SWH
SWSH
KIRIN !!!
CHOONK

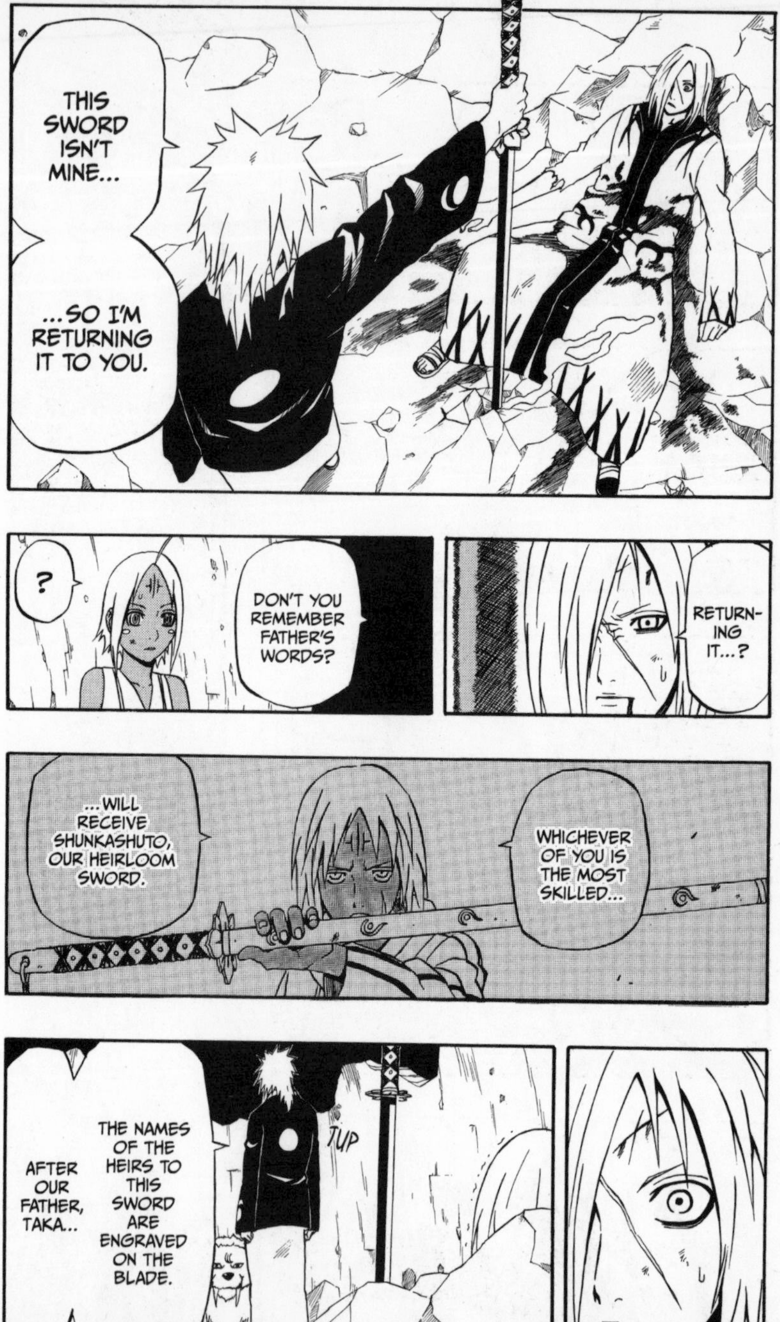
THIS SWORD ISN'T MINE...
...SO I'M RETURNING IT TO YOU.
RETURNING IT...?
DON'T YOU REMEMBER FATHER'S WORDS?
?
WHICHEVER OF YOU IS THE MOST SKILLED...
...WILL RECEIVE SHUNKASHUTO, OUR HEIRLOOM SWORD.
TUP
THE NAMES OF THE HEIRS TO THIS SWORD ARE ENGRAVED ON THE BLADE.
AFTER OUR FATHER, TAKA...

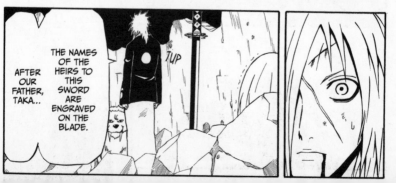

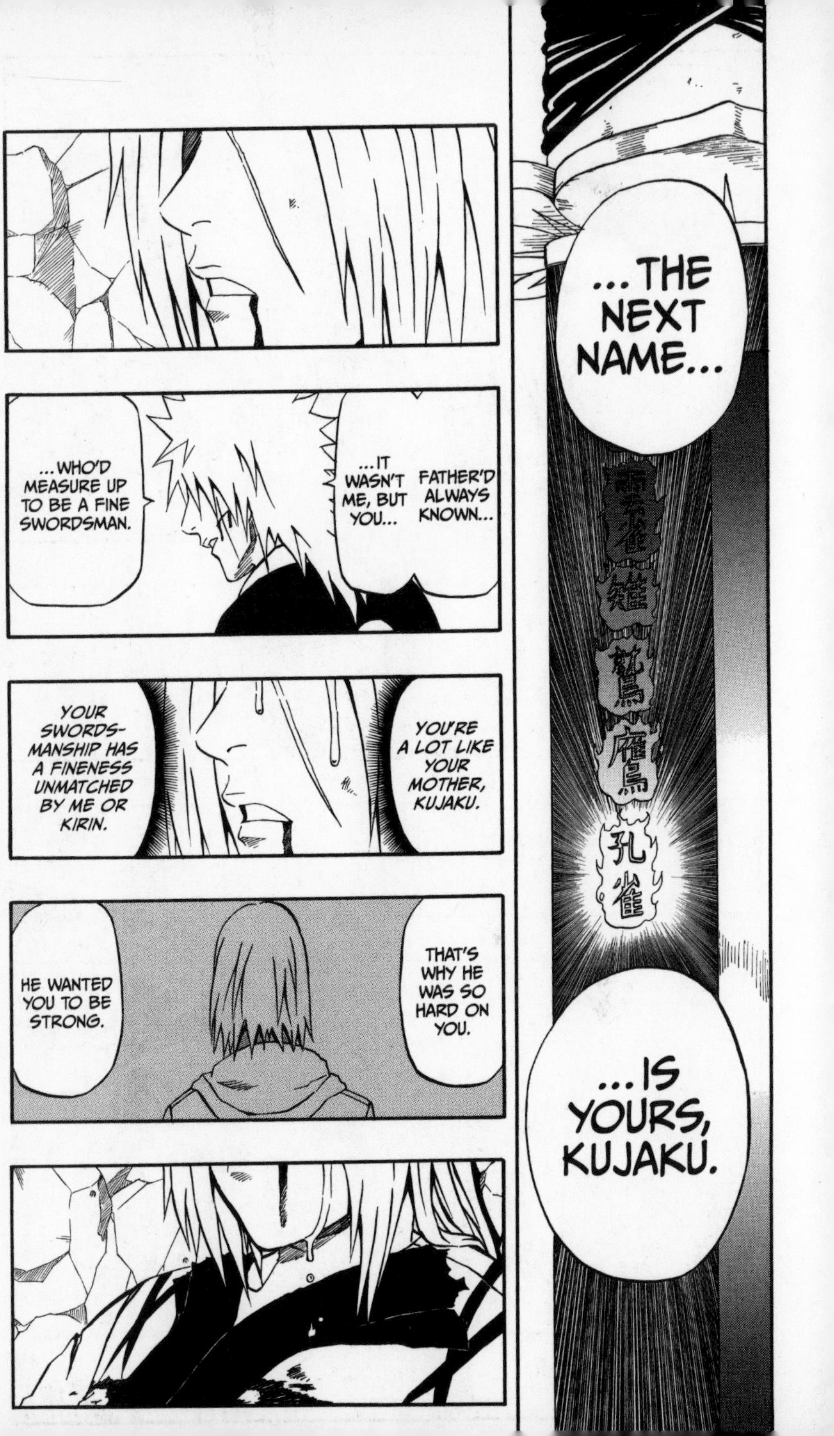
...THE NEXT NAME...
孔雀
...IS YOURS, KUJAKU.
FATHER'D ALWAYS KNOWN...
...IT WASN'T ME, BUT YOU...
...WHO'D MEASURE UP TO BE A FINE SWORDSMAN.
YOU'RE A LOT LIKE YOUR MOTHER, KUJAKU.
YOUR SWORDSMANSHIP HAS A FINENESS UNMATCHED BY ME OR KIRIN.
THAT'S WHY HE WAS SO HARD ON YOU.
HE WANTED YOU TO BE STRONG.

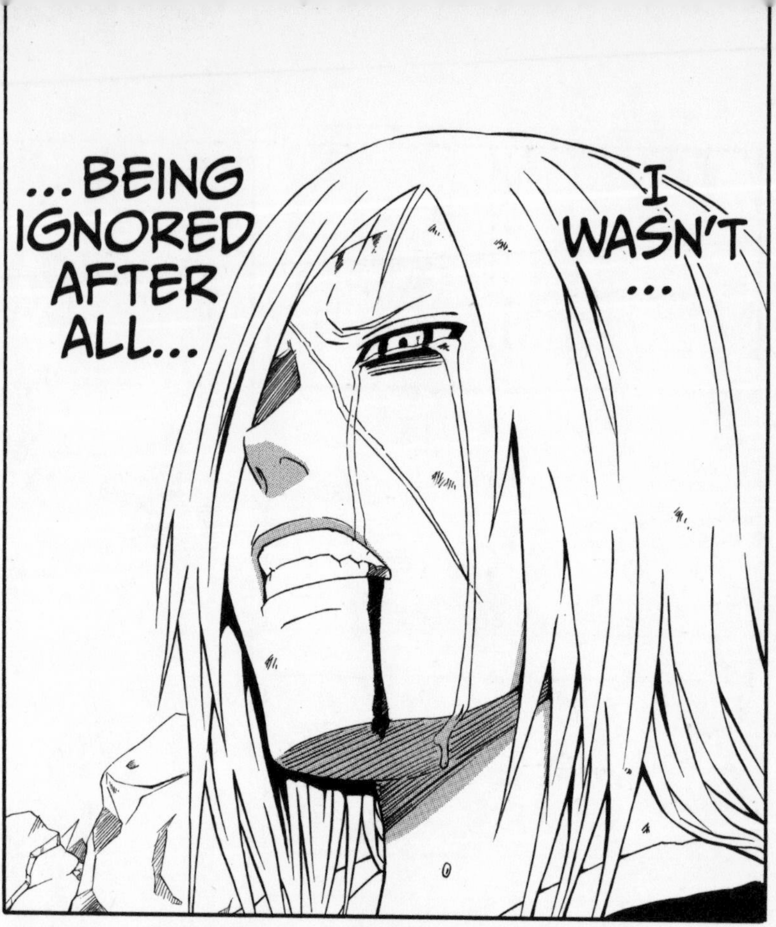
I WASN'T ...
...BEING IGNORED AFTER ALL...

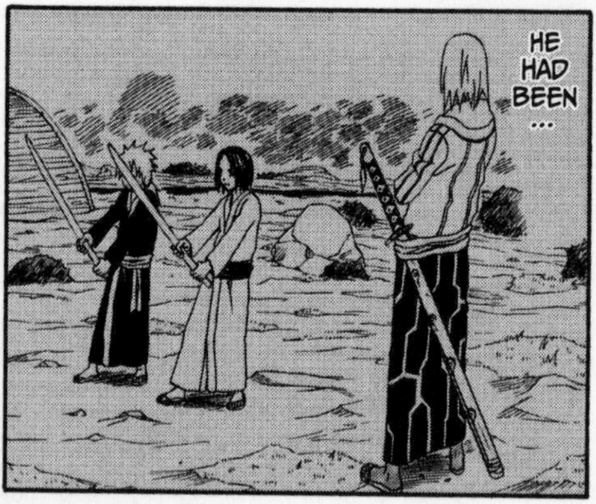
HE HAD BEEN ...

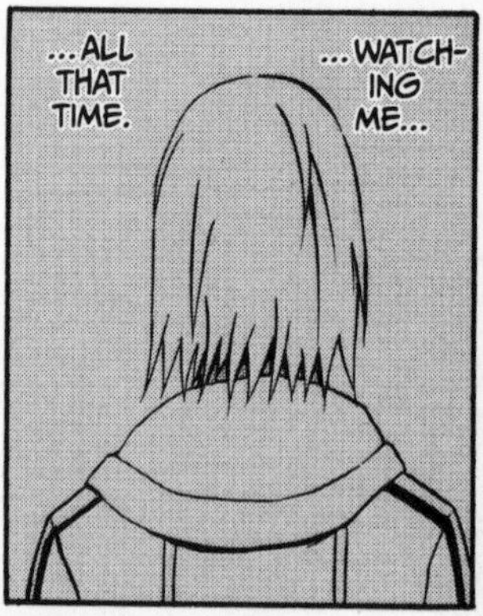
...WATCHING ME...
...ALL THAT TIME.

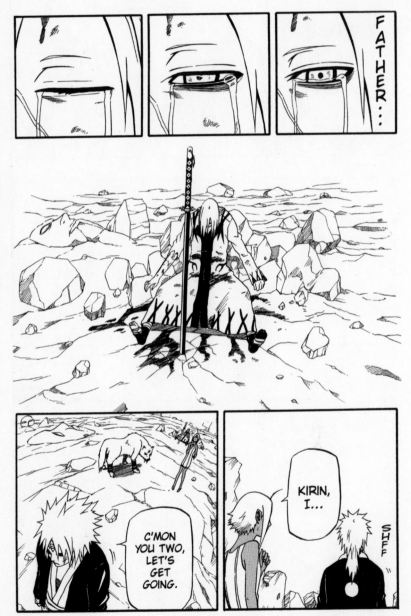

FATHER...

C'MON YOU TWO, LET'S GET GOING.

KIRIN, I...

SHFF

...IS GONE...

PT

THAT OLD ACHE IN THIS SCAR...

GOOD-BYE...

...COUS-IN...

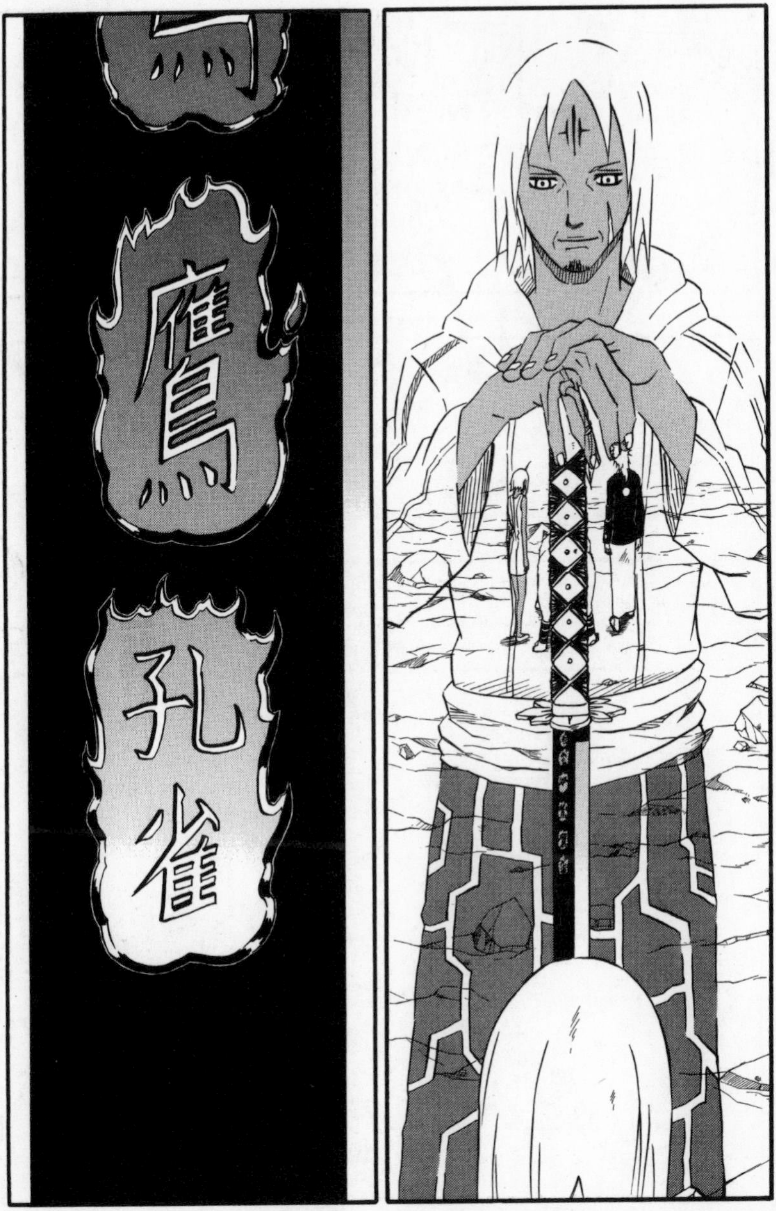
鷹
孔雀

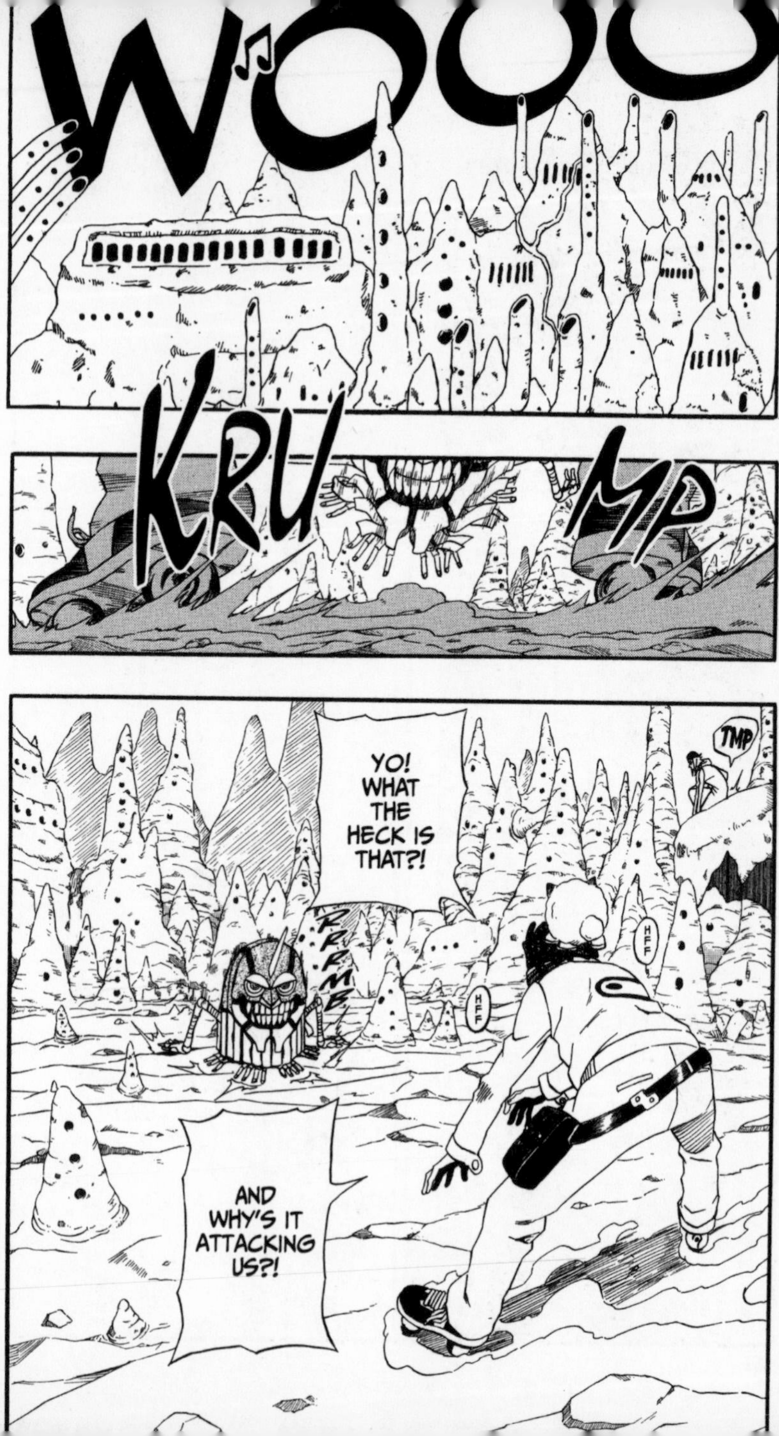
WOOO
KRUMP
TMP
YO! WHAT THE HECK IS THAT?!
HFF
HFF
RRRMB
AND WHY'S IT ATTACKING US?!

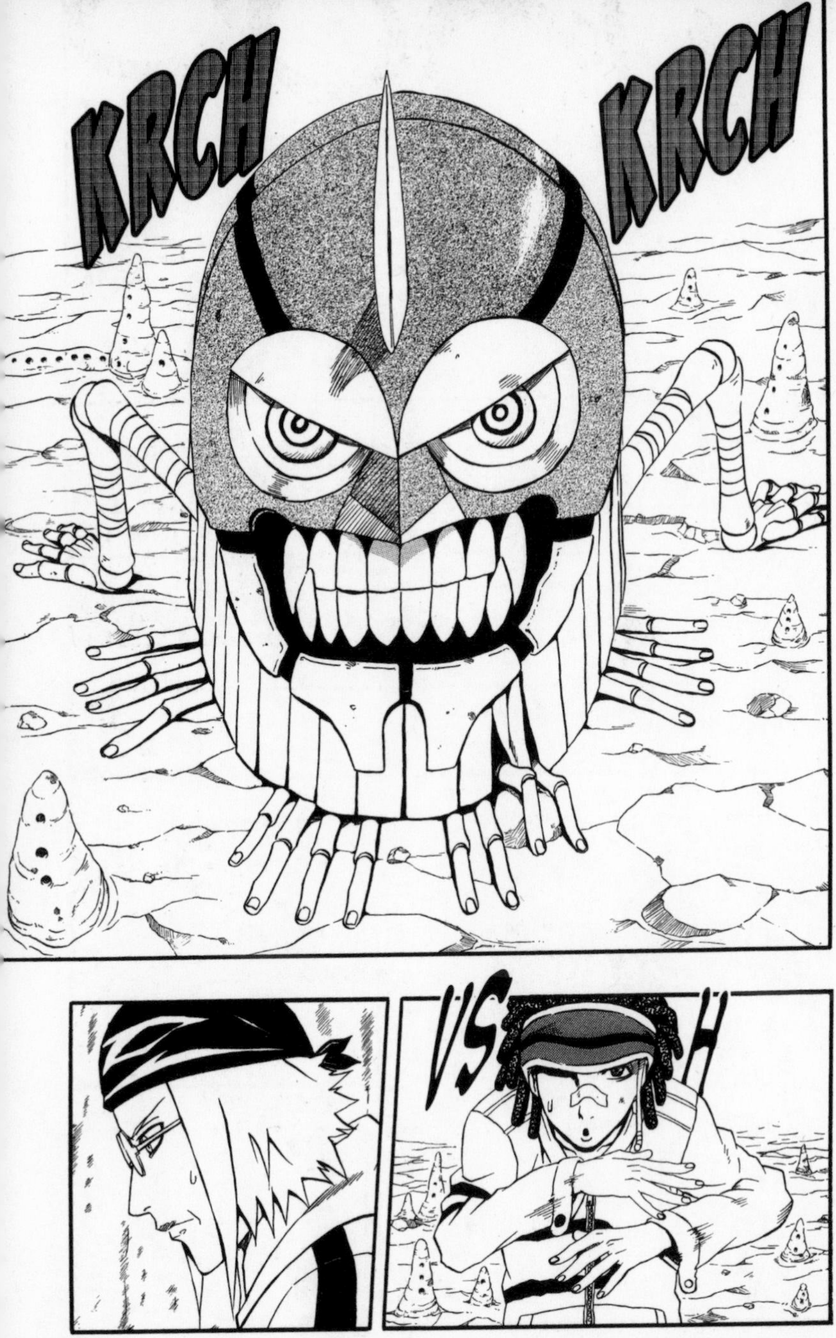
KRCH
KRCH
VS

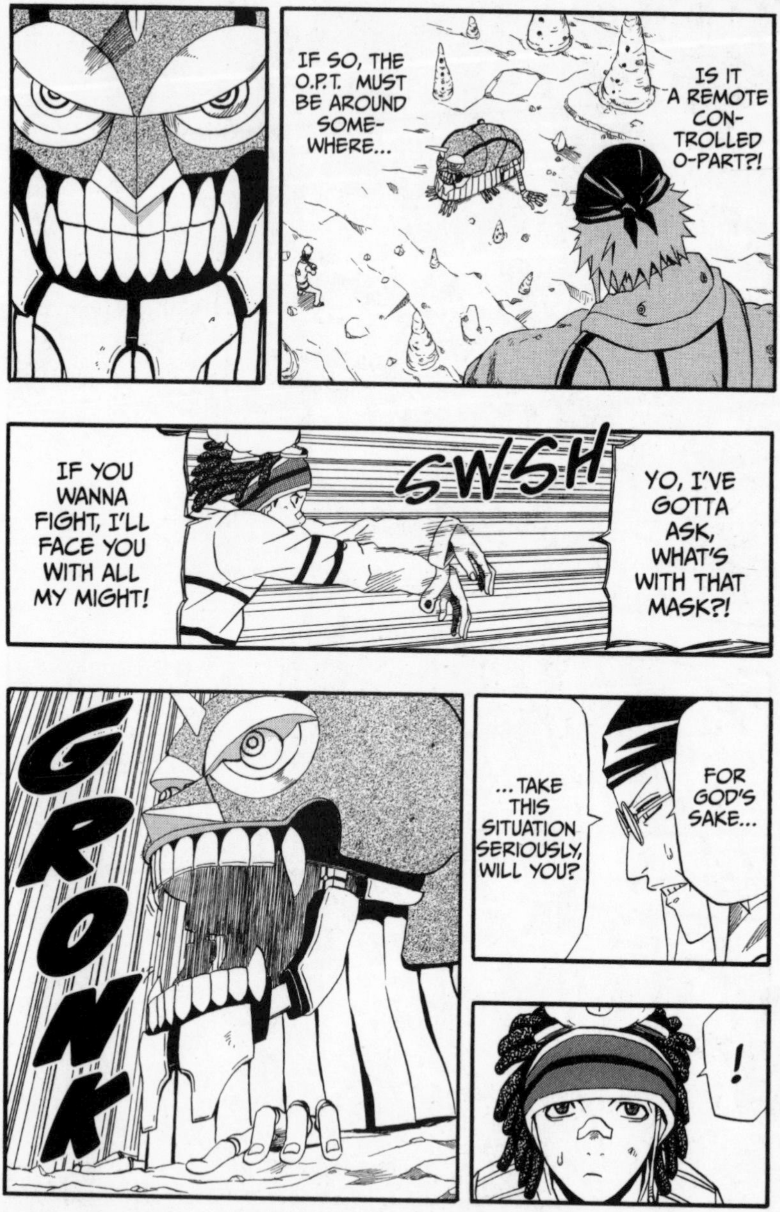
IS IT A REMOTE CON-TROLLED O-PART?!
IF SO, THE O.P.T. MUST BE AROUND SOME-WHERE...
YO, I'VE GOTTA ASK, WHAT'S WITH THAT MASK?!
SWSH
IF YOU WANNA FIGHT, I'LL FACE YOU WITH ALL MY MIGHT!
FOR GOD'S SAKE...
...TAKE THIS SITUATION SERIOUSLY, WILL YOU?
!
GRONK

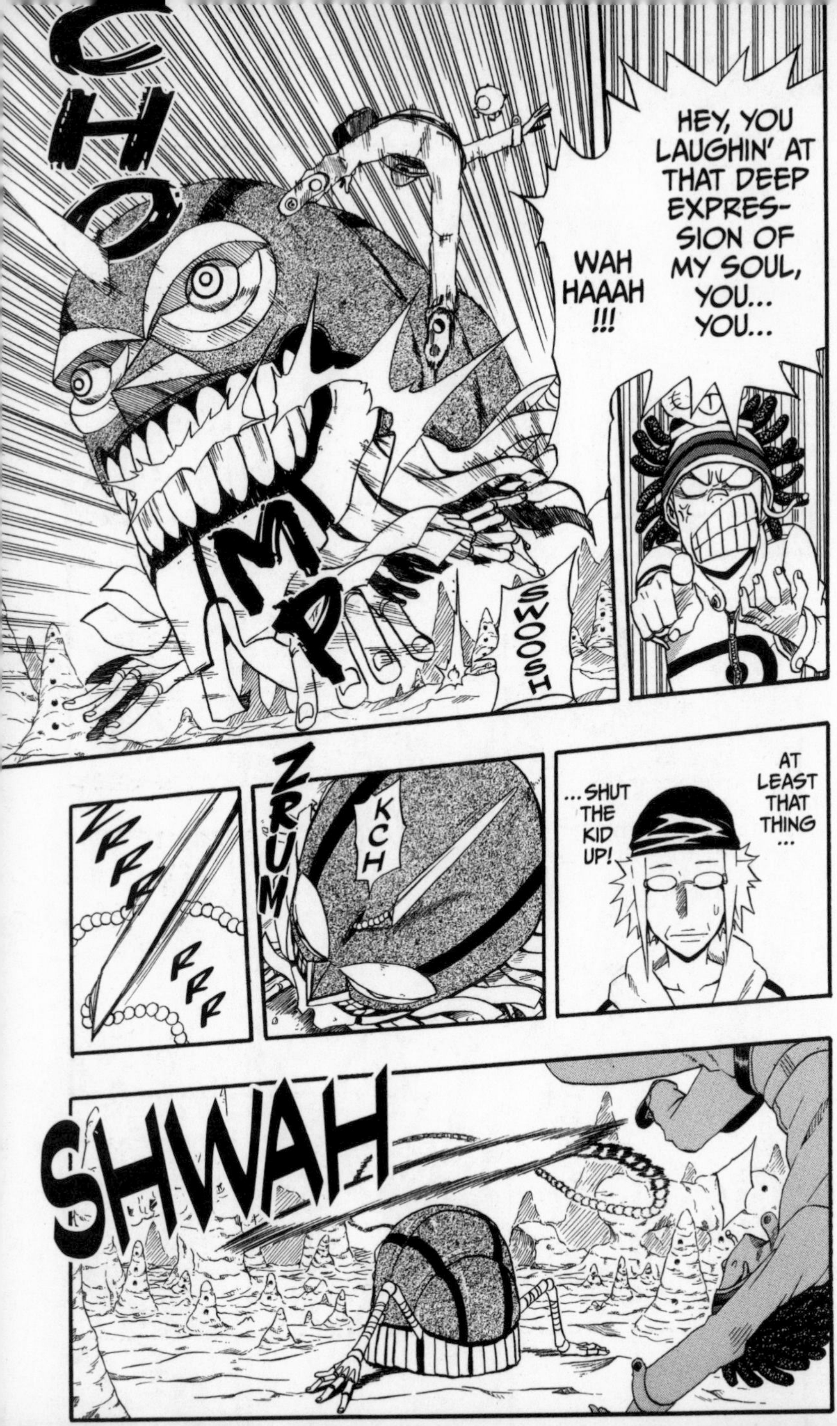
HEY, YOU LAUGHIN' AT THAT DEEP EXPRES-SION OF MY SOUL, YOU... YOU...
WAH HAAAH !!!
CHOMP
SWOOSH
AT LEAST THAT THING ...
...SHUT THE KID UP!
ZRUM
KCH
RRRR
RRR
SHWAH

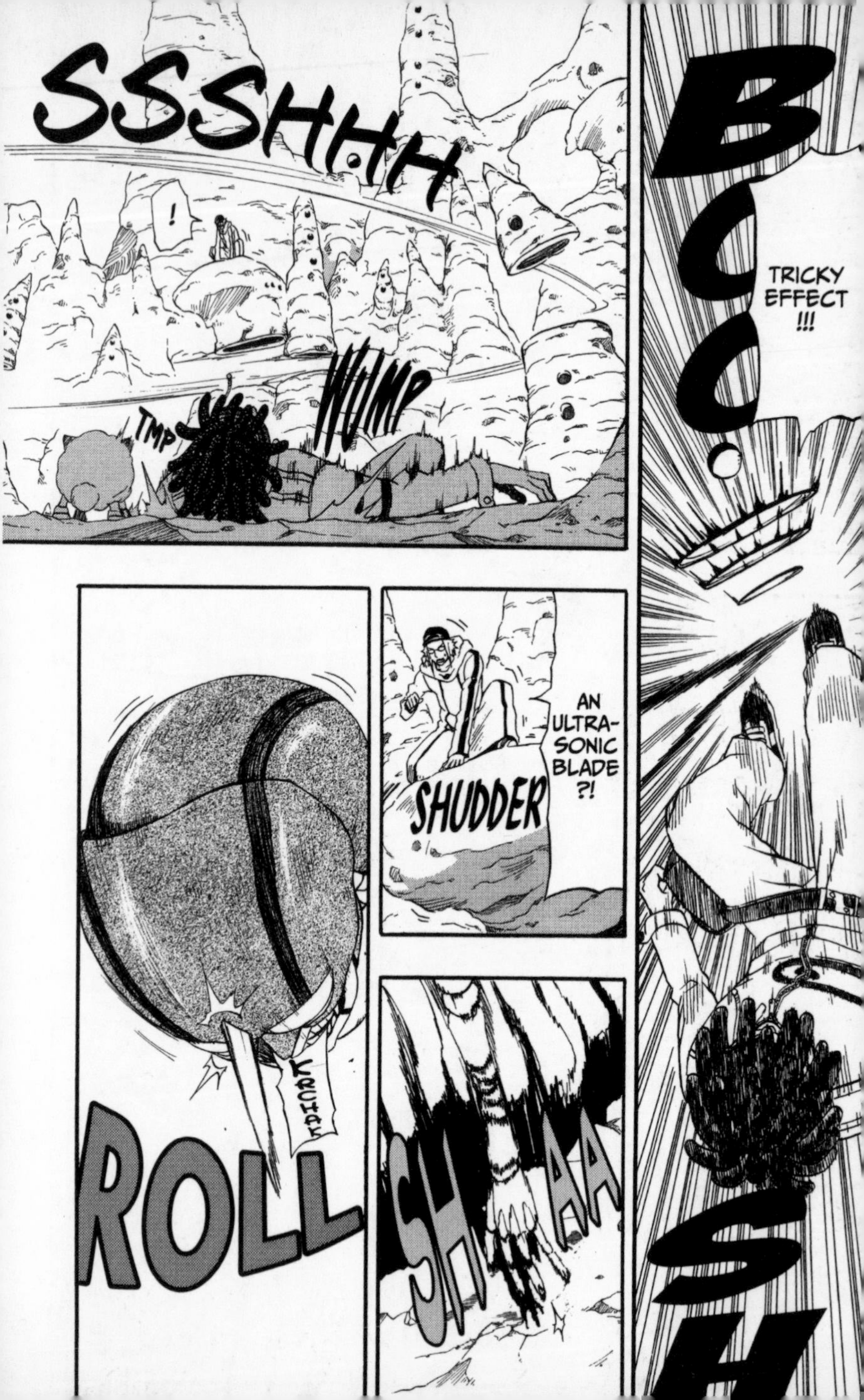
BOOSH
TRICKY EFFECT!!!
SSSHHH
!
WUMP
TMP
AN ULTRA-SONIC BLADE?!
SHUDDER
SHAA
KRCHAK
ROLL

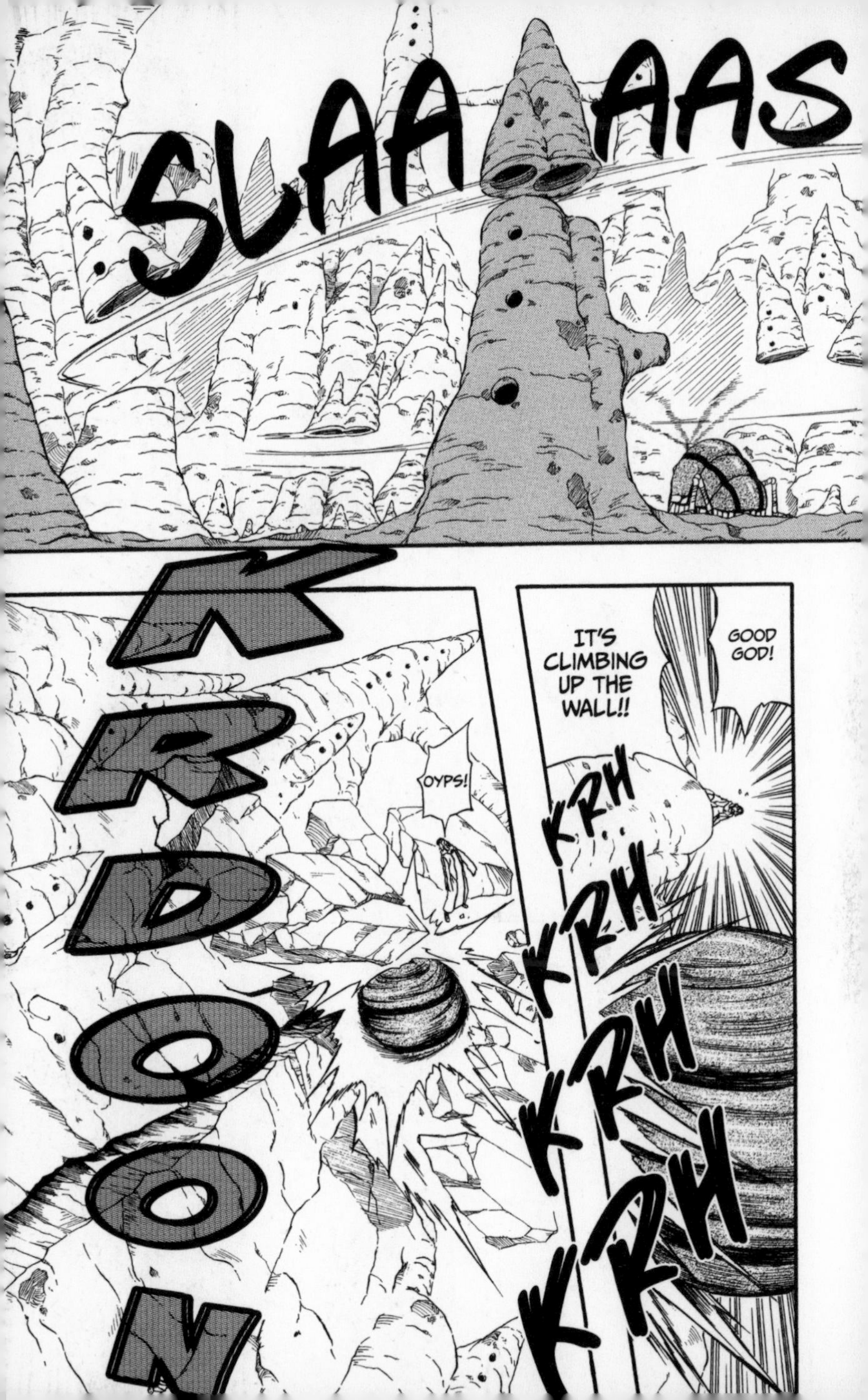
SLAAAAAS
GOOD GOD!
IT'S CLIMBING UP THE WALL!!
KRH KRH KRH KRH KRH
KRDOON
OYPS!

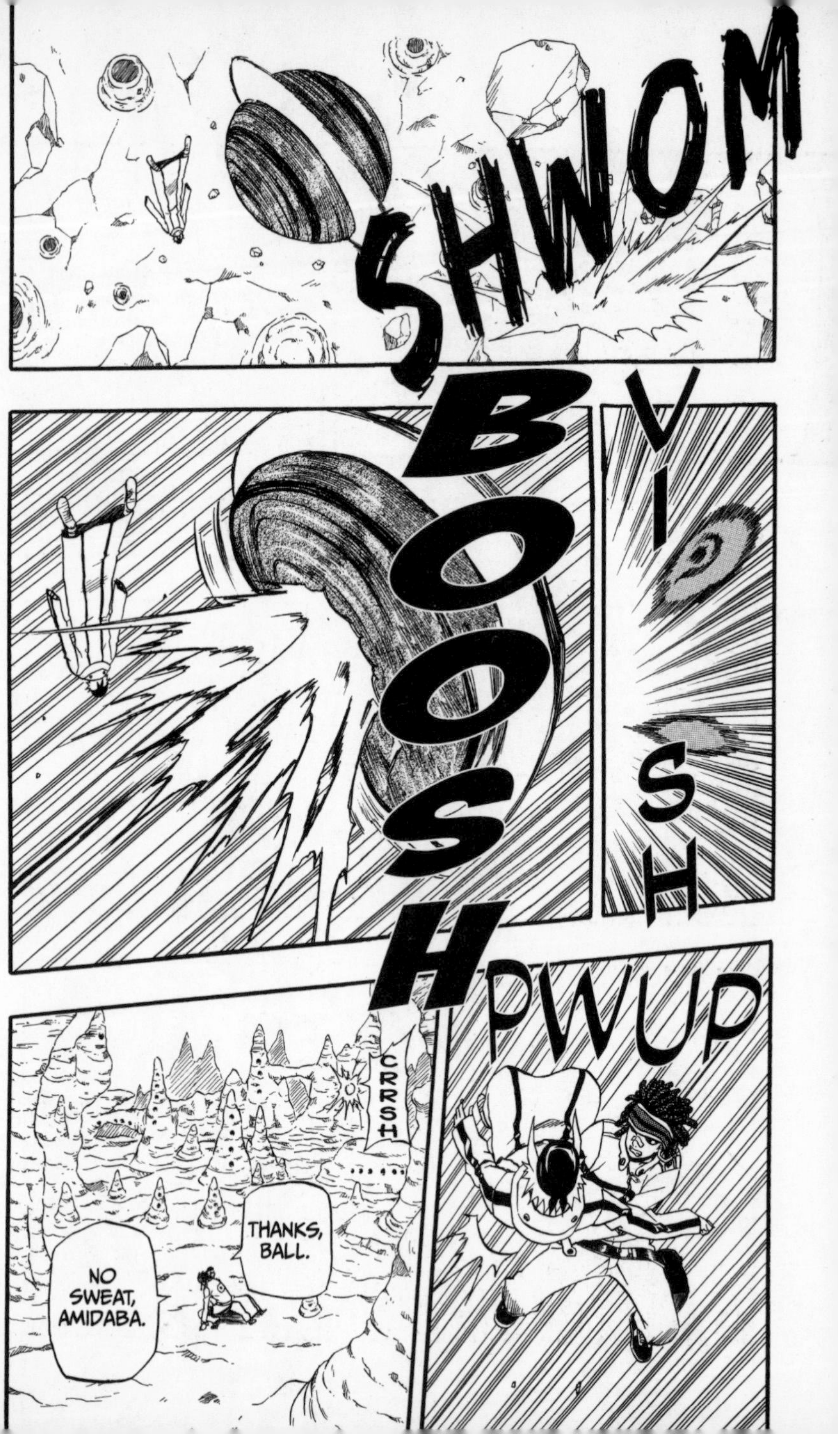
SHWOM
VISH
BOOSH
PWUP
CRRSH
THANKS, BALL.
NO SWEAT, AMIDABA.

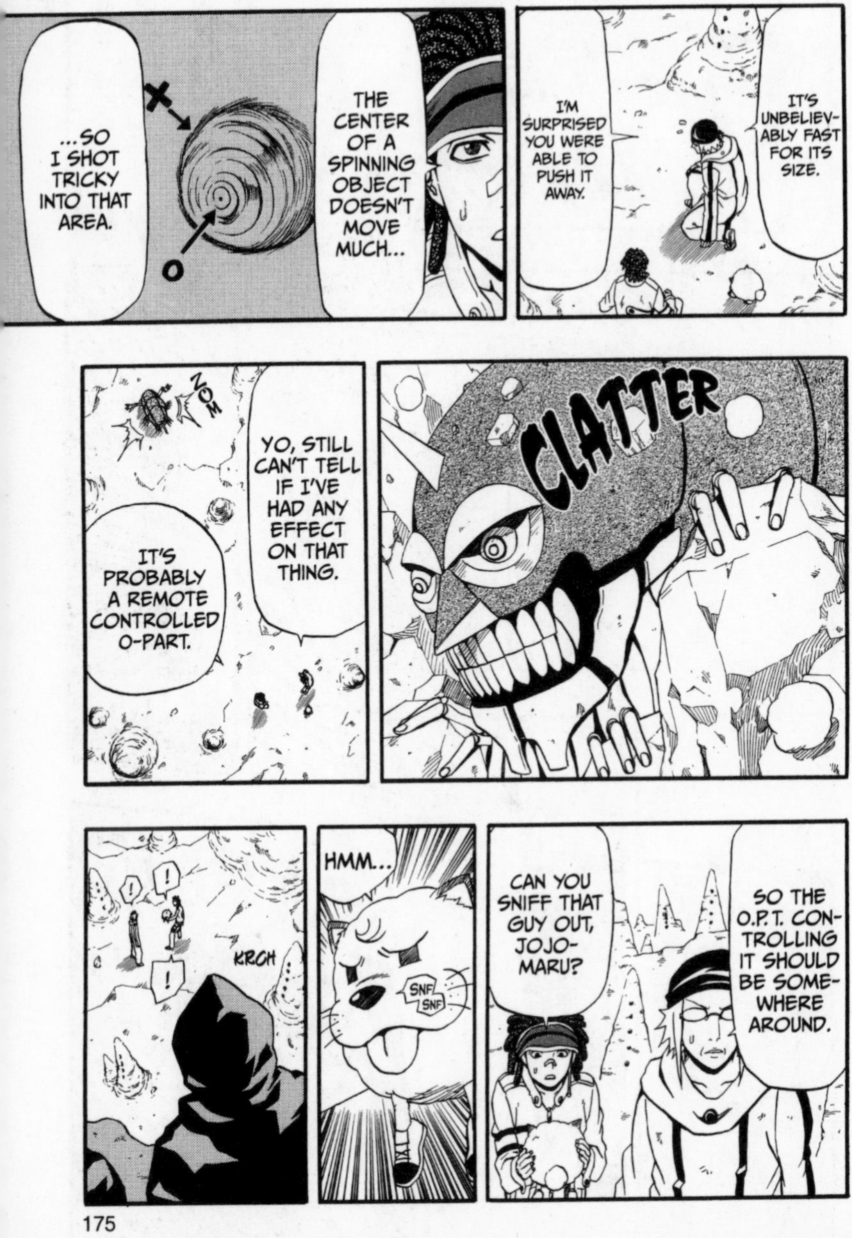
IT'S UNBELIEVABLY FAST FOR ITS SIZE.
I'M SURPRISED YOU WERE ABLE TO PUSH IT AWAY.
THE CENTER OF A SPINNING OBJECT DOESN'T MOVE MUCH...
X
O
...SO I SHOT TRICKY INTO THAT AREA.
CLATTER
ZOM
YO, STILL CAN'T TELL IF I'VE HAD ANY EFFECT ON THAT THING.
IT'S PROBABLY A REMOTE CONTROLLED O-PART.
SO THE O.P.T. CONTROLLING IT SHOULD BE SOMEWHERE AROUND.
CAN YOU SNIFF THAT GUY OUT, JOJOMARU?
HMM...
SNF SNF
!
!
!
KRCH

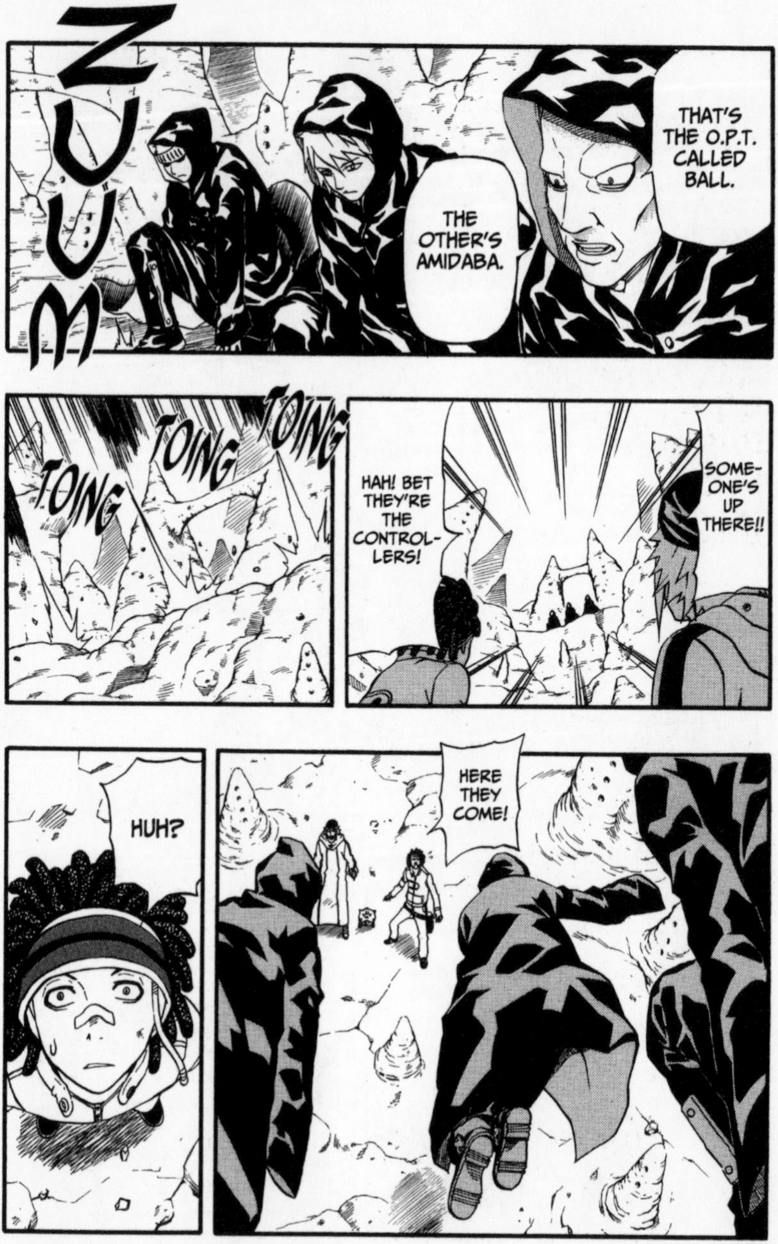
THAT'S THE O.P.T. CALLED BALL.
THE OTHER'S AMIDABA.
ZUUM
SOME-ONE'S UP THERE!!
HAH! BET THEY'RE THE CONTROL-LERS!
TOING
TOING
TOING
HERE THEY COME!
HUH?

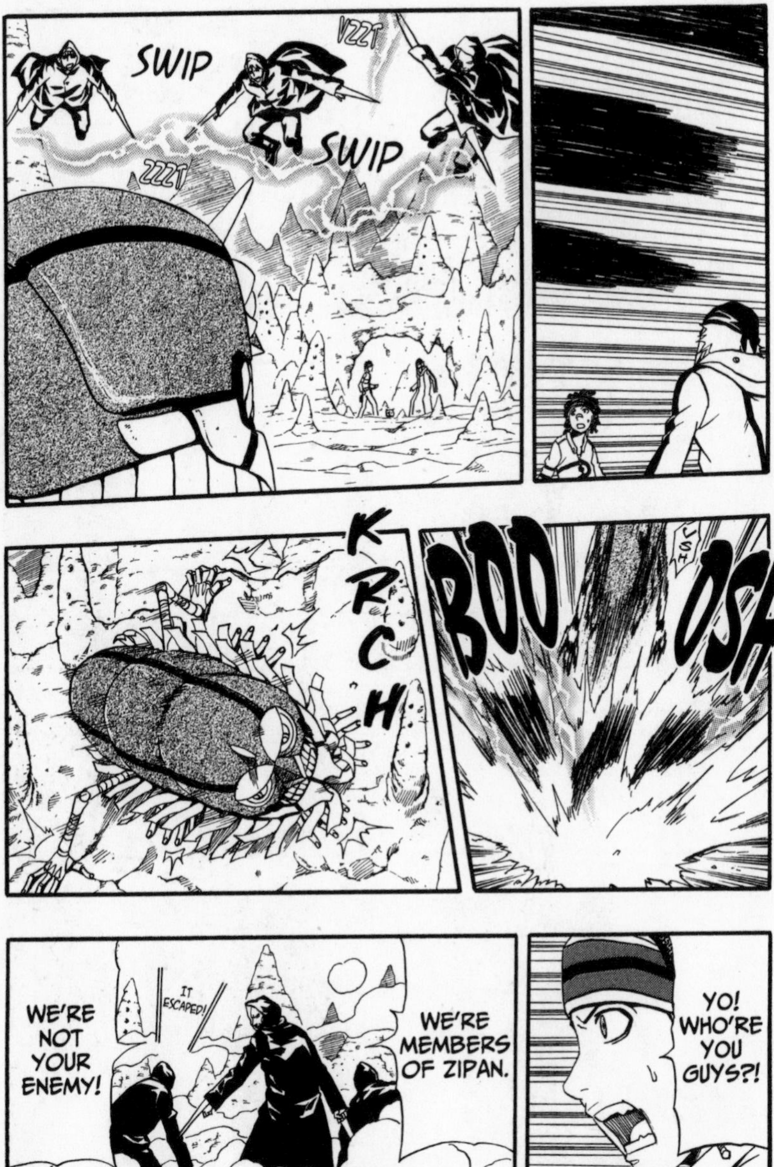
SWIP
VZZT
SWIP
ZZZT
BOOOSH
KRRCH
YO! WHO'RE YOU GUYS?!
WE'RE MEMBERS OF ZIPAN.
IT ESCAPED!
WE'RE NOT YOUR ENEMY!

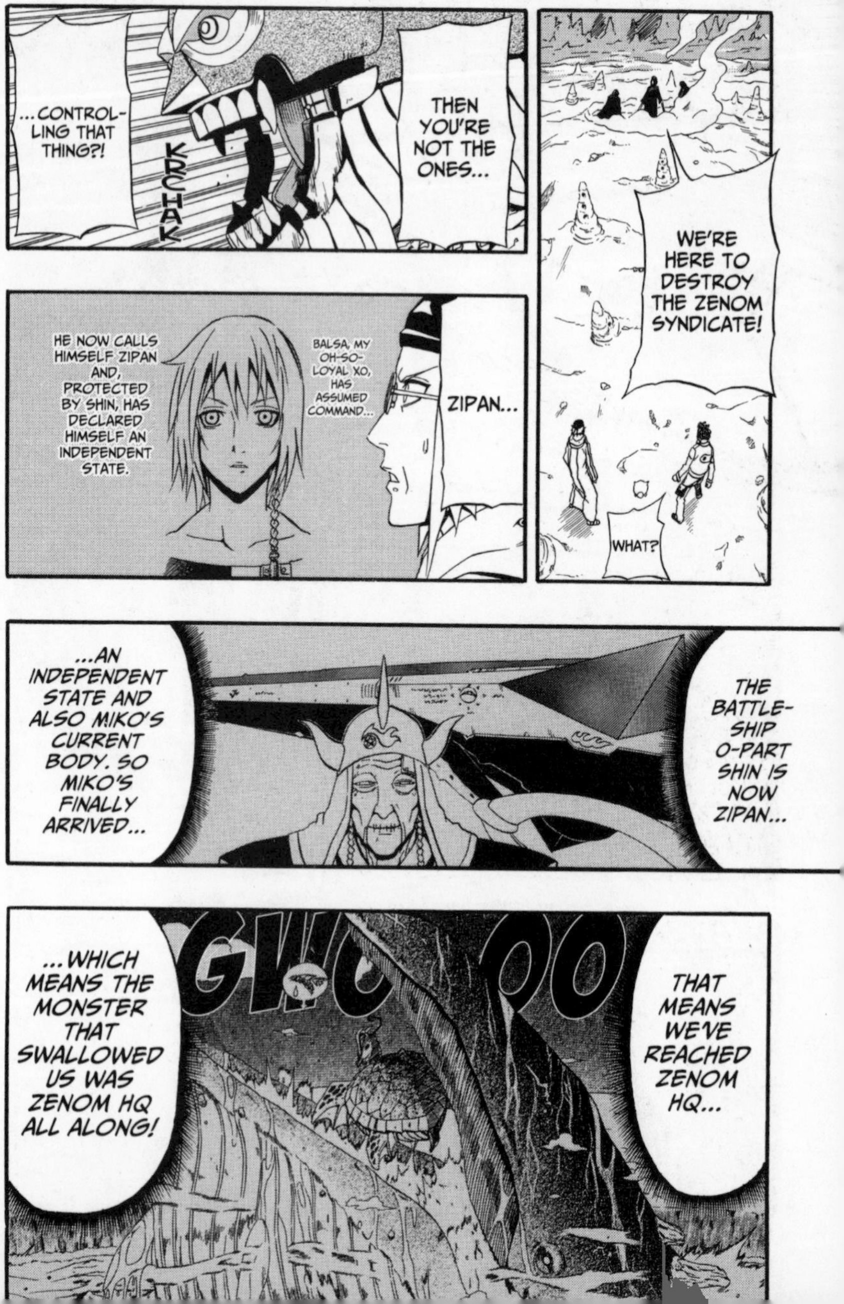
WE'RE HERE TO DESTROY THE ZENOM SYNDICATE!
WHAT?
THEN YOU'RE NOT THE ONES...
KRCHAK
...CONTROLLING THAT THING?!
ZIPAN...
BALSA, MY OH-SO-LOYAL XO, HAS ASSUMED COMMAND...
HE NOW CALLS HIMSELF ZIPAN AND, PROTECTED BY SHIN, HAS DECLARED HIMSELF AN INDEPENDENT STATE.
THE BATTLESHIP O-PART SHIN IS NOW ZIPAN...
...AN INDEPENDENT STATE AND ALSO MIKO'S CURRENT BODY. SO MIKO'S FINALLY ARRIVED...
THAT MEANS WE'VE REACHED ZENOM HQ...
...WHICH MEANS THE MONSTER THAT SWALLOWED US WAS ZENOM HQ ALL ALONG!

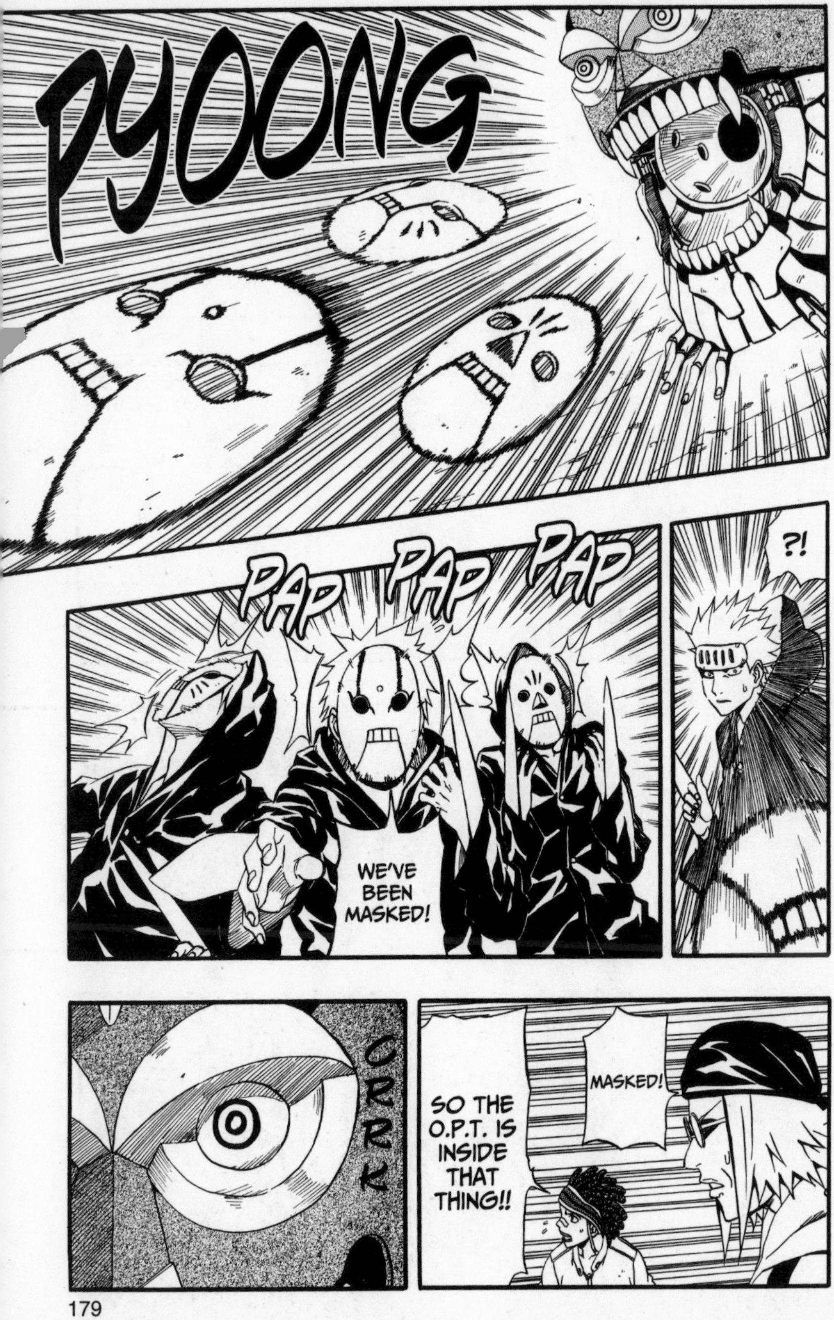
PYOONG
?!
PAP PAP PAP
WE'VE BEEN MASKED!
MASKED!
SO THE O.P.T. IS INSIDE THAT THING!!
CRRK

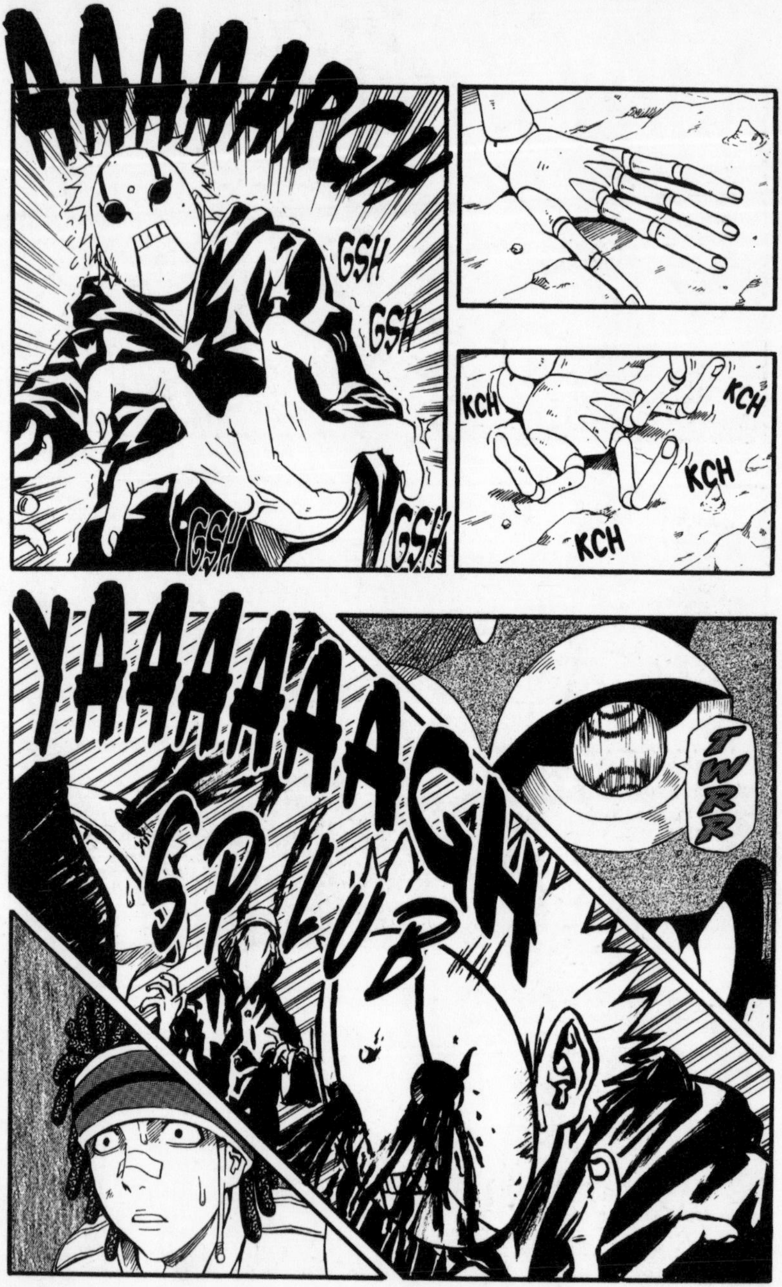
KCH
KCH
KCH
KCH
AAAAARGH
GSH
GSH
GSH
GSH
TWRR
YAAAAAAGH
SPLUB

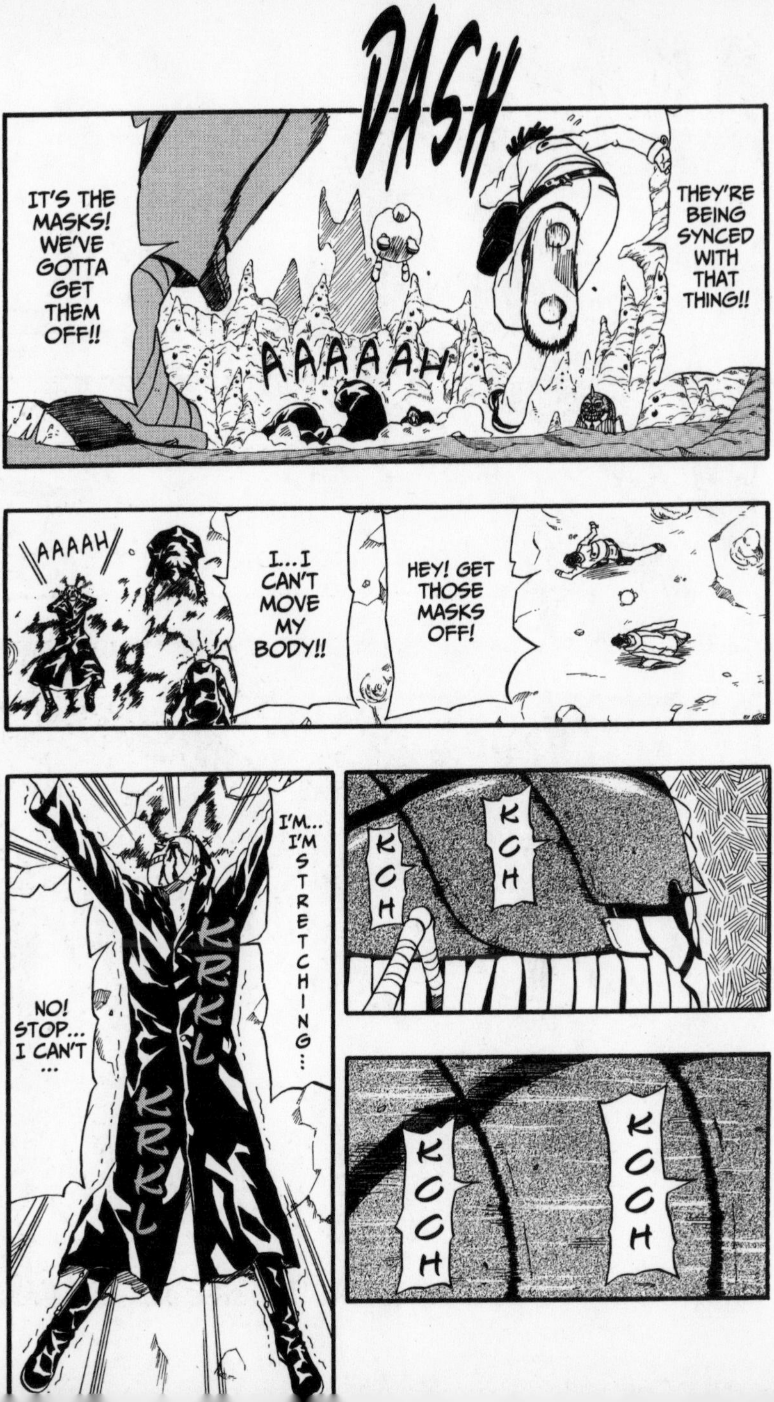
DASH
THEY'RE BEING SYNCED WITH THAT THING!!
IT'S THE MASKS! WE'VE GOTTA GET THEM OFF!!
AAAAAH
HEY! GET THOSE MASKS OFF!
I...I CAN'T MOVE MY BODY!!
AAAAH
KOH
KOH
KOOCH
KOOCH
I'M... I'M STRETCHING...
KRKL
KRKL
NO! STOP... I CAN'T ...

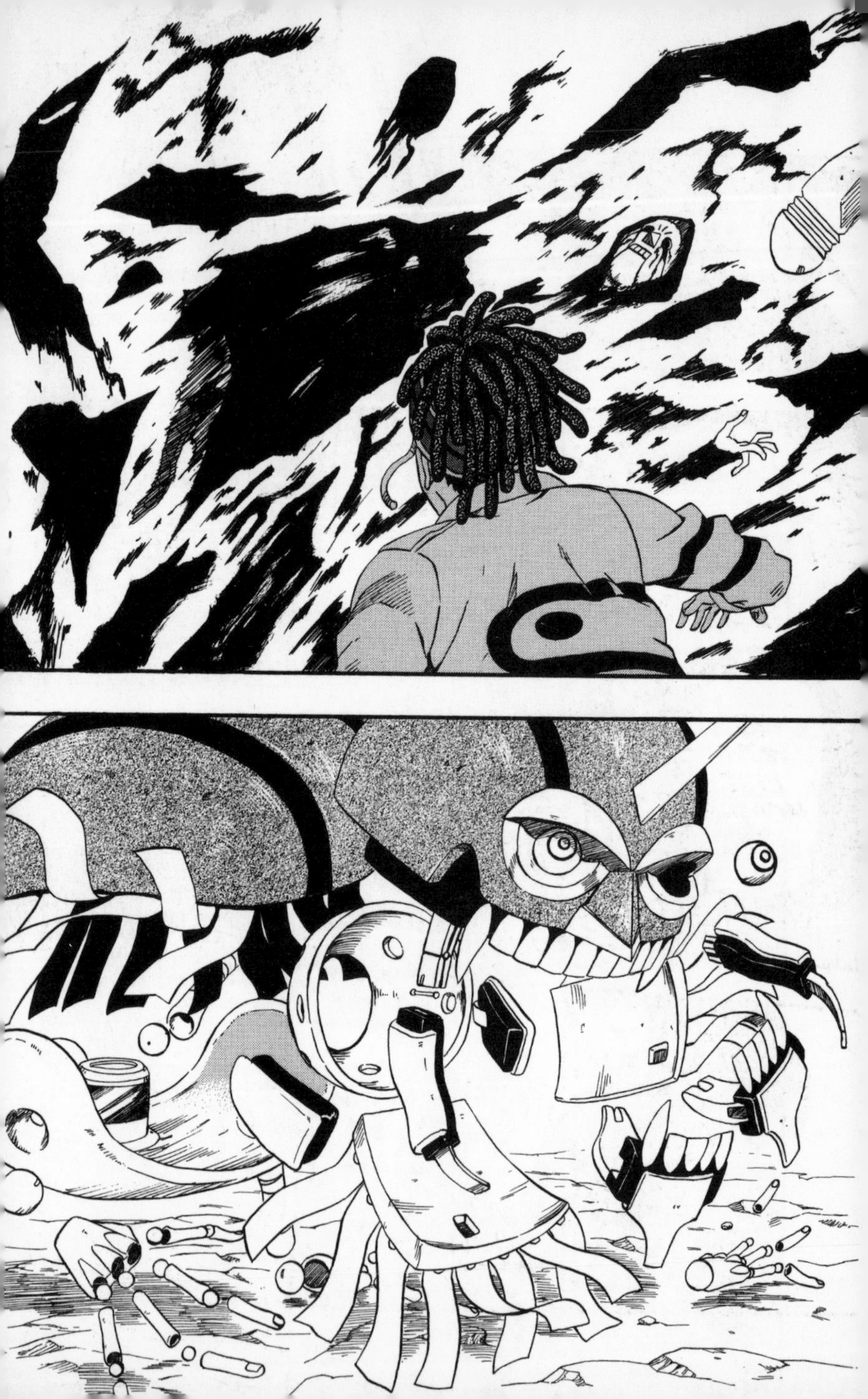

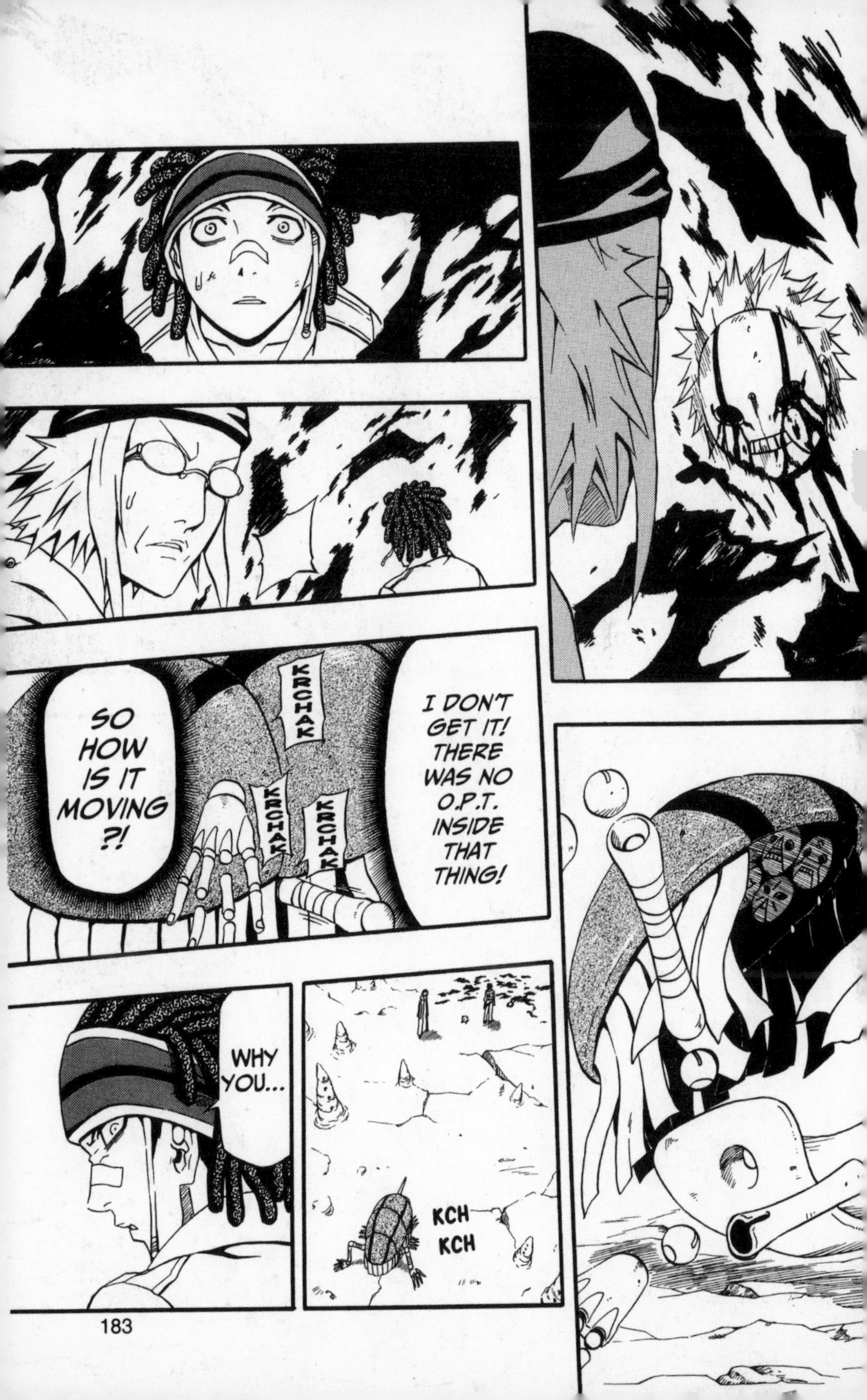
I DON'T GET IT! THERE WAS NO O.P.T. INSIDE THAT THING!
KRCHAK
KRCHAK
KRCHAK
SO HOW IS IT MOVING?!
KCH KCH
WHY YOU...

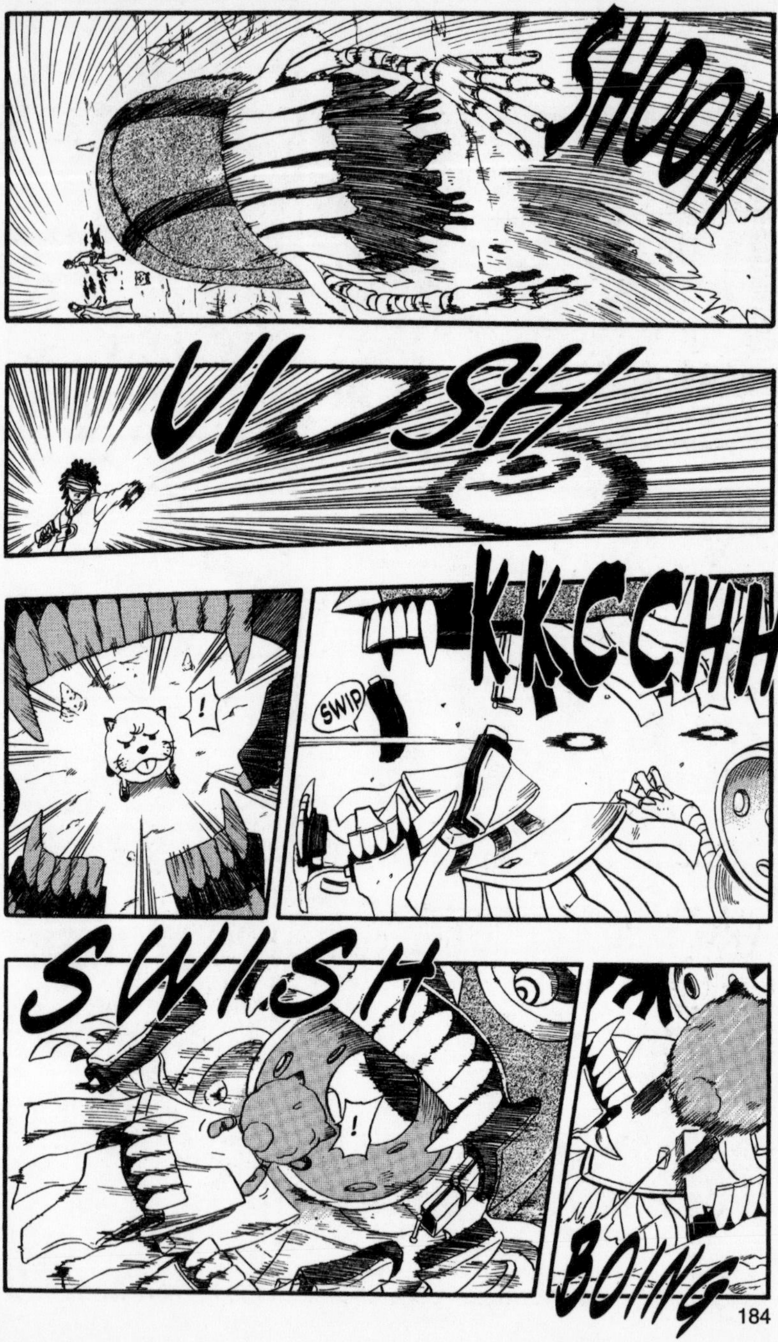
SHOOM
VOSH
KKCCHH
SWIP
!
BOING
SWISH
!

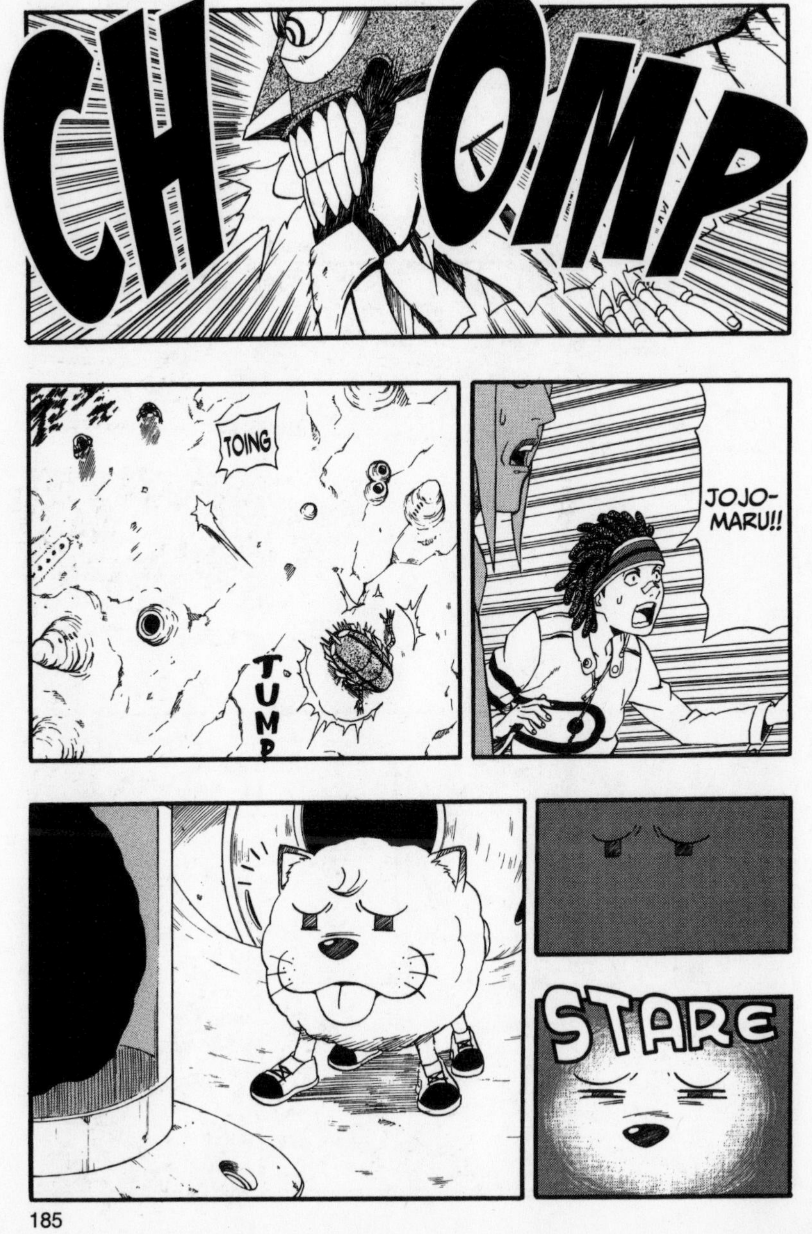
CHOMP
JOJO-MARU!!
TOING
TUMP
STARE

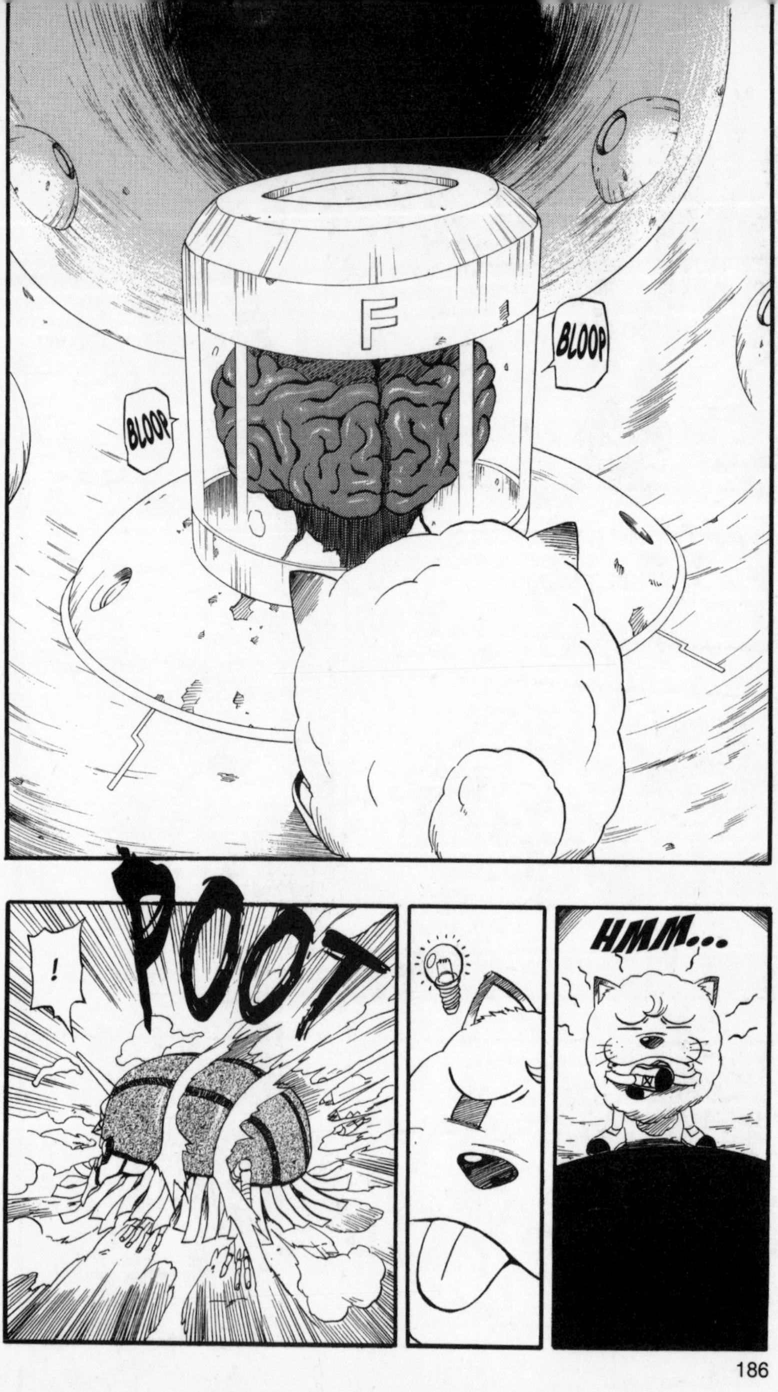
BLOOP
BLOOP
HMM...
POOT
!

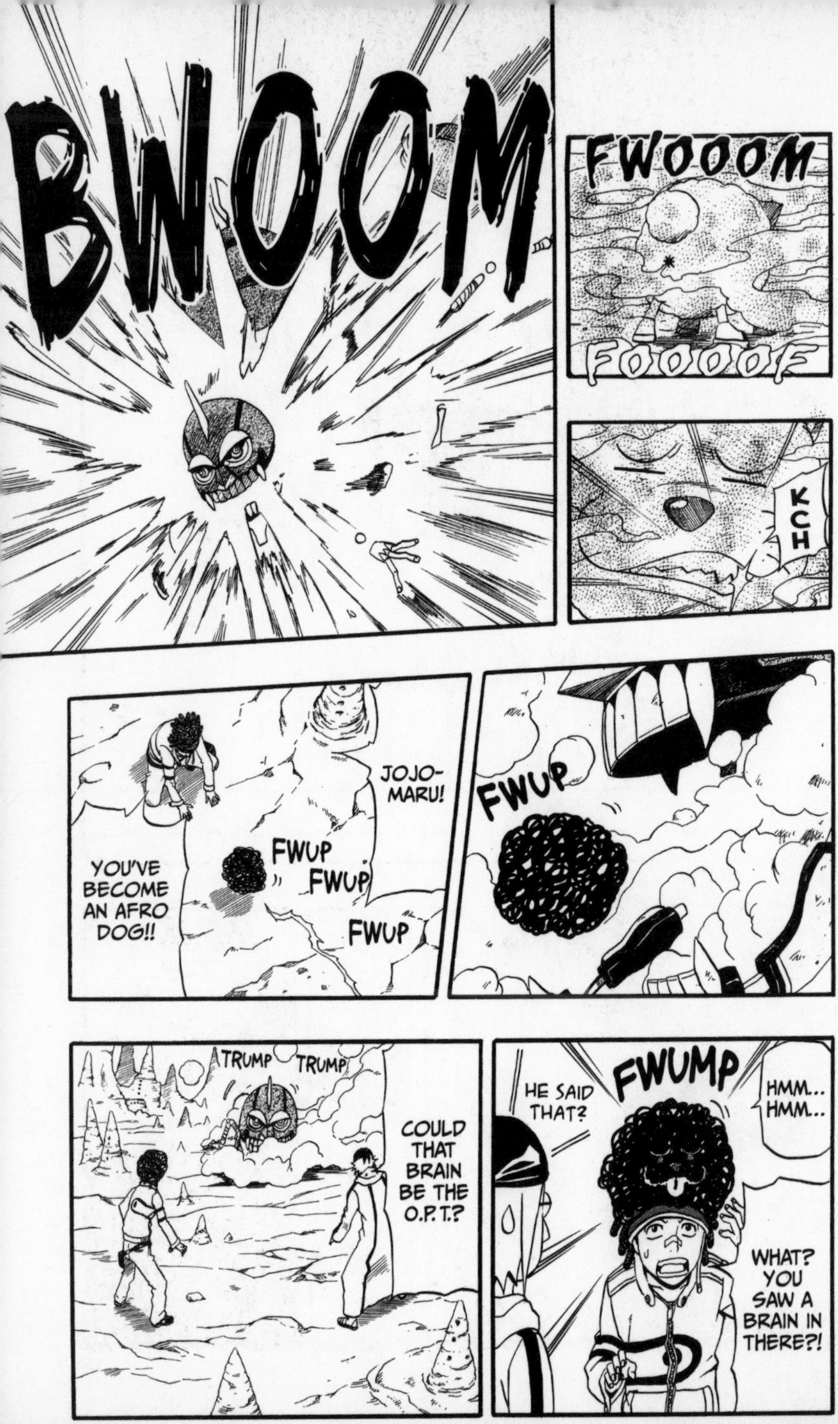
FWOOOM
FOOOOF
KCH
BWOOM
FWUP
JOJO-MARU!
FWUP
FWUP
FWUP
YOU'VE BECOME AN AFRO DOG!!
HMM... HMM...
FWUMP
HE SAID THAT?
WHAT? YOU SAW A BRAIN IN THERE?!
TRUMP TRUMP
COULD THAT BRAIN BE THE O.P.T.?

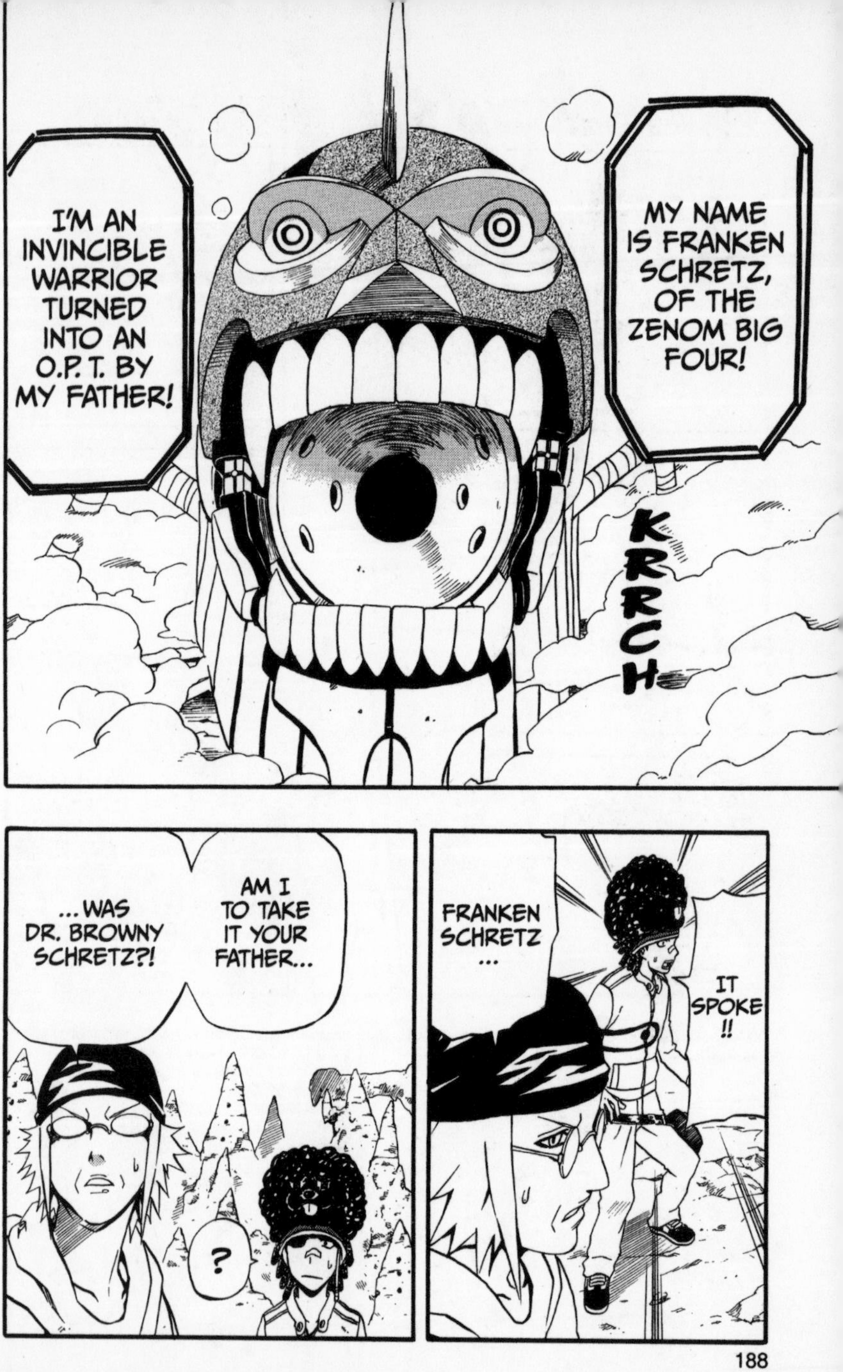
MY NAME IS FRANKEN SCHRETZ, OF THE ZENOM BIG FOUR!
I'M AN INVINCIBLE WARRIOR TURNED INTO AN O.P.T. BY MY FATHER!
KRRCH
FRANKEN SCHRETZ ...
IT SPOKE !!
AM I TO TAKE IT YOUR FATHER...
...WAS DR. BROWNY SCHRETZ?!
?

SEISHI AND HIS GAME CONSOLE PAL

SEISHI AND SANTA CLAUS

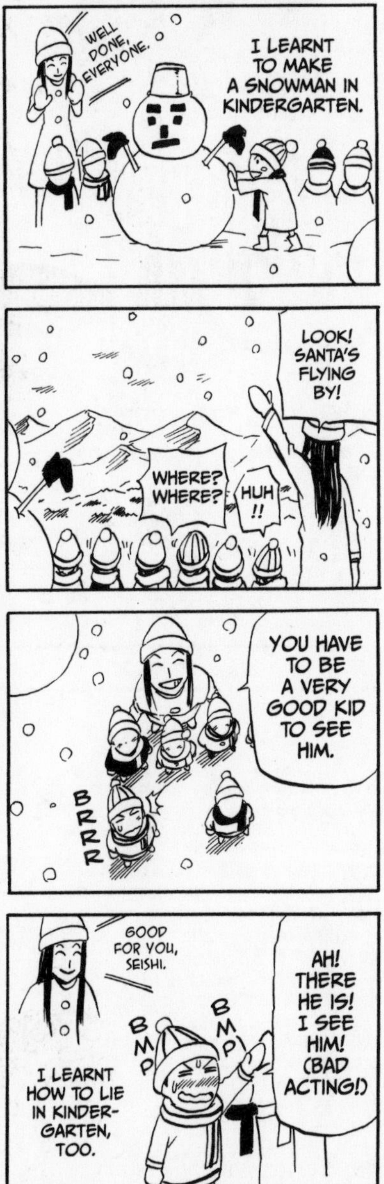

I LEARNT TO MAKE A SNOWMAN IN KINDERGARTEN.
WELL DONE, EVERYONE.
LOOK! SANTA'S FLYING BY!
HUH !!
WHERE? WHERE?
YOU HAVE TO BE A VERY GOOD KID TO SEE HIM.
BRRR
AH! THERE HE IS! I SEE HIM! (BAD ACTING!)
BMP
GOOD FOR YOU, SEISHI.
BMP
I LEARNT HOW TO LIE IN KINDERGARTEN, TOO.

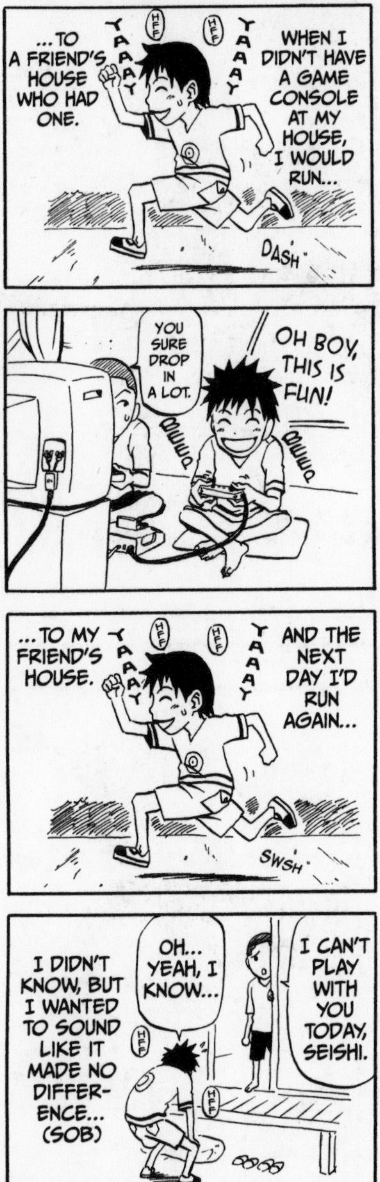

WHEN I DIDN'T HAVE A GAME CONSOLE AT MY HOUSE, I WOULD RUN...
YAAAY
HFF
HFF
YAAAY
...TO A FRIEND'S HOUSE WHO HAD ONE.
DASH
OH BOY, THIS IS FUN!
YOU SURE DROP IN A LOT.
AND THE NEXT DAY I'D RUN AGAIN...
YAAAY
HFF
HFF
YAAAY
...TO MY FRIEND'S HOUSE.
SWSH
I CAN'T PLAY WITH YOU TODAY, SEISHI.
HFF
OH... YEAH, I KNOW...
HFF
I DIDN'T KNOW, BUT I WANTED TO SOUND LIKE IT MADE NO DIFFER-ENCE... (SOB)

O-Parts CATALOGUE⑰

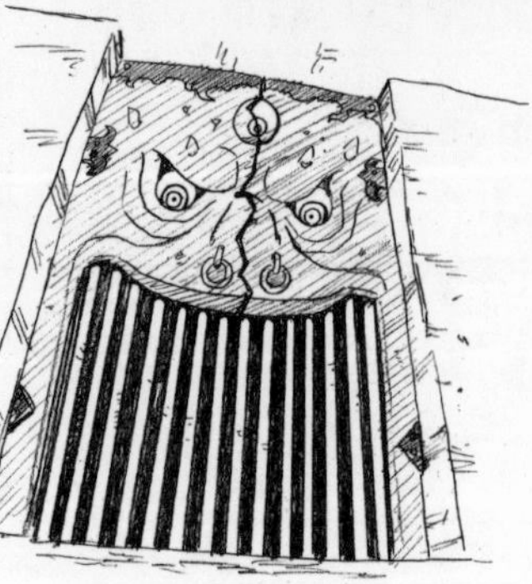

O-PART: GOMON
O-PART RANK: ?
EFFECT: ?
A BIOLOGICAL O-PART THAT CAN TALK AND IS MADE OF STEEL. IT CAN SPEAK IN EVERY LANGUAGE THAT HAS EVER EXISTED, BUT SEEMS TO PREFER MATHEMATICAL PROBLEMS. IT OFTEN TALKS TO ITSELF SINCE HARDLY ANYONE EVER DROPS BY, SO IT'S ACTUALLY PLEASED WHEN SOMEONE DOES.

O-PART: HEAVY METAL
O-PART RANK: A
EFFECT: METAL GUARD, WEIGHT CONTROL

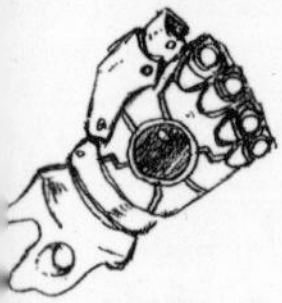

THE METAL GUARD EFFECT ENABLES ONE TO TRANSFORM. THIS IS BASICALLY A FULL-BODY VERSION OF THE GIANT'S KNIFE THAT KITE USED PREVIOUSLY. IT'S COLD.

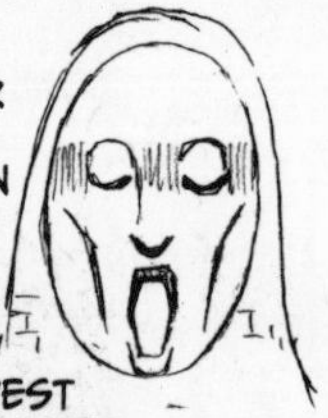

O-PART: STARING MIRROR
O-PART RANK: B
EFFECT: MATERIALIZATION OF THE INNER PSYCHE
A STONE MIRROR CREATED FROM GIL ORE. IT HAS THE POWER TO REFLECT EVEN THE DEEPEST AREAS OF ANY PERSON'S INNER PSYCHE, NO MATTER HOW POWERFUL THAT PERSON MAY BE. ACTUALLY, IF YOU WANT TO ESCAPE, YOU ONLY NEED TO SAY, "MIRROR, MIRROR ON THE WALL, WHO'S THE STUPIDEST ONE OF ALL?" WELL, PROBABLY...

REVERSE KABBALAH NUMBER 81, ADRAMELECH
O-PART RECIPE
A DEMON THAT IS SAID TO APPEAR IN THE FORM OF A MULE OR A PEACOCK. IT HAS THE GREATEST DISINTEGRATION ABILITY AMONGST ALL DEMONS AND CAN EVEN RECONSTRUCT OBJECTS. UNLIKE MICHAEL'S ABILITY TO BREAK THINGS DOWN, ADRAMELECH IS ABLE TO AFFECT EVERYTHING WITHIN RANGE OF ITS FLASHES OF LIGHT. IT CAN MOVE THROUGH PHYSICAL MATTER, AND PHYSICAL ATTACKS ARE PRETTY MUCH USELESS AGAINST IT.

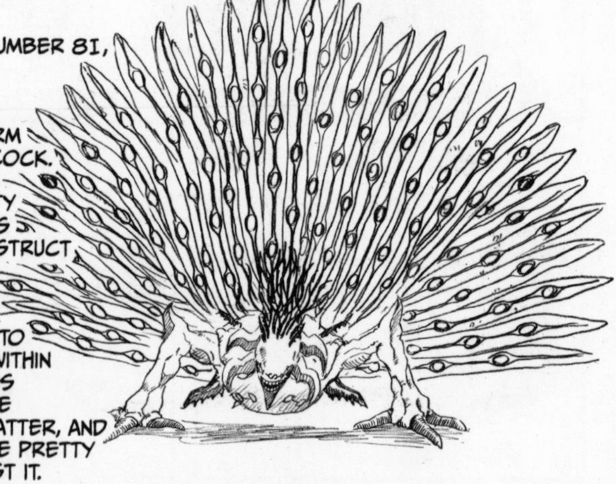

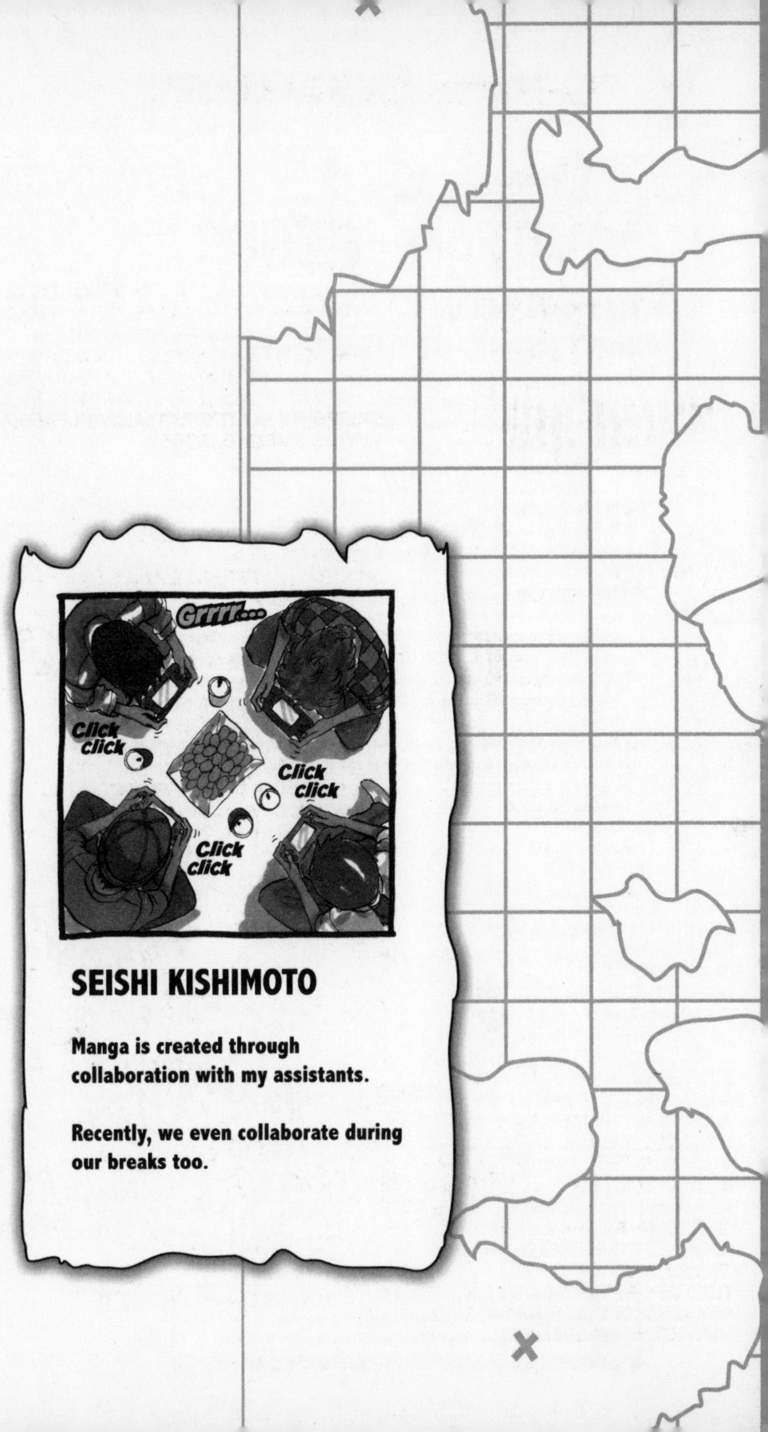
Grrrr...
Click click
Click click
Click click

SEISHI KISHIMOTO

Manga is created through collaboration with my assistants.

Recently, we even collaborate during our breaks too.

O-Parts HunteR 17

VIZ Media Edition
STORY AND ART BY SEISHI KISHIMOTO

English Adaptation/Tetsuichiro Miyaki
Touch-up Art & Lettering/HudsonYards
Design/Andrea Rice
Editor/Gary Leach

VP, Production/Alvin Lu
VP, Publishing Licensing/Rika Inouye
VP, Sales & Product Marketing/Gonzalo Ferreyra
VP, Creative/Linda Espinosa
Publisher/Hyoe Narita

Printed in the U.S.A.

Published by VIZ Media, LLC
P.O. Box 77010
San Francisco, CA 94107

10 9 8 7 6 5 4 3 2 1
First printing, August 2009

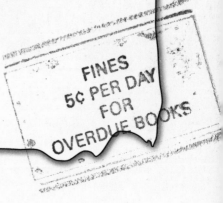

FINES
5¢ PER DAY
FOR
OVERDUE BOOKS

www.viz.com   store.viz.com